Thriving After Burnout

A Compilation of Real Stories and Strategies
to Reduce Female Physician Burnout

Copyright © 2023 Sharon T McLaughlin MD FACS
Female Physician Entrepreneurs Group
All rights reserved.

ISBN: 9798373333795

Co-Authors

To the members of the Female Physician Entrepreneurs group. Without you, this book could not have been written.

Co-authors
Gigi Abdel-Samed, MD, MBA
Carrie Atcheson, MD, MPH and
Rev. Dr. Eric Atcheson, MDiv, DMin
Puja Aggarwal, MD MBA
Heather Awad, M.D.
Ololade "Lola Day" Akintoye, MD
Ashley Albers, DO
Nadia Ali, M.D, M.B;B.S, MPH, ABHIM, FACP
Brittany S. Panico, DO, FACR
Gabriela Pichardo-Lafontaine, MD, ABOIM
Shilpi Pradhan, MD
Payal Ghayal, MD
Anupriya Grover-Wenk, DO, M.Med.Ed
Rita Gupta, D.O MPA
Melissa Hankins, MD, CPC
Julia M Huber, MD DipABLM, TIPC
Heather Awad, MD
Damilola Babaniji, DO
Param Baladandapani, MD
Tamara Beckford, MD MS
Tammie Chang, MD
Jenny Christner, MD FAAP
Diana Dumenko, MD
Lida Fatemi, DO MPH
Laura Fortner, MD
Beverly Joyce, MD, FACOG, NCMP
Mously Le Blanc, MD
Sadaf R Lodhi, DO FACOOG
Diana Cristina Londoño, MD
Winnie Mar, MD
Cecilia Minano, MD, MPH
Tracey O'Connell, MD
Chinyelu E. Oraedu, M.D.(Dr. Yel'Ora)
Chrissie Ott, MD,FAAP, FACP, CPC
Asha Padmanabhan, MD, FASA

Co-authors continued
Serene Shereef, MD FACS
Wendy Schofer, MD, FAAP, DipABLM
Sapna Shah-Haque, MD MBA
Christiana Jones, MD MPH
Jillian Rigert, DMD, MD
Zarya Rubin, MD
Susana Santos, DO
Olapeju Simoyan, MD, MPH, BDS, FAAFP, FASAM
Arpita Gupta DePalma, MD, FAAP
Radhika Sharma, MD, FACOG
Nandini Sunkireddy, MD
Santisree Tanikella, MD, FAAP, ABIMH, ABOIM
Robyn Tiger, MD, DipABLM
Avian L. Tisdale, MD, MBA, Paralegal
Mary Tran, DO
Kara Wada, MD
Anonymous contributors

Table of Contents

Table of Contents
5

The Price of Physician Burnout
9

Fostering Sustainable Well-being: Why I Chose Me Over Medicine By Tracey O'Connell, MD
18

Gigi Abdel-Samed, MD, MBA
36

Jillian Rigert, DMD, MD
43

Mary Tran, DO
49

Param Baladandapani, MD
53

Gabriela Pichardo-Lafontaine, MD, ABOIM
57

Diana Cristina Londoño, MD
64

Kara Wada, MD
68

Diana Dumenko, MD
71

Lida Fatemi, DO MPH
75

Nadia Ali M.D, M.B;B.S, MPH, ABHIM, FACP
81

Heather Awad, MD
92

Beverly Joyce, MD, FACOG, NCMP
97

Jenny Christner, MD FAAP
103

Avian L. Tisdale MD, MBA, Paralegal
109

Delia Chiaramonte, MD
116

Ann Huntington, MD, FACP
121

Ashley Albers, DO
130

Sapna Shah-Haque MD MBA
137

Wendy Schofer, MD, FAAP, DipABLM
142

Rita Gupta, DO MPA
149

Shilpi Pradhan, MD
154

Sadaf R Lodhi, DO FACOOG
161

Melissa Hankins, MD CPC
166

Zarya Rubin, MD
175

Arpita Gupta DePalma, MD, FAAP
179

Nandini Sunkireddy, MD
188

Olapeju Simoyan, MD, MPH, BDS, FAAFP, FASAM
191

Damilola Babaniji, DO
195

Asha Padmanabhan, MD, FASA
202

Chrissie Ott, MD, FAAP, FACP, CPC
210

Julia M Huber, MD DipABLM, TIPC
217

Tammie Chang, MD
224

Anupriya Grover-Wenk, DO, M.Med.Ed
230

Susana Santos, DO
239

Serene Shereef, MD FACS
244

Brittany S. Panico, DO, FACR
250

Christiana Jones, MD MPH
261

Tamara Beckford MD MS
266

Cecilia Minano, MD, MPH
270

Payal Ghayal MD
274

Santisree Tanikella, MD, FAAP, ABIMH, ABOIM
278

Winnie Mar, MD
300

Ololade "Lola Day" Akintoye, MD
303

Puja Aggarwal, MD MBA
307

Radhika Sharma, MD, FACOG
314

Mously Le Blanc, MD, FABPMR
324

Robyn Tiger, MD, DipABLM
328

Anonymous, MD 1
333

Anonymous, MD 2
336

Medical Malpractice-Laura Fortner, MD
342

Surviving Burnout as a Family By Dr. Carrie Atcheson, MD, MPH and Rev. Dr. Eric Atcheson, MDiv, DMin
346

How it All Started By Sharon T McLaughlin MD FACS
359

Resources
366

Final Note
367

The Price of Physician Burnout

Burnout is a psychological syndrome of emotional exhaustion, depersonalization, and reduced personal accomplishment that can occur among individuals who work with others (West). In the 1980s, social psychologist Christina Maslach developed a framework for identifying and measuring occupational burnout that is still in use today (Maslach Burnout Inventory). The goal is to assess an individual's experience of burnout.. Physician burnout is an under-recognized and under-reported problem (Lacy).

The Covid-19 pandemic sent the rates of physical burnout soaring. The American Medical Association estimated the prevalence of burnout among physicians in the United States to be 62.8% in 2021, much higher than the 38.2% measured in 2020 (AMA). Physicians have a higher rate of burnout compared to other fields and this has increased overall over the last two years. Each study on burnout consistently demonstrated that the overall prevalence of occupational burnout among physicians was higher relative to the U.S. workforce (AMA).

The impact of burnout is also economical as the cost of physician burnout adds more than $3.4 billion annually to the U.S. healthcare system (Mayo Clinic). The cost of physician burnout can range from $500,000 to more than $1 million per doctor. This estimate includes recruitment, sign-on bonuses, lost billing, and onboarding costs for replacement physicians (AMA).

What is the cause? Most physicians will point to charting and paperwork as the number one factor contributing to burnout, followed by a lack of respect from the administration (Medscape). Work inequality has led to even higher rates among women physicians. Women physicians in primary care are estimated to spend an extra 108 minutes more than their male counterparts for every eight hours of patient-scheduled time on the electronic health record (AMA). There has been a rise in patient portal messages to 157% of what they were at pre-pandemic levels. The American Medical Association is actively working to reduce inbox burdens on physicians.

Drivers of the physician burnout epidemic are largely rooted within healthcare organizations and systems. These factors include excessive workloads, inefficient work processes, clerical burdens, work-home conflicts, lack of physician autonomy, organizational support structures, and leadership culture (West). According to a 2018 meta-analysis (Jama-Data Entry) of 47 studies involving 42,473 physicians, occupational burnout is associated with an increased risk of patient safety incidents, decreased quality of care due to reduced professionalism, and reduced patient satisfaction. We all pay the price when a physician is burnt out.

Another factor is the lack of perceived access to self-care and mental health. Medical license applications include questions that reinforce the stigma of psychological stresses and discourage physicians from seeking appropriate care (Kuhn). Dr. Gigi Abdel-Samed openly shares her Ambien addiction. We hope that more physicians come forward and get the help they need. Depression and burnout are not the same things, although they could be associated. Over 60% of physicians responded that they had no history of depression before becoming a physician.

There are differences based on specialty. Medscape's report showed that those in Emergency Medicine had the highest rate of physician burnout at 60%, followed by Critical Care at 56% and OB/GYN at 53%. Dr. Huber shares her personal experience with emergency room medicine and PTSD.

If unrecognized, the costs to the physician and the healthcare system can be enormous because physician burnout is associated with increased rates of depression, alcohol, and drug abuse, divorce, suicide, medical errors, difficult relationships with coworkers, patient dissatisfaction, as well as physician attrition (Lacy). Each year, more than 400 physicians take their lives, likely related to increased depression and burnout (Stehman).

One in five physicians is now indicating that it is likely that they will leave their current practice in the next two years (AMA). One in three physicians anticipates cutting back on their work hours or going part-time, reducing patient access to care. Burnout is a major driving force behind those anticipated changes (AMA).

Additionally, physicians may not know that they are experiencing burnout. There may be overwhelming emotional exhaustion, feelings of cynicism, and detachment from the job defined as de-personalization. Doctors also develop a sense of ineffectiveness and little personal accomplishment. Their career engagement (job satisfaction, career choice regret, turnover intention, career development, and productivity loss) decline, and the quality of patient care (patient safety incidents, low professionalism, and patient satisfaction) also suffer (Hodkinson).

Fortunately, the problem is being recognized nationwide. In the past year, the U.S. Surgeon General issued an advisory on physician burnout. The National

Academy of Medicine suggested that healthcare leaders make an immediate widespread commitment to major systemic changes. The AMA's Recovery Plan for America's Physicians focuses on supporting physicians by, removing obstacles and burdens that interfere with patient care, and prioritizing physician well-being as an essential requirement to achieving national health goals (AMA). It is the healthcare system, not only the individual physician, that needs help. Dr. Wendt K Dean, MD President of Moral Injury Healthcare, stated it best, "it is time to stop holding individual clinicians responsible for the dysfunction of the U.S. healthcare system" (Medscape). Providing protected time for initiatives is a start with one-day seminars but ongoing check-ins are also needed.

Physicians do not need to become more resilient. As a whole, physicians are one of the most resilient groups I know. Our many years of training, sacrifice, and persistence require resilience. In multivariable analysis, resilience scores were higher among physicians than the general employed population. Resilience was inversely associated with burnout symptoms, but burnout rates were substantial even among the most resilient physicians (West 2020). This catchphrase of resilience has led to mandated physician resilience training but not giving them protected time to participate is also a failure of the system as it is increasing time demands and stress levels of physicians without the desired result.

Individually focused solutions such as mindfulness-based stress reduction and small-group programs to promote community, connectedness, and meaning are effective. While 48% of doctors mentioned that they were using exercise to help cope with burnout, 45% mentioned they were isolating themselves from others (Medscape). Mental health has come to the forefront of self-care. Spending time with family and friends, doing activities that one enjoys, and exercising can all help.

Increasing physician autonomy in the workplace is beneficial. We know that physicians who rated their control over their work environment as high had lower rates of burnout at 39% compared to physicians who rated their control as low with 75% burnout (AMA). Double and triple-booking patients cause undue stress on the physician and increase patient risk of errors.

Sneak Peak into our Stories:

With this as a backdrop of the state of physician health in the USA, we are fortunate to have over 50 female physicians contribute to this book on burnout and offer insights as to how we can learn to thrive in our current healthcare climate while more systemic changes are being implemented. We start our book with an in-depth exploration looking at the life of Dr. Tracey O'Connell, exploring feelings that "we are not good enough" and the toll it takes on our personal and professional life.

We know that physician rates of depression and anxiety are high. Dr. Tran openly shares her story that explores the high rates of depression and anxiety in physicians We know over 400 physicians commit suicide annually. Dr. Rigert and Dr. Chang share their stories about what led them to thoughts of suicide in their chapters.

At the time of this publication, an event occurred that many of us know. A young man playing football had a cardiac arrest on the field. The players huddled around him, and many of the players asked to not play after he was taken off the field. This is the NFL, professional football! In contrast, physicians run codes on unstable patients. However, when the code is over, we go on to the next patient regardless of the outcome as if nothing happened. Doing this over and over again. Can you imagine what a toll this traumatic event of a code has on all those involved in healthcare? Dr. Depalma, Dr. Huber, and Dr. Tanikella's stories speak to these scenarios and physician resilience.

We are doctors and scientists. We practice evidence-based medicine which includes standards for airborne and contact precautions with infectious diseases. The Covid-19 pandemic requires the use of personal protective equipment. Dr. Chiaramonte shares her story about being reprimanded for purchasing her own masks because she went against the administration's request for no masking. Physicians need to have better control over their safety and the environment they work in.

Dr. Panico shares the toll that metrics, charting, and pre-authorizations have on physicians. It is time-consuming and leads to de-personalization. Physicians could and should be doing the jobs that only physicians can do. We need to have ancillary staff who can assist in these mechanical tasks.

Dr. Dumenko shares chaotic and rushed encounters in the emergency room, where decisions can make the difference between life and death. However, administrators want high patient satisfaction scores, and this environment of short encounters and high-stakes medicine leads to lower patient satisfaction scores and less time to properly care for patients.

The Covid-19 pandemic has also brought a halt to life as we know it. Some of us had to slow down, and we realized what we had been missing. That time led to deep introspection and what was important to us. Dr. Huntington shares her story of leadership and the need for change. Dr. Anonymous 2 shares how this time led her to a path of reevaluation. Dr. Alber's and Dr. Sapna's stories share the importance of downtime.

Are women treated differently? Yes, we are. Dr. Schofer's story is one many of us can relate to and it reminds me of the term "beat into submission". The responsibility of childcare is placed more heavily on women. With almost 50% of physicians being women, there are concerns about time for parenting, pumping, breastfeeding, and fitting it all in when one is stretched to the max seeing many patients each day. Dr. Payal shares these concerns in her story. Infertility rates are higher among women physicians. Dr. Ott shares her experience with this as well as her experience leading important well-being work in her organization.

There is cultural bias in medicine, as shared in the stories of Dr. Shereef and Dr. Santos, and many of the other co-authors. We know that patients do better when their physicians are a similar background to them (Harvard Business Review). There are more minorities in medical school today, but will they stay in medicine? We hope so.

Stress causes physical ailments and poor concentration, as shared in Dr. Tiger's and my stories. Dr. Tiger mentioned her hands were so numb she had trouble operating the equipment. Dr. Gupta experienced chronic pain. There are illnesses such as autoimmune disease, as shared in Dr. Wada and Dr. Mar's stories. Dr. Grover-Wenk shares about chronic illness and leukemia. She is now practicing medicine on her own terms. I did not see any literature referencing higher rates of autoimmune disease in women physicians, although I did see reports of nurses having a higher incidence of autoimmune diseases.

The stress and pain caused some of us to look into integrative medicine, a more holistic approach to practicing medicine. Dr. Hankins uses EFT to help reduce stress, and many of our co-authors use an integrative approach to practice.

When is enough enough? There might be some event that stops us in our tracks when we say enough is enough and "no more". For Dr. Lola, it was swerving her car into a ditch while pregnant. For Dr. Le Blanc, it was having the rug ripped from under her. Many of us play it safe until we get to the point where that is no longer an option. This is true for Dr. Christner. She demonstrates how her beliefs impacted her choices until she said no more.

Perfectionism, with thoughts of "we can't fail" "we mustn't fail", is ingrained in us. As you read through the stories, you will see that they started as perceived feelings of high expectations as children. We were and are "people pleasers". We were pushed until we were at the breaking point. The system has taken advantage of this quality of physicians. Does this lead to higher rates of burnout as adults? I believe it does. It is up to us to set boundaries and realize "No" is a complete sentence, as Asha shares in her story. We fear we are not good enough, so we do more. If this constant pressure is not recognized, we are asked to do more, and the cycle repeats itself until it is no longer sustainable.

Perfectionism and our self-worth are demonstrated in Dr. DePalma's story. Dr. Anonymous 1's story shares about being a superhuman. Interestingly, the term superhuman comes up more than once in our stories. Why? Because we, women physicians, feel the need to do more to prove that we are capable. Dr. Sunkireddy shares with us how reducing hours, even a half day a week, can make a difference in productivity and life fulfillment.

Imposter syndrome plagues many women professionals. Dr. Pichardo-Lafontaine speaks about imposter syndrome in her story. As physicians and women, we naturally give until our bodies tell us we can no longer do anymore, yet society says otherwise. You will hear stories of altruism. We are physicians, and therefore we have to give it our all 24/7. Dr. Tisdale shares the story of a much-anticipated school trip and how she helped others with the business side of medical practice. Dr. Rubin shares that early childhood trauma can manifest later in life and that there are no wrong turns in life that cannot be turned back.

Too many of us feel guilty about spending time with our family, but what about when time is ticking, which it always is? Dr. Awad took time to visit her Grandma while her children played violin. Driving home, she knew she would never see her Grandma again.

You will hear stories from Dr. Pradhan, Dr. Radhika, and Dr. Aggarwal who continue to practice medicine but on their terms. Dr. Pradhan shares that it is okay if we don't start our surgeries at the break of dawn and spend the extra few minutes at home with our family in the mornings.

The average medical student has $200,000 in student loans by the time they graduate. Physicians are saddled with debt and strict workplace rules like non-competes which can be stressful. Many doctors feel trapped because of financial responsibilities. Dr. Beckford speaks to this in her story.

You will hear stories of tremendous support from spouses and family. Dr. Ali shared that her husband wrote her resignation letter, which I found heartwarming.

Many of us withdrew during our episode of burnout, as Dr. Sharma mentions in her story. If you notice your coworkers or friends withdrawing, ask if they are okay.

Our group, Female Physician Entrepreneurs, was created to help physicians develop their business interests. Interest outside of medicine can help us stay grounded. Creativity outside of medicine can help foster a sense of purpose and meaning especially if you have no autonomy at work. Dr. Simoyan shares her passions including book publishing, photo books, music, and art exhibits. Having an interest that you enjoy, and that keeps you grounded can be essential to helping burnout. Dr. Babaniji shared with us how she created her own lipstick company.

Dr. Yel'Ora shares her experience with overnight shifts and how she tackled this problem to provide a solution for others. Dr. Lodhi shares her story of burnout and walking away from her practice. She is now using social media to help Muslim women advocate for themselves and practice medicine on her terms.

Dr. Baladandapani shares her passion for real estate investing and how this helped provide a way out of burnout. We need to have compassion for one another within medicine. Dr. Padmanabhan shares her leadership stories and experience with different medical fields.

Dr. Christiana Jones shares about malpractice, long hours, and new adventures as a realtor and real estate investor.

Dr. Carrie Atcheson and her husband Dr. Eric Atcheson, offer insight to what helped their relationship when struggling with burnout.

This book contains many stories of burnout but also the positive stories of "Thriving After Burnout". The stories will warm your heart, and most of all, they will let you know that you are not alone. I'm privileged to know these physicians and share their stories. We hope you can reach out to our community and your community for support if you recognize burnout in your life and know you have the ability to thrive after burnout.

References

West CP, Dyrbye LN, Shanafelt TD. Physician burnout: contributors, consequences, and solutions. J Intern Med. 2018 Jun;283(6):516-529. doi: 10.1111/joim.12752. Epub 2018 Mar 24. PMID: 29505159.

Lacy BE, Chan JL. Physician Burnout: The Hidden Health Care Crisis. Clin Gastroenterol Hepatol. 2018 Mar;16(3):311-317. doi: 10.1016/j.cgh.2017.06.043. Epub 2017 Jun 30. PMID: 28669661.

Stehman CR, Testo Z, Gershaw RS, Kellogg AR. Burnout, Drop Out, Suicide: Physician Loss in Emergency Medicine, Part I. West J Emerg Med. 2019 May;20(3):485-494. doi: 10.5811/westjem.2019.4.40970. Epub 2019 Apr 23. Erratum in: West J Emerg Med. 2019 Aug 21;20(5):840-841. PMID: 31123550; PMCID: PMC6526882.

Rodrigues H, Cobucci R, Oliveira A, Cabral JV, Medeiros L, Gurgel K, Souza T, Gonçalves AK. Burnout syndrome among medical residents: A systematic review and meta-analysis. PLoS One. 2018 Nov 12;13(11):e0206840. doi: 10.1371/journal.pone.0206840. PMID: 30418984; PMCID: PMC6231624.

Kuhn CM, Flanagan EM. Self-care as a professional imperative: physician burnout, depression, and suicide. Can J Anaesth. 2017 Feb;64(2):158-168. English. doi: 10.1007/s12630-016-0781-0. Epub 2016 Dec 1. PMID: 27910035.

West CP, Dyrbye LN, Sinsky C, Trockel M, Tutty M, Nedelec L, Carlasare LE, Shanafelt TD. Resilience and Burnout Among Physicians and the General US Working Population. JAMA Netw Open. 2020 Jul 1;3(7):e209385. doi: 10.1001/jamanetworkopen.2020.9385. PMID: 32614425; PMCID: PMC7333021.

Hodkinson A, Zhou A, Johnson J, Geraghty K, Riley R, Zhou A, Panagopoulou E, Chew-Graham CA, Peters D, Esmail A, Panagioti M. Associations of physician burnout with career engagement and quality of patient care: systematic review and meta-analysis. BMJ. 2022 Sep 14;378:e070442. doi: 10.1136/bmj-2022-070442. PMID: 36104064; PMCID: PMC9472104.

National Academies of Sciences, Engineering, and Medicine; National Academy of Medicine; Committee on Systems Approaches to Improve Patient Care by Supporting Clinician Well-Being. Taking Action Against Clinician Burnout: A Systems Approach to Professional Well-Being. Washington (D.C.): National Academies Press (U.S.); 2019 Oct 23. 3, Extent and Consequences of Clinician Burnout. Available from: https://www.ncbi.nlm.nih.gov/books/NBK552628/

Panagioti M, Geraghty K, Johnson J, Zhou A, Panagopoulou E, Chew-Graham C, Peters D, Hodkinson A, Riley R, Esmail A. Association Between Physician Burnout and Patient Safety, Professionalism, and Patient Satisfaction: A Systematic Review and Meta-analysis. JAMA Intern Med. 2018 Oct 1;178(10):1317-1331. doi: 10.1001/jamainternmed.2018.3713. Retraction in: JAMA Intern Med. 2020 Jul 1;180(7):931. Erratum in: JAMA Intern Med. 2019 Apr 1;179(4):596. PMID: 30193239; PMCID: PMC6233757.

Errors in Data Entry and Figures. JAMA Intern Med. 2019 Apr 1;179(4):596. doi: 10.1001/jamainternmed.2019.0155. Erratum for: JAMA Intern Med. 2018 Oct 1;178(10):1317-1330. PMID: 30830146; PMCID: PMC6450298. https://hbr.org/2018/08/research-having-a-black-doctor-led-black-men-to-receive-more-effective-care

Health care worker Burnout. https://www.hhs.gov/surgeongeneral/priorities/health-worker-burnout/index.html

Marshall, Ariela L. MD; Arora, Vineet M. MD, MAPP; Salles, Arghavan MD, Ph.D. Physician Fertility: A Call to Action. Academic Medicine 95(5):p 679-681, May 2020. | DOI: 10.1097/ACM.0000000000003079

https://www.mayoclinicproceedings.org/article/S0025-6196(22)00515-8/fulltext#%20

Medscape 2022 Physical Burnout report https://www.medscape.com/slideshow/2022-lifestyle-burnout-6014664

Fostering Sustainable Well-being: Why I Chose Me Over Medicine By Tracey O'Connell, MD

It's been 5.5 years since I left my private practice radiology job. I've told my burnout story so many times, I'm tired of hearing it myself! What's neat to observe, though, is how much it's evolved over time; how my perspectives about what happened and why have changed since I've healed. There were signs early on, and all along, that medicine would not be a good fit for me. I ignored all of them because I was young and innocent. I now see my story through a clear, gentle, proud lens. No longer burned out, I have a newly acquired repertoire of skills for fostering sustainable well-being and self-trust.

Ironically, I never had a burning desire to be a doctor. I've always possessed a deep passion for learning, helping others, and making the world a better place, though. To this day, my favorite thing to do is to sit with other people and hear about their lives, the good stuff and the hard stuff. After my parents divorced when I was four, I traveled cross-country several times a year between them. Each time I deplaned I'd be animated with enchanting stories of the new BFF I'd sat next to on the flight. (Never thought to ask if they felt like talking but…). In school, I was the one who wanted to be friends with EVERYONE. I was popular, but not in an obnoxious way, by my interpretation. People are fascinating. Every person has something to offer the world: their own version of reality, their own lived experiences that shape them. I always befriended the "wounded bird," wanting to help them feel better. Really knowing people lets me understand them, their dreams and struggles. Connection enriches my life. I'll never know whether I was subconsciously seeking love from others because my parents had split, but it didn't feel that way. Most people agree that it feels really good to be seen and heard. I want others to have that feeling.

Whether high or low energy, when we're in connection, we lose track of time. We're in spiritual communion. Our needs are met. We're immersed in this moment, right here, and nothing else matters. No longer self-conscious about what we're saying or not saying or how we look as we're saying or not saying it. We're just present. Time is irrelevant, but we don't want it to end. It's effortless. It feels like play. We think to ourselves, "This is what it's like to be fully alive."

I went to college determined to be anything but a doctor. My father was a radiologist. My stepfather, a cardiologist. All of my parents' friends were doctors. Growing up around doctors in all specialties, I observed them living deeply rewarding lives. Yes, they worked hard. Sometimes they couldn't make it to the Christmas party. When my stepdad was on call, the phone rang at all hours of the night, and my mom slept in the guestroom. It wasn't easy. But there were visible signs that a career in medicine was stable, personally fulfilling, and highly valued by society.

I wanted to do something else, though, something different, outside of medicine. It's hard to remember life without the Internet, but the scope of what I could do with a psychology major at that time was limited to what I heard from professors, classmates, neighbors, and family. My understanding of what graduate school for psychology would involve was performing research on rats. And I'm allergic to rats. If I'd known what a licensed clinical social worker was at the time, I think I would've loved doing that. It also turns out that I really enjoy teaching when I'm excited about a topic, but at 21, I only knew folks who became elementary school teachers, and I knew that wasn't my niche.

With no other appealing options, I decided to go to medical school to be a psychiatrist. Family members and friends were excited for me and encouraging. I'd always performed well in school, was curious, and was repeatedly assured "you'll always have a stable job in medicine." It's too bad that I had no idea the emotional toll that career choice would take on me, right from the start.

The Dalai Lama, when asked what surprised him most about humanity, said: "Man. Because he sacrifices his health in order to make money. Then he sacrifices money to recuperate his health. And then he is so anxious about the future that he does not enjoy the present; the result being that he does not live in the present or the future; he lives as if he is never going to die, and then dies having never really lived."

I'd taken the bare minimum pre-med requirements. While my cohort was mastering microbiology and genetics, I'd been absorbed in liberal arts classes like The Study of Words, learning Greek and Latin roots of everyday language; anthropology; women's studies; The Geography of Apartheid. When it came time to sit for the MCAT, I was sorely unprepared. I went to Key West with my roommate for spring break a month before the exam, bringing my test-prep manual with me, ineffectively attempting to execute my "study plan" while friends went bar-hopping and chided me for being "lame." It became painfully apparent there was simply no way I could learn the content from only the test-prep materials. The night before the exam, I drove my dad's Subaru wagon into a cement pylon at a gas station, the kind intended to protect vehicles from hitting the gas pump. This random accident tipped off a shame spiral. I convinced myself I wasn't focused enough, out of control and inept; definitely unfit to take a medical school entrance exam. I didn't sleep at all before the test. I performed poorly.

As a non-STEM major, I spent the year after college working as a lab tech in a pathology lab at Yale, knowing that research experience would bolster my application. My Ivy League lab mentor insisted that I only apply to the "best" medical schools. At 22, I trusted his knowledge more than my own. I applied only to the most prestigious programs, including the University of North Carolina-Chapel Hill. The trouble was, I had no "safety school." My family had moved from my home state of Wisconsin to North Carolina while I was at college in Colorado, and at the time I was living in New Haven, Connecticut.

Just after submitting my applications in January, I met Tom. Six years older than me, he'd just finished his PhD and had come to Yale for a postdoctoral fellowship in Pathology. Shortly after introductions, I had our story written: *we'll go on a few dates, everyone in the lab will find out, it'll be really embarrassing, and then it will end, just as all my college relationships did.* But that's not what happened. We had fun together. We watched movies on campus. On one of our first dates, he came with me to an aerobics class and I thought *This guy is either a total goofball or he's completely comfortable with himself.* We took the train into NYC to see Broadway shows. And when each of the illustrious schools denied me admission, he comforted me and told me he was going to kick their asses for making such a colossal mistake. Come May, we'd just spent a dazzling romantic weekend together in Newport, Rhode Island, riding bikes and dining at sunset, when I returned to my studio apartment to learn that I'd been waitlisted at UNC. My plans for medical school were falling apart, and I had no back up plan. Tom helped me get a grip and soon, I began studying for the MCAT again.

Fortuitously, I was accepted into UNC off the waitlist. Tom stayed in New Haven, and I moved to Chapel Hill. We were committed to making it work. In many ways, I was relieved he was far away so I could better compartmentalize and focus on learning. But the seed of *I'm not good enough for medical school* had already been planted. Getting a B- on my first biochemistry exam cemented this belief. I was no longer "gifted and talented." I was average. As the anatomy professor stood in front of us pronouncing, "There are two types of students who will get Honors: those who are naturally brilliant, and those who work their asses off," I knew right away which category I fell into. Tom and I chatted on the phone when we could. We emailed occasionally, but email was new, and only possible using the common computer in my classroom lab.

I assumed a mantra: Please. Perform. Perfect. Those who knew me in medical school will remember me sitting in the front row in lecture halls, raising my hand frequently to make sure I understood *exactly* what was being said so that I could memorize it and be rewarded on the exam. I studied constantly. Instead of meeting friends on the weekends, I went to my parents' house and studied in the basement. I knew classmates saw me as a "gunner," but it didn't matter. I didn't cook, clean, or exercise. My mom would go to the grocery store to stock my refrigerator, and dinner was cereal eaten straight from the box.

For October's fall break, Tom and I met in Vermont. He'd made reservations at a darling bed & breakfast in the mountains. We were so excited to see each other again. But when he picked me up at the airport, it felt strange sitting next to him in the front seat of his Honda Civic. When he reached for my hand, I wanted to pull it away. After a brisk hike among the colorful leaves, we returned to our dimly lit room, to the antique canopy bed with white candlewick coverings. I knew the atmosphere and ambiance were set for romance. But when Tom handed me a fancy gift bag containing elegant, feminine lingerie, I froze. I couldn't step out of control mode. I couldn't relax. I couldn't be intimate because I didn't feel intimate. *I'm a med student. I am not sexy. I cannot be both.* This was the first of many, many fights to come about why I didn't feel like having sex, even when I wasn't studying or at the hospital.

As a first-year medical student interested in psychiatry, I'd been assigned to a small group with other potential psychiatrists, meeting bimonthly with a well-respected psychiatrist. In large lecture classes, this middle-aged man was charismatic. Charming. Funny. Engaging. In the small group setting, he was an excellent listener who set a tone of safety and trust. He led with deeply personal questions like, "How's medical life affecting you? How're you coping? What feelings are you experiencing? What's it like to be you?" Being who I am, I answered honestly. I said I was struggling. Not yet a reader, I wasn't able to keep up with the content. I felt inept. After the B- on my first test, how was I going to be a good doctor? The group bonded, but not everyone shared. During the many sessions when I cried, he'd escort me into the hall to console me, separating me from the others. At the end of the year, the only thing he wrote on my evaluation was, "Seemed younger than the rest of the group."

These words can be interpreted in many ways, but I took them to mean that how I'd shown up was immature and inappropriate. Unlike the natural impulse we have to show compassion in poignant moments, his ultimate assessment of me felt critical. My tears hadn't connected me to others; they'd isolated me. I felt safe sharing. Did the sagacious psychiatrist take me into the hall because he was concerned that my weeping would somehow psychologically damage the other group members? What made my sorrow something to hide? Regardless, I took away this message: *Such feelings aren't to be shown to others. Not here. Not now. Not ever.* My ordinary anguish was shameful and aberrant. Grief-stricken, I couldn't figure out how to stop feeling, trust my feelings, or where to safely show them. If not in a room of future psychiatrists, where do feelings belong? This experience changed the course of my career.

Meanwhile, Tom had secured a job in Raleigh. We'd had many radically honest phone conversations about whether it was wise for him to pick up his life and move to North Carolina. What if he moved in with me and we weren't compatible? What if we didn't last? Ever practical, Tom knew the job opportunity would advance his career regardless of what became of the two of us. We embraced this next step with cautious enthusiasm. But the joy of being together again was quickly replaced by resentment. I resented him for keeping me from studying all the time. He resented me for tacitly handing off all the cooking, cleaning, and shopping to him, leaving him to keep himself company while I was studying. I placated him with promises that this way of living was temporary: "It will get better third year. Everyone says so."

"If we want to get married, it has to be June 18, 1994," I told Tom in June of 1993. "I have two weeks between Part 1 of the Boards and the start of my third year Surgery rotation."

"Okay," he said, with a wink.

We went to Asheville in the Blue Ridge mountains a month later, and he formally proposed. Got down on one knee and everything. We were both giddy, and we both shed tears. We used the house phone at the B & B to call all of our family members. We toasted our future with champagne.

Studying for Boards while planning a wedding turned out to be a great way to balance two activities that could each be all-consuming. I'm not Catholic but Tom was (neither of us is now), and it was important to his family that we get married in a Catholic church. Doing so required that we go through premarital counseling with a priest. As a child of divorce (twice), this seemed like a very prudent plan to me. We were dubious about receiving counseling from someone who'll never marry, but he actually gave us sage advice:

"This person you're marrying will always remain a mystery. If you think you know all there is to know about this person, or you grow bored, or believe that someone better out there exists for you, dig deeper. Get to know this partner in a new way. Grow together."

"Put the marriage first. Put it before your career. Before your children. Before your extended families. If you have a healthy marriage, you'll be able to weather everything else life throws at you."

I completed my Board exam and our wedding went off without a hitch. We honeymooned in Charleston, SC, miles away from reality. We sang every song on the Counting Crows' first album while driving there and back.

I feel sad for myself now when I remember how hard it was to go from those intensely joyful moments as a newly married couple to my general surgery rotation. After only a few weeks of having to be at the hospital at 5 am, stay until 7 pm, and do it all again day after day, fights with Tom became daily occurrences. Consumed by work, I could see why he was upset with me, but I couldn't invest in him or his needs because I didn't have the energy. One night, things escalated. I was so bereft and frustrated, I just started screaming. I'm sure Marion, the 90-year-old neighbor in the apartment next door, thought one of us was being murdered. My screaming scared Tom, and it scared me. It was primal.

Our youth and vows helped us carry on, believing things would get easier after the surgery rotation. General medicine was less physically demanding but emotionally grueling. Pediatrics, family medicine, and psychiatry rotations were required to be done in other parts of the state, so Tom and I had to be apart for months at a time, settling once again for phone calls and occasional weekends together. By the OB-Gyn service, the last rotation of the year, I couldn't sleep. I went for a solid week without sleeping. (Sleep is non-negotiable for me, and ultimately, played a large role in my choice of medical specialty.) I had ruminations and was further distraught because my time in psychiatry hadn't turned out to be what I'd envisioned as a career. I was guilt-ridden for putting both of us through three years of hell for nothing. I didn't know what to do.

On our first wedding anniversary, we sat side-by-side on the cement stoop of our single-story apartment as the sun went down.

"Do you want to go out to dinner, honey?" Tom asked.
"No," I answered.
"Go to a movie?"
"No."
"Rent a movie?"
"No."
"Play tennis?"
"No! I don't play tennis, you do."
"Do you want me to leave you alone?"
"No. It's our anniversary. I can't spend our anniversary in this apartment by myself."
"Well, what do you want to do?"
"I don't know."

Tom turned to look at me. He took my hands in his. "Look. Listen to me. I love you. I am not leaving you. But you need help. And I can't help you."

I longed for my former self, who could work hard and play hard, without judging my feelings. No longer having the freedom for my happy-go-lucky personality to express herself, the stage was set for me to emotionally shut down. I was ashamed of being such a mess. We'd only been married a year and already we were falling apart. Although I knew I was the one who'd changed, I was simultaneously furious with him for making me take responsibility for fixing our relationship. I felt unjustly blamed for the state of our marriage, yet I knew he was right: I did need help. I was not okay.

Tom had been naturally able to embody Brené Brown's research findings long before she'd even contemplated her TED talk. He knew how to be vulnerable. He knew how to draw boundaries with love. He knew what to be accountable for, and what wasn't his responsibility. He knew himself, and he knew his own limitations. He stood by me without abandoning his own integrity.

At that time, there wasn't the socially acceptable term "burnout." The only term we had for what I was feeling was "depression," and it infuriates me that I took on the burden of seeing myself as mentally ill rather than having normal responses to significant emotional experiences. This is just one of many ways that medical culture "gaslights" us into believing that the system is normal, and that it is us, the student or practitioner, that has the problem.

In trying so desperately to be worthy in the eyes of others, I'd lost the most important connection of all: my connection to myself. The way I got through the loneliness and disconnection was to invest in therapy, medication, and lots of self-help books. In constantly trying to improve myself, I thought, at the very least, I could look back at the end of my life and know that I'd tried. The skills I learned then, and continued to expand upon over the next two decades, allowed me to embody my personal values, even subconsciously, as I made decisions in my personal and professional life. I stayed in my integrity, and I think that's what's helped me the most. Even when I wasn't "towing the party line," a part of me was very certain that I was doing what was personally right.

Remembering what the priest had said, I knew I had to put my marriage first. I could already see plain as day that the medical establishment wasn't going to approve of playing second fiddle to my personal life. I had to figure out a way to save my marriage, and somehow turn my three years of medical training into something useful. It was time to declare my specialty, and I had no idea how I was going to practice medicine.

I took two months off between third and fourth year, started seeing a psychiatrist and took an SSRI. I slept. A lot. I slept in. Got up to eat. Watered and deadheaded two potted plants on the front doorstep. Went back to bed. Slept until I woke up on my own. Did a word search. Sat outside listening to birds. Occasionally got dressed to go to the gym but rarely actually made it there. I stayed up late reading *Darkness Visible* by William Styron. I could relate to all of his feelings and felt comforted by his sharing of his own experience with depression. SSRIs helped me survive, numbing my hard feelings while also numbing any joyful ones, but Tom and I were able to spend quality time together in the evenings after he got home from work.

I knew I didn't want to be a cardiologist like my stepdad, who was rarely if ever truly "off" from work. At the encouragement of my birth father, his brother, and my aunt who are all radiologists, I declared radiology as my specialty before I'd actually even begun the radiology elective. They assured me I'd be able to have the work-life balance I wanted. I believed them based on their lived example.

Many radiologists choose the specialty because they don't like interacting with sick people. As a highly sensitive person, I rerouted to radiology to distance myself from patient suffering, from emotions altogether, as a means of self-protection. But that didn't stop me from thinking about others' feelings and opinions. As a resident, it's a wonder I learned anything at all because I was so preoccupied with making a good impression on attendings and colleagues. I had very little room in my head for information relevant to work; I even took a private practice job working part-time, choosing not to become a partner because I now had a personal psychiatric history and saw myself as fragile, unstable, ill.

Radiology has allowed me to compartmentalize, sort of. It allowed me to have three healthy babies: one in residency, one at the end of fellowship, and one 2 years into private practice. I went back to work after 6 weeks of maternity leave each time. Somehow, I was able to read cases, use the breast pump, do a biopsy, pump, pound fluids, stay late, maybe nurse the baby once before bed, and once before work the next day. This was also possible thanks to a committed spouse equally invested in family life.

Initially, the amount of patient contact and human interaction at work was enough to keep my "people-oriented" personality satisfied. It was helpful to be able to stay focused on a fascinating disease process, looking only at the images of the person with the illness, separate from the person suffering the disease. I was skilled at performing image-guided procedures when I could comfort Mrs. Jones through her fear during a biopsy, even get to chit-chat about her life briefly, and then walk away, back to the dark cave of black and white, rarely hearing about Mrs. Jones ever again. It was tidy. My role was brief, purposeful, and largely devoid of emotion. For a while, this was enough.

But images aren't just black and white, and neither is health; there are lots of gray areas rife with uncertainty and conflicting interpretations. Working in "the cave" was largely like working in a vacuum, because images only tell one aspect of a patient's illness. It was rare to ever hear any follow up about how Mrs. Jones was doing. This disconnected me from a sense of accomplishment or of having a meaningful impact on other humans through my work, and only exacerbated my emotional struggles. Surrounded by hyper-rational people who enjoyed spending 9+ hours in the dark didn't keep me from feeling. It only amplified my loneliness and self-loathing. When I cried at work, I was left alone.

One day, when my three kids were all under the age of 6, I was sleep-deprived and hijacked by postpartum hormones. After using the breast pump, I returned to read a few MRI cases before doing a CT-guided biopsy of the pancreas on a woman with probable pancreatic cancer. A colleague's unexpected entrance interrupted my focus. He closed the door behind him. My heart started pounding because a) I was on a tight schedule, and b) a closed door in this setting implied something serious to me. He wanted to let me know that his college roommate, an orthopedist in town, had called to express his annoyance that I had described abnormal signal in the subscapularis tendon; he didn't want me to read his cases anymore because he said the subscapularis tendon only rarely experiences pathology.

I'd like to think that under normal circumstances, I would have summoned my knowledge and expertise; I had just reviewed an article about the frequency of underdiagnosed subscapularis tears missed with an anterior arthroscopic approach. But this was not a normal circumstance for me. I was compromised.

I now know that the complaint was a "trigger" for me: the emotional response that followed was out of proportion to the inciting event. I completely lost it, crying uncontrollably. The patient with the pancreatic mass was waiting to be consented. I viewed myself as an observer: the news, the seriousness with which the news was delivered, the fact that I was crying at work, the discrepancy between the legitimate seriousness of the pancreatic mass and my trivial upset over a difference of opinion. It was all devastating to me. I didn't know how to compose myself. The patient was waiting. I couldn't pull myself together quickly. The shame was overwhelming: *I am bad. I don't belong here. I am not worthy of this job.*

I asked another partner to perform the biopsy, left the hospital, and drove 5 minutes to another colleague's house whom I considered a friend. She wasn't working that day. I wanted her to comfort me. When I arrived at her door, she looked at me with a blank stare and offered no consolation. As I sat on her couch, telling her I felt like I was falling apart, she responded, "Well, clearly, you're having a nervous breakdown." I suddenly realized: *This was a mistake. I shouldn't have come here.* I snapped out of my emotional frenzy, stood up, and returned to work.

Let me pause: How are you feeling at this moment? Are you having any visceral responses to my story? Are you feeling squeamish? Queasy? Maybe my story makes you cringe? Maybe even just reading my story fills you with shame for me? Sometimes just hearing about others' vulnerabilities and shame is too much.

I was gone for less than 30 minutes. The pancreatic mass had been biopsied. My partners were not empathetic. No one said a word to me the rest of the day. I stayed late and completed my work. No one called me at home to see if I was okay. Silence is the worst because it allows us to make up our own stories and further injure ourselves. The next day, I was back in the reading room. The head of the group called me to tell me that I needed to promise an event like this would never happen again. I reminded him that it had never happened before, was unplanned, and was not part of my future plans. I made my promise. These are the moments that, when left unresolved, send us into our lives searching desperately for belonging. I settled instead for trying to fit in.

I stayed in that job for another 12 years, becoming a robot, keeping my real self in check. But my work culture was toxic and weighed heavily on me, whether I was at work or at home. In radiology, competition has the potential to extend well beyond the training years. I worked in a highly lucrative private practice that prioritized revving up productivity over hiring when the economy tanked in 2008 and reimbursements plummeted. Many had joined the group envisioning a certain lifestyle, including luxury cars, multiple houses, and private schools, which wouldn't be possible with lower salaries. Rather than hiring more radiologists, the majority voted for a hiring freeze, agreeing to work faster, longer hours with less vacation. Physician assistants were later recruited to perform lower-value procedures, so rads were freed up to read more higher-value MRI cases.

A radiologist friend elsewhere said their group followed suit, encouraging RVU-productivity similar to incentives for kindergarteners. A colorful bulletin board assigned each radiologist a construction paper fish swimming from left to right in an ocean toward a finish line, placed according to productivity with the highest RVU fish furthest to the right. The same fish kept winning month after month, only by a narrow margin. Sadly, that partner also died of a glioblastoma multiforme a few years later, despite their RVU record. Cliques formed within my group, greed reigned supreme, and rivalries with other groups held everyone hostage as they relentlessly vied for referrals. I was perpetually exhausted and short-tempered, always living inside my own head, full of self-doubt. Tom had tolerated it because he'd slowly been brainwashed right along with me: *This is just the way adult life is.*

Post-pandemic, the landscape has radically changed. Like nursing, the global shortage of radiologists has practices struggling to find new hires willing to work the hours regardless of the pay. Those who've survived the trenches are tired. Love is lost. Did paper fish become less inspiring? Why aren't previous methods of operating yielding the same devotion?

It's been 18 years since "failed pancreas biopsy incident." I'm able to share my stories comfortably now, even the ugly, fall-down moments, because I've built up shame-resilience with Brené Brown's curriculum for helping professionals. I shudder to think where I'd be if I hadn't taken action to heal myself on my own behalf. I recognize now that my colleagues weren't equipped to deal with my vulnerability. I thought doctors were born with skills of compassion and empathy. But no one in my group had the skills to comfort me. Had anyone been concerned about my well-being, this story wouldn't be one that shaped my professional trajectory. Was it unprofessional for me to leave the hospital in the middle of a workday? Yes. Was it a mistake? I'm not sure. Would it have been wiser to go ahead and biopsy the patient's pancreas?

For decades, I'd seen myself as doing everything in my life half-ass. I'd viewed my sensitive, emotional self as an illness that needed to be managed so I didn't get depressed again. But now, with distance and clarity of mind, I see that all that inner conflict, all the deep feelings I had as I struggled, were actually gifts. My struggle was rooted in the battle between my identity as a doctor and my identity as a sentient being.

Medicine is hard. So is marriage. Marriage or medicine? Do we have to choose? In both, anger and sadness come up daily — we're only human, after all — but our conditioned emotional responses for survival in a medical setting are antithetical to inborn, evolutionarily favorable emotions outside of medicine. Sadness is a prosocial emotion, evolutionarily advantageous for building unity and love. My despair at work didn't evoke compassion from my peers as it does in ordinary life. In medical life, melancholy is deliberately avoided. It wasn't until I stepped away from medical life two decades later that I could see my struggle with sorrow isn't personal. It's cultural. Vulnerability is hard everywhere, but it's outright shamed in medicine. Opportunities to share how we're actually feeling exist only in private rooms with mental health professionals. Without intending to disparage all psychiatrists, my own experiences with them kept me believing there was something wrong with me that needed to be medicated and hidden.

Did I pick the wrong specialty for me? Perhaps. I made the decision that seemed best for me with the information I had at the time. As it turns out, you can try to take the emotions out of your circumstances, but you can't take the emotions out of yourself. Physicians don't receive any formal training around how to deal with our own emotions. Such "soft skills" take a back seat to memorizing facts and executing protocols. Assuming that we arrive in medicine with some degree of emotional intelligence from our upbringing (which is a hefty assumption to make), a life in medicine trains our own vulnerability right out of us.

The challenges of married life in medicine are the same challenges marriages experience outside of medicine, compromised further by the sense of ethical and moral obligation to the profession. It's not just about being employed or getting a paycheck, but the insatiable demands, responsibilities, and a code of ethics based on the premise that the physician will put the role of physician ahead of all other roles.

I will tell you this: I did not put my career first. I did not put my kids first. Remembering what that priest said, I put my marriage first. I stuck to my core values of authenticity (connection to the Self) and belonging (connection to others). At times, this cost me the respect of my co-residents and my co-workers in private practice. At times, this caused me extraordinary pain. I wanted so desperately to be the best doctor I could be and yet, I couldn't be bought. I craved meaningful connection with my work colleagues but they resented me for not being "all in," for working part-time, for not being a "team player" when they wanted me to work extra hours without extra pay. They called me "high-maintenance" when I questioned why the rotation start time was switched from 8 am to 7 am to benefit the division-head, requiring that Tom get all three of our kids to school by himself every time I worked. The male partners had wives that didn't work and took care of everything at home. The female partners had nannies that raised their children so they could work. I didn't want that.

I wanted Tom to know that I was committed to our partnership, and I wanted our children to see that, too. I worked diligently and conscientiously. I was never sued. But when my kids started asking, "Mom, why are you always tired? Always in a bad mood? Why don't you quit that job?" I had to really dig deep. Suddenly, my sizable paycheck and material wealth didn't matter. I didn't like myself. I didn't like the person I'd become. I didn't respect myself for preaching values of integrity, authenticity, and kindness, but not practicing them. I'd become a martyr, a person who undergoes severe or constant suffering. I'd justified my self-sacrifice as noble, but it was bullshit. I don't want to be a martyr for my family or society at large. I want to be a model. I want to embody what a good life looks like. When I thought about my babies, all grown up in the future, living the life I was living, it made my heart break. I'd never fit in with that work culture, and ultimately, I left that job setting. (I've since worked in other practice settings and have seen that the behaviors of my first group are prevalent, but not universal. I'm relieved to see that, and now have more lived experience to counsel residents as they transition from training to practice.)

In my opinion, what underlies the epidemic of burnout in medical life is the inundation with suffering without knowledge, permission, or opportunity to process or respond instinctively to the routine pain we experience. This keeps us in survival mode, afraid to do, say, or be like other humans. We're understandably bereft. We've normalized abnormal emotional responses to real life. What was adaptive for short-term success has become maladaptive for sustainable well-being. We don't feel like we're enough because we don't really know ourselves. If you knew what mattered most to you before medical training, you may have slowly and subtly betrayed yourself and your own needs after you made the tacit agreement to put medicine first. The inability to be authentic and autonomous is untenable. No one can keep so many balls in the air and still appear like they have their shit together. It's too much for any human to handle.

Outside of medicine, we can set boundaries around what's okay and what's not okay for us, boundaries that function to keep us safe and to meet our authentic wants and needs. The problem is, we don't get to create our own boundaries in medicine – medical culture creates boundaries for us. Even if we know who we are and what we value, the expectations and demands of our careers repeatedly trespass over these personal boundaries, requiring us to act in opposition to our own wants and needs. And when our behavior doesn't match our values, we lose our integrity. Did I just imply that physicians don't have integrity? Stay with me.

People who lack integrity and don't respect boundaries aren't trustworthy. So despite our ability to seamlessly navigate life-and-death circumstances daily, we don't actually trust ourselves or the people around us, making us feel perpetually unsafe. And no matter what we do, we can't overcome our anxiety that we're not enough. We're traumatized by self-betrayal and powerlessness against a near-constant fight-or-flight state which manifests as nervous system dysregulation and, ultimately, dissociation. Sadly, learning to manage shame in a healthy way isn't taught in school, and it's unlikely to be learned at home. It's absolutely up to each of us to stand up for ourselves and set boundaries to maintain our integrity. AND, it won't make us very popular in the short-term.

I left that job more than 5 years ago. Was it scary? Hell yes. It was also the best decision I've ever made. The crazy thing is that, as soon as I did, an amazing world of opportunities opened up for me; meaningful ways I could be the healer I set out to be early in my career. I am no longer a victim or a martyr. I have autonomy. I can look at myself in the mirror and like who I see. I sleep soundly at night. When I hear Harry Chapin's "Cat's in the Cradle" on the radio, I no longer feel sad when I think of my children growing up to be just like me.

I spent 6 months writing to my Future Self daily, with pen and paper. Writing long-hand has been shown by neuroscience studies to tap into a part of the brain that's not accessible any other way, not by speaking, typing, texting or thinking. Ultimately, writing to oneself allows us to answer the questions, "Who am I? What do I think? What's true for me?" All those years in therapy, trying to silence my anxiety and depression, I'd been ignoring my own body's messages trying to alert me that the way I was spending my time wasn't the right way for me.

I started listening to the messengers, giving them credibility rather than scorn, allowing them to speak on the page. I discovered what self-trust felt like: lighter, relaxed. Feelings I hadn't had since college. Opportunities began presenting themselves without the sheer grit and desperation I was used to. Once I stopped trying to control everything and play by the rules of others, life seemed to unfold with ease and flow.

I discovered that I hadn't changed. I was still the same person. I'd just lost connection to the parts of myself that felt natural and right. I'd covered up my true essence in an attempt to "fit" into a culture that wasn't right for me. It wasn't a "mistake," just a chapter in my own hero's journey. As I began to feel safe inside myself, I could remove the layers of mud and not only shine again, but be able to shine on others, help them process their own regrets, and rewrite their own life scripts.

Some friends and family can't believe I made such a bold move to pivot in such a drastic, risky way. My parents still introduce me to their friends as "the radiologist" rather than "the coach that fosters sustainable well-being." They struggle to believe my mantra that we can "have more joy in life by strengthening connection with self and others." I'm grateful I came to embody a new philosophy of success just as my own children are becoming adults. I no longer ask them, or anyone, "What're you going to do with your life?" Instead, I ask, "What're you going to do next?"

As a culture confronting epidemic loneliness, a killer worse than heart disease, we'd do well to heed Ashley C. Ford's words shared with Oprah Winfrey in an interview: "We can't heal unless we talk about what hurts." That conversation starts first with cultivating meaningful, trustworthy connection to ourselves and others.

Proximity is not what connects us to others. It's trust. Those in your circle may not be in your corner. Take inventory of the people in your life. Bodily sensations tell the truth about something important: whether you're actually connected to yourself or those around you. Pay attention. If you feel contracted, there may be issues around trust. Whenever you think about or spend time with others, check in with your body and ask yourself, *Do I feel at ease? Open? Free? Expanded? Or do I feel anxious? Closed? Contracted?*

We have lots of circles of people in our lives. I've learned to look out for and openly appreciate the ones who are also in my corner, those that don't require me to betray myself in order to be connected to them. Such people are rare. I intentionally cultivate such relationships.

In the end, self-worth is an inside job. Obtaining it outside of self is possible, but not sustainable. Many accomplished, high-achieving adults have no idea who they are outside of work. That used to be me, unable to sustain my own well-being in medical culture, but lacking any identity outside of it. Sustainable well-being relies on having the emotional tools to support one's self, regardless of circumstances, and requires time, energy, and attention to develop.

If you're looking for sustainable well-being, you can only do you, a task requiring a diet high in self-love. Nothing else works long-term. We've all sacrificed our well-being for what we believe is more important than our well-being. Achievements, fulfilling obligations, and winning approval are measures of success in our world, but are they sustainable on a personal level? The mass exodus from medicine suggests many are answering "no" and yet, they're confused about the role work is now supposed to play in their lives.

What's quite beautiful is that I am now grateful for my radiology skills. I'm able to do teleradiology from home a few hours a day- more than 2 hours and my skin literally starts to crawl. Radiology is my livelihood, it pays my bills, but it's not my identity. Radiology funds my dreams and passions. I'm back doing the thing my younger self loved: fostering connection. I've expanded my career to being an educator and coach, fostering positive self-worth and sustainable well-being with teens, physicians, and LGBTQ+. All those years of feeling "not enough" as a person, a physician, a parent, or partner kept me endlessly exploring any and all possible pathways to feeling better. On that journey, I learned that knowing how we actually feel, how we'd like to feel, how we don't want to feel, and how others feel, significantly helps sustain our well-being. Essentially, helping people FEEL better helps them feel BETTER.

I believe we can all access more joy in life by strengthening the connections we have with ourselves and with others. I prioritize "granting permission" to other physicians to stay committed to their own deep values rather than putting medicine first. I do this because I know that medicine is a fickle mistress. It can be deeply rewarding, and it will not remember you when you are gone. Don't betray yourself and what matters to you.

Who did you become when you loved your medical career more than you loved yourself? Did you choose medicine because you loved it, or because you couldn't love yourself if you didn't? How would you like to feel instead? How can I help you help yourself have that feeling?

Courage. Compassion. Connection. These are the reasons I'm here. The reasons I want to BE here.

What about you?

About Tracey O'Connell, MD

Dr. O'Connell is a self-described "recovering physician" who has expanded her career in radiology to being an educator, speaker, and coach, fostering positive self-worth and sustainable well-being with teens, physicians, and LGBTQ+. She is a certified facilitator of expressive writing and Brené Brown's shame resilience programs. You can learn more about her and her work at her website www.traceyoconnellmd.com . She can also be found on LinkedIn, Instagram, Facebook or her YouTube Channel.

www.traceyoconnellmd.com

"May our stories be a beacon of light to those who need it most, and may they inspire all those who are reading this, to be the voice of change."

-SHARON T MCLAUGHLIN MD FACS

Gigi Abdel-Samed, MD, MBA

How had I gotten here?

All I'd ever wanted since the age of eleven was to become a doctor. I wanted to help people. My life's mission since the age of 8 was to leave every life better for having been in it. All I desired was to be the person who, when I laid hands on a patient, the pain would stop... Yet here I was, in a rehab facility, sharing a small bedroom and ONE single bathroom with four other women. No computers or cell phones, just a television that barely gets cable on during limited (and supervised) hours and one landline phone in a communal room. I was the one who needed help.

Where had it all gone wrong?
I was miserable, exhausted, tired, and lonely. Though I had it all on paper — medical director of a community hospital emergency room, Associate director at a level 1 trauma center ER, a million-dollar dream home, a lake house —I had never felt emptier. I felt like it all owned me. I worked to pay for the things I had, but I wasn't enjoying them anymore.

I could pinpoint the moment it all began unraveling. I stood in my kitchen sometime after midnight, fully dressed, car keys and a crumpled receipt in one hand with my teeth sunk halfway into a Boston cream donut I didn't remember buying in the other. My heart sank. The last thing I remembered was being in my pajamas, in my bed, ready for sleep, but I couldn't refute what the receipt showed me: I had gotten dressed, driven to the 24-hour Dunkin' Donuts® drive-thru, and paid exact change for three donuts. Apparently, I'd eaten the first two donuts in a complete blackout and only came to as I was chowing down on the third.

I'd started taking Ambien to help me sleep for night shifts. It wasn't supposed to be addictive—after all, the only reason I even started taking it was because it was "safe", "non-addictive". I'd never even tried a drug in my life, and even the stress of repeatedly working through the night in an ER wasn't going to make me start.

But over the next few months, I gradually began using more and more Ambien. I wondered why I was always short at the end of the month, not realizing I'd been waking up in the middle of the night, blacked out, and taking more so I could sleep. There were mornings when I would wake up exhausted, wondering how on earth the laundry had gotten done and why the floors were vacuumed. I hadn't done it, right? I was sleeping!

I began to get prescriptions from my colleagues—"you work night shifts, of course," they said. But when that wasn't enough, I began writing prescriptions for myself. And then Ambien's effect on me lessened. It no longer made me sleepy, just calm, and before long, I couldn't even feel that. But I had to keep taking it because I would become nauseous and sweaty if I didn't.

One night, about six months into Ambien's regime over my life, I was working a twelve-hour shift. I had one dose of Ambien tucked safely in the breast pocket of my white coat, and I was counting down the hours to be off duty so I could take it in the car. That way, I wouldn't be shaky driving home. That night, I didn't make it. In the final hour of my shift, I began to sweat, I was nauseated, I couldn't speak, and my left arm wouldn't work. They thought I was having a stroke.

I've worked so hard to be successful. I graduated from Cornell with two majors and a minor in three years, getting by on loans and working part-time. I'd gotten into the second oldest residency for emergency medicine and survived 120-hour work weeks and no social life. And now, ten years later, practicing as an attending, it would seem I had it all. People respected me and treated me like I was the smartest person in the room. But I felt hollow. Broken. Like I was a fraud. How could I complain, with everything I'd ever dreamed of surrounding me? I felt trapped.

That night in the ER, unable to speak, unable to use my right arm, I faced the hard truth. Ambien was addictive, and I could no longer go even twelve hours without going into withdrawal. I didn't leave the hospital that night; instead, my colleague had to take care of me. Exhausted and feeling betrayed by my body, I endured an MRI, a spinal tap, labs, a urinalysis done by catheter so they could drug test it and be sure it was mine, and the humiliation of being sent to a detox facility against my will even though the drug test was negative. After all, Ambien "isn't addictive," so there was no drug test for it back then.

It was the end . . . and it was the beginning.

It certainly wasn't an easy street after that stay in the hospital. I stumbled and failed many times on my way back to myself. At first, it was frustrating because no one took my condition seriously. "Just Ambien?" they would say. "You can't be a drug addict." And yet I knew I was. When I finally found a facility with six pages of information on their website about Ambien addiction, I had hope again. I made the difficult decision to voluntarily surrender my medical license and enter what could be a year-long rehab. I knew I was at a turning point, and my life could be on the line—as well as the lives of my patients. And that was one line I would never intentionally cross. The withdrawal caused me to have a seizure and stop breathing. I couldn't go on like this.

During my first week in detox, I went three days without sleep, hallucinating all the while, and then had another seizure. But I'd decided, and I wasn't backing down. I would rather die having a seizure than ever put Ambien in my body again.

In the rehab facility, life was simplified. I shared a small space with those four other women, and beyond that room and the communal TV room, there wasn't much to do. There were maybe 30 of us in the program at a time, both men and women. It was a residential facility on the beach in California, and it was beautiful. They understood what it was like to be surfacing from an addiction, feeling like one raw nerve with the whole world standing on it. They understood that I felt so much shame at who I'd become that even holding eye contact with another human felt like unbearable agony. And so they brought us back to life, one day at a time. Eight 'modules' to move through at our own pace. To this day, I feel immense gratitude for that second step after detox, exercising, then sitting in the sauna to sweat out the drugs that had become stored in our fatty tissues—the surreal moments of watching someone tripping again from the release of those toxins still inside. Time became irrelevant and yet always present. From waking, to breakfast, to exercises to help us get back in our physical bodies and tolerate being there. It wasn't until the third or fourth module that we were asked to look at who we had wronged and what we had done. And by then, I was ready to face it. Simple exercises like eye gazing and holding eye contact without attempting to smile or relieve the 'tension' were profoundly life-altering.

Even though I knew the instruction was not to reveal emotion and to stay neutral and engaged, the critical committee in my head was in full force. I'll never forget that first one-minute session with a fellow person in detox... ALL of the stories in my head were revealed for the first time: 'why weren't they smiling at me? Was there something wrong with my hair?' The same committee that made me a 'high achiever' also made me afraid of disappointing anyone. Over those months in rehab, we built to hold that for 45 minutes at a time, which was transformative. And then there was the next level: 'bull-baiting' where we would hold that while others were encouraged to come in and out, saying outlandish comments and cutdowns, while we had to hold our poise and neutrality. Laughed? Start over. And oh how those exercises were the perfect training ground for later. I was taking back my power from the outside world and circumstances. Each day put into perspective all the things I had thought were so urgent.

I realized I had lost sight of who I truly was and what I stood for. I had forgotten what made me become a doctor in the first place. It wasn't the money, or the house, or the car. It was the service, the connection, the love. It was my way of serving God and love through medicine. And I had fallen into the rat race and the trap.

Before rehab, there had been days when I was at the effect of everything: emails I reacted to like a time bomb that had to be responded to immediately would keep me up at night. Preparing for tense meetings and losing sleep for days before and after.... An unhappy patient or bad outcome would keep me up playing it over and over... doing everything "stat", thinking it all needed to be done yesterday, and living on the knife's edge of anxiety and burnout— and I finally understood: it didn't really matter. None of it mattered.

I released the weight of those false pressures and stress. Mountains were just molehills.
And I became limitless. Weightless. Free. How far I had come from that powerless person. From a girl who wanted to hide and numb depending on the weather to a woman who, in her first year of sobriety, lost her dad unexpectedly, went through foreclosure and bankruptcy and stood strong in her freedom. None of that defined me. I knew I would never again use a substance to numb myself, to give me a false sense of calm and control.

 I had to wait two years to get my medical license reinstated, doing random drug tests up to six times a month to prove sobriety, and it wasn't even a sure thing. I didn't know if I would ever be allowed to practice medicine again, and that hurt. But I knew I couldn't sit home doing nothing, so I took a barista job at Starbucks. I had learned in rehab to take back my power from any circumstance or event. And I did. It was embarrassing to become a barista after 10 years of being a doctor, and yet, I didn't care. It was something new to learn, a place to belong. My coworkers were my family. Customers would look at me quizzically when they asked my story, and I shared... what was the doctor doing making their coffee? And I shared openly and vulnerably. I had learned the hard way: secrets kill. Pretending to be more or other than who and what I am led to illness. Each day, with each smile on a customer's face, as I handed them their coffee just the way they liked it and asked about their kids and their families, my self-esteem grew. I knew my place in the world again: one human being helping others. And it had nothing to do with the white coat.

I made the decision to get my MBA, in case I wasn't allowed to practice as a physician again.

The store where I worked approached me to become a manager. I declined, but in that moment, I realized I was not a survivor. I was a thriver.
Everything I needed was in my heart, head, and hands. I could be of service even when I was making coffee.

I finally knew who I was, with or without the white coat. I was a person who made every life better by being in it. In any way, big or small, I made a difference. And I would keep doing so. I had 'lost' everything, and yet I had everything. I never slept a day without food in my stomach, a roof over my head, and people who loved me.

I began the journey back to gratitude, back to that little girl who just wanted to make the pain stop when she would touch a patient. And I made a vow to never again lose sight of my inner compass, my north star. Two years later, my license was reinstated. By the grace of God, that was 15 years ago. And those lessons have never left me. I am free and limitless because I was willing to let go of those old beliefs, those false burdens, and pressures.

Today, twenty-seven years after first becoming a physician, I am still in the ER, and I am thriving. I embody the calm in the middle of chaos, the eye of the storm: at peace and fully aware no matter what. I create from my own being. I began my coaching business in 2017 and have touched the lives of over 250 one-on-one clients in the years since. My framework leads other physicians out of the pain, powerlessness, and pressure and into knowing themselves so deeply that nothing can stop them. I fully live what I teach, setting new records for myself without even realizing it, such as seeing thirty-five patients in ten hours just a few weeks ago with ease and energy. But the best part is that even on those fully packed days, it all feels manageable—because I put myself first. I feed myself first. I fill my cup with connection and love and service, and then it's easy to turn around and help others.

True freedom doesn't depend on any external circumstances. We all have the capacity to be anything. To create anything. But we hold ourselves back.
What's keeping you from your true potential?
I thought I "had it all", and I felt trapped.
Then I "lost it all" and became limitless.
Now I have it all and am truly free.

Question and Answers

Looking back, was there anything in your childhood or upbringing that you think led to your burnout?

Absolutely - people pleasing, caretaking, mothering all at a young age

Did anything occur in your training that led to your burnout?

Nothing during my training.
Joined a private group of all male ER physicians as my first job out of residency. Was the first ever female ER physician at that hospital and was treated like a zebra. This was in the south, and I'll never forget a cardiologist to whom I introduced myself saying 'Gigi. Sounds like a stripper's name or an orthopedist calling me 'girl' because I paged him at 2 am for a patient.

Was there anything about the system you worked in that led to your episode (s) of burnout?

Not being given equal credit as the men.

The first group was taken over by another physician. He doted on the guys. Never forget how he called to personally congratulate a new hire on seeing x number of patients in his first shift when I'd been there for 2-3 years, seeing 30% more every shift, and had never received recognition. He also gave shifts to his cronies and would tell me there were no shifts. Or when I helped them open six new ERs by traveling and working there because they knew I was good with both patients and staff - he put together a 'thank you' trip to either Tahoe or Vegas. He called me and said, 'you wouldn't be comfortable there with all guys, right? and I said, 'why not? I work with them every day, and it just means I'll have my own room'. Months go by, I hear nothing, and then one day, a doc who NEVER helped at any of the sites but is one of his buddies is telling the NP that he was 'pissed because I was taken off the schedule, but then I called, and they said 'yeah, Gerry wants you to go with them'." So he took them all, including men who did not even help open the new places, and left me behind. I was so hurt and angry. Or the time I said I wanted to be involved and sit on committees - and he said there were no available committees in spite of the fact that I was now privileged at SIX different hospitals with them. I mean, really? I started looking for another job after that. It definitely started the 'I'm not good enough' and compounded the childhood 'boys have value and girls don't' that led me to taking on more and more and burning out.

Did you feel that you had a support system?

During rehab, I had my family. Before the addiction and obvious burnout, no

Did anyone notice and reach out to you?

No

How are you thriving today?

Emergency Medicine still. Coaching other physicians as well as nurses.

What advice would you give to someone going through burnout?

Saying no doesn't make you selfish. You can take care of yourself and still be loved and of value.
What advice would you give to the facilities and administration who are trying to help decrease the rate of physician burnout?

Help physicians incorporate their unique ideas and meet their unique core values within the system.

What advice, if any, would you give to the facilities that can do better?

Taking care of physicians is the best metric for your bottom line.

About Dr. Gigi Abdel-Samed, MD, MBA
Dr. Gigi Abdel-Samed, MD, MBA is a Board Certified Emergency Medicine Physician of 27 years. She is the founder of Medical School for the Soul, an innovative coaching program using her signature method to help physicians and nurses struggling with heartache, burnout, and disillusionment to help them feel calm, centered, and empowered even amid the chaos that is life

www.drgigisamed.com

Jillian Rigert, DMD, MD

From 2013-2017, I was in the Air Force and training to become an oral and maxillofacial surgeon. I loved the Air Force, and I felt like all my dreams had come true. I was finally close to where I thought I would feel content with my level of achievement and role in life. However, reality would hit me as my brain did not tolerate the long hours of forced sleeplessness. Each call night was spent managing negative thought loops, including suicidal ideation, due to extreme exhaustion paired with high stress medical decision making. Additionally, while working in the civilian sector, having to alter my treatment plans according to patient's resources constantly weighed heavily on my heart. The healthcare inequities made me feel that I, as a clinician, was part of the problem and often helpless in the level of which I could be part of the solution which wasn't enough. Working in the system, I palpated the problems, and the vision that I had for being a clinician and healer were not in alignment with what I was now seeing.

How do I cope? At that time, I did not have enough tools to help manage the amount of energy coming in from all directions- the emotions of patients, family members, and healthcare professionals. It all felt like "too much" and that I would never be "enough." My whole life's meaning and purpose was in question, and the emptiness drove me further into the darkness of burnout/depression/moral injury. In response to the stresses, I lost my appetite and was eventually hospitalized for anorexia which almost took my life. While I was on the brink of giving up, there were unexpected losses of people close to me. One of these lovely humans was my ex-boyfriend, who called to check on me when he knew I was not well. I was exhausted, and for the first time in my life, I did not pick up the phone when I saw his name. He passed away unexpectedly that weekend, and I still have the voicemail on my phone to this day as a reminder of what really matters. What really matters to me is to be present for people... be present for those I love... be present for patients in need. And I was not present... not then, and not while putting my head down to chase the goals of getting to where I was.

Ultimately, my struggles would trigger my medical discharge from the military. When I found out the fate of my military career, I was completely empty. What if I had changed professions within the military sooner? What if I gave myself permission to pivot sooner to save at least the part of my career that I was confident in?

I didn't give myself permission to pivot, and I struggled to turn in my resignation letter to my oral and maxillofacial surgery program. It was a scary time, and I had no idea what the future would hold.

Rather than give myself time to consider, I jumped into my next residency with unprocessed grief and still very much burnout. As a marathon runner, it felt like running back to back to back marathons without adequate rest or fuel.

Through those experiences, I now advocate for people to give themselves permission to pivot and please take time off to rest when burned out Easier said than done, I know.

By 2021, I was at another crossroads professionally and was still just surviving. Facing existential crisis after existential crisis, I knew I needed to make big changes. At that time, I heard about coaching and how many physicians were benefitting. Just the thought that there may be something that helps that I haven't tried gave me the hope I needed to continue.

I also found Brené Brown and dove into all of her work on vulnerability. I finally sat long enough to feel the grief and start to process.

I joined Martha Beck's Wayfinder Life Coach training, sold most of what I owned, moved across the country for a completely new role, new institution, and new environment.

When I arrived, I sat in on a Burnout Committee meeting in my department. I asked the Chair if there may be a role for coaching in our department, and he informed me that coaching is a strong part of my institution! He connected me with the Leadership Institute where I had the opportunity to complete Professional Leadership Coach training in a group of wonderful and supportive people. This community and experience were pivotal in my healing journey.

However, I was still isolated in the guilt and shame of leaving my surgical residency until I finally decided to take Brené Brown's advice to be vulnerable. I shared my story openly on KevinMD, and the weight of my past began to lift off my shoulders. It only took one person to share their story with me in residency to help me step back and get off the SI merry-go-round long enough to find ground, and my hope is that sharing my story may help save others knowing that they are not alone, too.

Recovery from burnout has not been linear. The process has included multiple healing modalities from mental health support, coaching, to trauma-based psychosomatic and spiritual healing. My experience taught me what really matters in life, and getting more into alignment with my values has certainly contributed to deeper levels of healing.

Healing openly has connected me with the wonderful community of many individuals walking their own healing journey, and the ability to support and elevate their voices has given me a sense of meaning and purpose outside of my professional role. Professionally, I have found my way into a career path that allows me to be present... and holding space for people as they face challenging diagnoses and life changes is what I feel is a tremendous part of my greater purpose.

Through learning when my life is in conflict with my values, I learned my values and how to get back into alignment. When seeking a path towards a career that's in alignment, identifying core values is a key step I recommend for all.

Looking back, was there anything in your childhood or upbringing that you think led to your burnout?

Perfectionism and high reliance on grades and education to shape my self worth. Growing up, my family did not talk about emotions, and I was often isolated. Working gave me a sense of belonging and worthiness, so I was always working with very poor boundaries. Being a woman made me feel that I also had to take on the hardest jobs to prove my competence and strength, so I measured my goals by how hard they were and nothing was ever "enough."

Did anything occur in your training that led to your burnout?

Lack of sleep and inadequate nutrition, compromised physical and psychological safety in working environments at times, moral injury from patients not having access to care and unprocessed grief from deaths- including of people close to me and patients. Unable to have time to process and was isolated, so I thought I was the only one struggling. The sense that I was never doing enough and was trying to manage high-stress, high-risk patient cases without rest.

Was there anything about the system you worked in that led to your episode (s) of burnout?

My training environment, with the exception of a small few, was extremely supportive which I believe saved my life as I developed deep and pervasive SI during residency. The small few who did contribute created environments with compromised psychological safety through their preferred "leadership styles" which fed into my sense of inadequacy. Overall, my own underlying beliefs that I was incompetent and unworthy set me up for their comments to have a strong negative impact. I also was reliant on their mentorship and supervision, so the power hierarchy complicated the ability to set boundaries. The healthcare system in general contributed to my burnout- the moral injury from the inequity of the system in regards to access to care, the forced sleep deprivation, the long hours working on administrative tasks, the lack of time to devote to proper care and cultivation of connections, and lost sense of purpose and meaning. The system is made for robots, and we need to bring the humans back into the healing for the sake of all.

Describe your period of burnout out in depth? What did it feel like? What did burnout look like?

During that time, I was not aware that I was experiencing burnout. I thought I was incompetent, and that I was the only person that could not cut it in residency. My thoughts were full of negative self-criticisms, and I was diagnosed with major depression and had stopped eating which numbed the pain (though made everything else worse). Though my symptoms fit the diagnostic criteria for major depression, looking back, I was experiencing moral injury and was suicidal because I was exhausted, constantly stressed, isolated, and felt trapped. I was coping with eating disorder behaviors, which for people who may not understand that role- I equate the role of anorexia nervosa in my life to the role of a substance such as alcohol that may help others to numb.

Do you remember any specific incidents where your burnout was apparent?

Yes. I have PTSD, now, because I remember many deep times where I was so exhausted that I didn't think I could continue in life. My whole residency experiences were shaded by burnout, and I did not actually start to recover until I took a year off from the clinic. Clinic and the hospital setting often ignite my trauma response, and it's been a slow recovery process to get back into the environment. Boundaries have been essential to create my own sense of safety and trust that I have tools to support myself that I did not have during residency.

Did you feel that you had a support system?

Overall- yes. My program director and most attendings were very supportive, which I believed was the difference in life and death for me. I was also in the Air Force with supportive command.

Did anyone notice and reach out to you?

Yes. My upper level informed my program director that I asked if many people experienced SI while on call. This question and her support to get me help led me to professional help, and being open with my program director helped to make sure I continued to get help. Additionally, friends I met in training were extremely supportive, even visited me in the hospital and never made me feel weak.

What helped you overcome your burnout?

Professional mental health support, coaching (mindset work for sure!), community, my dog, resting, boundaries, and getting back into alignment with my values.

How are you thriving today?

I live in alignment with my values and stopped falling for what society tells us defines "success."

What advice would you give to someone going through burnout?

Rest. Rest. Rest. Find times to rest and process with a supportive community. Identify changes you can make in the immediate future and what changes may need to happen for long term sustainable living.

Give yourself permission to pivot as needed, and know you are never alone. Your worth is not defined by what you do.

Once you feel rested, find ways you can play and bring creativity and enjoyment back into your life.

If making big career decisions, I highly recommend doing so in a rested state rather than when feeling desperate and wanting to escape.

Identify your values and what feels out of alignment with your vision for your life.

Make small changes towards your ideal life. Making small, incremental changes are more likely to be successful over time than trying to make gigantic changes all at once.

What advice would you give to the facilities and administration who are trying to help decrease the rate of physician burnout?

Take responsibility for the systemic contributions and impact that the conditions have on the physicians. Bring the human back into the healing, for all.

What advice would you give to those facilities who appear to have lack of interest in helping to improve conditions?

Hum.. I'd leave those places. They have to be open to change or else others will leave, too. As physicians, we must normalize leaving and not enabling these conditions to persist without consequence.

About Jillian Rigert, DMD, MD

Dr. Jillian Rigert is an Oral Medicine Physician, Head and Neck Cancer Researcher, Life and Professional Leadership Coach, Air Force Veteran, Dog Mom, YouTube enthusiast, Writer, Human, Not Robot.

jillian.rigert@gmail.com

Mary Tran, DO

My story starts out similarly to so many others. I was ignoring self-care while trying to be everything to everyone else. I was barely holding it together, but I was still holding it together. I was getting through the day and taking care of everyone. I just didn't have anything left for myself.

Then, I went into preterm labor and landed on bed rest. The few weeks of bed rest led to depression. Then I had a crash c-section. My baby didn't sleep, had such bad tongue and lip tie, and each feed took 90 mins. She couldn't latch onto the nipple or bottle well. I got postpartum depression, and the burnout vs. depression just blurred together. I jumped back into work even though I was severely depressed and having suicidal thoughts. I was expected to be everything to everyone again. I tried to keep going just as I had done before. This time though, I couldn't do it. I didn't feel human anymore. I couldn't feel happy. I didn't feel any connection with others, including my daughter. My patients never knew. I gave them the best of me, just as I had always done. I barely had anything left to give my family or myself. My marriage suffered. I didn't feel that bond a mother should feel for her child. I didn't know if I could go on anymore.

The two people at work I tried to talk to both told me it couldn't be as bad as I made it seem. I thought there was something wrong with me. I tried therapy, and it didn't help. I felt weak and unworthy. Luckily I still had the insight to go part-time. I was still burned out, but as the months passed and I started to get a little more sleep, my suicidal thoughts started to get less strong. Then one day, I decided I would try to heal myself. I tried medication which somewhat helped. I read books, listened to podcasts, learned about coaching, and worked on my mental health and physical health. I started to heal.

Question and Answers

Looking back, was there anything in your childhood or upbringing that you think led to your burnout?

Being raised by very strict traditional Asian parents who taught me to suppress my feelings, not to speak up, and to stay in the background. They worried I would become big-headed or defiant, so they told me I wasn't worthy. I was abused physically and emotionally. I no longer blame them, though. They didn't have the tools to raise me differently. They were passing along what they knew. They're very supportive of me now.

Did anything occur in your training that led to your burnout?

What we all go through in training- ignore your humanness. Ignore your hunger and thirst. Ignore fatigue. Ignore self-care so you can care for others. Patients and colleagues come first, and self-care comes last. And the place where I trained was quite abusive to family medicine. Although my program was supportive, the specialties were not. Family medicine was seen as being inferior, and those in specialties did not hesitate to verbalize that.

What do you think caused the burnout?

The message is that we have to keep doing more. Just keep giving more and more, no matter how thinly you're stretched. I bought into that and kept giving when I had nothing left to give.

Did you feel that you had a support system?

Not until I was at my breaking point and was allowed to go part-time. I told a couple of colleagues how much I was struggling, and both told me that it couldn't be that bad. I had postpartum depression as well and was suicidal. Luckily, I decided to give it 1 last shot and tell one more person I couldn't handle it anymore. The postpartum depression, along with burnout or whatever you want to call it since everything blurred together, was too much. Fortunately, the last person I told happened to be someone who was in the position to help me go part-time.

My husband had depression after my daughter was born as well. He couldn't support me because of how he was feeling. We were both just trying to survive.

Describe your period of burnout? What did burnout look like?

Burnout felt like exhaustion. Like I barely had the strength to keep myself afloat. My head was barely above water, and I felt like I was going to drown any minute. Yet, I had to put on a smile for my patients. I still had to give them the best care. I had to take care of my daughter. I was taking care of everyone but myself. I felt alone. I didn't know what happiness felt like anymore during that period of my life.

Do you remember any specific incidents where your burnout was apparent?

I've always been very personable and friendly. I found myself very irritable when I was burned out. It was apparent in my email responses. When I didn't have a person in front of me for whom I had to put a performance on, I had no filter. I responded to group/administrative emails in a very angry demeanor, and people started to wonder what was going on with me. Yet, this didn't come to light until later. Part of me wonders if I would have reached out for help sooner had someone just approached me and asked if I was okay instead of whispering about it amongst each other.

Did anyone notice and reach out to you?

No one reached out to me that I can recall. Later, when I talked about my burnout and depression, I had people tell me they noticed something had seemed off, but no one reached out to me at the time.

What helped you overcome your burnout?

Getting enough sleep so I could think clearly enough to know I needed to get help. Once I realized I needed help, I set out on a self-help journey to heal myself. I immersed myself in a world filled with self-help books, podcasts, webinars, and anything I could get my hands on that would help me change my mindset.

How are you thriving today?

I am fortunate to say that I enjoy practicing medicine again. I no longer have panic attacks walking into work. I love seeing my patients. I no longer feel stressed at work. I finish my work during the clinical workday and come home with a clear separation between work and home life. I no longer work at home when I'm off. My marriage is stronger than it's ever been. I have the best relationship with my daughter. I have a true work-life balance.

I became a certified life coach and coach women physicians to help them finish their charting/clinical work within the workday without sacrificing patient satisfaction or quality of care. I help them get back their free time. The free time they can spend on self-care and with their family/friends. This mission is important to me because it helps me do my part to help with the burnout epidemic.

I am also writing and almost done with a book to help Asian women overcome the self-limiting beliefs so common in our culture.

I really feel like I'm thriving now.

What advice would you give to someone going through burnout?

Ask for help! There is so much help out there, and we don't always realize it. It's not your fault. You are not weak. There's nothing wrong with you. Some of it is due to issues with the healthcare system, but we do have control in so many aspects. We can look for where we have control and start there. There is hope. There is always hope, and that's always available to you. It can get better.

What advice would you give to the facilities and administration who are trying to help decrease the rate of physician burnout?

There needs to be more support and system-wide changes. It cannot be on the individual physician to reduce or overcome burnout. Keep reaching out and checking in on the physicians. Let the physicians know you care and you're listening. Give physicians autonomy and control. Be flexible. Let the physicians know that you see them as human beings and not just a cog in the wheel.

What advice, if any, would you give to the facilities that can do better when it comes to improving burnout rates of physicians (those facilities that appear to have a lack of interest in helping to improve conditions)?

Please stop asking the doctors to do more and more instead of allocating the necessary resources and support. An individual physician only has so much they can give before they break.

About Mary Tran, DO

Dr. Tran is a primary care physician and a certified life coach who helps women physicians finish their charting and clinical work within the workday so they get back their free time. It's her mission to do her part to fight the physician burnout epidemic. It's possible to do this without sacrificing patient satisfaction or quality of care.

www.drmarytranlifecoach.com

Param Baladandapani, MD

When I was born, my father knew that he wanted me to become a doctor. As the first-born daughter to Indian parents, that was the preferred career choice. As I grew up, I could think of becoming nothing else. I do recall a moment of uncertainty before entering medical school, but looking back, I consider it an immense privilege to have trained as a physician, to have insight into the miracle that is the human body, and to have the ability to heal and ease suffering and I would do it all over again many times over.

In school, I was always first in my class. I believe this was more because of my perseverance than my intelligence. I remember always wanting to be the best at everything extracurricular – and I worked hard to do so. Perseverance and people-pleasing are attributes I have embraced that, in hindsight, have caused me as much harm as they have good – if only the little child in me knew when and what to let go – it would have served me well as a physician.

I worked really hard to become a physician, burning the midnight oil – working many times harder than everyone else in high school. This also involved me moving to a boarding school in India because, at that time, there were no good medical schools in the United Arab Emirates, where my family was based. It was a huge transition, and I don't think I handled it well emotionally – and yet there was no time to waste – I had to be in the top 0.01% to get a full scholarship to medical school. Which I did – I was third in my state and got to attend the best school in the state. I loved every minute of it.

After medical school, I moved to the United States to learn from the very best in the field. Again I worked very hard, aced all the tests, and got into Radiology which is a very competitive specialty for Foreign Medical graduates. The specialty choice was hard – I loved procedural fields, but I always knew that work-life balance was very important for me, and I wanted enough vacation time to spend with my kids and family back home in India. Radiology had more than enough to stimulate me intellectually, gratifying procedural patient interaction, and as a breast imager, I loved that I was creating a world with more birthdays!

As I started my first job after my fellowship in a semi-academic practice, it was a nurturing environment, but I was still bothered by the limited flexibility around requesting time off, especially as I started getting more involved in administrative responsibilities. As an employee physician, I had little say in how things were done and what policies were instituted. The workflow was already in place, and I had to adhere to it while ensuring my patients were cared for to the best of my ability. In my second position, out of training, I took a significant pay cut to structure my job with the work-life flexibility that I wanted. This allowed me to take a few months off when I had my son – still nothing compared to a year off our counterparts were enjoying in Europe to bond with their children.

I placated myself with the thought that my son would not remember my having to drop him off with our nanny every morning when I had to go in to work, and I resented not having a choice in the matter every evening when I picked him up, and he smelled like the woman who got to care for him all day. A few years later, when my father was diagnosed with cancer, I was fortunate to be able to take a month off to help with his back to back surgeries, but I really couldn't sit with him through his subsequent chemotherapy. And then, to top it all, a merger at work meant that suddenly everything was changing – contracts were being renegotiated, admin and partners were being introduced while we were not on a partnership track – suddenly, I found myself in a position with no autonomy and no say. Attempting to negotiate terms ended up with my contract being rescinded.

It was a time of great professional and accompanying personal turmoil. I had another job lined up, but it meant staying away from my kids for a few months and losing childcare - it felt like I was starting from scratch. That's when I took a close look at what it would mean if I was forced to take a long break – what not getting another paycheck would look like? Even a half million in savings would only get me through 4 years before I had to find another position that afforded me a decent work-life balance. That's when I started exploring options for Financial Independence and fervently working towards it.

Not long after, the pandemic started. Suddenly, I lost child care, schools had to shut down, and while I was fortunate to be working from home a few days a week, I was suddenly burdened with RVU inefficient studies – and working on these from home while being completely responsible for two young kids who were 2 and 5 at the time meant that most days – I was reading cases till midnight and my kids were sleeping in the office next to me. That's when the full meaning of burnout hit me ... the anxiety, the feeling of never being able to catch up – of never having a moment to catch my breath. Many days I was anxious as I awoke in the morning and could feel the clamminess of my cold hands and my heart beating faster, filled with dread. I felt like I was being penalized for having devoted the majority of my life to medicine. I felt like I had fewer choices compared to my cousins, who chose to be stay-at-home moms. Was it wrong to want to be home and fully present with my babies?

More than others, I found myself judging myself. But I knew that in my heart, I wanted something different.

Fortunately, in the year between my initial career transition and this point of burnout – I had taken the time to accelerate my journey to Financial Independence through investing in real estate, and I was at the point where passive income from my real estate portfolio could completely cover my family's expenses including discretionary spending. I finally had a choice in the matter – after over a decade as a physician, I finally could practice medicine because I wanted to and not because I had to! I quit my full-time position as a Breast Imager and started working a day a week in medicine. At the time of writing this, I have had almost two years where I got to spend time with my little ones while still having the privilege of creating a world with more birthdays as a Mammographer.

Walking away from the prescribed path and giving up the lure of benefits and high pay (the proverbial golden handcuffs) wasn't easy. There are a lot of physicians who feel I abandoned medicine. But I honestly believe that in every season of life, our needs shift, and I truly believe having the choice to practice medicine as it fits into your life in each season is crucial. Maybe it's time for us to stop fitting our lives around our jobs in medicine and be able to fit medicine into our lives as it best suits us. There are others to whom my choices may not make sense. But it's not about walking away from medicine. It's about practicing medicine how you want to – so you are truly honoring yourself and aligned with your values. I truly believe separating medicine from its financial reward makes us better physicians, parents, and humans. That is what I want for all physicians. So we can practice medicine as we choose with total autonomy.

Once I made the transition, I started GenerationalwealthMD – a community aimed at educating other physicians about Financial Freedom through real estate – so that they wouldn't have to learn from decades of making mistakes. So they would have choices and autonomy – to practice medicine on their terms. I have helped thousands of physicians acquire hundreds of millions of dollars of real estate and create the lives of their dreams.

I know that there are institutional and individual practices and perspectives that promote physician burnout on so many levels. But what helped me the most when I went through burnout was Financial Freedom – it gave me back autonomy, the ability to say no, and the ability to draw boundaries. I find this to be an aspect of burnout that isn't really discussed much – just like we tend to stay away from talking about money and all things finance. It's also a topic that I wish someone had talked to me about and impressed upon me the significance of in my first few years as an attending. I regret having had to figure it out on my own after a decade of making money mistakes. But I now understand the Buddhist saying – "Every Obstacle is an Opportunity in disguise". Burnout is a symptom of an underlying imbalance and disarray – when we experience burnout at its worst, I know it's also an immense opportunity to flip the storyline – and I hope that in doing so, you also inspire and elevate others.

About Param Baladandapani, MD
Dr. Param Baladandapani is a Radiologist in Southern California who, while working full time and raising two young kids, built a multi-million dollar real estate portfolio that helped her become Financially Independent at 41.

She is the Founder & CEO of GenerationalWealthMD where she has helped thousands of physicians accelerate towards financial freedom by building a real estate portfolio that works for them. Over the last nine years, she has invested in Long Term and Short term rentals, Apartments as well as development projects in multiple domestic and international markets with over 800 doors under management. She brings this expertise to her Immersive small group coaching program- Creating Generational Freedom through real estate. Physicians in the community have acquired over $150 million of real estate in the last year and are building the life of their dreams.

www.generationalwealthmd.com

Gabriela Pichardo-Lafontaine, MD, ABOIM

Looking back, was there anything in your childhood or upbringing that you think led to your burnout?

I think so. I grew up with loving parents who are both physicians. My father was very strict and a perfectionist. He always wanted the best for me but expected me to be the best, so I always felt like I had big shoes to fill in. In my world, there was no room for mistakes. I always had to constantly prove to my parents that I was the best even though what I was doing was something I didn't feel passionate about or truly liked. I also saw their commitment from them to their roles as doctors. They were working nonstop and had more than one job (teaching, working in 2 different hospitals, having their outpatient clinics, doing conferences, etc.). I grew up mostly with my brothers watching over me since they were much older (12 years older than me) and with nannies. Both my parents were workaholics, so I grew up seeing this and considered it as the "norm" or how I should be.

Did anything occur in your training that led to your burnout?

I was married, and before my residency ended, I was getting a divorce. I think this drove me to immerse myself in my training and focus only on this. When I was in residency, I viewed burnout as normal as it was supposed to be that way. Actually, I didn't hear the word burnout until many years later. I kept hearing stories from other residents, and it was a collective thought that we all needed to go through this, that others before me did it so I could just push it through. I was also an Immigrant in a new country, so I felt I needed to prove myself and just push through it all.

What do you think caused the burnout?

During my residency, I didn't know what it was back then and only realized the things I went through after I had finished the residency and went on to the real world. It was a few years later that I realized how burned out I was feeling.

After residency and my divorce, I was excited to be going into the world and practicing medicine in a smaller town. I did receive some prejudice being a young Latina and newly single. I had people questioning me and started to develop this "imposter syndrome". I felt as if I wasn't good enough. I started to develop good friendships and had a good working environment, except for some patients not wanting to see me because they didn't know how to pronounce my last name or had someone asking in our clinic if I spoke good English.

I faced a lot of challenges, so I just felt a constant need to prove myself and validate how good I was. During this time, I met someone new, changed jobs, and moved to a different state (my current location in Texas) because I needed a change and wasn't truly happy where I was living at the time.

When I moved to Texas, it was like a dream job, but later on, I started to feel true burnout from it. The constant need to prove myself, working long hours and even after-hours charting. I was a good performer in the clinic and got nominated for a medical director. I took the position, not knowing it was truly going to affect me even more. I had more responsibilities than I could handle and also had a baby girl at home. It was challenging to find a good work-life balance during that time.

I started suffering from insomnia, my stress levels (and cortisol levels) were always high, and I started binge eating and drinking to find some sense of relief. I was also having difficulties with my marriage. I had an abusive spouse, and I was the sole breadwinner, which brought more tension and stress to my life.

I felt guilty about working so much and not being able to spend time with my little girl. I was working every day. After hours and weekends, I was just catching up with work and charting. It felt Never-ending. I wasn't happy. I started to notice I was suffering from depression and anxiety as well. I sought help and got a prescription, but it seemed like it was not enough or truly helping.

I accepted a medical director position in addition to all the work I had. This goes back to my "people-pleasing personality," same as what I did as a child with My parents. I couldn't say nor set boundaries. I didn't even know how to or where to begin. My husband at the time wasn't very supportive, and even though I thought about working less, I felt I couldn't because we had bills to pay, and I was the sole breadwinner.

I felt like I never had a break because when I was done with the clinic, I got home at 6 pm, and then It was my turn to take care of things at home and take care of our toddler since he was with her the whole day. After putting her to bed, I had the charting which I needed to finish so that I could fulfill a metric and avoid being penalized. I hated it. I was not happy during this time.

Sometimes I look back and think I would have felt the burnout if I had a better relationship with my husband, but that was just one variable in my life. I spent about three years in this situation. Then there was a breaking point, and I said no more. I would not endure this abusive relationship, and I filed for divorce.

It was an entire year of going to court and battling for custody. At that time, I had to step down from being the medical director. I couldn't manage it, and I was on my own. After hours I needed to go to meetings with staff and future candidates for our clinic and make dinner. I just couldn't do it. I needed to be there for My little girl.

After stepping down, things became more toxic around the workplace. Some other doctors were leaving. There was a lot of animosity. I was struggling and questioning where I was going and if this clinic was for me. I started to seek a part-time position, but that was not possible in the clinic where I was working at. They were very focused on metrics and generating income. It was all about performance and Press Ganey results, and I saw a lack of empathy even for other doctors and staff that were going through difficult times. I wanted to change this when I was the medical director, but with what I had going on in my personal life, I just couldn't.

In the midst of those 3 Years, I started a fellowship. Yes, I know more stuff to put on my plate, especially with an unhappy marriage and all I was going through. I went to a conference in San Diego which was a true eye-opener. I learned about burnout. I met other practitioners going through similar issues in their lives as me. I did a forest bathing session and meditation and learned about self-care. This was the AIHM conference. This was probably back in 2016. After this experience, I felt connected and decided to Join the fellowship.

During this time, I also filed for divorce. The fellowship helped me to go through a difficult time, and I also had some support with a new community even though we were doing these classes virtually and I was meeting and chatting with people from different parts of the world and then connecting in person for our retreats. It opened a whole new world for me, and learning different healing modalities not just for myself but also for my patients. I wasn't satisfied with the way I was practicing medicine. I was also getting my metrics affected because I was spending more time with patients, and this was a problem since they wanted me to see more patients in less time per day. I also was not happy with this.

I realized my days in this clinic were coming to an end since I wanted to have an opportunity to practice integrative medicine. Right after my divorce was final, I submitted my resignation letter. Since the divorce drained my finances, I found another job for a clinic which I thought would have a better work-life balance since they had less patient load and were also able to have more flexibility. They were open and interested in the whole integrative medicine Concept.

I had to move further down south since I also had a non-compete clause from my previous employer. During this time, I found a great guy. He was going through a difficult divorce too. I started liking this job, but shortly after, the workload and the charting became a nightmare. I thought I would face similar issues with any job in corporate medicine or a healthcare system.
They tried to compensate me well and listened to the issues, but I also realized I would not practice fully integrative medicine, which is what I wanted to do. They were pushing for metrics and a lot of utilization reviews dealing with Medicare Advantage programs. This became too stressful for me, and I didn't see myself practicing medicine this way. Since I was almost finishing my fellowship and getting ready for graduation, I went to my employer and decided to leave (in good spirits) since it was not for me, and they understood this well.

I was graduating, in a new, loving relationship, and leaving a job to find something more fulfilling. I found it. I am currently practicing medicine the way I want to. I feel better, and there is no more burnout. I am working the hours I do want to and am able to finish my charts before heading home so that I am able to spend more time with my family, doing things I love in my spare time.

Did you have a support system?

I do have a wonderful support system. My current husband is my number one: we just celebrated our one-year anniversary this past September, and we have been together for five years now. He has been my rock, and when I decided to shift gears from my work, he was there, holding my hand along the way. So he saw me when I was burned out and made things easier for me. When I was married to my ex, I felt I had no one except my work friends and my family who lived back in my country. They felt bad when I was single with a toddler, but they were happy since they knew how much he had hurt me. Back then, it was hard to find a support system, but I found it in complete strangers, believe it or not.

When I joined the fellowship, it felt like I had found my tribe. We confided in each other I was able to express and talk about my work, my relationships, and everything I was going through. When we did our retreats and were able to meet many of them in person, it was very nice. We bonded and also cried during our meeting. A lot of us were going through similar situations and had either felt lost or dealing with mental health issues or stress and burnout. I felt like I wasn't alone, and I wasn't the only one. I couldn't talk about these things with my own family because they wouldn't understand, and they were so far away.

Did anyone notice and reach out to you?

I had a few local friends who did. Some knew more when they found out about my divorce and what was truly going on since I kept all to myself. In the beginning, it wasn't noticeable, but certain work colleagues did notice over time and knew I wasn't doing OK. I was very depressed, and I wasn't happy doing my job and seeing patients.

How are your thriving today?

Currently, I am thriving! I managed to find a job where I can manage my own hours and work part-time. I am also practicing integrative medicine and primary care the way I had envisioned in doing so. I may not get paid as much as I did before, but I am truly much happier. No more long hours and charting and fulfilling a metric that, honestly, I don't believe in.

My voice is heard by managers and medical directors. I feel validated and respected more. I still have a hard time establishing boundaries and not thinking the job and work are everything (I still have that inner child that wants to please mom and dad) but working on it. I get to have some time off and spend time with my family. I feel now we can make more plans, travel, and do more things together. We have a blended family with my 2 stepsons and a little girl. I used to take prescriptions to handle my anxiety and depression but doing plenty of meditations, connecting with others, and doing a form of therapy every other week helps manage this. I honestly think leaving a toxic relationship, doing my fellowship, and changing the way I practice medicine has been good and almost healing me.

What advice would you give to someone going through burnout?

If you are struggling with burnout, try to get help. I didn't realize I needed help until I found that conference and decided to join the fellowship. Some may be going through therapy to help you realize what you need. For me, that was a form of therapy and opened me up to seeking therapy. Afterward, is when I realized I was going through burnout and I needed a change in my life.

Change is not easy and takes time. It took time for me. Several years but after five years, I am happier and in a much better place. You can get there too. It may be hard to realize at first, but to want you to acknowledge going through burnout and then deciding to take the steps in how to change it is huge. It doesn't happen overnight. This is how I look at health: health is never linear. There would be a lot of ups and downs and curves. Same with changing your mindset and getting yourself out of burnout.

What advice would you give to the facilities and administration who are trying to help decrease the rate of physician burnout?

Listen to your physicians: we often get judged, or we fear being labeled as weak: help your physicians not to feel this, help them feel empowered like they have a voice. Is not just about metrics. If the physician is going through some personal and difficult times, their job may get affected but scolding them and demanding for them to do better is not the way to do it. Take a step back and ask, "what can I do to help you" and if there is an entity they can go to, without fear of being judged, so they can open up. Well, that's a good start, at least in my book. I felt like I had no one I could trust or who could hear my voice. Not sure if this has changed now.

If they were less focused on metrics and data and really listened to their physicians. It is not doing certain workshops, bringing lunch to the office or special treats. We need to feel validated and not feel judged if we are depressed or going through burnout. We may all be going through some personal and difficult times. We are humans, not machines. This perception is what's got to change. Since some. of these bigger healthcare organizations are also driven by the insurance world, they would focus on the quality, not the quantity, when it comes to patient care. I am seeing some small changes here and there but still a lot to work on.

About Gabriela Pichardo-Lafontaine, MD, ABOIM
Dr. Pichardo-Lafontaine is a board-certified internal medicine and Integrative Medicine doctor who does holistic care, encourages meditation, and helps a lot of patients who deal with chronic diseases and mental health. She has helped patients with burnout recovery since they seek a more Holistic approach rather

than relying on a prescription to help manage their stress and mental health issues.

www.resilienthealthmedicine.com

Diana Cristina Londoño, MD

Did anything occur in your training that led to your burnout?

No, but I think discussions, information, resources, or training should be part of training programs. Burnout rates are actually higher in residents in many specialties (65% of second-year urology residents in 2022), and they also may not have the financial resources to do coaching programs or therapy out of pocket. Conversations and training regarding boundary settings, self-care, signs, symptoms, and resources for burnout/ chronic stress should be part of all residency training settings.

Was there anything about the system you worked in that led to your episode (s) of burnout?

1st time. Occurred due to not having rest. I worked five days a week and rounded every weekend for almost a year straight. Even if 1-2 patients were seen, I never had time for "mental rest." I was employed, and I was solo, so there was no one available to cover my patients on the weekend. It is important if you are starting a new position to ask questions about week and weekend coverage; otherwise, this situation can easily occur. Additionally, do not agree to anything unless it is noted in writing otherwise, it will never occur.

Due to a lack of "mental rest" and chronic worry about patients seven days a week, I began to feel foggy in my brain and had difficulties making decisions. I could not decide if I should put a foley on a patient I was consulted on in the hospital. I thought something was wrong physically and went to PMD to get blood tests. He said all is ok. Here is your Zoloft. What? I could not believe it. Clearly, there was another explanation for my symptoms.

I did go on it, started therapy, and quit my job way ahead of my 2-year contract since they were never going to have a weekend backup if I stayed in that job. Once I started therapy and medications, I felt the "fog" lift.

The second time, it occurred from a chronic fear of COVID and how I perceived the situations were being handled or not for the safety of all, whether nationally or locally. Fear, worry, and stress will all lead to the same path of activating the sympathetic (stress) system, and every single cell in your body will be bathed in cortisol.

For me, this led to physical manifestations of chronic stress/ fear, which were physical. I had insomnia, grinding teeth (bruxism) to the point of needing Botox injected in my jaw, damaging my molars which needed to be repaired with a root canal/ crown, and became infected with root abscess, GERD, newly diagnosed asthma at 42, debilitating chest pain and shortness of breath, hand joint pain with Rheumatoid factor elevated (seen in autoimmune diseases like Rheumatoid arthritis).

My mindset was always focused on what was wrong, how everything was terrible, and how everyone did not care. I had become Debbie Downer, a complete negativity vortex.

What helped you overcome your burnout?

Learning and understanding awareness. Learning about coaching principles, diving deep into reading and learning about the human brain, the stress response and sequela, spirituality, meditation, and yoga. Practicing daily gratitude, doing daily meditations, practicing asanas of yoga, and making sure I get plenty of sleep. It was also very helpful and healing to write and speak about my emotional experiences, as it helped me process my emotions.

Did you have a support system?

My coaches were my support, and I also began to reach out to physicians who I felt were on a similar wavelength of their healing journey, and they became my support system.

Did anyone notice and reach out to you?

My husband said, "Wow, you are really acting like someone you said is really negative you didn't want to be like, yet you are acting the same way." Made me pause and realize I needed to change something.

How are you thriving today?

I think every day is work to truly stay balanced and aligned and focus my attention and intention on things, thoughts, or activities that are uplifting and helpful.

I find speaking and writing about wellness, awareness, coaching, or other skills we can use fulfilling. I started www.physiciancoachsupport.com because I wanted to use my skills as a coach and organize other physicians who are coaches to give physicians a support system that could help them. This helps me find a purpose and a passion and pay forward with my skills to help others.

What advice would you give to someone going through burnout?

Symptoms can be sneaky, and we are so conditioned to think this is normal we really need to pause to check in with ourselves. Pushing through it or ignoring the signs our body is giving us will not make it get better. If you leave chronic stress, worry, or fear unattended, it will manifest into illness or disease. Pause and think about why you are not prioritizing yourself and what you are telling yourself why you don't think your mental, emotional, physical, or spiritual health is not important. Do not use others as examples, as the culture of medicine is not a healthy one and may not be the best one to model your actions. Listen TO YOU, your body, and what it needs.

Learn boundaries, and learn to say no to things, activities, or requests that do not serve you. You will be saying yes to yourself. If you find this challenging and need help, find a coach. A coach can help get you from point A to B faster than fumbling on your own. You are worth it.

What advice would you give to the facilities and administration who are trying to help decrease the rate of physician burnout?

Learn to be genuinely mindful and practice compassionate leadership. Listen to physicians and include them in decisions. Listen to what they need. We have to be part of decisions that affect our daily practice and the care of patients.

Decrease the burden of EMR tasks and or give support to answer questions/requests.
Decrease unnecessary early am, late pm, or WEEKEND meetings. Be respectful of time off that is protected, and do not continue to call or email during our times off.

What advice if any would you give to the facilities that can do better when it comes to improving the burnout rates of physicians?

Burnout affects care and leads to errors. It also leads to physician turnover and leaving medicine altogether. Each physician that leaves an institution can cost 500k to 1 million in lost revenue and recruiting costs.

More than 100K physicians left medicine in 2021 of 1 million physicians in the US. We already had a shortage of physicians, and it will only continue.

Physicians are no longer putting up with conditions that are weighing a heavy toll on our physical, emotional, or psychological health. It will not be sustainable if we continue on this path, and it is TIME to make a change. We are all patients.

About Diana Cristina Londoño, MD
Dr. Diana Londoño is the founder of Physician Coach Support.com, where doctors can get confidential peer support over Zoom 7 days a week.

She is a certified life coach and founded this platform to help her colleagues, as burnout rates are at 60% or greater for physicians. She received the Los Angeles Medical Association Physician Leadership Award for her work with Physician Coach Support.

She is one of the few female Latinx urologists in the country, making 0.5% of Urologists. She has experienced burnout twice herself, and because of that, she writes and speaks passionately about wellness and humanity in medicine, with more than 30 articles published last year in outlets such as Medscape, Doximity, Kevin MD, Giddy.com, and many others. She is also a regular guest on podcasts discussing these topics as well.

She is the co-host of a live stream podcast, "Supernova Sistas Physicians in Motion" in which the mission is to bring joy, positivity, and light to your day by discussing topics such as mindset, gratitude, self-care, connection, and integrating mind, body and spirit for optimal health.

She says if Physician Coach Support.com can pull just one doctor from the brink of burnout, it is all worth it.

https://dianalondonomd.com/

Kara Wada, MD

As an allergist/immunologist, our calendar is not dissimilar to my accountant friends. April and May kick off our busy season in the Midwest. In May 2019, I was nearing the end of my second year as an attending physician and nine months into being a mom to 2 energetic little girls, ages 4 and well, 9 months. I was also exhausted. Every inch of my body and even my soul felt like I was attempting to walk with concrete boots. I found it increasingly difficult to think clearly, noticing it was taking longer to recall words or names that should have been no problem at all, and I also noticed my ability to focus on tasks was nothing like it had been in the past. I was cynical and more snarky than usual. When seeing my patients that required more of me- more empathy, more care coordination, more validation—I felt numb. I was unable to lean in and help unburden them of their worries, frustrations, and fears. My cup was empty.

As it turns out, I was suffering from systemic Sjogren's and two weeks later my 9 month old infant daughter had an anaphylactic reaction- her first- to scrambled eggs.
That was the last straw.
My world imploded.

I wish I could say that was the turning point that helped me get everything back on track, but alas, it was another year of magical thinking before I actually started to emerge from a really dark space to a new and brighter reality.

So much of my magical thinking was fueled by the same perfectionism that I attributed to my academic and professional successes. If it worked for my grades, why wouldn't it fix my misbehaving immune system too? If I ate perfectly and worked out hard enough, maybe my Sjogren's would go away. Instead, the green smoothies I was drinking every morning led to acute hepatitis and a liver biopsy. As it turns out, not all superfoods are super. And when I then turned to a strict elimination diet protocol, thinking maybe less was more, all I ended up with was a whole lot less joy and significantly more anxiety.

Question and Answers

Did anything occur in your training that led to your burnout?

Like many, my childhood memories resurface in short snippets. My mom repeatedly told me that straight A's would not be rewarded because they were an expectation in the Simonson house. Sitting at the dinner table and my parents telling me once again that they had not saved for my or my little sister's college education- that it was up to us to earn scholarships to pay for it. The other perennial favorite is my dad recounting how he didn't get into medical school and regretted not trying again. I honestly don't recall a time prior to receiving my acceptance letter to medical school as a senior in college when I didn't feel this overwhelming sense of pressure. A constant heaviness was living in my shoulders- the expectation of doing something great with my life.

What do you think caused the burnout?

If I am honest, the reprieve from the overwhelming pressure was short-lived, only to return with a vengeance when I arrived on campus to start medical school that fall. Failing my first anatomy and embryology examinations only made it worse. When you bring some of the smartest, most successful, and most driven young adults on the planet into the same space, there is no avoiding comparison and competition. We all kept reaching for the next gold star and striving for perfection while sacrificing self-care and sleep. In reality, all we really needed was community, collaboration, and self-compassion.

Our medical education system is built for burnout. Working past the point of exhaustion is exalted, unfettered dedication deified, and perfection an expectation. And yet, despite our adult age, we had very little autonomy over our day to day schedule. I recall having no say in missing my dear cousin's wedding, which was planned for my intern orientation week 600 miles away.

How are you thriving today?

At some point along the way, I discovered a physician coaching podcast and was introduced to the "Model". The Model is just a new way to describe the ancient idea that our thoughts, feelings, actions, and results are interdependent. More importantly, I learned that we have control over how we show up in our lives, no matter what the circumstances are. I didn't have to turn over the reins to my misbehaving immune system or the broken medical system, or my inbox messages.

With the support of my husband, division director, and rheumatologist, I cut my clinic schedule in half. I prioritize my sleep.

I asked for help from a registered dietician with extensive knowledge in anti-inflammatory eating. She taught me how to approach my eating from a space of abundance rather than scarcity- a mindset that has been helpful to apply to so much of life.

Slowly, I learned I don't have to do exercise to the point of exhaustion or pain: moving my body is a privilege rather than punishment.

I am thriving today, having learned that saying yes to myself is the least selfish thing I can do. It is an act of self-preservation.

In place of my magical thinking, I share with others my formula for success:
Make ahead meals.
Mandatory me time
Mindfulness
Movement
Meaningful moments.

What advice would you give to the facilities and administration who are trying to help decrease the rate of physician burnout?

The system needs to change from the ground up. We need to keep working towards the goal of recognizing that physicians are human with real human struggles and needs. Physician well-being needs to be one of the core organizational strategies of the entire medical system. In doing so, I predict we will not only see more professional and personal satisfaction but also result in more compassionate, complete, and less expensive patient care.

About Kara Wada, MD

Dr. Wada is a board-certified pediatric and adult allergy, immunology, and lifestyle medicine physician, certified-life coach, TED speaker, and systemic Sjogren's patient. She is an Assistant Clinical Professor. Dr. Wada is a national expert and is called upon to speak, advise and coach on the topics of medical gaslighting, holistic care of chronic inflammatory illnesses, and how to navigate the healthcare and wellness industries with confidence.

www.drkarawada.com

Diana Dumenko, MD

I have always considered myself strong-willed, determined, and resilient. I thought I would be able to overcome any obstacle that was thrown my way. I even dived head first into projects and assignments that I either knew nothing about and were complicated or that scared me, just to expose myself to the beast and eventually tame it. I have always enjoyed a challenge. That is what drove me to the field of emergency medicine in the first place. I thought if I could treat the critically ill, if I could adapt to anything that walks through that door and just deal with it, then that would certainly make me a better physician, right?

In many ways, the challenges of the emergency medicine field made me stronger and more knowledgeable but also more apt at navigating the intricacies of the administrative and bureaucratic inferno that surrounds hospital practice. I have collected many stories over the years, success stories, moving stories, reality checks, and hard breaking defeats. I am happy I was given the opportunity to live through these moments and to be shaped by them.

When I decided to become an emergency room physician, I told myself it would be only for five years, I would not continue beyond that time, and I would not make a career out of it. I took the advice of older doctors and advisors scaring us with malpractice nightmares. I made a plan. But then, I failed to stick to it. I got caught up in the day-to-day demands of the job. In the scheduling requirements, I welcomed any break with a getaway vacation, refusing to think about the long term. And when I did picture the long term, I knew I would eventually transition to an office-based practice, but I was framing it more like retirement than the opportunity to embrace a new challenge. And who wants to think about retirement at the age of 30? That's right, I became an emergency physician by the age of 25, and that meant that I would need to retire by 30. Gloomy perspective. So I stuck with it. Then I gave myself reasons why continuing in the emergency department was actually better for me. I was familiar with the work, I was experienced by then, I could teach students and residents, and I would do challenging work every day. I would have the opportunity to save lives on a regular basis, I would continue to perfect my technical skills, etc. And I refused to think that I could not make it work. There is always a way, right?

The following three years were more difficult. I was eight years into the job at this point. I had managed to pull through working almost until the end of my first pregnancy, which was definitely an added challenge. Returning to work after taking a one-year maternity leave was probably more difficult even than being pregnant with my first child because, at this point, I was also sleep deprived and out of touch. But my decisive break came with my second pregnancy. Around that time, the hospital was undergoing major changes, an administrative merger with three other hospitals, and lots of personnel cuts and re-assignments, including in regards to nurses (our most valued team players in the ER) and secretaries. I remember a period when the ER only had one burnt-out and overworked secretary instead of the three secretaries we were used to. At that time, doctors needed to call patients into examining rooms, tell them to gown up, respond to distressed family members looking for their mother or for the toilet, call our own specialists through locating and wait endless minutes for a transfer, photocopy labs at patient's requests, see fewer patients because labs could not be done due to lack of nurses, etc. This extra administrative burden was in addition to our usual medical tasks of seeing and treating patients, gathering our own technical trays for procedures, running after the only antiquated ultrasound machine of the emergency department, which was always misplaced or borrowed by specialists, etc. The extra wait time was negatively impacting everyone involved, and patients and their loved ones were extra irritable and dissatisfied with the care, with the personnel, with the hospital. Occasionally in such a chaotic environment, mistakes were made, charts were switched, and patients were not triaged or were triaged and placed in a room with their chart misplaced, left there waiting for hours. It was a toxic environment to work in, that is for sure. We had lost some of our best nurses, our most experienced nurses, to other departments or to other hospitals, and the new nurses were unfamiliar with the tasks required and were overwhelmed by the work available.

It is in that kind of environment that my resilience was no longer sufficient. I had been dreading going to work for weeks and was feeling physically unwell as soon as I stepped foot into the emergency department. I could feel the angst building in my throat, would startle at loud noises, and become very emotional when something didn't check out. I was usually the person to welcome a challenge, but by that point, even the smallest problem was perceived as a mountain that could not be overcome. The work was painful. Every irritant was extra annoying and difficult to take, and my patience was running thin. I needed to take breaks between cases to recollect myself. I was suffering in silence. I knew I was in trouble but hoped it would pass and I would regain control. I always fell on my feet. But it was when I broke down in tears one day, in front of the new secretary, just because of some minor irritant, that I knew that I couldn't work there anymore, at least for the time being. So I decided to take a 10-day vacation and invited my sister to tag along. She was a

Ph.D. student at the time, and her time was her own. I pleaded with my colleagues to take over my shifts, and I freed my schedule. Hawaii was phenomenal. I could walk bare feet on the beach, could snorkel on a gorgeous bay overlooking an imposing mountain, could hike and explore nature. And also, my sister and I made some good friends, and hanging out with them was so refreshing! There were no problems for me to fix. In just a few days, I felt normal again. My throat tightness had gone, my hypervigilance had resolved, I was no longer an emotional wreck, and my energy was back. For me, just getting out of that toxic environment restored my joy to live.

A few days before we were due to fly back, I started thinking about the ER again, about the shifts that I had left to complete, and I felt such paralysis and anxiety over it that I realized that I could not do it. If I wanted to protect myself, I had to get out completely. I then spent the next few days sending emails and getting colleagues to take over my shifts and freed myself from that place. And when I did, when I knew that I didn't have to go back, I felt an enormous weight lift off my shoulders. There was a pang of guilt too, but the sensation of freedom was definitely greater. I sent my letter of resignation and my farewell message to my co-workers and never stepped foot there again.

I realize now that burnout was a blessing in disguise. If it weren't for that burnout, I likely would have put up with that toxic environment for longer despite the fact that I was deeply unhappy with it. The thing that was holding me back, surprisingly, was the fear of uncertainty and the fear of change. I was in my first trimester of my second pregnancy, months away from my maternity leave, and I could not see myself making such a drastic career change at that fragile time in my life. Paradoxically, despite all the stress and the toxicity, I knew what to expect from that work environment. I knew most of the people working there. It was predictable in its chaos. Working in a new place would mean reaching out, signing a new work contract, meeting new colleagues, new staff, learning to navigate new electronic medical records, getting used to new referral protocols, parking in a new parking lot, to a different commute. Change is difficult for most people, but change is extra hard when you feel tired and vulnerable. When you are burned out, it feels impossible because it requires so much new energy injected into this project. But there are great payoffs in the end. I saw that when I pulled the plug. Despite the dread of the change, the new work environment felt like a walk in the park in comparison with my previous ER job. The staff were nice and welcoming. The work was reasonable, no one seemed burned out, learning the new computer system was fast and smooth, etc. Most of my worries seemed ridiculous in retrospect. Overall, my daily stress decreased so much, and I felt like I regained control.

In my second and third trimester, I actually took not one but two new jobs. I flew to a rural and remote Northern Community on several work contracts, all being, in fact, in different communities, and did very varied and gratifying work while being well supported by competent nurses. The housing was close to the clinic, and while on duty, despite being on call all the time, I actually got a chance to rest most nights and slept better than I did while at home with a new baby. The second job I took was in my third trimester, deciding it was safer to be in the city in case I went into preterm labor, which was quite possible given the numerous contractions I was experiencing. The job I took was over the summer when the walk-in clinic next to my house was very understaffed due to vacations. I had no trouble working on most days two and sometimes even three shifts (each being 4 hours). The work felt so easy again. I stopped because it became unsafe for me to keep working due to the never-ending contractions. I ended up delivering at term, surprisingly. Then after my second maternity leave, I chose a new work environment that would offer a new challenge but with a measurably lower stress potential and that had the ability to grow over time and was also a business, something I had no prior experience with. I joined a private clinic and utterly enjoyed the next three years of my professional life, made strong connections with the staff, and strong therapeutic alliances with my patients. I know emphatically that I would not have achieved these goals had I not burned out in the emergency department years prior.

About Diana Dumenko, MD
Dr. Diana Dumenko is a Canadian medical doctor with a wide breath of clinical experience. She is the founder of Dr. Diana MD, a place to learn about health, longevity, nutrition, and how to live a healthy and fun life.

drdianamd.com

Lida Fatemi, DO MPH

As a first year hospitalist attending I became disillusioned with medicine. The hospital I once loved became dreadful. A few months went by, and my disdain grew stronger. The walls started closing up on me as I walked to my office. I felt lonely. I felt stuck, helpless, and stagnant. I felt turmoil inside. I could only see the flaws of the system. My lovely colleagues did not want to be around me. I sensed it. I did not want to be around me. I started feeling a gap between my family and me. I no longer had friends. I drove them away. I felt isolated and unloved.

I became depressed, anxious, and distrusting. I saw myself as a cog in a wheel. Going round and round without thought. The evidence-based medicine I was practicing became a script for pushing more and more medications on patients. I felt I was not helping anyone. In fact, I felt I was harming my patients with the toxicity of the perpetual prescription medications. The cognitive dissonance was eating away at my soul. How could I say I am not harming my patients? When in fact, there are many things I did in my job that could harm them. Including keeping them in the hospital for more days than necessary as their muscles atrophied and their chances of recovery decreased. During their prolonged stay, some would contract a hospital-acquired infection leading them to an ICU transfer and some to their death. Not to mention the patients who had been through the wringer at the end of life, and we kept sending them for more procedures and treatment without much thought about their quality of life. Why? Because there is a lot of money involved. This was all against my core ethics of humanism.

I was moving further and further away from my values. My job became about admitting, medicating, discharging, writing notes, and answering endless pages that pulled me away from building a sacred patient-doctor connection. I felt more and more disengaged from my patients.

Wasn't my purpose in working so hard to become a physician alleviating suffering? It used to be.

No one prepared me for my role in pleasing the system. My grandfather was an internal medicine physician for forty years in Iran. He practiced direct primary care. There were no administrators micromanaging him. He practiced evidenced based humanistic medicine. He nourished his sacred relationship with his patients. They loved him. I was under the impression my practice would be the same. I could not be further away from that utopic medical practice.

I finished my internal medicine residency as the resident of the year three years in a row. It was the first time anyone in our program received this honor. I loved every moment in residency. I was involved with many projects throughout the hospital, trying to fix system issues for doctors. I was the Regional Vice President of our resident union, the Committee of Interns and Residents. I attended many national conferences. Then, I became the first Doctor of Osteopathy University Chief Resident. It was during my chief year when I recognized the severe burnout in our residents. I presented on the topic of raising the alarm. At the time, we had not recognized physician coaching as a way through burnout.

The next year, one of our second year residents committed suicide. We were all shocked. Many of us started going to therapy. My quest to understand burnout, lack of fulfillment, dissatisfaction, depression, anxiety, and suicide in medicine started.

It took me two years of my direct personal experience with burnout to create a way through. I would do anything not to feel as I did. I started crawling my way out. Through my dark experiences, I gained many gems. I read the research on psychedelic medicines at Johns Hopkins for end-of-life fear with terminally ill patients. I read the book "How to Change your Mind" by Micheal Pollen. I decided I wanted to have a better life, so I tried psilocybin, where it was legal. I created and integrated the Conscious Life Practices with psilocybin. The combination changed my life. I was interested in life again. I was playing with my child more. I was engaged. I created a new community of incredible humans around us. I wanted to live and work again. I created a coaching program for female physicians to help them through their darkness into the light.

Using psychedelics in addition to spiritual practices was essential in becoming conscious of the effect of my childhood trauma and its manifestation into adulthood. We lived in a war for the first eight years of my life. Every day could be the day when our home would be bombarded. Every day we were concerned, we would not see my dad come back from his office. We did not have electricity for many days. We did not have running water for many days at a time. Food was rationed. It seemed as if we were constantly at a teenage boy's funeral who had forcefully been enlisted into fighting a fruitless war created by the government. We would all jump at the sound of the city alarms warning us of potential bombardment and flee to the shelters. We spent many nights when we had to leave our home and go to a relative's where we were safe. We would sleep in the living room like sardines in sleeping bags. As kids, we had a great time when we were all together. It was the epitome of a loving community holding each other through collective trauma. Toward the end of the war, we had to move over the Alborz mountains by the Caspian sea to seek safety. My family had the financial means to do so, but many did not have the luxury. This manifested as an inability to connect deeply with people later in life. Forming vulnerable relationships always ended painfully in a loss. As a young adult, I would avoid creating vulnerable relationships. This was shown to me in my psychedelic journeys.

Another large portion of my trauma growing up in Iran was living under a theocratic dictatorship regime for the first fourteen years of my life. The combination of state and religion is anti-human. Females were oppressed to unfathomable measures. As I write this, there is a women-led revolution occurring in Iran against this terrorist regime for the first time in human history.

I remember when I was six years old. My mom took me to my first day of school. I was excited and nervous. I entered the school courtyard with hundreds of other girls. The six year old girl in front of me had a tiny bit of hair showing from her head scarf. The religious woman barked at her that her hair was showing. She hit her on the head, screaming, "I'm taking you upstairs to shave your head!!!" I was speechless. I could not utter a word and froze in place. My six year old body and emotions could not understand why. I was told we were sinning by showing our hair because men were attracted to us. How horrific! How traumatic. I had a fever for the next three days, and my mom changed my school. That was the start of the micro traumas. The brainwashing with the message of "you're never good" because everything we did was a sin. We would be yelled at if we asked a question about the Quran in class. If there was a whisper of an anti-government sentiment from a reporter or a journalist, they would disappear. The society was utterly and completely run by fear. Fear of going to hell, fear of going to jail, fear of getting whipped, fear of death, fear of losing your family, fear of losing your job, fear, fear, and fear. The government used religion to control the masses with fear. This forced you to be "good." Though my family was very open minded and exposed us to all spiritual paths, such as Buddhism and Hinduism, it still left many small wounds.

I was a very good girl throughout my life. I listened to all the systems that forced me to do what was against my intuition. I entered a marriage I knew was not good for him or me because of fear of disappointing my family, fear of canceling the wedding, and not knowing what to tell people. Same story in medical school and residency. I was always the top student, top resident, and a lot of it was driven internally by wanting to be my best. A lot of it came from a place of pleasing others. Pleasing the patriarchy. This is what I was brainwashed with. It was a journey with psychedelics showing me the fears I had lived with all my life. They were shown to me as illusions I had carried for 37 years. I was pure consciousness walking inside the theater of my mind. I was the eye of the storm, and my fears were gigantic monsters that swirled around me. I looked at them and shed the weight of trauma. There was a separation. I was a curious observer. I saw how I was shackled by my empathy for others. I saw myself in a million mirrors looking back at me. It was through the darkness that I saw my own light.

Through my journeys into my darkness, I was shown my authentic self. This is how I created the Conscious Life Practices coaching program. It took years of experimenting with them every day with consistency to understand their worth in creating a life of freedom from inner turmoil. I was able to enter my current marriage with an incredible human who is fully present with me, empowers me, and co-creates a life of balance. A life of serenity. A life full of love. A life of courage. A life against violations, small or big. A life of vitality. A life with boundaries. A life of steadiness. A life of wholeness. A life of alignment with my intuition. A life in alignment with my body. A life of honoring myself. A life of self-compassion. A life of serving myself. A life of serving others. A life of connection between soul, mind, heart, and body.

In the past decade, I polished the practices. I created a coaching program for female physician moms with incredible results. I was recently on Bloom NBC, educating 36 million viewers on the topics of Conscious Life Practices and on Psychedelic medicines. We have a podcast, Conscious Physician: Medicine & Psychedelics, educating on the current research on psychedelics and their effect on mental health.

Those who have completed the program tell me they feel "blissful," and that their practice is finally thriving, and that they are able to be an "engaged parent without rage". Every person who has completed our program is thriving in their own unique way. They are no longer weighed down. They have "recognized things about themselves they never knew existed." They have the tools and skills to continue coaching themselves. I consider this a true success.

I am now practicing medicine as it is aligned with my core values. I get to alleviate suffering. I educate and speak at a national level on the intersection of medicine and psychedelics, as supported by research. I consult for practices in states where psilocybin is legal. I help people through their trauma with self-compassion. I am ecstatic and feel extreme gratitude for my life challenges and the wisdom I have gained through them. I am in awe of my daily family life and the gifts it brings me every moment. I have regained the sacred relationship with my patients. My grandfather would be proud.

Question and Answers

Was there anything about the system you worked in that led to your episodes of burnout?

The system I worked in encouraged saying "yes" to everything, which is a recipe for an empty vessel. The system's disregard for the physician's needs in workflow and having a balanced life is a major contributor. There are no boundaries. As if the medicine is our entire life. It's all-consuming, which is not natural or healthy.

What advice would you give someone going through burnout?

Seek help. Seek a coach, seek a mentor, seek a community. Talk about your experience without fear. Learn what you will and leave the toxic environment. Do what gives you meaning. You don't have to abide by any one system. You can create your own. You are never stuck. You are an executive.

What advice would you give to the facilities and administration who are trying to help decrease the rate of physician burnout?

Talk to your physicians. They have all the answers you are looking for. Ask them what they need to help them leave work early and be with their families without interruption. Take action. Just saying how much you appreciate your doctors does not mean you are making their life better. Wellness programs are not about a meeting or meditation. They are about how we treat each other at every level of interaction.

What advice, if any, would you give to the facilities that can do better when it comes to improving burnout rates of physicians (those facilities that appear to have a lack of interest in helping to improve conditions)?

Physician burnout costs between $500K to $2 million per physician. From a logical business perspective, it is best to take care of the currently employed physicians. Listen to them and take action. Words without action are a cause of burnout.

About Lida Fatemi, DO MPH
Dr. Fatemi conscious living tools dovetail with ancient plant remedies (psychedelics) to address trauma and optimize physiology and neurobiology profoundly, reconnecting her patients with their own spirituality and sense of belonging and contentment in as little as 3 months.

https://drlida.family/

Nadia Ali M.D, M.B;B.S, MPH, ABHIM, FACP

I was born and brought up in Karachi, Pakistan. We were a lower middle class family with limited resources. My mother was a typical house wife who worked very hard to take care of the three of us. My father was the sole bread earner. They loved us dearly and wanted to give us the best education from the very onset. My father wanted me to be a doctor but I was not so sure about it. My decision to become a physician came after I had several encounters with our family physician. He had a small clinic that would be jam packed with people. He was not simply a doctor who diagnosed patients and prescribed medications, but rather he was a healer. He could listen to what they could not say. His words were so soothing, and his demeanor was so compassionate that by the end of the visit, the patient would start to feel better. He was the messiah for so many people who would travel long distances because they felt they could trust him. I always wanted to be that healer and I thought that getting a degree from a medical school would do that. Of course, I was wrong.

I have always been a brilliant student, and I am very grateful to my parents, who invested in our education despite financial and social challenges. I was able to get into the best medical school (The Aga Khan University)in the country, and they helped us by giving me a loan for the first couple of years and then I earned a scholarship to cover the rest of my medical school. After completion of my medical school, my parents wanted me to practice medicine in Karachi, Pakistan. I wanted to do my residency in the United States because I knew that the quality of education there was much better. It was a lot of struggle to convince them but they finally agreed.

The three-year residency was not easy because there were a lot of cultural differences that I needed to adapt to in addition to the 80 hour workload. I had no friends or relatives except my spouse. I did not know how to drive, so I was dependent on my husband for transportation. We were newly married, and adjusting to our new relationship at the same time as all of the other changes was very tough.

After the completion of my residency, I was very happy and proud to have secured the position of an academic hospitalist at a reputable healthcare system. I was a little nervous but Confident at the same time. I loved the work I did because there was a lot to learn initially. It was a time when we saw a lot of readmissions, especially in the elderly population. These patients were on complex regimens of multiple medications, which led to confusion and reduced compliance. It was concerning to me because these patients and their families were struggling. I started to work with the Quality Improvement department voluntarily. I created a medication form to help patients and their families understand the purpose, form, and frequency of medications so as to increase their compliance, reduce confusion and reduce readmissions. Our committee won an award for our tools. Unfortunately, there was no recognition or appreciation for what I was doing. A new hire to the group was added who also was to have a part-time role in patient safety, but I was already working on it voluntarily, yet I was never approached or offered that position. I don't know if it was because of my gender or color, or lack of connections.

As time went by, I realized that I was just a cog in the wheel. Nobody was interested in addressing the needs of the hospitalized patients. It was all about making diagnoses and adding medications, and, most importantly, discharging them ASAP. Our lists of patients were getting longer and longer. We added mid-level providers-nurse practitioners to deal with the increased patient load. However, no matter how hard we tried, we could never make enough money for the hospital. I was beginning to notice that the number of patients I was being assigned was more than others. It was more work, no increase in pay, not even a note of thank you or even a remote possibility of growth. I kept a note of it for a week and then talked to one of my colleagues. He suggested that I talk to the team lead. When I called and asked him why I was being assigned more patients, he started yelling at me on the phone. I think no one had ever questioned him before since he was the team lead. I did not do anything about that, but I realized that I need to grow and prove myself in areas that I am passionate about so I can move into a different role. I started my MPH at Hopkins with a focus on health literacy. I loved teaching residents and students, and I was aware that this is a new concept that is not taught by residency programs, so I decided to assess and teach health literacy to the residents. Teaching students was getting more and more difficult due to the increasing workload. I had started keeping a log of the number of patients I was seeing. One day, one of my team leads met with me to give me feedback. I knew it would be something negative since I had never received any positive feedback for any of the volunteer stuff I had done. He told me that the students feel that they do not get a lot of didactic teaching on the floors. I showed my patient log that I was keeping to the lead to explain that it is not possible for me to teach if I am expected to see 22-24 patients a day. Of course, they were not happy with my response. I was thoroughly frustrated. The frustration made me irritable, angry, and depressed. It affected my relationship with my family to the extent that one Saturday, I almost could not stop crying. I felt I could not take it anymore, and I could not continue to survive like this. I called the Crises line to seek help. I just wanted someone to listen and to say that everything would be OK, just like my mom would say. My parents were not in the U.S., and I did not want to call and make them worried.

Interestingly I met a friend cum mentor after a number of years. She helped me start observing the fire inside me and how that affected my perception and my behavior. I started yoga and eating better. I used to work through my lunchtime, so I could get home ASAP. I stopped doing that, and I would get my lunch around noon before continuing to see the rest of the patients on my list.

I wanted to resign as soon as I could, and I gave them the notice per my contract, but I was forced to stay another two months or so. One of the program leaders threatened me by saying that if I left before they could find another person, it would adversely affect my ability to get citizenship. I recently received my green card.

I thought that all institutions are not the same and possibly an outpatient setting might be better. I got a faculty position in a community-based health system. Being on the faculty, I dedicated time to work with residents and students, and I loved it. I also had the opportunity to do research and create new knowledge. I went out of my way to work on multiple research projects, particularly related to health literacy. I created a curriculum on health literacy for our residents. Unfortunately, I realized over time that the same issues were happening all over again. It was all about the RVUs-income generated by physicians. We were expected to see more and more patients on the clinical side. I vividly remember seeing a woman who was crying and feeling depressed because of her marital issues. I was trying to comfort her. I was concerned about her depression and worried that this might get worse with life-threatening outcomes. I was getting knocked on my door every few minutes by the staff because there were patients waiting to be seen. I was frustrated and unsure how to deal with a situation when I could not even be with my patient during such a critical time. Every patient was a number. Every problem had one answer-prescribing more medications. The list of medications was simply going up. When we complained about how we could address multiple issues that the patient had over a 10-15 minutes time-frame, we were told that we should tell the patient that it is 1 issue per visit that we can discuss. Clearly, part of the problem is not the clinic or the health system but the insurance system and the healthcare model.

Patients were driving over an hour to see me because they wanted to have a physician who would listen, understand and help them address their lifestyles, teach them strategies to manage stress, and fulfill their needs for compassion and care during their time of suffering. These patients were assigned 15 minutes like everyone else. I informed my supervisors that I have obtained my certification as an integrative physician and would like to pursue this further. The option proposed was that I practice conventional medicine for those who cannot afford Functional medicine and practice Functional Medicine for those who can afford it. How could I possibly do that? Ethically, I cannot discriminate between treatment plans on the basis of affordability. I refused to move forward with that option.

In addition to the demand for seeing new patients, responsibilities were also being added to the faculty aspect of my job. I was asked to lead a critically important committee per the requirements of ACGME. I was not given any additional time and no increase in any form of incentive. I still agreed to do it. Interestingly, I was also forced to conduct those meetings at times that were suitable to my supervisor instead of me. I was excited to lead the committee, and when this announcement was made during the monthly faculty meeting, it was stated that I was chosen to lead because my supervisor could not be the lead according to ACGME's requirements. Clearly, I was not good enough for the job, and my supervisor had done a big favor by giving that position to me.

I never got a raise in my first job or my second job. I did not ask for a raise in my first job, and a failed attempt was made in my second job. New people were hired and given better salaries though they did not have any experience. I was not only beginning to lose my self-esteem but also my self-respect. I was not interested in intermingling with any of my colleagues. I did not care what policies were introduced and what the future plans were for the organization because that would not affect my personal or professional development. It was all about more revenue at the cost of physicians and other people who worked in the organization. Over 100 people were laid off during my stay at one of the health systems, but the salary of the CEO was not affected. The decisions were made by people who had no clinical background. Any additional resource requested to help patients, even if it was as low as $500, was not approved in the budget. All of these things made me more and more resentful. The breaking point was when I was directly humiliated in front of other faculty and members of the organization by one of my supervisors. Interestingly as members of the faculty, we receive training on providing feedback, and when I discussed this scenario with another supervisor, he/she refused to support me. I am very grateful that this happened. This was a blessing, and it woke me up to the reality that this organization and the people I work with have no integrity, no respect for those serving the organization, and no accountability for those in the leading position. I was a slave who had no value, no respect, no rights, and no voice. I was getting more and more irritable and frustrated, and this incident was the last straw that broke the camel's back. My spouse wrote my resignation, and I submitted that the following day.

I was anxious about giving my resignation because I was not prepared. I had not planned what I would do next and how I would practice Integrative Medicine. I knew how to treat patients with a better approach, an approach in which the whole picture is taken into account. What I did not have was the experience of working in an Integrative practice. Most importantly, I had no training on how to start a practice from scratch. However, as soon as I submitted my resignation, I felt relief as if a huge burden had been lifted off of my chest. I felt at peace. I felt proud to have stood up for myself. I deserved to be respected, heard, and valued for my contribution, just like any other employee of any organization. I regained my confidence, self-respect, and self-esteem that was sabotaged. I was free to create what was best for my patients. I could pursue my passion for personal and professional development. Rather, the resignation itself was a result of what I had learned the hard way. When we learn lessons through difficult times, we do not forget them. I was free to create my own schedule and have a work-life balance, just like I preach to my patients. I wanted to be a role model physician who walks the talk and who has experienced the difficulties of making lifestyle changes. This experience allowed me to understand the barriers, challenges, and strategies that can help my patients.

Question and Answers

Looking back, was there anything in your childhood or upbringing that you think led to your burnout?

I grew up in Karachi, Pakistan, and it is a patriarchal society. My parents were quite liberal, and they gave me a lot of confidence, and I was proud of my achievements.

Having said that, I was a product of a male-dominated society where women accept that it is OK for a man to get more, do less, throw a tantrum, and degrade women. In addition, I saw my father, who suffered a lot at the hands of his supervisors, and he endured all of that. I learned that subconsciously. Even though I did not like it and I opposed it, it was a norm. I think that this acceptance affected my ability to take a stand in my professional life. I had male attendings in my residency program who were disrespectful of my background (since I came from a third world country). I had a male boss who forced me to work longer than I needed to by threatening me. In another instance, my supervisor shouted and yelled at me over the phone. One of my male supervisors wrote an email to multiple people, including my colleagues and me, to let us all know that I was unprofessional because I was 15 minutes late one day. These incidents happened on an ongoing basis, and I often overlooked these kinds of behaviors till I lost all my patience and self-respect. Interestingly, in all of these instances, I left the position without complaining about these behaviors and reporting them to HR. I admit it was my mistake, but I was not even aware of my options for a long time.

Did anything occur in your training that led to your burnout?

If we look at the structure of the residency program, it is hierarchical in nature. We are constantly expected to agree and obey those above us since they are the ones who evaluate us. We are not assessed on our ability to think or be creative or ask questions pertaining to the policies and procedures, even if we think that they are inefficient, ineffective, and often not serving the patients. This environment is a systematic attempt to create submissiveness and subservience. We are creating robots that follow orders without questioning.

The workload during residency is another issue. Hard work needs to be appreciated, and I am proud of my parents, who taught us the value of hard work. All of us work hard in medical schools, and we take pride in our work and our ability to improve the quality of health and life of our patients. The area that is significantly lacking is training residents to understand the need to take a pause and assess their needs. It is wonderful to give of our time, knowledge, and skills for the improvement of those around us, but it is equally important to take care of oneself and one's own emotional, social and spiritual needs. I had no knowledge or training to assess my needs or resources to address them. I found all of those after I completely burnt myself out simply because I had no options at that time.

The last and most important missing area in residency training is the lack of training about our options post-residency, including serving in the pharmaceutical industry, being an entrepreneur, or working in social media. Most residents felt that they only had two options, being employed by a large healthcare system or by a private practice.

Was there anything about the system you worked in that led to your episode (s) of burnout?

Every system that I worked for had only one objective: making as much money as possible irrespective of how that will impact patients, physicians, and all the people that worked for the system. I was a number and a cog in the wheel. Every year, there was a session that informed us how we did not make as much money as the CEO or the system intended and how we would need to do more to achieve that goal next year.

There was no appreciation for the reason why we became physicians; to serve and heal patients. There was neither any discussion about how we can make patient care better, nor there was any budget allocated for that.

We were not considered humans; hence our needs are neither assessed nor addressed. We were physicians whose job was to be submissive and subservient to whatever was being asked of us.

Did you have a support system?

My only support system was my spouse. He also suffered due to my burnout. I did not have any colleagues or mentors to whom I could reach out. On the contrary, one of my colleagues made fun of me for expecting things to change. Others were proud of working long hours and being in the hospital for a long time. I could not dare talk about work-life balance. This is one of the primary reasons why I decided to be a coach for professional women, especially physicians who were going through difficult times in their professional lives.

Did anyone notice and reach out to you?

There was no time for people to notice you or even ask you about how satisfied you were with your job or with the work environment. I complained to one of my colleagues, and she told me that the best strategy was to either do what was asked of me or leave because the expectation of change was impossible. She was absolutely right. It became clear to me that a lot of people were doing their job as clerks who needed to get some money. No passion, no goals, no expectations except getting the job done. I did not belong to that category. I was a human being with hope, passion, goals, aspirations, and, most important of all, an intellect that asks questions and seeks rational answers. I cannot do something which does not make sense to me. I cannot follow a procedure that is inefficient and ineffective. I cannot stay stagnant. I want to grow and improve myself, my patients, my community, and the world at large.

What helped you overcome burnout?

There were a number of variables that helped me overcome my burnout. The most important being my spouse. He realized how I was suffering every single day. He could see how my supervisors were neither appreciative nor interested in supporting the initiatives that I wanted to take to improve patient care. Rather, they were disrespectful, degrading, and arrogant toward me. I felt as if they were doing me a favor by giving me the job. He saw that I deserved better. He realized that the price I was paying for these jobs was affecting my creativity, self-worth, health, and relationship. He wrote my resignation, and he said that he would support me in whatever I wanted to do even if I did not earn a penny. The value of my happiness, health, and self-worth was much greater than what anyone could pay me.

The second variable that helped me was the burnout itself. Every adversity comes with a lesson. My burnout came with a lot of lessons. The first lesson I learned when I was in a toxic environment was that I was expecting those around me to appreciate me and support my endeavors to improve the quality of life of my patients. That expectation was a mistake because my goals and the goals of the systems were not aligned and will never be aligned. I took responsibility for my growth, my needs, and my goals. No one, not even my spouse, can do this for me. I am grateful to all those people who pushed me, pulled me, and made my life difficult because they gave me the clarity, motivation, and determination to change my perceptions and my actions.

The third realization came when I searched and connected with my deeper self. I had to do that because I had so many questions but no answers. I saw that I had been blessed with so many strengths, and I realized my own self-worth. I was not born to be submissive or subservient. I am here to create, discover, conquer and connect with those who are like-minded. I love to learn, and the more I learn, the more I crave to learn. I knew that my creativity, learning, and compassion combined with my ability to connect with my patients, was more than enough for me to move forward and help my patients. Every adversity is meant to be a blessing for those who connect with their inner core.

How are you thriving today?

The process of burnout started roughly six years before I completely crashed. During this process, I had clinical experience in both inpatient and outpatient settings. I had gone through multiple health systems. It was clear to me that the concept of healing was completely lost in the current institutionalized form of medicine. When I intended to be a 'doctor', I envisioned a person who is sitting with the patient, listening carefully to every word, understanding the pain, the barriers, and the context that the patient is experiencing. My role was not simply to prescribe a pill but to be a healer who is compassionate and intelligent at the same time. If I see a patient with high blood sugar, then my role is not simply to write a prescription for Metformin, but I will try to understand the lifestyle, the stressors, the food choices, and the role of movement in the life of this patient. I want to help my patient understand how these factors interplay to cause disease and complications. I want to help my patient create lasting habits that will serve him/her, not just today but for many years to come. It would help the patient's family as well. This patient will then be the source of sharing his knowledge and experience with the community, and hence, we will have a healthier community. This led me to discover Functional medicine, a way to address the root cause of the problem, and use lifestyle, movement, meditation, and nutrients to address the root cause.

I started my Functional Practice with 0 patients, and I am humbled to be able to have served so many patients. I make a difference every day when I see them making healthier choices, feeling energetic and empowered. Each day is a new day to make a difference, and I am so grateful for this opportunity to serve and influence my community. The return on my burnout is much greater than I had expected. My knowledge, clinical experience in the field of Functional Medicine, and skill to create a healing space for those around me have not only benefited my family and community, but it has helped me tremendously. I am a better person today than I ever was. There is always room for improvement, and I learn from my patients every day.

I am healthier physically, financially, emotionally, and spiritually. I have connected with amazing physician entrepreneurs who have gone through similar burnout and transformed themselves completely. My learning has grown not only in the field of functional medicine but also personally and professionally. I have learned setting boundaries, identifying and communicating my needs clearly, saying no to those who do not realize my worth and value, and taking responsibility for my own needs and happiness.

I am passionate about educating my patients and my community, and I am actively engaging with everyone through different media platforms. This is the legacy I want to leave behind. I want health to be viewed not as an absence of disease but rather as the optimal functioning of the body, mind, and spirit. I am in the process of writing a book, and I am excited that this will be another intervention that will spread the message of hope and healing around the globe. I have no regrets and no hard feelings toward anyone or anything that has happened. I firmly believe everyone who touches our lives positively and negatively is a messenger, and we have the option to learn and grow or stay stagnant and suffer. I have decided to be the messenger of hope, and I will spread this message for as long as I live in as many ways as possible. I am proud to be blessed with the opportunity to do so.

What advice would you give to someone going through burnout?

The most important thing to remember is to not underestimate your own self-worth. If you do not learn to value yourself, no one will ever do that. It is important to take a pause and look at the bigger picture and ask yourselves some difficult questions about who you are, what are your values and goals in life, what is the legacy you want to leave behind, and what price you are willing to pay for it.

The second most important thing is to never give up on your dreams. No one gets what they want easily or quickly. It is a process where you build on your strengths and your skills. You fall and make mistakes but then rise again and again. The more you fall, the stronger your resilience is to deal with failure till a time comes when you are no longer seeking success because you have become the success and others around you are now interested to know you and your story. It does not happen overnight, but it happens eventually.

The third thing is to never care about what people think of you or what they say to you or behind your back. No one has the right to judge you, just like you cannot judge the intent, motive, or action of another person. You are living your values, goals, and aspirations irrespective of the perception of others. Your actions need to be sincere and based on what your values and life goals are. What truly makes you feel happy and fulfilled? It is possible that you may opt-out of practicing medicine or prefer an occupation that has no connection with medicine. You need to do that irrespective of the opinions of those around you. Those who truly love and care about you will support you in all the endeavors that bring joy to you.

Last but not least, you do not have to learn everything from scratch like some of us had to do. Seek help from physicians that have gone through this process and identify resources that can help you during this difficult time.

What advice would you give to the facilities and administration who are trying to help decrease the rate of physician burnout?

One of the most common mistakes that a lot of organizations that are trying to reduce burnout do is to band-aid the problem without addressing the root cause. An example of that is the emphasis on self-care as a strategy to reduce burnout. The underlying assumption is that lack of self-care is causing burnout. It is almost like an anxious person is asked to take Benzodiazepine for relief. A better option is to understand what is the underlying cause of the anxiety. Is there a work-related issue, a family issue, or a health issue that is causing the anxiety and addressing the real source of the problem? Every burnout case is different, and each of us has different needs, values, and coping strategies; hence we need to have customized solutions.

What advice if any, would you give to the facilities that can do better when it comes to improving burnout rates of physicians (those facilities that appear to have a lack of interest in helping to improve conditions)?

Unfortunately, change does not come from outside. It only happens when there is an inner need and desire for change. If physicians who work in these institutions do not openly express how they are suffering from burnout in a collective manner, these institutions will have no reason to make a change.

Just like we have Press Ganey scores available for all institutions to assess patient satisfaction, we need to have physician burnout scores for each institution with more than 10 physicians available for patients. We know that burnout affects the ability of a physician to provide patient care. This will allow these institutions to see the connection between the 2, and they will have the incentive to work to improve burnout.

About Nadia Ali M.D, M.B;B.S, MPH, ABHIM, FACP

Dr. Ali Is a Functional Integrative Physician, and her focus is to prevent, reverse and heal chronic diseases such as autoimmunity, gut issues, dementia, chronic fatigue, fibromyalgia, hormonal imbalances, obesity, heart disease, diabetes, cancer, and mental health disorders. The approach is to identify the root cause of the symptoms, such as nutritional deficiencies, dysbiosis, toxin exposures, chronic infections, hormonal changes, inflammation, and oxidative address. Reversing the root cause not only reverses symptoms and diseases but helps prevent complications and the development of other chronic diseases.

She offers mindfulness coaching for professional women undergoing burnout, feeling stuck in life, and facing barriers to achieving their goals and dreams. Her personal experience with burnout could have been so much better if she had found a mentor that could support and guide her during some of the most difficult times in her professional life. Dr. Ali decided to do this because she would not want anyone else to go through the same pain unnecessarily. She offers a complimentary 15 minutes to offer support to those seeking help as well as to identify if her coaching is a good fit for them.

https://www.theholistichealing.org/about-coaching

Heather Awad, MD

"I try not to tell everyone how much pain I have." Grandma looked up at me with a furrowed brow. She wanted me to scratch her back as well. That day we would discover that she was allergic to the morphine that was treating her leukemia pain. That itch would blossom into full body hives. It was a difficult situation as morphine was quick pain relief. I recalled that my grandma had planned to be a doctor when she was a young woman, but the man at the pre-med office at the university told her 'no' and walked her down to the teacher's college. She and I were both glad that I got to make my choice.

I looked across the room at my four small children, sitting in the sunshine in front of her hospice room windows, drawing bright colorful crayon pictures on blank paper. Their futures seemed limitless. Three violin cases were scattered about as well, and one blue violin made out of foam for the three year old, who didn't play a real one yet.

I had received a call last week from my mother in Michigan that Grandma's myelodysplastic syndrome, an autoimmune disorder of the blood cell lines, had turned into acute myeloid leukemia. The family knew this day would likely come, but the time was now. She would not turn ninety. Death strikes slowly or quickly at its whim, so I canceled my patients, gathered up my children and their little violins, and drove the ten hours from Minnesota to Michigan.

It had been a hard year. I took a family doctor job near my house, and the company had one of those new electronic medical records. I had good training with it, with an IT support team to call with questions, as well as customizable SMART SETS. These allowed me to enter a little phrase, and a whole visit for a child with abdominal pain would pop up on the screen. I could click through the symptoms and record my plan easily for a straightforward problem like this. Office days ran fairly smoothly with this new tool at first. Then a few months later the company fired one third of the staff. Now that we had the computer system, the doctor could answer all the questions. Instead of two nurses to field phone questions from patients, those could go electronically to the doctors. This added to the workload for the day. And all the messages waited for the doctors, even if they weren't at work. If I took a week off with my little family, my choice was to keep working the computer during time off, or face an insurmountable pile of inbox messages when I came back. The number of nurses working in the actual clinic decreased, so if I needed someone with medical knowledge to help with a patient, or to help communicate with a patient, that just wasn't possible anymore. And of course they wanted us to see more patients in a day since the electronic record theoretically made visits faster. Lab reports came straight to me without review from a nurse. Report cards were emailed to me to tell me to print out more papers for patients to take home, and to get more of my patients with heart disease to quit smoking. It didn't matter if they refused to quit when I counseled them. There was no humanity in the system for the caregivers.

No study ever showed that the computer made anyone healthier, nor made working with patients better for doctors or staff.

I rushed home at the end of each day to care for my children, help with their spelling lists and violin practice, and tuck them in their beds. Then I was back to my computer to review lab reports, finish typing out visits that weren't simple, and answer messages. I slumped over the desk when I wasn't physically able to stay awake any longer, then woke due to a crick in my neck or other pain. I'd stumble to my bed, knowing I had to start it all over again in a few hours. I felt so relieved one day to find that a friend at my office was also falling asleep at her laptop at one in the morning. I had thought I was bad at the work, but this was just the job. Neither of us questioned why we weren't sleeping in our beds all night, next to our husbands.

It felt like a rubber band inside me stretched tighter as my sleep hours shortened. I had a hard time depositing memories of time with my children, I ate poorly, and I became anxious about my patients and loved ones. I remember calling a woman with Type I diabetes at home to see how she was feeling after a visit with fever and cough earlier in the day. "I'm feeling much better now," she said. "It's so kind of you to call." I didn't tell her that the reason I called was so that I didn't wake in the night with my heart racing with worry over her. These experiences were to be expected with insufficient sleep and chronic stress, and were common among the doctors at my office.

When I left my job abruptly to see my grandmother, we brought the violins because she loved music so much. She spoke fondly of her childhood when relatives would visit, bringing all sorts of instruments to jam together for the weekend in the Upper Peninsula of Michigan where she grew up. My little ones played their Suzuki pieces for her with their tiny fingers on miniature violins, swaying to the music. Grandma would sit with her eyes closed, head back on her pillow and smile. I slept full nights that week, left my computer in its bag, and that taut band inside me relaxed. As we left I embraced my grandma and whispered how good it was to have the time with her. My children put their small hands in her large soft ones as she thanked them for their music and drawings. We drove home to Minnesota, and I knew I wouldn't see Grandma again, whether her death was slow or quick. I felt better, because I took this time with her instead of work. And there was music that was a comfort to my grandma, and an important family experience for all of us. I noticed that I only had this one life, and death would come slow or quick at its whim for me too. I chose to quit my job, and never work in primary care medicine again. I didn't know what burnout was, but I couldn't go back to living with that tight rubber band that always felt in danger of breaking. I would find other meaningful work to do with my medical degree.

Over the years, I felt an ache in my heart some days for the loss of the joys of primary care. I sometimes wondered what would have happened if I'd had a physician coach while working there. Could I have discovered another way to do the work or fight the system? I wonder how it could have been different if the corporate medical practice had valued the lives of the doctors as well as the patients. I wondered why medical training had taught us to put the job first.

So what did I do? I trained in medical acupuncture, but then some insurance laws changed in my state, and the reimbursements went too low. I became a clinic administrator, but I didn't enjoy it enough to stay with that work. Thankfully, I found a physician-led wound care company, and enjoyed years of this meaningful work. I cared for patients at skilled nursing facilities and rehab centers, with the ability to choose how long I rounded each day, and never had work to bring home at night. I hired career coaches to help me along my journey after primary care, so it's not surprising that I eventually became a coach myself. I currently have my own business helping women over 50 achieve permanent weight loss. I'm in charge of my work week, my boundaries, and my family life, while helping others as a doctor.

Question and Answers

Did anything occur in your training that led to your burnout?

The job always came first. I remember taking every other night call for a week at a time sometimes, which was working 36 hours on, going home to sleep, and returning the next morning. The program psychologist we were required to meet with was a detriment rather than a support--she seemed to be trying to just get personal details to share with the directors. It wasn't confidential.

Was there anything about the system you worked in that led to your episode (s) of burnout?

The importance of families was ignored. I remember a med student who constantly talked of her baby, and she didn't match in a residency. I remember thinking that she didn't know to make medical work the biggest priority. In residency, I took it as a compliment when someone would say, "I just found out you have a child. I can't believe I didn't know you had a kid." When my husband was out of town, I needed to hire a second nanny for evenings and overnights, because our main nanny already worked 50 hours a week. Spouses were meant to be disregarded and to know that family was a second place behind work.

What helped you overcome your burnout?

Quitting primary care. I wish I had known other ways, but I didn't in 2009.

Did anyone notice and reach out to you?

No. I hear about doctor suicides and I think about that tight rubber band I had inside me and how one really bad day could have broken me as it has in other doctors.

How are you thriving today?

Having my own businesses has been a way to thrive. I have been able to schedule around caring for my children and myself. I love helping other women free their minds and thrive through my current weight loss coaching program.

What advice would you give to someone going through burnout?

Get help--a medical therapist or a doctor coach. You are worth it. This "normal" feeling isn't something you have to live with.

What advice would you give to the facilities and administration who are trying to help decrease the rate of physician burnout and those who could do better?

Time stress is the systemic part, in my opinion. This has a different flavor every decade but is always the same. Change systems, so there is more support and also bring in coaches to help doctors do their work and deal with stress. Find all the ways so that patient care can be done during the day and left at night.

You will lose money with physician turnover.

About Heather Awad, MD
Dr. Awad is a family doctor in Minnesota who helps women aged 50 plus find permanent weight loss. She is the host of the Vibrant-MD podcast, where she discusses weight loss, women's health, and food.

https://www.vibrant-md.com/

Beverly Joyce, MD, FACOG, NCMP

After finishing my residency, I stayed in the large healthcare system in which I trained. I had a distinct advantage being a female OBGYN, and several facilities wanted me, but not my boyfriend, so we ended up in different locations. I thought this was IT- my life would be as an employed physician within this system, without any business responsibilities and with benefits and a pension. When I started, I was the physician with the least seniority in the group, but being female meant that my panel was immediately full. My male colleagues, who made considerably more money than I did because of their seniority, were often seen with their feet up, reading the newspaper and drinking coffee, while I was racing around trying to keep up with my duties for that day. When I was on call, I covered labor and delivery, the postpartum and GYN floor patients, the ER (where every female patient was referred to GYN first, even if she had a non-GYN complaint), and also clinic patients who requested a female doc, because the patient-now-customer always got what they wanted (even though the more senior male doctors had schedule openings). These clinic visits could be for something easy like a vaginitis complaint or for a "rule-out ectopic" that needed labs, ultrasound, and possibly surgery, and often took a lot of time and energy away from my primary focus, L&D. It was supremely unfair, and after 5 years, this inequity eventually led me to join a private OB/GYN practice across town. I didn't call this burnout at the time, but it was.

In my new practice, I was still the physician with the least seniority, but at least I was being paid for my hard work. By this time, I had a husband and kids (not the residency boyfriend- that was an ugly breakup), and I was very lucky that in the early days of my practice, the kids went to daycare with my husband in the morning and came home with him in the evening. This left me available for my patients all the time. And because our practice of 4 physicians competed with another 4-physician practice across town, everyone delivered their own patients, regardless of whether they were on call. So that is what I did. And I LOVED it! I loved the continuity of care and the gratification it brought both to the families I took care of and me. I loved getting the gifts they brought me, and my practice was booming. At one point, I had 20 patients due in a month and was turning patients away. I had long-lasting relationships with my patients, and I had patients who stayed with me through several pregnancies and beyond.

And life was great until it wasn't. I found myself with ever-competing interests- my patients versus my family. When my kids no longer went to daycare, we had a daytime sitter three days a week. I often found myself calling her for pickups on her days off because I was stuck with a patient in labor, and thank god she was almost always available. When the kids started after-school sports, I was their driver/chauffeur. Unfortunately, when our sitter moved away, we went through several babysitters, none of whom wanted to just be a driver. They would start and then quit. The constant interviewing and vetting of people were exhausting. There were negotiations with other families to arrange carpools, and, of course, this scheduling was all up to me. I was the master of the calendar, with color-coding for every member of the family. My type-A personality was in overdrive. Rides, dental appointments, doctor's visits--God forbid if either kid was sick or had to be picked up from school. They called me the mom. And my appointments?? HA, half the time I had to cancel them. And when, as would inevitably happen, a patient screwed up my master plan, I became a whirling dervish, scrambling to figure out how to make it all work. I began to resent my patients.

At one point, to make my life more predictable, I approached my partners (now totaling eight) and suggested a share-call type of coverage. Although some agreed that might be ok, none were fully on-board. This left me feeling like I was the only one struggling, that I couldn't hack it, and I felt ashamed that I no longer loved the life I had chosen. I felt stuck and thought, "I just need to keep going, and eventually, it will get better."

It didn't get better. I was on constant edge. My nervous system was in constant fight-or-flight mode. My family, office staff, and everyone else around me got the brunt of it. I would curse, yell, and scream at people. I was a total BIT*H. I'm surprised I never got written up by nurses at the hospital for being a disruptive physician.

I had a therapist whom I saw intermittently. We had started with her for family therapy before a European trip with the kids, then did couples therapy for a while, but my husband dropped out, and then it was just me. She encouraged me to find ways to "put air in my cushion" because it was always deflated. She provided some coaching, which was very helpful. My husband was supportive and would say things like "but I love you," as if that would make it all better, and honestly, this was just infuriating. It was not the kind of support I needed. He didn't understand the struggle I was having. And no one in my practice seemed to understand either. I felt alone.

The incident that helped me recognize my burnout and start my subsequent life transformation was the most painful, insulting, and demeaning experience of my life.

My senior partner (wife of the husband-wife practice owners) texted me that she needed to talk to me and asked if she could come over to my house to talk. I figured it must be something serious if she needed to meet me in person. My mind was racing with thoughts like- she has cancer, they're getting divorced, something terrible…

What followed was a barrage of screaming - attacks on my behavior, my personality, and threats to my job of the "shape up or ship out" variety. She said I needed to apologize to her, the front desk staff, and the nursing staff, or else. Of course, in my mind, this screaming attack was like those I had suffered during my childhood, and I reacted in exactly the same way- I cowered, visibly shaken, and did what she told me to do. (see paragraph about childhood impact.)

As awful as it was, this tongue-lashing was also the impetus I needed to make a major change in my life. When I look back on it now, eight years later, I consider it the pivotal turning point in my journey. I am still angry at the way she talked to me in a way that was in no way empathic. Had she asked me what was going on or why I was acting like I was, it would have been a very different experience, one where I could have opened up to her and possibly come up with a solution.

At that point, I knew I couldn't go on the way things were. I took time off work and went to Canyon Ranch in Arizona for a week of reflection and rejuvenation. I came back with a list of possible options that included quitting my job altogether or changing the job. Finally, I decided that I wanted to stay in my practice but work less and stop doing deliveries because it was the 24/7/365 on-call expectation that was killing me. I wanted to be able to spend time with my kids and husband without the constant anxiety and fear of getting called away. What I didn't realize until I looked back a few years later was that some of the anxiety was also menopause-related. Once I recognized that a light bulb had gone off and I decided I needed to change my practice to focus more on perimenopause and menopause.

Question and Answers

Looking back, was there anything in your childhood or upbringing that you think led to your burnout?

I was the only child of a high-achieving single parent (my mother was a Ph.D. psychologist). She had "high standards" (her words), which, to me, meant perfection. Everything I did in my childhood, AND young adult life, had to please her. When she was angry with me, she would scream. I never screamed back; that was just not my nature. I would cower and apologize, promising that it would never happen again, or I would do better next time, pay attention better next time, and not make that mistake again.

She was also a larger-than-life personality. She threw parties where she was the center of attention, singing and playing the piano. Everyone loved her, including my friends, who would say things like, "Your mom is so cool.". This made ME feel bad like somehow I was supposed to be like her so that people would like me.

My strive for perfection, my people-pleasing, and my avoidance of confrontation became a significant problem later in my life because I lost ME.

Did anything occur in your training that led to your burnout?

I loved my OB-GYN residency training. I worked hard because that is what you were supposed to do, and I soaked up the learning. I trained before resident work-hour restrictions, so I would often work 24 hours and then the whole next day. Days off were a godsend, and I took full advantage. I was dating one of my fellow residents, and we kept it secret for over a year. Our clandestine rendezvous was not as steamy as those in "Grey's Anatomy," but they definitely kept life interesting! We were each other's support system during a time that was pretty stressful.

What helped you overcome your burnout?

Once I recognized my own burnout and made the decision to change my practice to GYN-only, I was like a woman on a mission. I became obsessed with everything related to physician burnout and physician wellness. I figured if I had experienced it, there must be a large number of women physicians having similar issues. I attended conferences, started a wellness committee at my hospital, and learned HeartMath, a tool I use every day to calm the sympathetic nervous system overdrive. An SSRI was also very helpful. I invested in a course on physician coaching (Physician Coaching Institute) and became a coach for other women physicians.

How are you thriving today?

I am thriving today by having space in my brain to think, learn, create, socialize, exercise and golf. As a life-long learner, I have thrived in my current pursuits- coaching and writing. I am thrilled to have become friends with so many women physicians through Facebook groups like FPE. And I am grateful to be able to help other women who may be struggling.

What advice would you give to someone going through burnout?

First and foremost, you have to let people know you are struggling. They can't read your mind. If you don't feel comfortable talking to your work partners, then find a therapist, a coach, or both to assist you in coping and understanding the ways you are thinking and feeling about your situation. Often just a few tweaks in either of these things can make a huge difference. Physicians are incredibly hard-working and will sacrifice so much for their patients, at the expense of themselves. They tend to think in all-or-none, black-or-white, and it can be very helpful to get outside help in the form of a coach, therapist, or clergy. As they say on airplanes, you need to put on your own oxygen mask first before you help others. Self-care is critical to living a fulfilled life.

Second- learn to say no. You do not need to be on every committee. It may feel like they value you (yea!), but you may just be a sucker they can pick who doesn't know better than to say no. At least, give yourself time to contemplate if it's something you want or something you think you "should" do.

What advice would you give to the facilities and administration who are trying to help decrease the rate of physician burnout?

I think there needs to be a change in the fee-for-service model and RVU compensation which just encourages a higher number of appointments, with less time allowed for each. For a physician to feel like you are providing good care, you need to have adequate time with patients to address all their concerns. Support services like nutrition, social services, and mental health services need to be more readily accessible to patients. There should be nursing support services in the office to take care of orders, documentation, prescriptions, and in-box management.
Facility leaders need to spend a day in the shoes of the physician to see what they do daily and to see the types of annoying and pointless tasks they have to do that have nothing to do with patient care.

About Beverly Joyce, MD, FACOG, NCMP
Dr. Joyce is currently a practicing gynecologist with expertise in menopause, infertility, and minimally-invasive surgery. She has a coaching practice in which she helps women physicians, especially those in midlife or mid-career who feel like they are dissatisfied with their current situation and are looking to find

more passion in their lives, both in medicine and in life.

www.DrJoyCoaching.net

Jenny Christner, MD FAAP

I never wanted to be a doctor. It was not my life's dream. What I really wanted was to be a ballet dancer. Or Connie Chung – during my youth, she was the leading lady journalist/newscaster. However, being a doctor was a safe, sure path, one I considered to be a non-risky option given the circumstances I grew up in. Or so I thought....

At an early age, I began ballet lessons and fell in love with precision, movement, and beauty – I was enamored by all of it. I desperately wanted to be a prima ballerina with the New York City Ballet. These were the years of the great Baryshnikov and Nureyev. It was spellbinding to me. I read books about ballet, hung posters about ballet (I still have one from National Geographic in my den to this day), and I did every school report about ballet. Eventually, I received a summer scholarship from the preeminent dance company in the city to fully immerse myself in dance. After that experience, I could choose to become part of an intense program for those who wished to make dance their career, where I would attend high school for half a day and then the dance company for the other half of the day. Guess what I chose? I chose to stay in regular high school. It was a pivotal moment for me. I chose this route because it was the safe and steady route. I saw my parents struggle financially every day. Argue and yell about it. We never went on vacations. My first vacation was one that I paid for myself in college. Sometimes I could feel (and hear spoken out loud) an undercurrent of resentment from my mother that they were supporting me in ballet due to the expense – classes, driving downtown, leotards, tights, pointe shoes, lamb's wool – it all added up. And there was no guarantee I'd be a prima ballerina. My body was changing; I was not long and lean. I was curvy. With a heavy heart, I chose the safe and steady route. A path I would keep choosing over and over in various ways.

I did enjoy science, but it was not my passion. I became a doctor so that I could always provide for myself. Something my mom said to me often. After a fight with my dad over money or worrying about paying bills, she would say to me, "Jenny – never end up like me. Always be able to take care of yourself." So that's what I set out to do. I dabbled in the arts – performing in community theater, modeling, and creative writing - and while I did well as a pre-med in college, it was not what I wanted. In fact, I changed my major to communications for about one month in my sophomore year. But there was no guarantee that I'd be Connie Chung and successful, just like there had been no guarantee I'd get into the New York City Ballet – so – I chose the safe and steady route yet again – and went to medical school.

I remember interviewing for medical school and stating what everyone wanted to hear – "I want to help people." Really, I wanted to help myself never be in the financial mess that my parents were. I completed my residency in pediatrics and that time period remains one of the best and most fond memories of my life as a physician. I was actually pretty darn good at it. I would make one pagers of all the items you needed to know for a particular rotation and give them to my fellow residents. Those "cheat sheets" really made a mark. I'll never forget, after joining the faculty where I had been a resident, seeing one of my summary sheets in the hands of a fellow junior faculty member! A resident had given it to her, and she pulled it out and ACTUALLY REFERRED TO IT during a rotation I was co-precepting with her. Wow, I thought. Maybe safe and steady is the way to go.

In time, I forgot about the time I turned down a modeling job that would have made me miss a couple of months of college. I forgot about how empty and cowardly I felt after turning down a chance to go to Los Angeles and meet a few influential people. I forgot the thrilling feeling of performing in front of a live audience. I just did what I thought I was supposed to do. A non-risky route. Why? Why was being a doctor the "right" way to go? I have no idea. While on one hand, I wish I could change so many things, I also know that living with regret is not healthy. There is only one way to go – and this is forward.

After residency, I was off to academic medicine, where I successfully wrote papers, built a practice, taught residents and students, won awards, and began to make a name for myself. All the safe and steady academic routes. I remember thinking that medical school had beaten all the creative juices and spirit out of me. Academics continued in the same vein. The pressures to produce spectacularly in all three missions – education, research, and clinical are profoundly unrealistic. The praise when someone was sick, on vacation, AT A FUNERAL, but still answering emails, getting the grant in, and reviewing a paper, maybe one of the most harmful things about the culture of medicine. You are only good if you never ever take a break. Frankly, there are also unrealistic expectations about whom we are supposed to be as doctors. We put ourselves on a pedestal – we teach it as part of our professional identity – we are "special." Really? Are we more special than teachers to who we entrust our children to? Are we more special than pilots whom we trust will land us safely? Are we more special than 100s and 100s of other professions? If you ask me, no, we are not. Our own pride is part of our problem. There were so many times I had the chance to take a risk – personally or professionally- but I never could say yes. What would the profession think? I always took the safe and steady route. The non-risky route. While inside, I was slowly dying. Finally, I'm late mid-career. I've done everything "right." I was pretty darn successful. I had forged a path for myself in medicine – by choosing medical education as my passion - where I could be pretty happy, or so I thought. So here I was – a dean, a mom of 3 amazing children, married to a man for over 25 years – nice house, nice vacations – from the outside – I should have been in a constant state of bliss. I wasn't. I felt like something was massively missing from my life despite all the outward signs of success. I couldn't figure it out. I ruthlessly pursued changing things outside of myself - my job, my physical appearance, and considered changing my family situation. Nothing was helping; frankly, it was getting worse. I didn't want to go to work anymore. I was tired of playing the academic game. I was tired of the never-ending email inbox. didn't want to keep doing the sure and steady thing. I was filled with regret. I was filled with if onlys. I was miserable. I was burned out.

Over the years, I had a lot of dreams. At one point, I thought about starting a scrapbooking business and actually had business cards and an intake form created. Every idea I had seemed like a lot of work on top of what I was already doing for not a very big payoff. In 2018, I found a couple of podcasts that I listened to on my very long and painful commute to and from work. The themes addressed ultimately brought me out of my burnout and completely changed my life. One podcast was a weight loss coach who really focused on how your thoughts drive everything. No one else was responsible for my happiness but me. Nothing external that I could change would bring lasting contentment. It was MY OWN THOUGHTS that were sabotaging me. I could change my thoughts and change my life. How did I not know this before? The second podcast was from another highly successful woman entrepreneur who guided people to follow through on their dreams and eventually leave their day jobs. Her manner and the stories of the guests she interviewed gave me hope that things could be different. That I could wake up with joy. That I was in charge of my own destiny. That maybe playing it safe and steady was actually one of the riskiest, most dangerous and most devastating things I had ever done.

In 2020, I began to take risks and "own" my life. I took an acting class and followed that up with improv classes. I began my own business – doing three things that I did well but that also brought me true joy. None were guaranteed to succeed. I didn't care. I was going to do it anyway and see what happened. First, I became a certified professional coach. I wasn't sure exactly what my niche would be. However, I quickly found my secret sauce – helping folks realize that "No one promotes you better than you!" Second – I do love to perform! Speaking engagements allowed me to connect with an audience and be "on stage" again. My "risky" move to complete five levels of improv training and graduate has added to my speaking repertoire – allowing me to showcase how the principles of improv are key to communication and functioning teams. Lastly, my rather odd love of precision and attention to detail rounds out the third leg of my business - accreditation consulting.

I am absolutely passionate about my business – which is successful beyond my wildest dreams. While you might think it just adds to more burnout, as for now, I'm still working full-time in academics, it does not. It leads to pure joy and has saved me. It is truly my happy place. I am still working on taking risks, and it remains difficult for me. I know my next move is to likely leave academic medicine and grow my business while pursuing a whole host of other interests. I'm not quite ready to take that leap – but slow and steady – by incorporating risk-taking - I'm getting there.

Questions and Answers

Looking back, was there anything in your childhood or upbringing that you think led to your burnout?

I did not feel "safe" in childhood. Both my parents struggled with mental illness. I knew that I had to take care of myself. I did not want to make all the mistakes my parents made financially. I had great trouble respecting them for the situations they found themselves in. I realize now I had and have carried with me a scarcity mindset. It's really hard to get over that – but I'm trying.

Did anything occur in your training that led to your burnout?

Not really in my training. Except I loved the ICU and knew I'd never do it for a career as my faculty, I so admired never ever seemed to go home. Ever. Not the life I wanted.

Was there anything about the system you worked in that led to your episode (s) of burnout?

The idea that you had to be good at research, clinical and education missions is just unrealistically ridiculous. I feel I was "lucky" because in academics, I didn't have to be in an office 9-5, so I could attend my kid's activities and just work nights and weekends – as in every night and weekend to make up for that. Not OK. It goes back to the whole idea of a "busy" culture. Whoever is the busiest – if you are not busy and working 12 hours a day, you are not worthy, you are not doing your job. People were praised for being ill and still answering emails and showing up for meetings. For being on vacation and answering emails. For being at a funeral and answering emails, turning in the grant, writing the policy – it's not OK. It's just not OK.

What helped you overcome your burnout?

I was miserable internally. I didn't want to be around my kids or my husband. I thought they were contributing to my unhappiness. But it wasn't them. I had to learn that changing my circumstance wasn't going to make me happy. I had to make myself happy.

Did you have a support system?

Yes – my husband. A friend outside of medicine. Groups like this.

Did anyone notice and reach out to you?

No, not at all. In fact my "success" was encouraged.

How are you thriving today?

My side gig business and doing interests outside of work is what fulfill me.
What advice would you give to someone going through burnout?
There are no Supposed to's, must do's, have to do's. You are the owner of your own life. Don't let anyone make you do things you don't want to. There is life on the other side. And it is SO MUCH BETTER.

What advice would you give to the facilities and administration who are trying to help decrease the rate of physician burnout?

Don't allow emails after 5 PM and on weekends. Discourage the use of email at all.

Let people go on real vacations or professional development. Not - yes – you can go to that conference and then work triple shifts for a week when you get back to "make up" for being gone. Train people not to email or reach out to folks when they are off. Provide time to get charts done during the work week or hire scribes.

About Jenny Christner, MD FAAP
Dr. Christner has served in a variety of roles in her 20+ years as an adolescent medicine physician and leader in medical

education. Currently, she is the Senior Dean. In this role she oversees the continuum of medical education – Medical Students, Residents/Fellows and Continuing Professional Development for physicians, as well as the Health Professions Programs—DNP (Nurse Anesthesia), Physician Assistant, Orthotics and Prosthetics, and Genetic Counseling.

In 2020, Dr. Christner founded Christner Strategies. Consultative services focus on: 1) Executive /Life coaching – specializing in helping mid-career professionals who feel stuck in their professional/personal lives achieve the results they desire 2) Event Speaking -Engaging and motivating audiences on topics such as (but not limited to): No one Promotes You Like You: Creating Your Personal Brand, How A Life Coach can Change Your Life, and Utilizing Improv to Improve Communication and Teamwork in the Workplace and finally, 3) LCME accreditation consultations (she has been recruited to remove 2 schools from LCME probation and served on the LCME committee)

www.christnercoaching.com
www.christner-strat.com

Avian L. Tisdale MD, MBA, Paralegal

AS IT TURNS OUT, DO NO HARM APPLIES TO US TOO
That's how I end most of my presentations to physicians, it almost always stops them in their tracks. People literally freeze as their minds breathe in the concept of us being human beings, just as worthy of protection and compassion as those we empty our emotional cups for every day. As I write this, I picture my colleagues re-reading that sentence. They never realized while pledging to commit our lives to care, we promised never to harm ourselves either. As it turns out, do no harm applies to us too.
I know what you're thinking. What are we whining about? How hard is it to be a 'rich doctor'? No one will listen. We are not supposed to complain because we have it so much better than most people. We just need to be tougher.

There are powerful stories being shared here, but not every physician in the world will share my experience. Indeed, some will have spirited opinions about it. And me. What fascinates me most about that is if I were their patient, I'd likely be a concerned gaze and bullet pointed plan away from their compassion.

That's sort of how it starts. Believing fully in the concept that we can give in unlimited quantities to other people without giving or receiving anything for ourselves. Our own mental separation from the rest of humanity and care are emotionally compartmentalized for delivery to everyone else.

In the process of giving and serving others, we are depleted. Like any human would be but wait, we are supposed to be superhuman. If we don't feel superhuman, we must be doing something wrong. But physicians can never be wrong, right?

We refill everything when it's empty, at times well before it gets there, because we need more of it. Gas tanks, coffee cups, medications for our patients, school lunch accounts. Not physicians?

I have always said physicians do not have a sympathetic narrative, and I still believe that. The fact that we are listened to most when we are talking about everyone except ourselves has always fascinated me. I think people want to know what they don't know, which is why movies and television shows about our profession are so successful. But viewing us as human beings with real stories, challenging people to connect to us the way we connect with 30+ people and families per day, is not as straightforward.

We often say doctors and patients, as if there is a realm of humanity between the two where only we live, instead of the fact that physicians are people who often bring our burnout to their doctor (each other) for help. Not realizing that our physicians may be struggling too..
That's the duality I want to write about, the fact that we carve a line between people who are worthy of help and then physicians, the by us but not for us approach to our profession that leads people to a place well beyond human capacity coined as 'burnout'.

I am not here to blame anyone else.I am here to do something I believe we should do more often. I am here to talk about what it feels like to be us.

In May of 2006, I graduated from medical school, my now husband and family were present, and it was the day I'd always dreamed about. Three years later, I finished training, and we moved to another state for work. My husband had just completed school to become a surgical technician, we had a 1 year old, and we were flat broke. It took every penny we had and a pulled bbq sale to pay for the moving truck, but off we went.
I don't think I have ever loved a job more than being a hospitalist. Even as I write this, I can feel my heart skip a beat at how much I miss that type of medicine. I used everything I learned every single day. I worked so hard people noticed, and I was given the opportunity to lead after about 3 years. I was extremely young compared to my peers, but I couldn't wait to say yes. It was a new venture, and like many, I expected leading as a hospitalist to be even better than my clinical work.
I would carry a full-time around the clock clinical schedule and serve as the physician leader for a multi-system partnership. Shortly before accepting the role, I decided to go back to school for an MBA in finance. We also had another surprise, a baby boy born barely two years after our first. So with my husband working full-time, two kids under 2, a 24/7 role, and a full-time degree, off we went.

I don't come from wealth, and I am the first physician in the family. That means people did everything they could think of to support me, but no one could tell me what to do from experience. Still, the sense of pride beams from your loved ones at every turn. It is the only fuel I have left sometimes during school and training. I will spare you the many definitions of finished (which we never truly are in this profession), but when everyone else thinks you are, there is a tremendous amount of relief. She did it. She's a doctor! There is a palpable release of concern about any future challenge, failure, or struggle because you are 'finished'. School and training are the most guided parts of our journeys, our lives after we finish are the least...

Just like any working person, your daily life isn't finished when your workday ends. Most of it is just getting started. But what if we had already given more than we had before we got there? And what makes our experience so different?

As a pediatrician, I am often presumed to have superhuman parenting powers. Meaning my children must have perfect everything, do everything perfectly, and never get sick. My husband and I have a plan for everything, and I never second guess what I am doing as a Mom. None of that is true because everyone in my family, including me, is human.

The one assumption that takes a bit more context is that no matter what, I am always ready to give people something, even if I don't have it.

When my kids were younger, our oldest went on a field trip. I was looking forward to it, and so was my daughter. She squealed and ran excitedly to me as I walked into the school foyer. As young as she was, she realized Mommy coming along for the field trip was a treat. We boarded the school bus and proceeded to laugh and giggle 'whoa' every time the seat bounced at us. The sun was warm and bright yellow through the window, just enough to see her fingerprints all over it.. I took a deep breath and sank into the seat.
Dr. Tisdale!
Oh God.
I froze. I am not at work. Who is calling me that, and why?
I felt a firm tapping on my knee as the school bus rounded a corner. I swung my eyes open to find a child's arm barely an inch from my face.
What do you think this rash is on his arm?
What in the world, who are you? What is happening? Did I somehow dream about a bus, but I am actually at work?
To this day, I am unsure how she found out I was a physician, but she'd come to our seat for a stat consult.
My shoulders tightened as I stuck my back straight into the seat.
Miss, I'm sorry, but I'm not sure. I'm super tired……….. and I'm really not prepared to do this right now.
She sat back, surprised but silent.
But you're a pediatrician, right?
Yes, I am.
So can't you just-
No, I can't. I am a pediatrician most of the time. Today, right now, I am Mommy.
Please.
Mommy, whoa, whoa, my daughter squealed as we bounced into the parking lot.

Whoa indeed.
I did not have it, but I was still expected to give it on demand. We were all Moms, but I was the pediatrician, so I must want to go to work on the field trip school bus.
I don't, though.. She never spoke to me again.

When we are talking with our patients, we often advise them to avoid stress, be honest when their needs are not being met, etc. When we do it, sometimes even with each other (competitive environment), we are met with doubts about our commitment to the profession. Or encouraged to give an emotional dissertation instead of an honest answer.

In my current world as a consultant, I meet many physicians who see patients and own businesses or have left the clinical world altogether. Common conversations involve the tangible guilt many feel around transitioning into another role. When did your caring bone break? How could you? What else could you possibly do? How will you pay your bills now? It's hard to find a physician who does not have these thoughts. Not being able to discuss them openly frequently pushes people to their personal and professional breaking points.

That's what makes our experience so different. There are concrete expectations around physicians and our obligation to be superhuman. Questioning means there must be something wrong with us, not the expectations themselves. Nothing is sustainable when it is empty. 'Fill the tank before you press it,' we were often taught. We are always pressed but rarely filled, and every physician knows that never works out well.

It may surprise some to learn that we have physicians too. When we are concerned or in pain, we see each other. 2 years ago, I became curious about how well we are cared for as physicians. The most consistent answer I found is it has not been well studied. No kidding, feel free to check for yourself. We study everything, and everyone in our profession ad nauseum except ourselves.

So I decided to start studying for myself. What were people talking about, and what were their experiences? How can people who are trained to think for a living find a different way to think about their life's work? How much of our identity is securely fastened to our work as physicians? What happens to us when that identity changes? How do we stay connected to other human beings? How do we sustain all of the other things we love in our lives without shame and guilt?

The more I did that, the more I began to think differently myself. Changing the way I thought changed my behavior. Not the quality of my work as a physician- its placement in my life as a whole.

I started learning more about the business of healthcare and the effect it has on the practice of medicine. This made me think about how those things affect us as human beings and how if anyone can make that better, it's us. Some people watch movies for a good time. I read, listen, and process what other physicians are saying and doing about their everyday lives. Podcasts, social media, and curbside conversations, we are telling everyone what we need, whether anyone else is listening or not.
At some point, I started answering people with my thoughts to see what would happen. I am a physician, and the joy of a good experiment is not lost on me.

I met a pediatrician recently who was terrified about taking on the business end of her practice. She knew about my work as a consultant, and we have been friends for years. She called me while waiting for an Uber ready to quit her project on the spot. I was repotting a plant in my backyard. I have learned the value of strategic silence and kept quiet until I felt she'd yelled most of the fear into the phone.
I don't know what to do, I just don't.
Hmmm, I replied.
That's all you're going to say?
Silence.
I am just going to quit now.
Hmmm. I have a question for you. If one of your patients just randomly needed a spinal tap, a baby, right now. Would you do it?
Silence from her followed by more silence from me.
What are you talking about? What does this have to do with anything?
Would you do it?
Yeah, I mean of course I would, it's my patient.
Hmmm, and since most babies and their parents are doing this for the first time, they're scared. So you'd comfort them, reassure them, right?
Do you remember the very first time you even saw a lumbar puncture? You felt that way because you'd never done it before. Now years of experience later, you would jump in an Uber to help your patient by doing something most people never do in their lifetime, complete with authentic pediatrician compassion. How can all of that come from you but not apply to you and what you're passionate about?
Her signal dropped. No kidding. She texted me back moments later.
I dunno Ave……..just tell me……..how can you be so confident?

I replied with a screenshot of those exact words from the inside cover of my old notebook. I memorized it and tell it to myself every time I try something new.

During my adult medicine rotation in NYC, we assisted in end-of-life care for a man who'd recently arrived in the United States. He told us all he wanted to do was go home. He had no family here, just a few friends who were helping us translate over the phone. A group of students decided to help him get home. We all gave what we could, along with many others and before he died, we sent him home to be with his family. We can't put that on our CV. There are no awards or certifications for something like that. Just a reminder that our help comes in many forms, often when no one is watching. It wasn't my idea, but it was one of the purest things I've experienced in my career.

I didn't have health insurance back then. I had about $12 dollars available on a credit card that I used to buy tuna and crackers from the drugstore on my way home. I was renting a room the size of a closet in a Brooklyn brownstone that sat right over the subway, and my only window opened to a brick wall. I didn't know how I would pay my rent the next month or buy groceries for the week.. Sitting there with my tuna, crackers, and DVD of classic 80's sitcoms, I was content. I am here to help people, and that's what I did today.

As a consultant, I help physicians, trainees, and students all over the country. In order to do so, I have to listen to their stories. In that moment, I have to see beyond their degrees and deep into who they really are as people. Sometimes we empathize with how being a physician can be painful. Sometimes I am overwhelmed by how joyful they are at what they've already accomplished and how well they understand the difference between completion and failure in their careers.
Twenty years ago, I sat down in front of a medical school interviewer and said I wanted to help people. That includes us too.
Dr. Honeymom®

Question and Answers

What helped you overcome your burnout?

Learning a different way to think about my profession.
Did you have a support system?
My husband and two children have lived every moment of this journey with me. They are awesome.

Did anyone notice and reach out to you?

I have a wonderful circle. They do their best to keep me lifted up.

How are you thriving today?
I still see patients, but I started my own business, and it was the best decision I ever made.

What advice would you give to someone going through burnout?

You are not crazy, it really isn't supposed to be this way. Change starts with you, one tiny step at a time.
What advice would you give to the facilities and administration who are trying to help decrease the rate of physician burnout?
Take a look at your org chart and find the person responsible for physician health. If you cannot find one, make that a priority.

What advice if any, would you give to the facilities that can do better when it comes to improving the burnout rates of physicians?

Investing meaningful dollars into physician health is good for business, physicians, and patients.

About Avian L. Tisdale MD, MBA, Paralegal
Dr. Avian Tisdale serves as a consultant for physicians and systems nationwide. She holds an MBA in Finance from Drexel University and completed her paralegal studies at the University of Texas at Austin. She is a board certified pediatrician and owns her own practice.

Dr. Tisdale has held many leadership roles, including Regional Director, Chief Medical Officer, and Clinical Assistant Professor.
In 2016 she trademarked Dr. Honeymom® as an experiment with all of her titles-wife, Mom, and pediatrician. She launched her consulting firm to help physicians at the intersection of medicine, business, and employment.

www.drhoneymom.com

Delia Chiaramonte, MD

I saw the number of coughing, and febrile patients in our hospital increase, and I developed a feeling of impending doom. The general message from the administration was, "there is nothing to see here." I seemed to be the only one who was concerned.

As the gaslighting from leadership increased, my well-being plummeted.

There were signs posted at the hospital stating that wearing masks all day was dangerous. In fact, physicians and other healthcare providers were NOT ALLOWED to wear masks to examine patients unless the patient had a positive or pending COVID-19 test. I don't mean that there weren't enough masks to go around, although there weren't, I mean that even if we had our own masks, we weren't allowed to wear them. We were told that if we wore a mask, it would imply that we thought we were more important than other people, and since we were compassionate physicians who cared about our patients, we wouldn't want to imply that we were somehow special, would we? Gaslighting.

One morning I spent an hour, unmasked, in the room with a coughing, febrile patient. I knew that this was wrong. I was caught between following the rules and protecting my own safety. I didn't take efforts to protect myself, and I am ashamed of my cowardice.

I knew what was coming. I knew how absurdly dangerous this no-masking rule was. There was a profound disconnect between the messages from above and the dangerous freight train that was barreling towards us. I felt profoundly disrespected by a leadership that cared more about appearances than about the safety of their clinical workforce.

I expressed my concerns and could feel their annoyance.

"This isn't Italy, Delia," the medical director said to me condescendingly.

"Why not?" I thought. "It may not be Italy today, but it will be. It's coming. It's definitely coming." I got a reputation as the girl who cried wolf, except the wolf was really there, and no one could see it but me.

The patient and family's suffering continued to grow. The news said that only elderly patients were dying, and many of them were. However, we also listened to heartbreaking sobs as people heard that their beloved 30 -or 40- or 50-year-old loved one had died of COVID. Family members screamed at us when they weren't allowed into the hospital to say goodbye to someone dear to them. I didn't blame them. We knew that our offer of an iPad farewell was woefully inadequate.

I asked if my team could wear scrubs so we didn't have to put our COVID-contaminated clothes back in our closets at the end of a long day. It wasn't reasonable to dry clean slacks and dress shirts every day. The leadership said scrubs were unnecessary and wouldn't look professional. This time I listened to my own compass instead of theirs, and I wore them anyway.

My husband discovered that we could order masks through the AMA. I ordered enough for the entire palliative care team and asked leadership, respectfully, if the team could wear them for all of our patient encounters. I wasn't asking the hospital to provide masks, I simply wanted permission for us to use our own masks so we could protect ourselves. We had seen patients younger than us die, and we were all afraid.

I got called to the administrative office.

I will never forget that meeting. I was verbally whipped and told that I was unprofessional for going against the administration party line. I was hurt and furious and incredulous. It took enormous effort not to cry.

That night I updated my CV and searched "non-clinical jobs for physicians."

After that meeting leadership scheduled a standing half-hour meeting with me every day, for months.

Every day.

Every day.

I counseled young adult children who had just lost both their mom and dad to COVID. Then I had a meeting with leadership to talk about minutiae.

I participated in a planning meeting to determine how we would triage patients if we didn't have enough ventilators for everyone who needed one. Then I had a meeting with leadership to talk about minutiae.

The ethics committee debated whether our own physicians and nurses if they got COVID, should have any priority if ventilators were scarce. Then I had a meeting with leadership to talk about minutiae.

It was the contrast that got to me.

In my more generous moments, I can acknowledge that leadership was overwhelmed and frightened too. They didn't know what to do, and their head-in-the-sand, micromanaging, gaslighting approach must have seemed like a good idea to them at the time.

It didn't work for me.

Our trust was fractured. They couldn't trust me to be a loyal foot soldier and I couldn't trust them to have my back. We were polite, but we never found our way back to each other. Like a marriage wracked by infidelity, even once the acute distress has passed, the trust was irreparably damaged.

I felt personally damaged too, and I committed to trying to repair myself.

I reduced my hours and changed to outpatient clinical work. I took a medical editing job that I could do from home. I was still passionate about growing the integrative palliative program that I had created, but the well had been poisoned, and leadership decided to go in another direction. I resigned.

I gave myself one week to cry and feel hurt and betrayed. Then I wiped my snotty nose, took some deep, cleansing breaths, and got busy creating my new future.

Questions and Answers

Looking back, was there anything in your childhood or upbringing that you think led to your burnout?

Actually, yes. I was raised by a narcissistic and rejecting mother who did not prioritize my wellbeing. I became a pleaser who overperformed to get acceptance as a substitute for love. This experience was reminiscent of being with a mother who prioritized her own wellbeing over mine and rejected me when I didn't make her feel good about herself. I think that the shadow of childhood trauma made this experience more painful for me than it might have been for someone else.

Did anything occur in your training that led to your burnout?

I do think that I got burned out in training, too because I had very loose boundaries. I spent way too much time with people and therefore was always behind and overwhelmed.

What helped you overcome your burnout?

Getting away from the scene of the crime has helped the most. I was actually trying to stay at that hospital and was sad when it didn't work out. But it has absolutely been for the best because leaving has healed my burnout. I will be more thoughtful in the future about how I allow people to treat me and how long I stick around once I see that things aren't going well. I stayed for two years after that ugly meeting. In retrospect that was probably too long.

Did you have a support system?

My husband was extremely supportive and allowed me to do whatever I thought would be best for me. I vented to friends a lot, and that helped too.

Did anyone notice and reach out to you?

I had a team that I was leading that was very supportive, but it wasn't their place to make things better for me. I tried hard to make things better for them.

How are you thriving today?

I started the Integrative Palliative Institute, which provides education and support to allow people with serious illnesses to live their best life. I also host The Integrative Palliative Podcast. I mentor physicians in integrative symptom management and coach people who feel overwhelmed because they have a loved one with a serious illness.

I also work in medical education as an Executive Editor for McGraw Hill.

I couldn't continue my practice, but I have found other ways to meaningfully promote the field of integrative palliative medicine. I describe it as "whole person care for people with serious illness using all the tools that work." The work feels important, and I love the improved quality of life that working from home provides me.

What advice would you give to someone going through burnout?

You aren't trapped. There are a million ways to be a doctor, and you should keep working at it until you find a situation that makes you happy. Feeling miserable isn't necessary, and it isn't good. You deserve to be happy.

What advice would you give to the facilities and administration who are trying to help decrease the rate of physician burnout?

Express empathy and respect for your physicians. They work extremely hard and are dedicated. Don't take them for granted or minimize their contribution. Also, please do not imply that NPs are the same as physicians. Please respect the education, experience, and expertise of your physicians.

About Delia Chiaramonte, MD

Dr. Chiaramonte is an integrative palliative medicine physician. She is the Founder and CEO of the Integrative Palliative Institute and host of The Integrative Palliative Podcast. She is an experienced clinician and medical educator with expertise in serious illness care, end-of-life issues, office counseling, and physician well being.

She mentors physicians in integrative symptom management (including tools for managing their own stress and anxiety) and supports physicians who have a loved one with a serious illness.

www.integrativepalliative.com

Ann Huntington, MD, FACP

"My story of burnout and of achieving post-burnout growth"

My burnout story began as a child. I grew up in a loving, safe family, for which I will always be grateful. As the oldest child, I was conscientious and responsible and tried to please my parents and other adults around me. Through interactions at home, church, and in society, I was conditioned to believe that women were always in a supportive role to men and that they were not as smart or as important as men. Consequently, I didn't grow up with much confidence in myself, and I rebelled against the notion that females should be subservient to men. I studied hard and jumped through all the hoops to make it to medical school.

My medical school and internal medicine residency training were life-changing, and I began to overcome my lack of confidence which was positive. However, as with many physicians, training created an element of burnout for me. Taking overnight call every third to fourth night, waking up at 4 AM to pre-round on patients, staying awake for 30+ hours straight, and working for more than 14 days straight, etc., took a toll on all of us. I recall feeling exhausted even during my morning commutes *to* the hospital. We were expected to work through illness and were once told the only exception to miss work was if we had bacterial meningitis (which is deadly and transmissible). We didn't take time to process the sad situations and suffering that we witnessed, and there was no debriefing after traumatic cases. The first patient I pronounced dead as a new intern was my age, 28.

I somehow made it through two pregnancies during my training. The only time I recall missing an overnight call shift was when I had a threatened miscarriage. When my oldest was breastfeeding, keeping up a milk supply was difficult due to my schedule, stress, and lack of sleep and proper nutrition. Because of what I went through during training due to the rigor of my program, my pregnancies, and an infant who didn't sleep well, there is much I don't remember. My husband occasionally reminds me of a person we knew or a gathering we attended, and I have no memory of it. Most of the pillars of a healthy lifestyle (proper nutrition, adequate sleep, regular exercise, stress management) were non-existent for me. I lived in survival mode for years. I also carried a significant amount of guilt at not being the mother I had been taught to be. This guilt was unfortunately reinforced by my in-laws during the first decade of our marriage, although this has since improved. As the seeds of burnout grew, these experiences shaped my career decisions and my outlook on my future, which ended up not helping my family or me.

As I looked toward graduation from residency, I had opportunities to extend to a chief resident year or do a fellowship, and I also had offers for local jobs where I trained. My young family was not able to support a fellowship at the time, and despite the pressure from my attendings to stay on and do critical care, I finished training and took a position at a large community health system where I grew up. I built a "hybrid" internal medicine practice, where I had an outpatient clinic and was able to do a stretch of inpatient shifts every couple of months. This fit my family's needs, and I was able to keep up my inpatient skills.

A few years later, we added two more children to our family. Those pregnancies were much easier than during training, but it was still not easy. I was committed to building my career and slowly became involved in extra-clinical work, including leadership council, quality, peer review, and credentials committees. I worked hard, sometimes at the expense of family time and self-care, as I had seen modeled in my childhood. So deep was the conditioning ingrained within me on what women were supposed to do that once I joined a quality committee meeting virtually at the beginning of the induction of labor with my third baby. Our quality committee was surprised that I joined. My family was present with me, and I regret that I didn't savor the moment with them as much as I could have, although in fairness, it was nice to have an additional distraction from the discomfort.

As an outpatient primary care doc, everything seemed to fall on my shoulders with the help of just one medical assistant - the health coaching, the counseling, all the preventative care, managing the EMR inbox, home health, and other paperwork, in addition to diagnosing, working up, and managing often more than a dozen health conditions and that many or more medications. I read many notes from physicians of other specialties - they would manage one or two conditions, and their notes would conclude with something like "PCP is managing" everything else (all the other 15 problems) or "defer to PCP." Because most of these chronic diseases are due to unhealthy lifestyles and polypharmacy, I spent a great deal of time counseling and coaching my patients. Many were able to lose weight, control their diseases, and stop unnecessary medications. However, my efforts came at a significant personal cost due to the practice model at that time. I was incredibly frustrated with the burdens placed on primary care and the inefficiencies of a broken healthcare system. I made the difficult decision to leave my outpatient clinic in search of a more sustainable situation.

Transitioning to inpatient hospital medicine was the right move at the time. I enjoyed the ability to save lives and help patients have a meaningful clinical improvement in a short period of time without having an EMR inbox to constantly manage. However, over time, patients and patient care became more complex and demanding, and the amount of clerical work increased. Nationwide, as the specialty of hospital medicine grew, physicians in other inpatient specialties stepped away from wanting to manage in-hospital care and provide overnight coverage, which has led to the demoralizing treatment of hospitalists by physicians of other specialties. This trend worsened significantly during the early stages of the pandemic. Financially, due to current reimbursement models, hospital medicine physicians do not typically bill a lot of work RVUs outside of procedures, despite caring for many of the most complex and acutely ill patients in the hospital. Thus, these programs typically lose money when considering labor costs, and many hospitalists must care for more patients than the research deems safe.

Despite and perhaps because of these frustrations and concerns, I stepped into leadership. As before, this was the right move at the time. I became the medical director of a group of over 50 hospitalist physicians and 15+ advanced practice providers at two tertiary care hospitals. Two talented and fun women physicians allowed me to recruit them as site leads at each hospital, and together we created a powerful leadership team that became respected throughout the health system. The medical director to whom I reported was one of the most positive leaders I have ever worked with. We were able to create a culture of trust and of solidarity that increased our ability to effect positive change.

At the time, our group was at a dangerous point for several reasons, and many docs were talking about leaving. This also happened to be right before the Covid delta wave hit us. I focused on messaging that was respectful, and we produced workflows that attempted to make their jobs easier. I advocated for improved communication, patient safety, appropriate care, and efficient use of resources. We built relationships within our service line and across specialties, disciplines, and throughout the health system. Things began to turn around. Then Covid hit again.

During the Covid surges and when we were under crisis standards of care, multiple additional wings of the hospitals were opened to care for the influx of patients that were hospitalized due to Covid-related complications. To be able to provide safe care for that many additional patients, we stood up multiple additional teams of physicians, and our group of physicians worked 90 extra shifts per month in addition to our usual work schedule for approximately six months. I, along with an infectious disease colleague, trained all the adult primary care physicians in our system, as well as some surgeons and others, to take care of covid patients in the hospital because we ran out of enough hospitalists to care for the volume of very sick folks. I also devised workflows for other inpatient specialties to offload from us more patients in their areas of expertise, so we could handle the increased volume of patients with respiratory failure and other Covid-related complications. Senior leadership was very supportive. Our surgery leaders even voluntarily met with us regularly during the crisis to add support. In addition to systemwide wellness resources, one of my colleagues helped me implement an informal wellness check-in process within our group to regularly check in on each other and provide emotional support. Along with our nursing colleagues, we arranged video chats for patients with their families who could not see them due to visiting restrictions, helped a man participate in his daughter's wedding virtually not long before he passed away, and we sat at the bedside with patients as they passed. Everyone throughout the health system (nurses, physicians, APPs, operational leaders, environmental services, therapists, etc.) worked so hard to care for our community. It truly was a team lift, and many lives were improved and saved.

These efforts paid off. Not only were we able to take care of our community, but we were able to support our physicians and APPs compared with what occurred elsewhere. Only 3 out of over 50 physicians left our group, and all for reasons other than group dynamics. However, there was plenty of burnout from the extra shifts, from missing time with our families, and from the trauma sustained by seeing so many relatively young folks crash into full respiratory failure in a matter of minutes and hours. We have memories of calling family members to share difficult news and hearing screams of anguish. We signed far too many death certificates in such a short period of time. Unfortunately, our docs and our fellow critical care physicians also sustained threats from patients and their families - verbal abuse, threats of legal action, and even physical threats. We recognized their fear, stress, and their sense of loss. We also knew that the threats couldn't have led to any better care. They just served to further demoralize our docs. We did the best we could to provide compassionate and high-quality care, despite receiving very few useful tools to fight the virus and the resultant pneumonia and acute hypoxic respiratory failure once it took hold in the body. Hearing what we went through, one of our state legislators invited me to testify at a committee meeting about our pandemic experience.

After the worst of the Covid surges, life and work adjusted to the post-pandemic state. We all quickly realized it was not "back to normal." Many children and teenagers worldwide continue to suffer significant mental health challenges from bearing the brunt of the stress of being isolated, trying to learn virtually, and having critical developmental years disrupted. More adults than usual ended up in the hospital with mental health challenges, progression of malignancies or other diseases, and liver failure from too much alcohol consumed to cope with pandemic stress. Our inpatient nursing colleagues, who also sustained burnout, threats, and trauma during the pandemic surges, moved on to other roles or left the nursing field, forcing a monumental effort to train a whole new generation of nurses. Surgical and medical teams focused on catching up on the great backlog of hundreds to thousands of procedures and consults that were delayed during the pandemic.

Projects resurfaced that had been put on hold during the pandemic. My attention as a leader was pulled to address these and to limit and/or prevent added burden to my team, which unfortunately was not always successful. Some of my docs struggled with significant burnout, and I tried to support them and provide resources to stay safe. New regulations, including for documentation, necessitated changes in workflow for physicians, APPs, and nursing staff. These led to additional stress on our physicians and APPs and on our leaders to advocate for proper workflows. Financial woes in numerous health systems nationwide began stretching leaders/administrators and cascading down to frontline workers. The middle-distance race of the pandemic, with impressive sprints during the surges, is stretching into a marathon with an unclear endpoint.

Over time, the cumulative burden of working as a frontline physician and leading a large team with such significant external pressures took a great personal toll on me. I had to acknowledge the additional stress, the disrupted sleep, the fatigue, and the weight I carried. There was constant change and significant headwinds in healthcare looming on the horizon. I knew we were still doing really good work and that we were still needed, but I became increasingly aware of my frustrations with certain projects and situations and of the physical manifestations of stress I was sustaining. I realized I had lost myself in a way. I was angry sometimes, especially at the state of healthcare and at a career that was much different from when I started.

On the home front, as the wife and mother, despite my busy schedule and heavy work responsibilities, I still bore a significantly higher burden of household work and cognitive energy compared with my male colleagues. In addition, I had given up quite a bit of family time and focus, and there was an element of regret. Working with a coach really helped me identify what was occurring and opened my eyes to the need to set some boundaries and change my trajectory. Ultimately, despite the benefit of various positive outlets, including exercise, uplifting books, and podcasts, blocks in my meetings' schedule for family time, etc., nothing could fully overcome the weight I felt. The following scenario from months prior was increasingly present in my mind (see this excerpt from my journal):

Jan 28-29 (12:38 AM)
"I just finished an admitter shift... Hospital volumes are crazy high, lots of ED admits. ED docs and hospitalists are tired. As I prepared for my shift and the meeting preceding it, [my daughter] looked at me and said, "Mommy, you belong to me more than to the hospital." Mic drop. Moment of truth, pure truth from a 5-year-old. Of course, she is correct. I belong to her... She needs me to teach her and guide her and spend time with her. That single statement by my little [one] holds so much wisdom and a realization of how I want to spend the next few years. I am not owned by the hospital; my identity is much more than a physician or hospital employee or even a leader. I am her mother, and I need to hold onto these times of little chats, hugs, learning how to read and write, telling jokes, going places together."

I told my husband I was burned out. His efforts to support me bore much more fruit when he started life coach training and employed some of his training in our conversations. My friends were supportive but could not understand what I was experiencing, so I withdrew from many of them. Ultimately, I spoke with one of my mentors who previously led this large group, and I told her I was feeling burned out. She said, "I get it. You are the only one who is miserable. You are doing such a great job that everyone else is happy." Wow. She put into words what I was thinking and feeling. I knew I had been far from perfect as a leader, but I also knew I had given my best and that my team was in a much better place than it was when I took over. It was time; I announced that I was stepping away from leadership.

Around the same time, I also finished my time as chair of our credentials committee of nearly 2200 medical staff, and for one of the few times in my career, I am not on a single committee or workgroup. I went back to clinical medicine part-time, which is still frustrating at times, though much easier without the burden of leadership and committee work. What a relief. At a Christmas party, one of my friends commented on how much lighter and brighter I appeared. She was correct. I felt lighter. I loved leading, but I was grateful to offload the stress and dissatisfaction of navigating a broken healthcare system. I recognized that my time was one of my most valued possessions and that I had not protected it as I should have. So, by making this big transition, I gave myself a "time raise." I began to focus my efforts in earnest toward investing in myself and creating time freedom.

In the last few years, I have engaged in entrepreneurial activities and have found these to be most in line with my authentic self. I invest heavily in my personal development with books, podcasts, courses, coaching, and networking with like-minded physicians and others. As a proponent of lifestyle medicine, I am re-prioritizing rest, quiet time, family time, improved nutrition, and regular exercise. As a lifelong goal-setter, I have set short- and long-term goals, including a lifetime reflection for my future 90th birthday party of whom I wish to have become. And as an entrepreneur, among other projects, I am building a CME course on the evidence-based use of essential oils (yes, it sounds crazy), to teach physicians and others not only about aromatherapy but about the science, the safety, the shortcuts of the industry, and the future possibilities of essential oils as an integrative tool.

Questions and Answers

What advice would you give to someone going through burnout?

Stay safe. Have a support system. Put into words/write in a journal about what you are going through to help you identify it and put a name to it. Your story is unique to you, but please recognize that the healthcare, AKA sickcare, the system is flawed and broken. If necessary, step back and reassess what you are doing. Write down what your dream job or ideal practice would look like. Know that there are many options for you to earn money to provide for your family.

Invest in yourself. Get coaching and/or counseling. Advance your career in a way that is authentic to you. Brand yourself, even if you are an employed physician. Whom do you want to be known as? What do you want to be known for? Learn to speak in public. Learn boundaries and when to say no or not now to something that doesn't serve your highest purpose. Gain additional skill sets outside of clinical medicine. Be financially wise. Surround yourself with people who will uplift you and inspire you to be a better version of yourself.

What advice would you give to healthcare practices and institutions to reduce burnout?

I recently attended a leadership training in which the facilitator asked physician leaders to rate their own level of burnout and that of their teams. The results weren't encouraging. We are on the verge of a precipice nationwide.

Physicians are fed up with being held to unreasonable standards (that are usually different from other roles in healthcare):

unlimited numbers of patients at any time; repeated high-stress situations; decreasing reimbursement for increasingly complex patients, especially in non-procedural specialties; multiple federally-mandated trainings that eat up personal time; patients and families that are understandably stressed and demanding; increasing documentation, coding, and insurance requirements; budget cuts; and being asked to do more work with fewer resources. Don't count on physicians and patients tolerating the American model of healthcare much longer.

-Analyze projects that affect clinicians (including nurses) to make sure they meaningfully improve the lives of both clinicians and patients.
-Don't ask for additional work without providing additional resources.
-Administrators, HR, and med staff personnel that interact with frontline physicians and clinicians should be trauma trained.
-Expect these employees to be helpful, compassionate, and respectful of the difficult experiences of frontline clinicians.
-Listening is a critical skill.
-Hold administrators accountable for unprofessional, inappropriate behavior. Offer coaching.
-Eliminate discrimination to your female physicians and others who are discriminated against.

This story by a woman physician would not be complete without mention of the elephant in the room, perhaps the most demoralizing, unfair, and hurtful part of all - the disrespectful, demeaning treatment of women, specifically women physicians, by some (not all) patients and family members, some administrators, some nursing and operating room staff, some case managers, some advanced practice providers, and some male physicians. Physicians from minorities in the US have had similar experiences. The mistreatment is so pervasive that any female physician can probably speak to dozens of experiences in her career in which she was not accepted as a physician, spoken down to, not listened to, called by her first name or "Honey or Sweetie" when the male physicians were referred to as Doctor..., paid less than male colleagues, called names for speaking up assertively (when her male counterparts were praised for their assertion), or not offered leadership positions or academic appointments though she was better qualified and/or experienced than the male applicants.

Here are a few examples from my career and those of others:

-A female medical resident who was deaf was referred to as "deaf girl" and treated disrespectfully by a nurse. Her colleagues spoke up for her and reminded the nurse how many things she must have overcome and how many ignorant people she must have endured to even become a doctor.

-I was in a hospital patient's room discussing my patient's serious condition with him and his family when a man walked into the room. He looked at me and immediately started talking over me, asking the patient how they liked their food throughout their hospital stay. I politely and calmly told him that I was the physician and was in the middle of an important conversation about their reason for being hospitalized. He excused himself. He later apologized to me, to which I replied, "you probably saw that I was a woman and thought it was ok to interrupt me". No response.

-A full-time female physician discovered she was paid nearly 20% less than her male colleagues for the same work. She attempted to address it with her administration and then through an attorney, but there was no reciprocal acknowledgment and no rectification. It wasn't until her male colleague sent an email widely to senior leadership, making clear the discrimination, that the situation was finally addressed.

Advice to everyone
Help fix the broken system before it completely breaks.

About Ann Huntington, MD, FACP
Dr. Huntington is an Internal Medicine physician currently in the field of Hospital Medicine. She has expertise in quality, patient safety, peer review, privileging, credentials, and leadership. She has special interests in lifestyle medicine, integrative medicine, physician wellness, and coaching. At the time of this writing, she is launching a CME course for physicians on the safety of essential oils and their evidence as an integrative tool, as well as a consulting practice.
Dr. Huntington is also engaged in coaching, business, and leadership training.

www.givemorenaturally.com

Ashley Albers, DO

It all looked so perfect. Once I set my sights on medical school, I never looked back. I worked at it, as we all do. Studying in the library until midnight, in bed by around 1, and back up at 6 to study some more. Third and fourth year rotations brought call nights and little sleep. It paid off with a good residency slot that I believed would lead to a fellowship.

Talk about work! Work hour restrictions limited us to 80 hours/week (averaged over 4 weeks) and 30 hours/day. They weren't followed. Some rotations were particularly challenging, and if complaints were made, then the interns tracked into that specialty would deny that they had a similar experience. So nothing changed. Of course, as a trainee, I saw those experiences as representing the dues everyone has to pay. I often recalled my surgeon father's lesson that you can survive anything with an end date. No matter how bad the rotation is, it'll be over in 30 days. Growing up, I had always been taught to do my best, and so I did. I learned to work for hours on end, to switch from days to nights and back without falling asleep at the wheel, and to rush on to the next crisis without ever processing the last one.

It all seemed to pay off when I was accepted into a fellowship program close to home. I was able to see my family and work less-crazy hours. With my training complete, I took a job for a nonprofit hospice organization in my hometown. Talk about a story! Local girl comes back and…

I learned a lot of lessons in that first role. I learned that we should "do more with less" and that additional help would not be coming. I learned that one-to-one meetings with my boss really weren't that important, which became very clear when they didn't show up, and the meeting was never rescheduled. Most dangerously, I learned that I had to accept whatever was offered if I liked my job.

With changes on the horizon, I switched roles within the company while my teammates became hospital employees. In that new role, I met many incredible people who helped me to grow personally and professionally. One-to-ones continued to be a challenge. We had them this time, and my supervisor asked what was keeping me up at night. It's a popular question there. They weren't the only people to ask me that. I answered honestly and spent the next several years believing that I had made a huge mistake. I felt that the response to my answer was to blow it - and me - off with the abrupt assertion that it would be "fine". At that moment, I learned that this person did not care at all about me and that revealing any part of myself was to be avoided at all costs. I figured out a safe answer and offered that every single time I was asked that question. It felt safer that way.

Over a few years, multiple things changed. There were staffing changes, growth in the number of patients we were serving, and changes in my role. I was promoted and on a path to chief medical officer. Five years after starting there, I already knew I wanted out. I wasn't burned out yet, but I wasn't happy, and I didn't see how that could change. The founder of the organization was of the opinion that if you weren't thrilled to be there, you should quit. So it was probably better not to appear unhappy. The culture is still one of many hours of work. I'd get an email from one person until somewhere between 11 PM and midnight, and then someone else would start sending them at about 3 AM. While they didn't explicitly demand answers at those hours, the implication was that you would always be on and available. I did, in fact, get calls after 10 PM asking whether I'd seen an email and was quite upset that I hadn't answered.

The culture of always on was pervasive. I got a call from an out-of-state discharge planner while I was on FMLA because someone hadn't been taught how to read the schedule. HR didn't want to be told about that one. Others would call me on vacation because, apparently, nothing could wait. The COVID-19 pandemic only made matters worse. Everyone who could pack their workstations up and went home, where the meetings continued well past business hours ended, and the emails flew all weekend.

Looking back, I was probably already burned out when the pandemic hit, and it only got worse from there. At the worst point, I was only capable of doing what had the next due date. I constantly felt behind and unable to get help. I'd had to fight to hire physicians as we grew, and my role had outgrown what one person could handle. I was exhausted, not sleeping enough, not performing my best, and incapable of showing up for my family in the way that I desired. If I took Sunday afternoon off, I would come back to a lengthy email string that I had missed and needed to respond to. I wanted out and needed out and felt stuck. The only option I could see was to leave and go to a similar role in a different organization, and what if it was worse?

After a time, things started to shift. Somehow I moved through the worst of it and was able to regain some of my function. Some of myself. I ended up getting the promotion to CMO with additional responsibilities and without additional help. I also got an executive coach, and he, along with a close friend, helped me to get unstuck. I realized that I really liked remote work and that opened up other career options.

I'm grateful that it did. While I was getting unstuck, some things were getting worse. When I reported abuse, the response was "oh no" and silence. I realized that as the world opened back up, I had spent a great deal of time multitasking. I had been working almost constantly, even while engaging in virtual events. It struck me that I was starting to resent the things that I love for taking away my work time as we started to return in person, and I couldn't multitask anymore. When I interviewed for my current role, my interviewer commented that I was at the "pinnacle of my career". On paper, maybe, but I was still miserable.

Coming out of burnout happened over time. I moved through the worst of it about a year before I left my job. I thought I was better, but I had no idea what was actually possible. Working with the executive coach helped me to see that I had work to do if I didn't want to take some of my habits and thought processes into my new job. That's when I found life coaching and joined a program. Within that, I got to see physicians who were thriving. They were satisfied in their careers, and even better, they loved themselves. I chose to hope that would be possible for me, and kept doing the work.

It's been over a year since I left my CMO role, and I have a new perspective on all of it. I see now that when I thought I had gotten through burnout, I wasn't actually out of it yet. There was so much healing that I needed to do for that to fully lift. I have compassion for the person I was and the decisions I made, and I believe that I did the best that I could with the lessons I had learned and the tools I had available to me. I can imagine that it might be wonderful if the systems and the organization were different, without having to fight with the reality of what they were. The same goes for people - I can allow them to be without trying to make them be different.

Looking around at the world now, I see options and possibilities. Things that I can create, and become, and choose. I have so much hope and peace. And it is my wish that every physician will reclaim the hope and optimism they possessed the day they were accepted into medical school.

Questions and Answers

Looking back, was there anything in your childhood or upbringing that you think led to your burnout?

Both of my parents are healthcare professionals. My dad, a general surgeon, and my mom, an occupational therapist. Growing up, birthday parties were scheduled around the call schedule. Middle of the night disappearances were not uncommon, because surgeons sometimes operate in the middle of the night. There is not a single event that stands out, but years of learning that medicine is one of the highest priorities and that we do not settle for anything less than the best we can do.

Did anything occur in your training that led to your burnout?

Looking back, everything did, although that may be my own bias. My training taught me that it's expected to work 30+ hours a day, 80+ hours a week, no matter what work hour restrictions were in place. There were days that it took someone else complaining to the residency director's office to get me sent home after the laws said my shift should have ended - but nobody wanted to take the pager and instead kept piling on work. Events like that taught me that asking for what I needed, for what was right, for what was safe, was pointless. And just because someone reported it once didn't mean that it would be better the next time. On the contrary, nothing changed. I recall sleeping for four solid hours in the hospital one night and being terrified that I had missed calls or a code or something important. We were expected to be up all night. I called in sick one - once! - in my entire residency because I could not get out of bed, and when I returned to work the next day, my attending laughed at my paperwork, saying "too sick to work". And I learned well that my body's need for sleep, for rest when I am sick, for not working more than 30 hours really should be ignored. Medicine demands all.

What do you think caused the burnout?

The organization I was working in at the time of my burnout mandated monthly one-to-one meetings between boss and employee. My first boss typically didn't bother to schedule them, and if they were scheduled, he didn't come. But the next one dutifully asked the much-beloved question, "what keeps you up at night?". I answered honestly, and her response was to tell me, "oh, you'll be fine," and move on to her agenda. I quickly surmised that 1) she didn't care and 2) it wasn't safe to share anything. To this day, I have never asked an employee that question, and I never answered it honestly again. So there I was, believing that my boss didn't care at all about me and that it wasn't safe to go to her for anything. Meanwhile, she started sending emails around 3 AM, and the CEO stopped sending them somewhere between 11pm-midnight. Take a Sunday "off," and there would be a full-blown email string waiting when I came back. I got called on FMLA because someone wasn't taught to read the schedule and gave my number to an out-of-state discharge planner. I got called on multiple vacations because someone wasn't happy about something. I was never off. Sadly, while I was in a leadership role, I did not have control through any sort of reporting relationship to address the problems that I saw. So I dealt with the aftermath without being able to address the root causes and didn't ever feel heard. There was no accountability for the problems that existed.

When I finally left that role (post-burnout), my position was split into two full-time roles with the addition of administrative support that I did not have. The tendency is for leaders within that organization to perform 2-3 roles until they simply cannot, and when I could not, one of the people I was reporting to became verbally abusive.

What helped you overcome your burnout?

I didn't overcome burnout. Neither did I recover or bounce back. I think about overcoming or recovering from in terms of an illness - you heal and return to your prior state of health. I have not done that, and I am grateful. The experience of being burned out has forever changed me. It rewired my neural pathways and my nervous system. And one day I was a little better and a little less burned out, and then one day I wasn't burned out anymore. I was still suffering abuse and in an untenable situation. A very close friend, an executive coach, and my therapist helped me to find within myself what I needed to leave that job.

I was not magically better when I left. I felt broken and unworthy and incapable of doing anything right. I have since spent hours in coaching and have done a lot of healing. Coaching and therapy and friends who understand have helped me to heal and to see that I am not alone.

Did you have a support system?

No. I have always believed that my family supports me, but nobody knew how bad it was. And without people actually seeing it, nobody could push me to get out.

Did anyone notice and reach out to you?

No. Even after the fact, anyone who says something will admit that they didn't know or understand what was going on.

How are you thriving today?

Right now, I am in a job with boundaries! I have learned just how much is available to me in this life if I am willing to choose it, and I continue to learn how much I do get to choose. I stayed in an as-needed role at the organization I was in during my burnout and am now days away from the end of that contract. I have freed myself from the hold that that organization and some of the people within it had on me, and now believe that I am worth so much more than I was being offered. Knowing how much I have benefited from coaching, I pursued a coaching certification and am working with individuals in career transitions to help them harness their own beautiful brains to create a life that they love.

I still moonlight at a company I've been with for about five years and love showing up as my authentic self to care for patients. I enjoy my interactions with staff and am able to be more fully present with everyone while I am working there.

What advice would you give to someone going through burnout?

Tell someone. NOT someone at your company. Find a coach or other physicians who have been there. Borrow their belief that it can and will get better.

And if all of that feels like too much, that's ok. Just don't give up. You are far too important and if all you can do is survive right now, do that.

What advice would you give to the facilities and administration who are trying to help decrease the rate of physician burnout?

If you are not actively part of the solution, then you are the problem. So, thank you for choosing to be part of the solution! All of the things that we like to think will help in wellness programs - rewards, massages, etc. - are worthless in the face of burnout. If you want to combat physician burnout, you have to see that your physicians have boundaries and autonomy. The training we go through is designed very specifically to push physicians past a normal breaking point, and we will work until we literally break. So don't get near that point. Make it possible for physicians to have a reasonable workload, to finish charting at work and not at midnight, and to make sure there's actually enough staff. Physicians should be doing only the things that only a physician can do - if a medical assistant can do it, don't put it on the physicians. If you hear complaints from physicians, listen. This is not a group that's going to complain just because - if you're hearing from them, you have a problem that you need to fix.

Time off matters. OFF. Not charting, not fielding calls, not dealing with messages, and definitely not coming back to more work. If they believe that taking time off will only make their life worse, you have a problem and need to fix your policies.

Think of burnout like a malignancy. If it isn't found and treated early, it will spread and destroy the body. Left unchecked, burnout will claim the best of your workforce and put your organization at risk. If you are in healthcare, there is an assumption that you care about people. Caring about your physicians doesn't make them or you weak, it doesn't mean they won't be productive and work to high standards, and it won't cause any of the harms you might be trying to use as objections. What it will do is make them more loyal, healthier, and probably more productive, and more likely to stay with your organization in the long term. Whether you choose to care about physician burnout says everything about you, and if you're not actively working to be a part of the solution, then you are the problem.

About Ashley Albers, DO

Dr. Albers is an internal medicine physician who subspecialized in Hospice & Palliative Medicine. She served as the chief medical officer of a nonprofit before leaving for saner territory. In addition to her day job and moonlight roles, she also coaches individuals in career transitions, whether new jobs or promotions, helping them to find fulfillment in their work. When burnout is part of the story, we work on that too.

Rfscoaching.mykajabi.com

Sapna Shah-Haque MD MBA

My first journey through burnout was in 2016. It was a culmination of a rigorous outpatient clinic schedule, inpatient, consults, and covering for other physicians as the new kid on the block. Initially, I thought it was great. I felt like I was a real doctor. This is what I trained for. This is why I went to medical school and to residency. But about a year and a half into practicing, it became unsustainable. Not only was the clinic completely full of double, triple books or covering for a partner, I also had inpatient, consults and also covered the patients that were unassigned or even patients n the hospital that would normally be seen by the physician for whom I was covering. I tried to decrease some of this, and I received pushback. I remember being told that my generation didn't like to work hard. My response was it's not that we didn't like to work hard, it was just that we had realized that there was more to life than working. I remember getting home at 8 or 9:00 PM. I remember going in at 6:00 in the morning. I remember going in at 3:00 AM for an ICU admit or consult. I remember getting called on my days off or my holidays off while I was on vacation. I remember getting reprimanded for losing my temper when I was being paged while I was off to celebrate holidays with a family member. I remember being told when my mother had a stroke. Why would you want to go up there? What can you do differently? It was a fact that I could be a daughter and be at bedside. I did not get to see her until she was being dismissed from the hospital. It was such a large stroke that she required 24-hour care. Our family life was completely turned upside down within a very short time.

I remember during my burnout in 2016, I would come home, and I would not want to talk to even my beloved greyhounds for at least an hour because I could not turn my mind off. I could not fall asleep. I could not stay asleep. I was fearful of missing a page, and as soon as I fell asleep, I would get paged. I remember several nights upon the end of having completely interrupted sleep. I remember being irritable even with the dogs with everybody I loved. I remember not liking to be questioned. I did not like to repeat myself more than once even if somebody did not hear, it aggravated me to have to repeat such a simple sentence or task. On my days off. I did not want to be bothered. I did not even want to be bothered at one point by friends or family, and I became socially isolated. I think the biggest thing was I was incredibly irritable, where normally I'm a very happy-go-lucky person. I like to have fun. I like to laugh. I couldn't even find a reason to laugh at times.

I never asked for help. Looking back. I wish I really would have looked into counseling. I was smarter the second time around. I ended up taking a job closer to my mother as well as an outpatient only. There was no call. No weekends. It allowed me to have time to be a physician as well as to step up to the plate when my family needed me.

The second time I went through burnout, it was after the death of my best friend from medical school and residency. She died by suicide. She was also a physician in my hometown while I was there then practicing. One week we were planning a wine evening, and the next week it was her celebration of life. With the news, I was completely shocked and heartbroken. I really don't think that there are words to quantify or qualify the emotions. There are some things that words do not do justice to, and this is one of them. With her death, it really made me think about what in the hell I was doing. Medicine did not deserve such a caring soul that my friend embodied. It was then that I became aware of the astronomical rate at which physicians take their own lives. I became completely disgusted with medicine. I think in 2019 and in 2016, I had contemplated becoming a mixologist but there was no mixology school or coursework in my hometown. Wildlife photography would not pay the bills with small kids at home. I really decided in 2019 to take a step back and go part-time. Part-time. Not only did I not want to continue working for a system that did not give a damn about physicians, but I also wanted to try to make it better. I decided to work part-time because that way, I could ensure a roof over my kids' heads and also have a very hands-on approach to their upbringing.

I remember going to work about a week after my friend's death, and we were training a new nurse. This nurse could not recall a darn thing. Time management on her part was horrible. It should not take 30 minutes to check in a patient that was just there for his annual exam. I lost my temper and told the head nurse it was either that nurse training or me. And if I walked off the job for the day, she would have to see my patients or tell them why I was not there, and it was because the system was inefficient. I'm sorry I made that nurse cry, but I'm not sorry for standing up for myself. Usually, I am more tactful but after going through such a traumatic loss might give a damn was quite busted. The administration asked me to apologize to that nurse, and I refused. It was then that I decided I was going to practice on my own terms. If someone did not like it, then I'm not the doctor for them, and there's the door.

Question and Answers

Did anything occur in your training that led to your burnout?

During medical school, there was a culture of never saying no. I have always been up for challenges, but it was absolutely ridiculous to expect a med student to do a 24-hour trauma call followed by a trauma clinic resulting in 36 hours straight. Then to drive home...

In residency, there were two attendings that, when I was around, I developed a stutter and tremor. Anything I said was incorrect. This did not happen with other attendings. I loathed those months. Eventually, some of us that were having issues, all females, went to admin and had the rotations switched. I wish I had done so sooner. It took about a year to go forward with my concerns.

What helped you overcome your burnout?

The first time, cutting back on my hours and finding a position where I was not on call or did not have weekends, and I had time to recharge. The second time, I had to cut back further. About a year after my friend's suicide, when the first anniversary of her death was approaching, I started having flashbacks and nightmares. The irritability increased. This is also during the pandemic. In 2020, I formally sought counseling/ therapy and have maintained it as part of my health and wellness program for myself. I am very proud to say in 2023. I still go to therapy just for my mental sanity. If nothing else, it is my tune-up. Just as I take my vehicle in for tune-ups, I take myself into a mental tune-up. I can also say that proper nutrition, lifestyle, and family support, as well as from friends and my co-workers where I am currently, have ensured that I do well and I stay well. I work at a place where the well-being of physicians is actually cared about. If we don't take care of ourselves, they ensure that we take time off that we need and do have an employee assistance program with mental health.

Did you have a support system?

Definitely family, friends as well as co-workers where I am currently. And my previous position. I did have support as well with co-workers and my boss. But a lot was too little too late. I have never had suicidal ideation, but I have felt isolated. Irritable, and why in the hell did I waste 10 years of medical school residency and then on those days when I have hard days, I have great co-workers currently where I can walk into my clinic manager's office, close the door and just vent. The administration at this hospital that owns the clinic has been incredibly supportive through rocky times. And when I have had personal losses, they do ask how I'm doing and what I need to succeed. For that, I am incredibly grateful.

Did anyone notice and reach out to you?

I did have people ask about how I was doing after my mom's stroke or after the loss of my friend. But besides being told that I was slightly irritable at home, nobody reached out. To be fair, I thought they just thought it was stress, and even I, myself, was not familiar with the term burnout.

How are you thriving today?

Today I'm thriving because I work part-time. I work in an environment that actually cares about me as an individual, not just a physician. I have some control over my schedule. I am employed by choice with a non-profit. I find that working in an area that aligns with my values adds purpose to what I do as a physician. I also have achieved a work-life balance or life-work balance for myself. I am able to explore areas of myself that I thought I would never see again, such as reading, art, and history. Those were interests of mine as I was growing up and even in medical school, but died during maybe the second year or third year of medical school because of the training. I draw boundaries. I allow myself not to have to be perfect. I ask for help. I maintain my counseling/ therapy schedule very regularly. I also have found a way to grieve by producing a podcast. I have found it very cathartic and enlightening to know that I'm not alone in what I've gone through.

What advice would you give to someone going through burnout?

Once you recognize it, do something about it. Push the pause button. Get help. You are replaceable at work but not with your family. You are not replaceable with your friends. There is nobody else that can be you. There are people that are similar to you, but there is only one of you. As we tell our patients, take time for yourself, draw boundaries, and go to therapy. Get on medication, and seek help. We need to follow our own advice.

What advice would you give to the facilities and administration who are trying to help decrease the rate of physician burnout?

If you want solutions, don't just look to a wellness officer. Don't ask physicians to do yoga or meditate their way out of burnout. While yoga and meditation are excellent daily practices for mindfulness and decreasing stress, it is not a tool for overcoming burnout. It is maybe a tool for overwhelm or for a really crappy time in life that is not burnout. When someone is burned out, they are so deep in a hole. Really look at the person and ask them with genuine intent if they are okay. If you sense that they are not okay, ask again. Ask the next day or the next week again. Keep tabs on that person. Keep tabs on that person as to how they are doing with their mental health. Ask the individual what they need to succeed. Ask physicians for solutions because we are problem solvers. We do better when we can actually be part of the solution, not be handed a solution. Do not shame a physician if they ask for help. Do not shame a physician for saying no to a double book. I am sorry that the system is the way it is, but that does not mean that we should have to work around it all the time. Find other ways other than asking physicians to double-book. Triage urgency. Triage the clinic flow or the hospital flow to address things that might need to be seen immediately, but asking a physician to overextend themselves when they are already overextended, and unless you are a physician, this is nothing that the administration would understand at all. Because with a physician and administration, the job description and the stakes are different. Do not assume that physicians are resilient and will bounce back. Physicians die by suicide at a higher rate than the average population. Keep that in mind when you are looking at the well-being of your physicians.

What advice, if any, would you give to the facilities that can do better when it comes to improving the burnout rates of physicians?

If you cannot take care of your physicians, why are you at your job? Would you want a rundown, disgruntled physician taking care of you? The answer is no. So why would you want to keep that type of work culture? Remember, burnout equals more medical mistakes, which equals more lawsuits which equals decreased profitability. If you want to look at the bottom line, you also have to look at the well-being of your physicians. They are a huge part of that equation. You cannot have health care without physicians. Value them.

About Sapna Shah-Haque, MD

Dr. Sapna Shah-Haque is a board certified Internal Medicine physician. She was born and raised in Kansas, and attended medical school at the University of Kansas [KU] School of Medicine. She completed her Internal Medicine residency at KU-Wichita as well. After experiencing burnout herself and watching other physician colleagues burn out, it became a passion of hers to look into different aspects of burnout. She started a podcast, The Worthy Physician. While the system does need to change, as it is broken, this podcast is a way to reach physicians and possibly shed light on what is not an isolated situation.

www.theworthyphysician.com

Wendy Schofer, MD, FAAP, DipABLM

There was nothing damaging or traumatic in my childhood that specifically led to my burnout, yet I am a product of my childhood, and having experienced burnout multiple times before I had the language to describe what I had experienced, I revisit it. I worked hard in my early school years, as I heard that I was bright and I craved the accolades. I reaped the benefits of my hard work in the form of promotions, good grades, and leadership roles throughout my schooling. I was outspoken, very outspoken. While there were times that I found myself working to prove myself, that I was worthy or even more worthy of a position than someone else, but I do not see this as anything beyond what every child experiences. I saw that striving to prove myself as the key to my success as the 8th grade Spelling Bee Champion, ranking third in my senior class and persisting in running for student office until I won the election to become Class President my senior year. I earned a full scholarship to college.

In college I didn't feel the need to prove myself, as much as found a place where I blossomed while being myself. I found my people, including a very special group of women I now call my Sisters. I thrived in the biological sciences and dabbled in the social sciences, including a minor in sociology. While I thought that I was going to go into the FBI to become a forensic scientist, I later discovered two things: one, I don't like bench laboratory work, and two, genetic fingerprinting in the FBI did not involve the field work and firearms I pictured. I did find that genetics and biology were keenly lining me up to pursue medicine, which was confirmed by my volunteer experiences. Medical school was my next step.

My medical training was the playground for my burnout story. I went to medical school with my college boyfriend. We had both been high achievers in college. I found that medical school was very time-intensive, and he found that it was easy. I went to class and worked so hard to learn all the material, and he stayed home to play video games, just read the scribe's notes and he aced it all. It could have been a case of just 2 different styles, but I noticed how I started comparing our experiences more and more.

He was outspoken, and I found myself taking more and more of a quiet role. It was nothing that he had done. It was more of me finding or maybe actually creating a distinction between the two of us. But yet, I learned. We were on clinical rotations together, and I found out how he was received as an outspoken (male) medical student. He was never confused by any patient for being a nurse. He was never talked over at conferences.

I learned from these observations.

During my 4th year of medical school, I completed a pediatric infectious disease sub-internship along with two female medical classmates. At the mid-point, we received feedback. I was asked by the accomplished attending, "Have you taken assertiveness training? You talk too much. You need not ask so many questions." Those words have haunted me since then.

I was devastated. I do recall that both of my classmates, very quiet, studious women, also received the same feedback about asking too many questions, minus the question about assertiveness. Instead of wondering why this feedback was given across the board, I shut down. I squeaked through the rotation and decided that I would never do infectious disease as I had more questions than could ever be answered.

My husband and I had our first child during the Spring of our fourth year of medical school. We matched in military residencies. We moved across the country with our 3-month-old daughter, and I became a pediatric intern momma.

Holy smokes, I had no idea what awaited me. I was perpetually exhausted. I recall falling asleep at a red light while driving home and being horrified when awoken by the honking horn of the car behind me. There was nothing to do but to keep going. I remember receiving feedback after feedback about how I needed to read more, especially when I went home in the evenings. One particular feedback session stands out in my mind from my second year of residency. I was on a NICU rotation, where I was functioning as the senior resident. And I was clearly not functioning the way that my attending wanted. My single male attending told me that I needed to go home and stop playing with my child at night. I needed to stay awake and read more.

What he didn't know is that I went home and I completely crashed from exhaustion. I was reminded of the evening one year prior, where as an intern, I took call in the NICU and was responsible for the stabilization of three sets of micro-preemie twins that were all born after midnight. Later that morning, I could not keep Twin A and Twin B from Family X, Y, and Z straight. I was still rounding and writing notes at 6 PM the next evening and crying in the workroom. A senior resident connected with me and told me to just get through the day. Or was it night at that point? I was back in the NICU the next morning by 5:00 AM to start rounding again.

What I took away from these experiences was that I wasn't good enough, wasn't working hard enough, and wasn't smart enough to be a good resident. I did have a mentor during residency who was just a few years older than me. He rode his bicycle to work every day, had a wife who also practiced medicine, and a child the same age as mine. I looked up to him as someone who let all the rules and regulations of military medicine just roll off his back as he rode his bike home to his loving family. He is the one who modeled leaving work at work. He reminded me that I was the only intern with a child and the only female resident with a family in later years. His words, while meaningful, seemed so quiet in comparison to the voices of the critical attendings. However, his words and modeling would be important to me later.

After I graduated from residency, I was assigned to the Naval Hospital Camp Pendleton in the pediatric clinic. It was full-scope pediatrics, with minimal specialists at the hospital, but close enough to San Diego that families who had children with complex medical needs lived in the area and were my patients.

All of my insecurities about not being a good enough doctor (and mom) and not working hard enough, or long enough followed me and intensified. I would round in the hospital all day after filling the pockets of my white coat with Peanut M&Ms and Pepsi One (not recommended). I learned that I could lose weight on this horrific diet as I was stressed and climbing stairs all day. I developed palpitations, and my mind raced. I was about to self-refer to psychiatry because I couldn't do it anymore when I was deployed with 48-hour notice. There was no time to seek help.

I was deployed on the USNS Mercy hospital ship to provide humanitarian relief to the residents of Nias, Indonesia. I missed my family dearly and was gone for my son's first birthday. I was treating very sick patients, and yet… my palpitations went away.

I collaborated with numerous specialties, including pediatric intensive care, general peds, anesthesiology, and surgery on the ship. We were all in it together. And when I wasn't on duty, I slept. At night, I would hang out with my new friend, who happened to be a psychiatrist. We would talk under the stars on the ship's deck. I was healing.

A year after returning home, I was transferred to the Naval Hospital in Okinawa, Japan, with my family. The old ways returned. I worked long hours, finding that I was always on the run to grab my kids from preschool. My colleagues insisted that I should get a "mamasan," a Japanese nanny, so I could work more without having to rush. The only part that I heard there was "so I could work more." I had valued the time that my mother spent raising my sister and me, and I did not want to outsource that just so I could work more.

Instead, I nearly killed my marriage. My husband and I worked opposite shifts so that one of us was home with the kids at night. We were strained by frequent military taskers, "Heads-up, we may need for you to go to (insert remote location) in a few days." We were both stressed, understaffed, and overburdened clinically. I served the role of the pediatrician, social worker, and therapist for my patients and their families. I gave 150% in the office and had *zero* left over for my family. When I got home, I just wanted to sleep or blame my husband for... everything.

I counted down the days until my active duty tour was done in Okinawa, which was conveniently the end of my military obligation. I could not leave fast enough. I learned that I wasn't good enough or put together enough to be able to juggle full-time medical practice and being the wife and mother that I wanted to be.

Fast-forward a few years and a number of transitions later. I was working very part-time as a contractor for the military clinics in Portsmouth, Virginia. I volunteered for a local population health nonprofit and assumed the leadership role. In truth, it was a role that I enjoyed, yet I found that it was taking more and more of my time, and I thought that I wasn't the doctor I was trained to be. I heard slights from others about how I was a volunteer versus people who "actually had to work." I felt devalued and tendered my resignation.

It was rejected. I could not resign from a volunteer position.

The unbelievable part is that I went along with it and kept trudging along. My heart was no longer in it, and I found myself growing to resent the work.

And then a funny thing happened, something called COVID. The world changed seemingly overnight. Our programs were put on hold. Money was shifted in the budget. And I tendered my 2-week notice and stuck to it.

During the early days of COVID, I found myself working 0.25 FTE clinically as an urgent care pediatrician and otherwise having a lot of time at home. I suddenly had sleep and time with my family that I had never experienced before.

I also started online classes, because... COVID. I took the Science of Happiness (thank you, Dr. Laurie Santos), and I heard about coaching. My world changed as I learned the language of positive psychology, motivation, and perceptions. And then a new word came up: Burnout.

When I first heard of burnout, I scoffed at it. I was skeptical because it seemed that everyone was talking about it. It felt like everyone was saying, "Me too!" I brushed off the conversations. And then, one day, I was cleaning out my closet (because of COVID!) and found a bin from my time in Okinawa. I pulled out a T-shirt that my husband had made at the time and gifted me for Christmas.

It is embarrassing to tell, but it is the truth: the T-shirt said "F*** 'EM ALL (edited for purposes of this book)" on the back, and the hospital logo on the front. It suddenly came back to me. My husband made this ridiculous T-shirt, not because of his off-brand of humor but to commemorate something that I said every single day when I came home from work. Every.single.day.

I do not recall swearing much at all prior to this time, and definitely not in this way that I was practicing every single day.

It hit me: "F*** 'EM ALL (edited for purposes of this book):" Depersonalization. Exhaustion. Feelings of ineffectiveness.

I had experienced the triad of burnout. While I had concluded that I wasn't good enough, smart enough, or a hard enough worker, it was actually burnout. And that's why it kept coming up everywhere I went: in training, practice, and even as a volunteer in the nonprofit sector.

Now folks will talk about the institutional and cultural contributors to burnout. What I learned right away was that there was one consistent that went wherever I went: and that was me. I kept trying to leave the "toxic systems" and the "bad fits." But at the end of the day, I was in each of these stories.

I dove into exploring burnout and each of my personal experiences. I found that the story that I told: the feelings of inadequacy, of having to prove myself, of being a woman in a patriarchal medical system that I either blamed the system or told myself that I wasn't enough.

What I had never done was ask myself: where do I thrive? What are my strengths? What do I want?

I had been trained to fix it. I had been trained to find the faults and address them, including my own. It meant that I was continually focusing on my own inadequacies and shortcomings. My fix had been to withdraw and contract myself.

I got a coach and started consuming psychology and cognitive-behavioral tools. What I found was that my training had been one-sided: find the problems and fix them. I had never had the opportunity to tune into what *was working* in my life, let alone explore my strengths and how I could use them every day.

And in the middle of COVID, I found that there was a lot working in my life. My family was experiencing grief from the death of beloved family members, disruption of routines and schooling, and mental health strain. And yet, I was calmer than ever. I kept telling myself that my training as a pediatrician had completely prepared me for this moment to best support my children. My psychology training was being used daily in personal practice.

The biggest changes in my life were my relationships: with my kids, my work, and with myself. I changed the story I was telling myself about being inadequate. Suddenly, I found that I was in a place where I was the perfect person for the job at hand. In my clinical practice, I shifted from being cautious about which patients I picked up (I have a visceral reaction to certain orthopedic injuries like dislocations, which is a challenge for an urgent care pediatrician) to own that I am totally the doc who wants to see the teen with several-months of abdominal pain and anxiety. That is my jam! I embraced working to my strengths instead of shying away from my perceived inadequacies.

I decided to certify as a coach, at first a health and well-being coach, and then as a life coach. I wanted to explore the tools and use them more and more. But when I saw that I was using the tools clinically to help anxious parents and leaning into my ability to connect with families with chronic conditions, I knew I had found a new path forward.

I created a business that suits my strengths: connecting with parents and families, helping them find health at home, with humor (and a bit of a sailor's mouth, just not to the degree of what was on the T-shirt!). I founded the Family in Focus program to help parents who are worried about their children's weight so they can rewrite the story of their family's health by building better relationships with food and body. I also work with physicians who are experiencing burnout and work-life stressors so they can create a life they don't need to escape.

I don't have to fit my business into a tidy box, just like I don't fit into a lot of people's molds of what it looks like to be a physician, a coach, or a parent. Instead of turning down my voice, I am practicing using it to speak up and out. My challenges in training, the things that I thought of as wounds, have helped me become so much stronger. I speak up. I get a lot of sleep every night. And I've learned that in order to be the mom, wife, physician, and coach that I want to be, I get to focus on what I need. These are the practices that I keep every day. I learned them because of my experiences with burnout, and I practice them to recognize and avoid having those experiences again.

I am grateful for my experiences with burnout.

About Wendy Schofer, MD
Dr. Schofer is a pediatrician-coach who specializes in cultivating health at home. She is the Founder of Family in Focus, where she helps parents who are worried about their children's weight build healthy relationships with food and body. She also helps women physicians who feel trapped in the daily juggle of work and family create a life they don't need to escape. www.wendyschofermd.com

Rita Gupta, DO MPA

I had a bunch of life changes all at once. I got married, six months later got pregnant, and my Dad had a massive stroke. All these things placed a lot of strain on me. I was happy to find a wonderful partner and fulfill my dream of being a mom. I had gone through some relationships in the past that left me feeling that it might not be a possibility to be a mom. I was lucky to get pregnant within the first 6 months of marriage at age 40.

The burnout started happening when my chronic neck pain started becoming more intense. About five years prior, I had severe cervical radiculopathy from C5/C6 disc extrusion. I was advised to have surgery at that time but was too scared to undergo ACDF. I would see it took about two years of searing pain and endless hours of PT that I was able to move past the radicular symptoms.

I continued to have pain, but it was manageable, and I could gauge what activities were going to flare it up.

Fast forward to my Dad's stroke and having to move geographically for my husband's job and better quality of life. Our move, overall, in retrospect, has been a good decision, but that first year was so terrible with housing issues (a long story, we lost a significant amount of money from a home that we later found out was not livable). We had to go into a small apartment and lived there for 18 months until we found our home.

When we moved into our home, my neck pain was at its peak, and the radicular symptoms were shooting down my arm. I was in so much pain that I felt exhausted and hopeless. I found an acupuncturist who was helpful, but as it flared up more, he said he wasn't able to help me. I saw PM&R, and they got another MRI. Steroid epidural initially and possibly surgery were recommended. While awaiting the ESI, I awoke one morning and could not get up to move. I had no choice and was taken out of work. Prior to that point, the specialist recommended I take some time off while awaiting the steroid injection. I wish I had done that, but I was so afraid of what they might think. I was afraid to speak up.

I also felt emotionally drained and sad. I couldn't be a mom to my daughter, who I had wished for so long. My husband tried to help but couldn't understand the severity of my symptoms. I didn't tell him much about the pain I experienced in the past, but he knew about the neck issues. I didn't talk about it much until it got to the point I couldn't function anymore.

The PM&R doctor was understanding. I remember his words that the system would be able to function without me. His kindness was my first step to realizing that I needed to take care of myself. I was so in my head and disconnected from my body. My body would only scream louder and louder. He also said that it is hardest for moms not to be able to be present for their children. It made me stop and reflect on what matters to me the most.

I returned to work after doing a series of epidurals and PT. I have had surgical consults, and the overwhelming consensus is that doing surgery may or may not help at this point now that I am so far from the initial insult. I manage my pain. With Covid, I was able to do a lot of virtual work and have continued to adjust my work environment so that I can continue to work even though I have daily pain. I have learned how to manage it, plan for it and stay on top of it.

Learning mindfulness has been a game changer. I feel less emotionally tied to the pain and can observe it. I feel I accept the pain instead of fighting against it.

After seeing the limited options for helping me, I turned to Integrative Medicine. I found Acupuncture, Spinal therapies, and Mindful Based Stress reduction to be helpful. This further expanded my interests and led me to pursue a fellowship in Integrative Medicine. I feel excited about what I am learning.

Question and Answers

Looking back, was there anything in your childhood or upbringing that you think led to your burnout?

Being the oldest to immigrant parents, I felt an unspoken responsibility to act according to the traditions my parents grew up with. I never fully understood what that meant until situations arose, like the high school prom or dating. I didn't know how to express what I was feeling, but I wanted to be accepted. I felt like being invisible was the only way to clear myself from judgment and scrutiny. I tried to avoid attention and stay under the radar.

Did anything occur in your training that led to your burnout?

I took a transitional year out of school and was confused regarding what specialty I wanted. I was interested in Radiology and felt the competition was too fierce to find a program, especially without going directly into it after med school. I came across a website and submitted my resume. Within a few days, I got numerous recruiters contacting me for jobs. To make a long story short, I ended up taking a consulting position for a large healthcare company and got trained in Six Sigma and Lean methodologies. I enjoyed traveling all over the country to analyze throughput in the radiology department and also looking at other projects, such as bed capacity in the Emergency department. After doing this for two years, I longed to be in patient care again and completed two additional years of training in Family Medicine. I was very excited to be a resident again. Being away from clinical medicine made me appreciate being back at it and seeing patients. So I wouldn't say anything specific in residency or training that led to it.

Was there anything about the system you worked in that led to your episode (s) of burnout?

Over time I felt I had less autonomy. I felt I had to prove myself over and over. I think transferring service areas hurt me. I didn't have those relationships I built with my original setting and faced coupled personal issues. I had a family illness and financial issues at that time. My Dad had a massive bilateral hemisphere stroke, and my husband was having a hard time with his job after moving cross country to get settled. I couldn't find the support I needed at the time.

What helped you overcome your burnout?

Being an integrative fellow has given me a community of health professionals who have a holistic view of care. Feeling that I have options has helped me. Tools of mindfulness, self-compassion, and mind-body medicine have been so useful. The epidural steroid shots I got were very effective in getting me from no function to functional. I felt invisible, but now I feel I matter. I am allowed to take up space, and my feelings are valid. Chronic pain is invisible, but it is real. As a patient, I felt the bias out there against chronic pain. I believe it is an unconscious bias that needs to be brought to light. Integrative medicine modules and lectures taught the pathophysiology of chronic pain, the upregulation of receptors, and patterns of pain that occur.

Did you have a support system?

I have a few good friends to whom I can talk. I am mindful of being around others who are more uplifting.

My husband and daughter understand when I can't participate the way I like to at times because I am having increased symptoms. We have learned to cherish and enjoy the times I am feeling well.

Did anyone notice and reach out to you?

When my Dad had the stroke, a peer physician supporter reached out to me. This was at my first location before I transferred. It was very helpful, and we kept in touch for a little while after the transfer. No one reached out to me after the move to my new location.

How are you thriving today?

Doing the fellowship is helping me. I am also managing my pain by seeing a PT that does spinal manipulation, keeping a ritual, and managing the flare-ups. Practicing mindfulness and self-compassion.

What advice would you give to someone going through burnout?

I would tell them that right now, it feels like there is no way out, but there are many options. There are people who care and can help. You are allowed to take a break and rest. The world will keep going on, and time will not stop for you.

You matter, and you deserve to listen to what your soul is telling you. No one else's opinions matter at the end of the day. Everyone is involved with their issues. Do what is right for you. Listen to your body. Listen to your heart.

What advice would you give to the facilities and administration who are trying to help decrease the rate of physician burnout?

Mentoring sessions and training sessions on mindfulness, self-care, and mind/body medicine that were ongoing would be helpful. I would incorporate it in CME or educational time.

Have less stringent requirements on metrics and more emphasis on the entire healthcare team. This will include the well-being of the patient, health practitioner, and healthcare team as one.

About Rita Gupta D.O MPA
Dr. Gupta is a Family Medicine and finishing up fellowship in Integrative Medicine. She offers coaching to women to help guide them to feel better in control of their life and live well with health challenges.

Rkg85260@gmail.com

Shilpi Pradhan, MD

Why is it so hard to write about burnout or moral injury or whatever you want to call it? Is it because it's still stigmatized in my head? Is it because I'm afraid to acknowledge it? Is it because I want to move on from it? But I'm compelled to write to share and help others who may be going through the same thing. It is not a one-and-done thing. It lives with you, inside of you, sitting in the shadows, submissive but still present.

Thinking back, when was the first time...probably in private practice. When was the last time, maybe a few years ago at the start of the pandemic when I cried myself to sleep every night, afraid I would bring home Covid and die a suffocating death and spread it which would kill my entire family. How do we move past it? We just do. We're resilient by nature, especially physicians. But support is everything.

The first time of overwhelm, just steps before burnout, was in 3rd year of medical school, trying to learn, apply our written knowledge to taking care of patients, learning how to write a note, use the computer system, and keeping up with the scut demands of running to the cafeteria to get ketchup for residents. But senior residents who grade you don't see all the crap and don't remember what it was like. But each change of rotation, each break of vacation helps reset the clock.

In residency, I remember having to be responsible for "the phone". It was still the time of pagers and we had one portable phone for the clinic that the first-year Ophthalmology resident was responsible for. No one else would answer it, even if they were sitting right next to it, no help. After one outcry to ask for help, and being told to suck it up, I would just become cold, a shell of a person. Perhaps I was in burnout but I was able to keep going. I completed tasks to finish the day, get patients scheduled, and out the door, stone-faced, cold, and probably rude to some. It was the only way to stay alive. Shut out the whole world and shut up, no complaints. It was a good method to deal with clinic days that ended at 9 pm sometimes and just keep going. Breaks and rotation changes with changing senior residents and attendings help reset the clock of overwhelm.

In fellowship, it all came to a head when I had an unplanned pregnancy and the loss of my twins at 21 weeks gestation sending me into my first real suicidal ideations. There were many other factors but after taking one month off and listening to too many rumors of too many things being said about me, coming back and finishing my duties in bilateral wrist braces for bilateral de Quervain's tendonitis would eventually require surgery on both wrists. These rumors still sometimes swirled in my head but I was grieving, crying myself to sleep with the wooden square urn of my twins' ashes. Depression was my constant companion behind the familiar cold mask of getting the work done. I was doing more Lasik with the new practice I was joining, and then taking one month off for secret bilateral wrist surgeries and taking and passing my oral board exam. No one knew. No one needed to know. Breaks again helped reset the overwhelm, the grief. Writing helped. Setting up our Twin Angels Scholarship Fund at my alma mater helped. Time helped. It saved me from burnout.

Then one day, months later, in the middle of my surgery day, I knew I was pregnant again, I started contracting, feeling dizzy, and weak. My staff urged me to lie down. They helped me make the difficult decision to cancel the rest of my surgeries for the day, and talk to patients. One couple, without caring for my well-being or even theirs by wanting to have surgery with a surgeon who was feeling dizzy, yelled at me…only concerned for the inconvenience of not having their cataract surgery. A verbal slap in the face. Figuratively face-planting me into burnout deep in the earth. Heavy with their words hanging in the air, words degrading me, and my surgical expertise, everything hit me hard. The sacrifices I'd made, the babies I'd lost, the pain and surgeries I had to endure and survive. It was the first time I was in burnout. I just quit. It wasn't the first time I felt like I had to be cold-faced to continue. However, it was the first time I refused to accept it. Probably because there was another life on the line, my unborn child's. There was nothing else to do. My practice supported me. But I lived in fear. Fear of losing another baby. Fear of wasting my education. Fear of needing to pay my large malpractice tail. Fear of how I would pay my student loans back. Fear was a constant companion. Slowly with time, burnout led the way back to overwhelm; which in turn allowed me to return to "normal" in my PTSD and pregnant state.

I read voraciously about miscarriages and preterm labor. I found a high-risk OB and saw him, putting all my hopes for a miracle baby on his expertise. I learned that I was gluten intolerant and gluten gave me severe diarrhea and had been linked to preterm labor, contractions, and miscarriages. I went gluten-free for the first time and started on injections and medications. I didn't do anything that would put a strain on my body. I didn't fly, I didn't go down into our basement, and I didn't lift anything heavy. I didn't even stand for extended periods. Living with flashbacks of holding my lifeless twins, I fought back the tears for the health of my new baby. My husband and I were relieved that the labor and delivery period went by and we were blessed with our child. Afterwards, I struggled with when to go back to work, where to go back to work, and how to go back to work. After over 18 months off, I restarted with trepidation but open arms from an amazing university. It was good for my soul. I was operating again. I was teaching and loved it. I had my beautiful baby. But with my husband's fellowship completed, and after months apart, I moved to a new state, new practice, and started over.

Everything seemed ok until I got pregnant again. Now it was an active choice to stop practicing and put this new baby's health over my work again. But I had to leave that practice as an extended time off was not acceptable. I tried to find another position but ultimately started my practice, which allowed me to thrive initially but there was a downward spiral. I could go home during lunch break and nurse my baby and bond. I didn't pay myself for the first 4 years of practice (a huge mistake) as my husband made enough for us but it led to me feeling less than worthy. I fought for fair contracts with insurance carriers. I fought and lost a battle to get paid for taking 24/7 calls for a local hospital after 6 years of free work. I started working all the time. Charting in the middle of the night, seeing patients in the ER instead of putting my kids to bed.
Once on vacation, I spent 12 hours in an ER and inpatient for chest pain. Thereafter, I found plant-based medicine. I became vegan for a few months and my irregular PCOS cycles regulated and I had a surprise pregnancy at age 40. I was seeing 25+ patients per day and doing 4-8 cataract surgeries per week and sleeping from 12-2 am, then charting from 2-4 am every night while 21 weeks pregnant. I was trying to finish notes and billing from 2-4 months ago. I thought I was superhuman but I was tired. I thought I could handle it all. I stopped paying myself again anticipating needing to stop working, knowing I still had to pay the office rent and pay my staff.

Then it happened again…contractions. I was surrounded by the support this time. Supporting husband, parents, staff, and patients who cared. I stopped working, hugged my babies, and had our third child. I went back to work 6 weeks postpartum after my first C-section and decided something must change. I changed our schedule and limited the max number of patients per day to 18 with an average of 12. I just couldn't do it anymore. But I was trying to be happy, struggling with the worst postpartum depression I'd ever had. I actively made a decision to slow down my work schedule and it was helping. Damn the pandemic. The worldwide Covid-19 pandemic of 2020 brought factors we could not control. It brought fear back into my life. I could not get N95 masks, supposedly the only thing that would prevent us from getting this deadly virus. Every time I was able to place an order for the masks, they would get canceled. I was constantly hunting for gloves, hand sanitizer and Clorox wipes to stock my clinic to see patients. I was scrambling to get personal protective equipment (PPE). I kept our doors open for all emergencies to keep my practice afloat.

It was the second time I was in burnout, worried about everything, life, death, money and battling postpartum depression, which is unlike any other depression I had experienced. The physician communities on Facebook were supportive and listening to coaching calls and engaging in anything to control my life helped. This pulled me out slowly like a lifesaver raft on a rope that I just kept holding onto, one grasp of the rope at a time, one foot in front of the other. I read and went from plant-based medicine to studying and passing the Lifestyle Medicine boards. It gave me something to do, a goal to complete. This episode of burnout was in some ways better and some ways worse than the first. With family and friends' support, I was able to climb out quicker than prior, and the time off from work due to the pandemic gave me a chance to reset. Time off and being away from work do help to heal.

Overwhelm is when you are given too many things to deal with but can muster the strength to conquer and keep going. You can handle it, maybe with some emotions and tears but you can keep going. With burnout, it's to the point where you cannot even muster that strength. Like I experienced, one just becomes cold, maybe unresponsive, somewhat lifeless. You must recognize when you are both overwhelmed and in burnout and must take a moment or sometimes months to reset. The pandemic, despite its challenges, helped give me the time at home I needed to reset, to step away from the stress at work and the world, and to take care of myself and my kids.

Being vegan and gluten-free again, cycles regulated again, I was shocked to be pregnant again at the age of 42 with my 4th child. So much fear of how to support my growing family, and my practice but having done this before kept me out of burnout. Somehow, even when I got Covid pneumonia and was hospitalized struggling to breathe (pregnancy and post-partum is a higher risk of severe Covid), my 4-week-old baby was hospitalized with Covid, somehow, we kept going. Only because I had a community and friends willing to help feed my kids home-cooked food when I was not able to, with money for groceries or a meal train, we were able to grasp straws and stay afloat.
In reflecting what threw me into deep burnout was the lack of human care for me and my lack of care for myself. We can take care of each other and help prevent burnout. Social connectedness is one of the pillars of Lifestyle

Medicine and truly may be the most important pillar to help support ourselves from burnout. Humans need each other. Each time I was thrown into overwhelm or full-fledged burnout, it was because of a lack of compassion from my fellow human. Each time I was pulled out, it was by being surrounded by the love of my husband, my family and fellow doctors. With this love, I was able to continue to thrive and restructure my life and my practice. I have strict limits now on my time in the office. I will not stay there after 4 pm except in emergencies only. I needed to help with the morning routine at home, so I moved my clinic start time to 9 am. When leaving early for surgery created strain for months, I brainstormed and moved my surgery start time down to 9 am from 8 am. Yes, it's unusual. Who starts operating at 9 am? I do. I am accommodating to the needs of my family and it keeps me centered on the most important part of my life. Sometimes, we don't even realize how we can help ourselves until we step back and look at each strain and how to relieve it. I'm not sure how else to explain it but hopefully reading my story helps you. Inhale. Exhale out. Re-center. However long it takes. Change what you need to thrive. Constantly re-evaluate what is needed. And continue, together and supported.

Questions and Answers

Did anything occur in your training that led to your burnout?

Answer: The residency had an unwritten strict definition of who does what without any leeway and help. As I understood the system with a stark awakening that had not occurred in medical school or internship, I knew not to ask for help. The culture of medicine, especially in the surgical subspecialties with the typical statement "You can call me if you need me, but know it is seen as a sign of weakness", is a culture that forces you to learn what to do by yourself unless necessary. Fortunately, this culture is dying with the current times and better support of the training residents.

Was there anything about the system you worked in that led to your episode (s) of burnout?

Answer: I would say the above answer explains the old system well from when I was in residency almost 20 years ago. The specific episode that forced my realization was about the emergency phone in the resident clinic as mentioned in my story. This carried true on-call seeing patients in the ER as well. I learned my senior residents and attendings were available if I needed them and they were required to be present, especially for emergency surgery. My fear that I couldn't call them unless necessary was beneficial in helping me learn and look up many things on my own and learn when I truly needed help. I did not burn out in residency so I'm not sure this applies as it was a good teaching tool for me. It may be different for others.

What do you think caused the burnout?

Answer: I think the lack of support and compassion from my surgery patient is what led to my first episode of burnout. The lack of support for small private practices during the pandemic without access to proper PPE led to the second episode. Yes, the small PPP loan program from the government helped pay my staff salary for 8 weeks but as I had not paid myself, it did not help with any salary for myself or any other expenses for keeping the doors open of my office. The access to PPE to help keep me and my family safe is what led to the second episode. I also had a 4-month-old baby at that time so I was juggling baby needs, breastfeeding, and zoom/school coordination for my older two kids at that time as well.

What helped you overcome your burnout?

Support. Human compassion. People caring about me and taking time for myself helped the most. In my two major episodes of burnout, my family and husband's support helped so much as well as the concern from other people including my practice of being understanding during my first episode and my patients for my second episode.

How are you thriving today?

Answer: I am thriving by making my schedule, allowing me to put my children and my family first. My staff and patients' understanding of my schedule and the surgery center's understanding of my start times helps me thrive.

What work are you doing that you find fulfilling?

Answer: I enjoy Ophthalmology and I love talking to patients about their eye condition, especially dry eyes. With my education and board certification in Lifestyle Medicine (LM), I also enjoy talking to patients about the six pillars of LM

What advice would you give to someone going through burnout?
Answer: I would say to reach out to your support system. People may not know you need help. It may be hard but reach out to them and you will be surprised how much your family and friends will be willing to help if they know you are struggling. Consider coaching or listening to coaching podcasts as even just listening to other people being coached or struggling with the same things you are can be immensely beneficial. People, including doctors, can consider therapy from qualified individuals.

What advice would you give to the facilities and administration who are trying to help decrease the rate of physician burnout?

Answer: The support from the leadership in each field is critical to helping residents and physicians feel as if they are more than a cog in a wheel but an individual who matters. I'm not sure what system changes have already occurred in the last 20 years as I've been in solo private practice for over 7 years but perhaps an interview at the start and end of each rotation or quarter to get feedback and see what additional support the doctor needs and what can be done to meet those needs.

What advice, if any, would you give to the facilities that can do better when it comes to improving burnout rates of physicians (those facilities that appear to have a lack of interest in helping to improve conditions)?

Answer: I know many facilities are engaging coaching experts to provide physician group coaching, and that would be a great start.

About Shilpi Pradhan, MD

Dr. Pradhan is solo private practice board-certified Ophthalmologist, board-certified Lifestyle Medicine doctor, small business entrepreneur, mom of four children with her husband, Dr. Kumar Abhishek, mom of self-published authors Shreya Pradhan and Ankit Pradhan, philanthropist including the Twin Angels Abhishek Pradhan Endowed Scholarship at Washington University in St. Louis School of Medicine, donates monthly to the local food bank FeedMore, and personal finance enthusiast and real estate investor.

www.eyedoctormd.org

Sadaf R Lodhi, DO FACOOG

What do you want to be when you grow up? Before I could even answer that question, my mother would answer for me. "She wants to become a doctor." Ever since I was 5 years old, I remember being told that I would be a doctor. My parents always wanted at least one of their children to become a physician. My father had wanted to be a doctor when he was younger himself and had gotten into medical school, but due to unforeseen circumstances was not able to attend. So now it was up to one of the children to fulfill his wish. We all had the same opportunity. However, I was determined to be the one that would fulfill my father's dream.

In undergraduate, I did well in the sciences. I got into medical school right after undergrad. As soon as I entered medical school, I felt a sense of overwhelm. Everyone seemed to be much smarter than me and seemed to know just how to study. I was failing my first semester of medical school. I was so ashamed I didn't know whom to talk to or ask for help. I went to the medical school advisor and asked him what I could do. He suggested I find some friends to study with. I didn't know very many people and was living in the graduate student dorms. Every other day we would hear about someone dropping out of medical school. I questioned if I should drop out of medical school myself and would call up my mother and cry to her on the phone. I soon found a group to study with and graduated from medical school.

I went on to do an OBGYN residency. OB is a specialty that either you hate or love. Unfortunately for me, I loved it. The residency was very grueling, with early mornings and late evenings. I sacrificed a lot of personal freedom, time, energy, and youth in my residency, as do most physicians in training. Mental health and wellness was not something discussed back then - had it been, I definitely would have had a diagnosis of burnout after my first year. I hated the residency, and my senior residents did a lot of hazing of the junior residents. Eventually, I became a senior resident and vowed never to treat my junior residents the same. Fast forward to my first few years as an attending. I enjoyed what I did most of the time, but taking call took all I had. I hated call. I hated the stress of being on and not knowing what could walk through the doors at any point of day or night.

I did this for 12 years as an attending and then decided to open up my own medispa and gynecology practice. I always wanted to do something more than be an OBGYN. I worked hard at this practice, but it never became profitable. I ended up doing laborist work just so I could keep my doors open at the clinic.

Eventually, it became too much to work in the evening as a laborist and in the day as a private practice owner. I was getting exhausted and decided to close down my private practice. When it came time to liquidate the furniture in the office, I felt as if I was giving up my baby for adoption. Every piece of the office represented my sweat equity in trying to establish my own private practice. My autonomy. I felt as if I had failed and let myself down. The process of selling off my office piecemeal was so difficult that I never wanted to own another brick-and-mortar for any business that I would start in the future. I quit private practice and went all in on my laborist job but became tired of being on call and the politics of laborists vs. private practice doctors vs. nurses.

I decided to do locums. The year that I did locums was by far one of the best years I have ever had. I was able to travel, spend time with family, and practice medicine on my own terms. I loved it but wanted to be a part of a hospital system again, so I worked for one. I enjoyed the people that I worked with at the hospital. I also discovered that I loved teaching, speaking, and writing. I taught medical students and residents. I spoke at grand rounds and at collaborations with other hospitals, and I wrote policies for the hospital. It was great until it wasn't. I decided to leave and found my real love, which was to be on social media to educate and empower women on sexual health and wellness. I was still doing locums so my clinical skills would not lapse; however, my time was split between social media, podcasting, and locums. I also became a life coach but specifically an intimacy coach for women. I found that diversifying what I did and giving breath to what I love made me feel passionate about medicine again. I didn't feel the overbearing weight of call or having to deal with birth control refills in the middle of the night. I could practice medicine on my own terms and have the autonomy to decide my own schedule. I felt in control of my life by being able to schedule work around my life instead of scheduling my life around my work. I fell in love with medicine all over again. I felt that I could live out my dream of helping others while at the same time helping myself. By struggling to reinvent myself over the course of several years, I see now that I was burned out. Now I am creating a life for myself where I can practice medicine, empower and educate women and make a global impact. It took time and lots of wrong turns to discover my truth, but in retrospect, I would not change a thing except to be more kind and compassionate to myself.

Questions and Answers

Looking back, was there anything in your childhood or upbringing that you think led to your burnout?

Being highly driven and competitive. Constantly comparing my achievements to those of others.

Did anything occur in your training that led to your burnout?

The first year of residency was very difficult, and there definitely was some hazing that happened by the senior residents toward the junior residents. We would get told to do all the menial work with no one to help us. It was expected to do 36 hours of call. That was customary, and to do it without complaining.

Was there anything about the system you worked in that led to your episode (s) of burnout? What do you think caused the burnout?

OBGYN is a very demanding specialty, thus the people that go into this specialty are also very demanding. There were two incidents when my children were young and hospitalized for RSV, I was not able to take time off. I felt awful as a parent and decided that I would never let my job get in the way of taking care of my children. Also being part of an academic hospital where the environment was toxic and punitive. There was constant turnover of physicians and staff within the span of one year. I was hired to lead a program for which there was no support and the other disciplines were not on board. I came up with the processes to run the collaborative program, but no one to run the program with.

Even with all of that, I kept going. I think what caused the burnout was the idea that physicians - no matter what happens to them, personal or professional - must keep working. It did not matter that I had sick children at home or that I was tasked to create a program for postpartum women that never had any support, I was expected to make it successful anyway. The physician is seen as a superhuman being that is expected to neglect all needs.

To ask for help is seen as a sign of weakness, especially in surgical specialties. To that end, physicians and myself included, have a hard time asking for help, even when we are drowning. Physicians put themselves last when they should be putting themselves first.

What helped you overcome your burnout?

Finding a life coach to help me to go over the feelings that I was having and the lies that I was telling myself. Discovering what resonated with me and finding a community of like-minded professionals helped me uncover what I truly enjoyed and what I wanted to do.

Did you have a support system?

I found a few coaching programs. One was a one: one program, and the other was a group coaching program.

Did anyone notice and reach out to you?

No, but I wish they would have so the experience would not have been so isolating.

How are you thriving today?

I joined a coaching program that has helped. I also have revamped what I want to do. I started teaching sexual health on social media and recording podcasts. I have diversified what I do so that I am not doing the same things over and over again. I am creating a space for myself that does not involve the hospital, call, or having to put myself in high stakes situations where there is constant stress and somebody's life on the line. A position where I can make a global impact without ever having to leave my family.

What advice would you give to someone going through burnout?

Find time to connect with family and friends. Plan dates with friends. Do things outside of medicine. Travel. Practice mindfulness and yoga. Exercise. There is hope outside of burnout. Find a life/career coach that will help you to find the things that you love and how you can incorporate that into your job.

What advice would you give to the facilities and administration who are trying to help decrease the rate of physician burnout?

Encourage physicians to find communities, go outside, and do things that they enjoy that are outside of medicine.

What advice if any, would you give to the facilities that can do better when it comes to improving burnout rates of physicians (those facilities that appear to have a lack of interest in helping to improve conditions)

Paid time off for mental health days - at least one per month

About Sadaf R Lodhi, DO FACOOG

Dr. Lodhi is a board-certified OBGYN and executive coach for women based in New York. She graduated from the University of Michigan with honors, receiving a Bachelor of Science in Biochemistry. She acquired her Doctorate in Osteopathic Medicine at Michigan State University and completed her residency in gynecology and obstetrics in Michigan. Dr. Lodhi earned her certification as a life and executive coach from Rutgers University. She is a sex counselor and educator. As a practicing OBGYN in New York for over 20 years, her mission has always been to empower and educate women. She helps women with sexual confidence through coaching so that they can find pleasure in their relationships. She believes that all women, regardless of their backgrounds, have the potential to live life to its fullest.

www.drsadaf.com

Melissa Hankins, MD CPC

"He would just be better off if I wasn't around anymore. He'd have his dad to take care of him, and at least his dad would show up for him. He wouldn't be constantly disappointed the way I disappoint him because I'm never around for him or for things in his life. I'm always disappointing him, telling him, "No, Mommy doesn't have time. I have to work." Even at home, at night, and on weekends, I tell him this because I just can't catch up with everything—it's impossible. I just can't keep doing this to him."

Those were the thoughts I had the day after my son's fourth birthday—thoughts that my son was actually better off with me dead. Those were the thoughts going through my head as I got dressed to leave the house to go to the outpatient clinic where I worked as a full-time psychiatrist. Those were the thoughts I had as I continued to put work first in my life above all else--above my son, above my relationship with my fiancé, above anyone and anything else in my life, and certainly above myself (hell, anything for myself wasn't even on the playing field).

I didn't kill myself (a fact that may be obvious because you are reading this). What I DID do was to notice that, as fleeting as those thoughts were, they were thoughts that weren't okay for me to be having. I said to myself, "Well, that's not good. Here you are, a psychiatrist helping people with their own mental health, and you're having thoughts that your son would be better off if you were dead. That's not cool." At that moment, I made the decision that I was going to tell my supervisor that I needed to take an immediate medical leave—however, I needed to tell him after my clinic ended because patients, of course, come first.

I didn't think it would come as a complete surprise to him. My supervisor had known for a while that I was completely overwhelmed with my workload and trying to balance work and home life. Add to that the many other factors that culminated in my reaching my breaking point. I wasn't allowed to close my panel to new patients because "behavioral health wasn't a money-maker, and we had to justify our existence to the other medical specialties" in the clinic. I was chronically exhausted, typically up until 2 or 3 AM, trying to finish charting (and was still well over 100 charts behind), answer patient messages, and follow up on lab results. My relationship with my fiancé had imploded, and he had moved out three months prior. Despite my trying to maintain my professionalism in front of colleagues, I had cried on various occasions at work (including during various meetings with my supervisor) because I just couldn't hold it all in. The backdrop to all of this was that I had increasingly felt for some time that my values and the ways in which I felt patients needed to be helped were not in alignment with those of the organization.

I met with my supervisor at the end of the day and with tears in my eyes, told him I needed to take an immediate medical leave. I didn't tell him that I had some brief suicidal ideation, but I did tell him I wasn't doing well at all, and I just couldn't keep all of this up. This happened on a Wednesday. I remember that distinctly because he looked at me and said awkwardly, "Okay, I guess I'll need to find out what to do to make that happen. In the meantime, can you come in for the rest of the week because you have a lot of patients scheduled, and they need to be seen? We can't give them to anyone else because they're already seeing patients."

Being the very well-conditioned physician I was, having endured years of medical school, residency, and being an attending during which it was constantly drilled into my head that patients ALWAYS come first (unless you are actively dying), followed by your colleagues and organization, I, of course, said that I would come in to see patients for the next two days. That's what a good physician is supposed to do, and I was nothing if not a good physician.

The next morning, while attempting to get dressed to take my son to school and get myself to work, I had my first (and only) MAJOR panic attack. I couldn't get dressed. There was no way I could even attempt to leave the house. I called the office, sobbing on the phone to the administrative assistant, trying to explain what was happening and that there was no way I could come in that day. I told her I had already told the clinical supervisor I was taking a leave of absence. She said, "Okay. We'll take care of it. You just feel better."

I hung up the phone, and after about 15 minutes, I was much calmer and was able to get dressed. It then occurred to me that I could see my son's ice-skating lesson. It was his last day of lessons sponsored by his school, and for the first time, I didn't have patients to see. I had missed all the previous lessons because I had to work, and it had broken my heart to miss them. However, I was finally free to go watch him. The panic was gone, and in its place was joy and excitement. I took him to school, went and watched his lesson, and loved and was fully present for every second of it.

When I got home and went near my work laptop, I started to feel anxious and mildly panicky again. When I was away from it, I felt fine. There was a clear link between my anxiety and panic being tied to work.

I thought I was going to be out of work for two weeks (because, of course, I HAD to get back to my patients and couldn't leave my colleagues in the lurch). As it turned out, I was on leave for ten months before resigning. During those ten months, for the first time ever, I invested time, energy, and money in ME and my well-being—my self-care, my healing, and my growth (in all ways, including spiritual). I meditated, journaled, received energy work (and did some on myself), worked with an EFT (Emotional Freedom Techniques; an evidence-based mind-body-energy technique) "tapping" practitioner (which I myself was becoming trained in), a coach, and a therapist. I uncovered, acknowledged, and released several of my limiting beliefs and the emotions that had anchored them in place. I exercised, ate well, slept, and played. I spent time with my son, time with friends, and time alone. I went on walks, connected with nature, and explored and deepened my connection with The Divine and with myself.

I thought about the ways I REALLY wanted to be helping people and the people I wanted to be helping. I knew I didn't want to continue to practice medicine as a psychiatrist in the same ways I had been doing up until that point. I was truly convinced that if I did that, psychiatry would literally kill me. I also knew that I wanted to find ways to support others in healthcare, particularly physicians (this was in 2012—before "physician coaching" was available and prevalent as it is now).

I began thinking about what skills, talents, and expertise I had gathered over time that might serve me (and help me to serve others) in charting a new path —one outside of psychiatry. I had obtained my certification as an executive coach five years prior, in 2007, while pregnant with my son (because even then, something told me that I didn't want to remain working in healthcare forever), and I began to think of ways I could use it in a way that felt authentic to whom I had become. I wanted to combine it somehow with the skills and expertise I had gained as a psychiatrist in recognizing and understanding patterns in human behavior and use that knowledge to help people understand the reasons behind their actions and change the ones that no longer served them. I further wanted to combine all of that with my exponentially increasing fascination with and love for Emotional Freedom Techniques (or, EFT Tapping, which I was training in to become certified), and the power it has in creating deep levels of transformation in the emotions, beliefs, thought patterns, and behaviors in people. However, I wasn't quite sure how to meld all of these interests into a cohesive new career path (to be honest, I was also still a bit scared to do so), so I returned to working as a psychiatrist, this time at a different organization that was slightly more aligned with my values at the time, while I figured it all out.

While at my new outpatient clinic job, I began incorporating EFT Tapping into several of my appointments with various patients, with amazing results. Not only were the patients amazed, the therapists and nurses who sat in on some of these meetings with our mutual patients were amazed at the shifts they witnessed. Soon, some of the staff began to approach me, asking if I would do EFT Tapping with them to help them manage the daily and ongoing stresses and overwhelm many of them experienced working in a strained healthcare system with an unending workload and limited resources. I began offering group tapping sessions at lunchtime, after which various staff asked to continue to work with me privately for individual EFT Tapping and coaching services.

That was the beginning of my entrepreneurial career as a coach and EFT Tapping practitioner. Fast forward several years, and now, my EFT Tapping and Coaching business (Melissa Hankins Coaching) is my full-time work (having transitioned out of working as a physician). Through my business, I focus on working with physicians and other high performers to address burnout and perfectionism and empower self-agency and well-being, and with organizations (including healthcare organizations) in creating psychologically safe work environments. I have spoken at a number of organizations on the topics of managing stress, addressing burnout, connecting with the power of emotions, releasing perfectionism, and identifying and managing trauma when coaching clients and in the workplace. I also serve as faculty at an accredited coach-training organization that utilizes a coaching model that focuses on training coaches to acknowledge and incorporate a whole-person approach when working with coaching clients.

I love what I do, and I've been able to combine all the parts of psychiatry, coaching, and energy work that I love and enjoy, creating a way of helping people that truly resonates with my values, my interests, and who I am as a human being. I have the freedom to evolve and grow in ways that I find fulfilling and that allows me to better serve my clients, while also making a bigger impact in the world by helping individuals, groups, and organizations create higher levels of personal and professional transformation, improve individual and collective well-being, and educate and work with others in supporting and optimizing emotional and mental health in work environments.

As difficult as it was to go through my burnout journey, I'm very grateful to have experienced it. It was the wake-up call I needed to truly show up and actively and consciously be present in and create my life with intentionality, love, and compassion for the human being and soul that I am. That panic attack that prevented me from going to work that day in 2012 is something I've come

to refer to as "God taking me out when I couldn't or wouldn't take myself out." It gave me an opportunity to finally listen to the many messages my mind, body, and soul had been telling me for months (if not years)—messages telling me to:
slow down,
enjoy life,
be present in the now,
you are worthy and deserving of love, peace, and happiness,
you are enough just as you are.

Looking back, I've come to recognize that much of my burnout stemmed from my own "need" to be perfect and the fear and shame tied to being seen by others as anything other than perfect. While I'm not negating the fact that my work environment and the systems within it most certainly did contribute to my burnout (including the unending workload, not having enough support staff to delegate to, and the increasing values mismatch), I truly believe that if I had had less of a need to seek and receive the approval of others, I would have either been more vocal about expressing my own needs for more support and desires to pilot new programs for patients and staff that better used my newly acquired and increasing skill sets and interests, or left that job and created something of my own before the situation became so dire for me. I would have had the courage, the confidence, and the self-love to simply be and trust in myself—the version of myself that I truly am (vs. the version that I had felt I needed to be in order to be liked, loved, and accepted by others).

It has been through consistently engaging in and doing the deep and transformative internal work through EFT Tapping (primarily), coaching, and some therapy that has helped me to acknowledge, identify, and release many of the self-limiting beliefs, subconscious thought patterns, emotional anchors, and no-longer-helpful behaviors and actions that were preventing me from creating, working, and living in ways that were much more aligned with the ways I TRULY want to be experiencing all aspects of my life. While I do have more work to do in continuing to uncover and release the beliefs and patterns that no longer serve the person I consciously choose to be, I have come so far in embracing, honoring, appreciating, accepting, and loving the person I am, which has given me tremendous freedom in allowing myself to show up professionally and personally as the totality of ME.

I love being on this journey of self-discovery and uncovering (not changing—I spent most of my life changing and hiding to appease other people and protect myself from their rejection or judgment) the truth of me. While it's not always easy, it is always fascinating and absolutely rewarding. It has given me inner peace, increased confidence, greater self-love and love for others, more acceptance and compassion for myself and others, more joy, deeper levels of connectedness with myself and others, and more willingness to do, try, and create new things in my life and business/career. And I truly love helping other physicians to do the same.

To that end, some KEY TAKEAWAYS I've discovered on my journey through burnout and self-discovery that may help others are:

You do not have to be everything to everyone (in fact, it is impossible to do so). Most people (including employers) will try to convince you that their "asks" and demands are needs that must be fulfilled by only you when, in truth, many of those asks are actually "wants" that, if fulfilled, may make their lives easier but often at your expense. Take your time to sift through the many "asks" by others in your life, and decide if it is something you truly want to do. (If it truly is something you "must" do—keep in mind, there are very few "must do"s in life--find a way to make it more enjoyable, and look for the ways that it may help you learn something new about yourself, the other person, or the situation.)

Know that YOU ARE ENOUGH, JUST AS YOU ARE. Trying to fit into someone else's idea of who you "should" be is not about you; it is about that other person and the belief system that they are using to guide and shape their life. You get to choose whether or not you want to define yourself, your decisions, and your life (professionally or personally) by the "shoulds" of other people (including the people—dead or alive--you allow to take up space inside your own head).

You are allowed to have boundaries for what you will and will not do. Learn to set and honor your boundaries for what is a YES vs. what is a NO. It's less about you setting boundaries with others, and more about you knowing for yourself what your boundaries are and honoring and loving yourself enough to maintain them. Always keep in mind that when you are saying "Yes" to one thing, you are saying "No" to something else. Make sure you are saying "Yes" because you truly want to, not simply because you think you "should" or because you're worried about what other people may think of you if you don't do it.

Perfectionism is a made-up, impossible, unachievable construct—do not waste your precious time or energy trying to reach it. If perfectionism is something you struggle with (as many of us physicians and high performers do), work on uncovering and understanding what need is driving it. Perfectionism generally develops in childhood, and while it may seem to have aided us on our journeys to becoming physicians, perfectionism actually robs us of our ability to experience joy, fulfillment, and the ability to be fully present and to be our true selves.

For me, perfectionism was rooted in childhood feelings and beliefs that in order for me to be loved, accepted, and feel safe and secure in my family, I had to be the "perfect" child. This translated into my trying to make the life of my mom (a single mother struggling with raising three children while working as a nurse in the midst of battling depression, anxiety, a history of abuse, very low self-esteem, and systemic lupus until she succumbed to the latter when I was 16yo) easier and happier through my being the "perfect" daughter, student, and the "perfect White girl in a Black girl's body" (I'm bi-racial, having much of my childhood in Utah with my White mother and her extended family, some of whom were openly racist and not always safe for me to be around as a Black girl). While your "need to be perfect" may not have the same roots as mine, perfectionism stems from needing to feel a sense of belonging, being loved, and/or feeling safe, which is often done through attempting to control outcomes. I encourage you to explore your drivers for perfectionism and find other, healthier ways to fulfill those needs.

Emotions are data--they are messengers signaling to us what our needs and true desires are vs the ways our limiting beliefs, thoughts, and actions are leading us to show up in our lives. Learn to tune into your emotions and use them to help guide you to transform beliefs, shift thoughts, develop behaviors, and take action that is truly aligned with your desired outcomes, personally and professionally. Unfortunately, as physicians, we have been conditioned to suppress our emotions, hampering us from not only connecting with our negative emotions but also dampening our ability to fully feel and express our positive emotions. This cuts us off from a key component of our internal guidance system as we try to navigate our life's journey and our desire for joy, balance, and fulfillment (and anything else you truly desire). Experiencing emotions is a somatic experience, a "felt sense." It's important to engage in practices that help you to be more present in your body, not just inside your head. EFT Tapping and other mindfulness-based activities can help with that.

Don't go it alone. Working with a coach, EFT Tapping practitioner, or therapist can offer you support, offer a place for self-discovery, healing, and self-empowerment, and literally change your life for the better. As physicians, we are used to being experts and leaders and doing things on our own. However, working with one of the aforementioned types of professionals can help you identify your blind spots (areas where your subconscious, often limiting, beliefs are hiding out, yet are guiding many—if not most—of your thoughts, behaviors, actions, and outcomes), which is often KEY to creating real change in your life. It can save you time (saving years, not simply months), create more money (while it does cost money to hire these individuals, the resulting changes in mindset that occur when working with an EFT Tapping practitioner and/or coach often allow you to make decisions that result in greater income opportunities and/or pursuing and achieving your dreams in other areas, which is often priceless), improve your mental, physical, and emotional energy, and help you feel more fulfilled and joyful, both personally and professionally.

And, finally, if you are a healthcare organization wanting to better support your staff, it is vital that you have a process by which you regularly CHECK IN with your physicians, providers, and other staff, ASK QUESTIONS, TRULY LISTEN TO THEIR ANSWERS, and TAKE ACTION BASED ON THOSE ANSWERS. Find out what they need in order to feel more supported in their day-to-day work, as well as in their longer-term professional goals. While you may not be able to make large-scale changes right away (though it is important to gradually work towards those things), it is important that you take immediate action on any of the smaller, easier to implement requests that could make a significant difference in how a physician or provider is able to manage their clinical day or workload. And, if you aren't getting feedback from your staff, it's because they either do not feel safe to do so (meaning, there is a lack of psychological safety in your workplace, and you need to take immediate steps to work on creating a psychologically safe workplace), or there is a significant lack of trust that anything the staff says they need will be acted upon by the organization (this is often due to a lack of transparency and history of inaction on the part of the organization), or both.

While my life and story are ever-evolving (as are all of our lives and stories), I truly love the freedom and the willingness to embrace and TRULY BE MYSELF in all areas of my life. My transitioning out of medicine into creating my own path and business as an EFT Tapping practitioner and coach certainly is not the path for most physicians. However, the path that I hope to help other physicians take is one in which they recognize and value their true worth, honor their true desires in creating and experiencing life and work that is joyful and fulfilling, and that they have the courage to embrace and utilize the totality of their gifts, talents, and expertise (even, or, perhaps, especially those things that fall outside the bounds of medicine as we've been taught to practice it) both inside and outside of medicine.

If that is something that you want support in doing or are simply curious about how that might be possible for you (or, if you are an organization if you want to help your physicians and staff experience that for their own benefit and for the benefit of your organization as a whole), please reach out to me to have a conversation. I'd love to discuss with you how I could help support you in living and working as the TRUE AND BEST VERSION OF YOU.

About Melissa Hankins, MD, CPC

Dr. Hankins, is a Mindset and certified Executive Coach, Trauma-Informed EFT Tapping (Emotional Freedom Techniques) practitioner, and Harvard-trained psychiatrist. She is the founder and CEO of Melissa Hankins Coaching, where she coaches physicians and other high performers who often "look great on the outside" but are struggling on the inside. Her clients are wanting to experience more joy and freedom, yet find themselves weighed down with perfectionism, workaholism, burnout, and "should-ing" all over themselves. Dr Hankins supports her clients in identifying and releasing the limiting beliefs and behavior patterns that no longer serve them, helping them rediscover and reconnect to their authentic self as they move forward creating the life and lifestyle they truly desire to live, both inside and outside of work. In addition to leading her own coaching organization, Dr Hankins also serves as faculty for an accredited coach training organization.

In her roles as both coach and educator, Dr Hankins is committed to helping her clients and others understand the impact that traumatic experiences (including experiences that may not be considered traumatic in the traditional sense) from both childhood and adulthood have in the shaping of their thought and behavior patterns, and the results in their adult lives. She is also dedicated to teaching and supporting them in developing skills to shift these patterns to create more desirable outcomes in their professional and personal lives.

Dr Hankins provides individual and group coaching, interactive workshops, and is available for speaking engagements. She has spoken at several healthcare and coaching organizations and corporations, and has appeared on numerous podcasts discussing issues related to burnout, stress, trauma, perfectionism, managing emotions, mindset, and EFT tapping.

Hello@MelissaHankinsCoaching.com

Zarya Rubin, MD

When I was five years old, I was diagnosed with a malignant tumor in my leg and given several months to live. Since I'm still here writing this 45 years later, it was clearly a misdiagnosis, but it planted the seed from a very young age that I would pursue a career in medicine.

A few years later, the tumor recurred, only I kept it a secret, certain that this time it really would kill me. Each night I would go to sleep wondering if I would wake up in the morning or not.

By the time I was 14 years old, the anxiety and grief got to be too much to bear; I finally broke down and confessed to my mother, and we made our way back to the general surgeon to find the same benign hemangioma. I was in the clear, and aside from a nasty scar on the back of my right leg that I often told people was the result of a bear mauling, I continued down the path of becoming a doctor.

A year later, I put my own diagnostic skills to the test and diagnosed myself with scoliosis, and this time I didn't wait. A voice inside me told me that this was actually something very serious that had somehow been missed by everyone around me.
I didn't expect to end up in the office of the orthopedic surgeon that same afternoon, being told that I had very advanced scoliosis and would need surgery and a spinal fusion.

"But, will she be able to be a doctor?" My mother asked. With hesitation, the surgeon replied, "She will," and I breathed a sigh of relief, knowing my dream was still alive.

In retrospect, childhood trauma probably isn't the best way to choose a career path, but I didn't realize that at the time and barreled along full-steam ahead. Well, not quite. I took a rather circuitous route into medicine, stopping at Harvard to study liberal arts and Biology, then on to opera school and a year spent traveling around and working as an au pair in Europe. Clearly, I was running from something, not towards the career I thought I so desperately wanted.

And yet, I wasn't able to put medicine out of my mind. I applied, was accepted, and headed off to medical school, the dream finally becoming a reality. During the first day of Anatomy Lab, I had an emotional breakdown over the cadaver. I wasn't excited to wield a scalpel like my classmates - I wept at the sadness of the lightning bolt rainbow tattoo on the hip of my cadaver. It was once a human being. Someone's mother or grandmother, sister or lover. I wasn't able to divorce the medicine from humanity like we were being groomed to do in an almost militaristic fashion. My anatomy instructor pulled me aside and asked if I had experienced a recent death in the family. I hadn't. Then she gently suggested that maybe this wasn't the right career path for me. The sheer audacity! I doubled down, determined to be the best doctor they had ever seen.

Despite some initial struggles (I had never taken anatomy or physiology or many of the prerequisites my colleagues had), I soon sailed to the top of my class. I was masterful at book learning and problem-solving. I might just be able to do this medicine thing. That was until we got to the clinical rotations and the panic attacks began.

I assumed I was just an anxious person, Jewish, neurotic, or any number of excuses were fabricated for why the sight and smell of a hospital made me want to pass out, vomit, and run for the nearest exit. I began CBT, Cognitive Behavioral Therapy, to try to "fix" my anxiety so I could go back to doctoring. Not once did it occur to anyone (until nearly 25 years later) that I was suffering from PTSD as a result of my childhood trauma and that may be a hospital was the last place on earth I should be.

Somehow, I made it through medical school, but unlike my gunner surgical colleagues who knew exactly what they wanted to do, my bleeding heart pediatric and family medicine colleagues, my antisocial pathology and radiology colleagues, and my I-prefer-talking-to-blood psychiatry colleagues, there was absolutely nothing I enjoyed in medicine. Every rotation was torture, and I couldn't wait for them to end. I dreaded being on call, praying that my pager would not go off. I walked as slowly as I could to CODES, never wanting to be the one to run them and have to pound on the chest of the dying, hearing the crunch of ribs under my fingertips. On surgical rotations, I would pass out in the OR, so they sent me to run the wards since I was adept at dealing with labs and insulin sliding scales and generally had a natural bedside manner that the surgeons lacked.

Somehow, I settled on neurology as a specialization - it was very intellectual, it was so hard that no one wanted to do it (hence the relentless consults), and there wasn't a lot of blood and guts (lumbar punctures are beautifully clean), and I figured that if you had to choose a body part, why the kidney instead of the brain?

Residency was far worse than medical school for myriad reasons; I was far from home, away from family and friends, and I was in a city I hated, where it was bitterly cold most of the year without much daylight. I trudged along. I didn't sleep. I had constant nightmares that often involved being dissected in a cadaver lab, being in a war zone, being shot at, or being murdered. I ran several hours a day just to get out of my own head. I drank too much on the weekends. Anything to escape the horrors of medicine and the toll it took on my empath's heart. I cried with families. I held patient's hands. I made them food on call while the nurses looked at me like I was insane.

I ended up transferring to another neurology residency program in my hometown, thinking that would fix things. It didn't. I was a zombie in the clinic, doing the best I could, but was questioned by my attendings "Are you sure you even *want* to be a neurologist?" Which only made me fight harder to prove them wrong. The support of having all of my family and close friends around did keep the threads of my sanity together long enough to believe that the solution to my problems was more medicine; I would pursue a fellowship.

And so I moved to New York City, to the prestigious Columbia Presbyterian Neurological Institute, and thought if I could just keep specializing, maybe I wouldn't have to see patients anymore. Maybe I could just do research and teach? Maybe I could retire early? Is next year too early? I was in my early 30s and already dreaming about retirement. But I told no one. I was too ashamed.

How do you even begin to entertain the idea that you might leave medicine? That the career you've invested your entire life and bank accounts you don't even have in, was the wrong choice? It was unfathomable. Even when I would get up every morning, drag myself to work, always late, always behind in my charting and EEG reading, staring down the barrel of the subway tunnel and asking myself, "Should I get on the train? Or jump in front of it?" Even then, I still knew I could never leave.

Until one day in June, my best friend called me catatonic and inconsolable. Her husband had been playing frisbee, collapsed on the field, went into cardiac arrest, and died. "But they were able to resuscitate him," I said. "No, he's dead," she whispered. I nearly dropped the phone.

At that moment, my life screeched to a halt, the earth spun on its axis in reverse, and I thought to myself, "I have to get out. If I don't, this will kill me." And so, bit by bit, day by day, I started to allow the idea of leaving medicine in. I gave it room to breathe. My mother sent me a Turkish proverb she found in a cookbook *"No matter how far you've gone down the wrong road, turn back."*

And that was how I finally left. Knowing it was the wrong road. It always had been. I just kept driving. I went on to work in the pharmaceutical industry as the director of research at a healthcare technology startup, I even tried to go back to clinical medicine a decade later and quickly thought better of it. When I first decided to leave medicine, I took up tango dancing, which allowed me to feel something for the first time in decades. I'm now a functional medicine health coach, helping smart, driven, passionate women like myself heal from burnout. I've come full circle, and I've never looked back.

About Zarya Rubin, MD

Dr. Zarya Rubin is a Harvard-educated physician, keynote speaker, and functional medicine health coach specializing in helping smart women heal from burnout. She studied neurology at McGill University and the Neurological Institute at Columbia in New York City. She received her health coach training at the Institute for Integrative Nutrition and went on to train in Functional Medicine at the School of Applied Functional Medicine.

After serving patients in clinical medicine and working in the industry, she realized her true calling was helping others to experience optimal health and wellness. She is a writer, speaker, and private health coach, helping high-achieving women struggling with anxiety, overwhelm, and burnout break the stress cycle and heal from the inside out so they can truly THRIVE.

www.drzarya.com

Arpita Gupta DePalma, MD, FAAP

Every physician has experienced trauma in some way during their training and career. This book is a compilation that demonstrates the wide range in which trauma and burnout can present. It shares the stories of numerous female physicians and what was painful for them before, during, and after their training and practice. What is painful and traumatic for one individual may have no impact at all on another. Each person has their own individual circumstances that may activate their trauma, and there is no reason for comparison of what is painful for one person versus another. As I wrote this manuscript, I found myself debating whether to share my story, as I believe that I have generally had a very blessed life and have no intention of offending others by my own unique experience and portrayal of burnout. But what one person defines as being painful and traumatic can look so different to another. The gift is having the awareness and ability to support one another through whatever is causing the pain, without measuring the magnitude with our individual scales. As Dr. Edith Eger wrote, 'There is no hierarchy of suffering. There's nothing that makes my pain worse or better than yours.'

This is my story, to give insight on my experience and maybe provide a few nuggets of wisdom that you may be able to relate to within your own life. I graduated from The Ohio State University Nationwide Children's Pediatric Residency Program in 2002, and I was so proud of everything I had accomplished up to that point. I worked in urgent care for a year while my husband finished his residency. We then moved to Philadelphia for his fellowship, and due to his demanding hours, we decided it would be best if I stayed home during the first year after the birth of our first child. After he completed his training, we moved to Virginia, where I began working part-time as an outpatient pediatrician, two days a week, while my husband became the medical director of a local hospital's spine center. He was becoming an expert in his field and a big wig in the interventional spine community. I was practicing while still being a mom to our littles. I loved it and all the pieces of my life, as they fit perfectly.

Then, after eight years of living the dream, the senior partner in my practice submitted her resignation and buyout request... My practice gave me an ultimatum to take her place full-time, as they could not afford to buy her out, hire a new full-time doctor, and also keep me on part-time. I couldn't do it. I praise myself now for sticking to my guns and putting my family first. And, I remember feeling the urgency to immediately start interviewing for other part-time positions, thinking I needed to go back to work right away.

Although, at the time, I did not know that I would never again return to practicing pediatrics in a traditional manner, I remember feeling that I needed to return to practicing pediatrics as quickly as possible. I never paused to understand why I was telling myself this on repeat. I just knew I wanted a part-time option so I could take care of our young kids while simultaneously overseeing Virginia iSpine Physicians - our interventional spine practice that I had since co-founded with my husband with his career growth. I believed it would be wasteful to discard my education, disappoint my parents, and not utilize my degree to its full potential if I stopped working as a physician. In the meantime, I was disregarding all the other things I was accomplishing because in my mind, nothing was as high of an honor as being a practicing physician.

When the job options were slim and didn't meet my schedule needs, I started thinking that I had been forced to quit more and more often. And with time, that thought turned into an untrue belief. I felt it was all happening to me, not for me. I had loved practicing but was not able to fit it into the puzzle of my life. And that piece not fitting was becoming everyone else's fault. I was annoyed that other people didn't want to work with my schedule and didn't seem to understand how to meet my definition of flexible. I was frustrated that the world was not more accommodating to young working moms. (I was a pediatrician, for god's sake - shouldn't other pediatricians understand this?) Although I was smart enough to know my boundaries, I really was not at peace with what my boundaries were.

To add to it, my father was always an extremely supportive Indian dad who was gushingly proud. I was the first generation in his family born in the USA, and he believed I had exemplified success by becoming a doctor. I thought he believed that, so naturally, I did as well. Yet, despite all the loving words he said to me over my life, these ones still resonated in my head... 'You better not quit your pediatric career and throw it all away to become an office manager.' It may not be exactly what he said, but it is the story I told myself and what I had heard. I had worked so hard to practice medicine, and after not finding the perfect job, I also started to believe that I was throwing my success away. Surprisingly, the anxiety I had was mostly about disappointing my father and about what other people would think of me if I stopped practicing. I also didn't want to tell people I really didn't want to practice anymore for fear of what falsehoods they would make that mean. What if they thought I was not good at it? What if they gossiped about possible patient complaints or the possibility of lawsuits? What if they said I wasted someone else's chance to become a physician? And worst of all, what if they thought I had been terminated for poor performance or errors?

My practical side was aware that my husband's practice was what was paying the bills. I justified my stepping away from pediatrics by knowing this. I had a love for practicing pediatrics, but I also believed I brought more value at that time to our household as our practice manager because my oversight translated into more earnings generated by his office. Gradually, instead of continuing my pediatric job search, I overworked and oversaw my husband's practice, for now over 12 years. It was mostly trivial work compared to practicing medicine, but I thought it made me feel needed and important. I micromanaged, thinking it was creating value. I buffered by overworking to feel the false pleasure of being needed to avoid the negative feelings of low self-worth. It became my skewed view of my essentialism.

In the process, I pushed away managers, telling myself that they couldn't do the work as well as I could. The turnover in that position was high, and the feedback I received was that my micromanagement of managers was driving them away. Ultimately, I started carrying a very heavy purse that was filled with the underlying thought that I was disappointing so many people and was failing. I grew tired, bitter, and resentful towards everyone, including my husband - I reacted with misdirected anger towards my loved ones, avoiding my underlying feelings. I felt like I was failing at everything I was doing since I wasn't practicing pediatrics. Silently, I started blaming my husband and our office for preventing me from being able to do the one thing I was good at (pediatrics) even though my decision to leave my practice and take the path I did had all been my choice and doing. It's amazing how powerful our thoughts can be. It's intriguing how our beliefs about reality can become so skewed after we repeat unproductive sentences in our brain over and over, to the point that we can't separate facts from our stories about them.

To add to my new administrative role and workload, I made sure that I kept all my medical credentials and licenses up to date and active. After all, they were my only real badges of accomplishment and my certificates of worth, so I clung to them for dear life. In effort to maintain my worth, I founded Peds Proxy, MD, my local pediatrics locum's business, to allow me to practice pediatrics again on my own schedule and on my own terms. I reasoned that with this new entity, I would not overwork on work nights or weekends, and I'd be able to avoid taking any call. Looking back now, I question how much I truly wanted to practice pediatrics rather than showcase that I was just CAPABLE of being a doctor.

Ironically, I was unaware that I was now working approximately 10-12 hours a day at our medical office while still trying to practice pediatrics on my own terms. I couldn't see that I was using overworking as an administrator to avoid feeling the pain of my low self-worth. Although I had the awareness to walk away from the ultimatum my pediatric partners presented to me in 2012, I felt forced to do so and was unable to accept it for reasons that were right for me. I was not at peace because I was tying my self-worth to having a 'commendable, honorable career' and because of the monetary contributions I wanted to bring into our home to feel equal. I justified giving up pediatrics as a way to sacrifice for the good of the household at the time but didn't truly accept it. And as years passed, I found myself asking, if I wasn't using my education and I wasn't contributing to the household income in some other way, why should I be worthy enough to enjoy the fruits of my successes? I was discounting everything else I was doing to support and maintain our business, our household, and our livelihood, and I was completely oblivious to how I was always my own worst enemy.

Coaching after leaving medicine has helped me come to peace and give myself permission to see that I was intelligent enough to recognize my boundaries ten years ago. It helped me see that I could release my resistance to accepting my choices as being sufficient, for no one else's sake but my own. It has allowed me to celebrate how intuitive I was then, even though I may not have fully recognized it until more recently.

Coaching has shown me that it's okay that I accomplished all these things AND that I am now choosing to do something else outside of medicine. That practicing as a medical doctor doesn't define my success and worth. It has shown me that I am worthy no matter what I do with my education or career. I am worthy because I am.

Coaching has empowered me to give myself permission to believe that my value comes from more than just the money I bring into the household to provide for our family. My value comes from so much more. Coaching has helped me remember that no one can replace what a mom brings if that is her path of priority and what she chooses to focus on first in that phase of life. It has reinforced what is important to me and allowed me to shift my career onto a new path that truly brings me joy, by healing my physician colleagues in a non-traditional yet completely appropriate manner. It incentivized me to form my coaching entity, Thought Work, MD, where I can now offer coaching to women physicians and professionals to help them with their struggles, including anger and low self-worth, while still upholding the boundaries I have put in place for my work-life balance.

Coaching has given me permission to believe that I am a badass and has allowed me to give myself credit for my past and future accomplishments, even if I am no longer actively practicing clinical medicine. It has allowed me to re-write my thoughts about my past, accept it, and love it. It has shown me that we all continue to evolve and that this is the true purpose of living a full authentic life. Finally, coaching has shown me that my dad's love for me is not conditional upon his approval of me. That was just my belief. And, man, is he proud of me.

I've shared how coaching has helped me heal after I made the decision to stop practicing medicine and struggled with low self-worth. Sometimes I wonder how life would have been different had I come upon coaching years ago instead. I truly believe that everything happens exactly how it is supposed to. I have grown stronger and wiser from my experiences, and they have enabled me to become exactly who I am today. And I am still growing.

Question and Answers

Looking back, was there anything in your childhood or upbringing that you think led to your burnout?

My parents immigrated to the USA in 1970 from India. My father came over first, by himself, with $8 in his pocket. He lived with his college buddy who had just come over from India a few months earlier, and they lived as bachelors, focusing on their studies and working odd jobs to make ends meet and save for a better life. He believed that hard work, diligence, integrity, and perseverance would lead to success and allow for an honorable career. He was an overachiever in all aspects. His first job was in a photo mart where he developed camera film, as he is an avid amateur photographer. However, he also went to school for his master's in engineering at the same time. His boss noticed how he was able to do the work of two people in half the time of others, so he encouraged him to interview with engineering firms after finishing his photo mart work, while still on the clock. This kindness from his boss has always stood out to me, as it showed how he recognized a young immigrant trying to start his dream life in a foreign country. Seeing how hard he worked and allowing him to further his career while still being paid for his hourly job was truly impactful. A year later, after saving up and securing a job at Bell South, my dad brought my mom over to join him. A few years later, they had started a family and bought their first home. He was living his dream.

Over the next 20+ years, through school, residency, and beyond, I didn't realize how I had structured my life in such a seamlessly perfect way. It was a balance that was almost always under my control. In my mind, there was little room for error, minimal flexibility to account for other people, and certainly no room for a worldwide pandemic like COVID in 2020. Whenever unexpected problems arose in the past, I simply applied myself and overcame them, just as my father had demonstrated and modeled for me.

The COVID-related circumstances left me feeling completely out of control. Despite all my accomplishments and a sense of control in other areas of my life, I became increasingly anxious as I tried to maintain high standards in all aspects of my life, including my businesses, home life, and emotional well-being. I didn't realize how much I was blaming unexpected events for my growing resentment and agitation towards others.

It became clear to me that, despite my achievements, I was always overly critical of myself and falsely believed that everything could have been done better. I was too hard on myself for not fully utilizing my training, for not being a perfect parent, for not completing my never-ending to-do list, and for anything else I deemed as not being done perfectly. My pursuit of perfection in every aspect of my life prevented me from enjoying the simple pleasures in life. I was blindly pursuing a future promise of happiness without realizing how unhappy I was in the present. I was starting to understand the concept of the "arrival fallacy" and knew that this pattern would continue unless I made a change.

Sometimes I do wonder if my dad's tenacious perseverance contributed in some way to my previous burnout. As a comical example, I received the Perseverance Award from my home builder for always securing the best deal on supplies and ensuring everything was done perfectly during the build. I may have taken this quality too far in multiple areas of my life, including my medical practice. However, it is a part of who I am and how I got to where I am now. I am grateful to see the benefits that have come from this quality and the benefits that will continue to come as I work on being more mindful when it is not serving me while still appreciating the journey.
Did anything occur in your training that led to your burnout?

I'm not sure if any specific factor contributed to my burnout during my residency training. However, I do remember that the call check-in and checkout process with my fellow residents was often extremely stressful for me. At the time, I wasn't aware that my perfectionism, partially fueled by this routine, would eventually lead to anger issues later in life. My anxiety came from my co-residents not following my checkout list or from receiving an incomplete list from them. This worry stemmed from a fear that if I wasn't perfect in my performance because of someone else's communication (or my tendency to blame others), it would reflect poorly on me and tarnish my perfect reputation.

Was there anything about the system you worked in that led to your episode (s) of burnout?

I sometimes wonder if all my micro-traumas have been blocked from my memory. One specific example that comes to mind is when I was the senior resident on the pediatric rehab service. A repeat patient was admitted who had been badly burned in an accident. He looked like the white ghost face from horror movies, with black cape and hood, and was bedridden with deformed and contractured extremities that had only nubs left as hands and feet. He was unable to speak or do anything for himself and lay in bed crying in misery. Despite this, his parents again refused to sign a do-not-resuscitate (DNR) order.

The trauma of trying to intubate and keep this suffering human alive, while he repeatedly extubated himself with the help of the ENT and anesthesia team throughout the day, still haunts me with overwhelming nausea.

I question why I didn't do more to honor the patient's wishes, why I didn't speak up and say something about how inhumane this was, why I felt like I didn't have a voice for this patient who was burned so badly that he couldn't speak, and why I didn't just say "This isn't right." That patient died that week after numerous attempts to keep him alive, despite his horrific quality of life. As I write this, I am realizing that there is probably more for me to uncover and process about this trauma. Our brains do what they are meant to do – keep us safe – by avoiding processing of past traumas.

What helped you overcome your burnout?

Coaching, my friends, my husband, my family and meditation.

Did you have a support system?

My incredibly supportive and loving husband and children

My amazing Doctors Mastermind group, which consists of 10 amazing physician coaches who I gathered to collaborate, grow, and learn from each other.

My invaluable UniPeg group – a group of 10 female badass physicians from my group coaching experience who offer unconditional support and love that I won't find anywhere else.

My friends and family.

How are you thriving today?

I have learned to let go of micromanaging and the need for everything to be perfect. I have come to understand that not everything is a reflection of me and that it's okay to not be perfect. We can never control what other people think, say, or do. They will have their own thoughts and beliefs, just as I have mine. The only thing I can control is how I choose to think about things. As a mindset coach, I am now thriving as I help other female physicians and women professionals transform into their true, beautiful selves by recognizing that they have full control over what they choose to think and believe, and ultimately what they create in their life.

What advice would you give to someone going through burnout?

If you don't know what's wrong, if you have brain fog, if you don't feel good, or if you no longer enjoy things you used to or feel happy about them, you may be experiencing burnout. Often times, we don't know what's wrong, we just know something isn't right. It's important to listen to yourself when you have this realization and trust your gut. Make the investment in prioritizing yourself and not worrying about what others think
of you. It can change and potentially save your life.

What advice would you give to the facilities and administration who are trying to help decrease the rate of physician burnout?

Implement a physician coaching and wellness program using external resources such as certified life coaches to foster trust and confidentiality among physicians. Everyone needs a coach.

What advice if any, would you give to the facilities that can do better when it comes to improving burnout rates of physicians (those facilities that appear to have a lack of interest in helping to improve conditions)?

I would ask physicians to consider the cost of replacing one of their colleagues, and then ask them to compare that to the cost of implementing a coaching and wellness program (which now has evidence based benefits). I would encourage them to think about the future of healthcare and the potential impact on the availability and quality of care for their own loved ones if the current trend continues. Finally, I would suggest that implementing a coaching program may help to mitigate the need for replacement by supporting the well-being and retention of the current physician workforce.

About Arpita Gupta DePalma, MD

Dr. DePalma founded Thought Work, MD to provide transformational mindset coaching for physicians and professional women. Through one-to-one and group coaching programs, she helps clients identify and manage negative thoughts and behaviors, and teaches them how to let go of what is not serving them in order to lead and execute with poise. Arpita specializes in helping clients with anger management, time management, burnout, perfectionism, self-worth issues, parenting, cultural disparities, business development, and any other areas they wish to improve. As a woman, she understands the challenges of balancing multiple roles and responsibilities and the importance of self-care. She is dedicated to helping her clients empower themselves to become exceptional and achieve their goals.

https://thoughtworkmd.com

Nandini Sunkireddy, MD

I am a board certified family medicine, obesity, and lifestyle physician. I am a mother of 2 kids 10 and 6 yrs old. My younger son was born with a rare disorder called biliary atresia, which led to liver transplant when he was 6 months old. We as a family went through a lot, going through a transplant, coping with post transplant new normal life where he is on immunosuppressants, he ended up having frequent infections, several surgeries post transplant, his medical condition had a huge impact on his development, led to several developmental delays, which led to several therapies. Until he turned 3, I worked part-time urgent care. After his condition started to improve, I took a job as a full-time primary care physician, which I always loved and enjoyed. Later I got certified in obesity and lifestyle, which helped me to grow my practice. As my practice started growing, I felt that it was taking a toll on me. I was working 4.5 days, trying to manage my special needs child, the activities of my older son, and chores at home. My husband and me we were constantly on a roll, weekends are really short, and at work, I was always trying to play catch up with charting and handling the IN basket. At the end of the day, I felt guilty because my husband was taking my son to all his appointments. It was stressing him out as well. We are constantly measured for productivity, so I could not take off or block my schedule. At one point, I felt I was a failure. I am unable to do justice to either of the jobs. Finally, 6 months ago, I decided to go 0.9, where I am working 4 days a week.

Question and Answers

Looking back, was there anything in your childhood or upbringing that you think led to your burnout?

My Mom always told me nothing is easy in life and that I need to always work hard. She wanted me to become a doctor, so she told me I could never say no to work, and I think never saying no had led to burnout.

Did anything occur in your training that led to your burnout?

I have always been eager to learn and prioritize work over my personal needs during residency. I never called in sick. I used to feel like I committed a crime if I called in sick. I would feel guilty and beat myself up if I did that. I did work a few hours before going into labor.

Was there anything about the system you worked in that led to your episode (s) of burnout? Please give specific examples.

What do you think caused the burnout?

Bureaucracy of the health care system often leads to physician burnout.

What helped you overcome your burnout?

Cutting back on hours, going four days a week. My productivity went up when I started working four days a week. I have a day to work on my YouTube channel and grow my public speaking skills.

Did you have a support system?

My husband, my aunt

Did anyone notice and reach out to you?
none

How are you thriving today?

I have a YouTube channel on a healthy lifestyle and growing my paid speaker side gig.

What advice would you give to someone going through burnout?

Try to prioritize your wellbeing and your family's needs over your work.

What advice would you give to the facilities and administration that are trying to help decrease the rate of physician burnout?

Please listen to the doctors. When a doctor complains about something, please take it seriously.

What advice, if any, would you give to the facilities that can do better when it comes to improving burnout rates of physicians (those facilities that appear to have a lack of interest in helping to improve conditions)

Please try to let doctors take control over the healthcare

About Nandini Sunkireddy MD
Dr. Sunkireddy is a Family Physician, board certified in obesity and lifestyle, founder of styleyourhealthmd, and a paid speaker. She is passionate about treating obesity.

https://styleyourhealthmd.com

Olapeju Simoyan, MD, MPH, BDS, FAAFP, FASAM

Looking back, was there anything in your childhood or upbringing that you think led to your burnout?

I'm not sure if this contributed to burnout specifically, but I grew up in an environment where there were very high expectations, and this may have contributed to a situation where I put myself under undue pressure and was very critical of myself.

Did anything occur in your training that led to your burnout?

The first episode of burnout that I was able to clearly identify was during my training. I was in a city where I didn't have a support system and in a combined (dual specialty) training program that had just started, which complicated things. In addition to being far away from family and friends, additional stressors included things like having to be at two different hospitals in opposite parts of town on the same day. It got to the point where the situation was just not sustainable for me.

What do you think caused the burnout?

Another episode occurred several years later. I had cut down on my academic work, though I still had significant responsibilities at the medical school and was seeing patients four full days a week. I also had administrative responsibilities in the clinical setting with little or no protected time. When I indicated that I wanted to go part-time, the administration decided I couldn't do that right away. Then something happened….. I went for a Fourth of July walk with a friend who was volunteering for the event. I was not participating in the marathon – I was just walking and got to the point where I was just too weak to walk anymore, and someone had to call for a vehicle to take me back to the starting point. It turns out that I was severely anemic. And now that I had a medical reason, of course, I was allowed to cut back my hours significantly. I worked on a part–time basis for several months after that and realized that working flexible hours was something that should have been possible all along. I also had the time to pursue other interests, including self-publishing my second book and helping my father get one of his books published, something I am grateful for, as he passed away a few years later.

Looking back, I don't think it should have taken a medical problem to get me to the point where I realized that I didn't have to work full time, but I am grateful for the lessons I learned.

The cause of burnout was likely a combination of factors, including being overworked and not having the time I needed to fulfill my administrative responsibilities in the clinical setting, in addition to having several academic responsibilities at the same time.

What helped you overcome your burnout?

Fortunately, during the first episode, I was able to switch residency programs and move closer to family and friends. Addiction medicine is a field that is open to all medical specialties, so I was still able to specialize in this field without completing a psychiatry residency. I eventually got board certified in family medicine and addiction medicine.

The second episode of burnout led to my working on a part-time basis for several months, and I was able to keep my benefits, support myself and pursue other interests at the same time.

Did you have a support system?

My family and friends have always been important and supportive, but unfortunately, sometimes, the physical distance between us limits our interactions.

Did anyone notice and reach out to you?

Since I was physically far away from my family and closest friends, I had to "notice" what I was experiencing and be my own advocate.

How are you thriving today?
 I have several interests outside of medicine and previously struggled to find ways of incorporating them into my work. My academic work has involved co-teaching medical humanities courses and being a faculty advisor to a medical student arts and music interest group. More recently, I have incorporated music into group sessions at an addiction treatment facility. I have also concluded professional presentations with musical performances. I have published three photobooks in which I combined my writing and photography. I am preparing to release the second editions of Scranton, A Place to Call Home, and The Amazing World of Butterflies. My third photobook, Living Foolproof, Wisdom

for Daily Living, was published in the fall of 2022 and is available on Amazon. I am also in the process of recording a Christmas album.

What work are you doing that you find fulfilling?

Pursuing an academic career has allowed me to combine patient care, teaching, and research, each of which can be fulfilling on its own, but in my case, I really believe I needed the combination. Right now, I am on a break from medicine and finding fulfillment by pursuing my creative and artistic passions, which are equally important. I am also working on expanding my Women in Medicine exhibit and plan to publish a book highlighting female physicians, their professional accomplishments, and their creative endeavors.

What advice would you give to someone going through burnout?

It's okay to ask for help. If you need to take time off to get perspective or take care of yourself or a family member, it's okay. You shouldn't feel guilty about this. Life doesn't come to a standstill while we're in medical training - or afterward. It's important to have and pursue interests outside of medicine - they help us maintain balance in our lives. Try to focus on the big picture - determine what matters most to you - and try to focus on those things.

What advice would you give to the facilities and administration who are trying to help decrease the rate of physician burnout?

My advice to administrators is that they should listen to physicians' concerns and work with them to create a working environment that truly fosters well-being without jeopardizing productivity. I would also suggest that they focus on truly meaningful outcomes and de-emphasize metrics that are purely subjective, such as patient satisfaction scores.

About Olapeju Simoyan, MD, MPH, BDS, FAAFP, FASAM
Dr. Olapeju Simoyan is an addiction medicine specialist and a full professor in the department of psychiatry. A member of the American Medical Women Association's music and medicine committee, Dr. Simoyan curated a photographic exhibit featuring prominent women in medicine. She plays several musical instruments and has combined her interests in writing and photography in three photobooks: Scranton, A Place to Call Home, and The Amazing World of Butterflies and Living Foolproof. She was a 2022 recipient of the Arnold Gold Foundation Humanism in Medicine award and a 2012 recipient of the AAMC's Herbert Nickens faculty fellowship, in addition to several other awards.

Dr. Simoyan strongly believes in the need to transform the way we educate students across the educational spectrum, with a focus on creativity, problem-solving, and integration of the arts and sciences. Her upcoming book will feature women in medicine, with a focus on creativity.

www.thedoctorwriter.com

Damilola Babaniji, DO

I began my career as a freshly minted attending physician working right in the middle of the pandemic surge with my husband, a 4-month-old, and my other two kids, ages 4 & 9, in tow. After the long, laborious, and grueling process of medical education and training, I finally began my dream job! I was excited about what I called my LIP service (Legacy, Impact, Purpose) to the world. Life was busy, and I naively went to work with rose-colored glasses and my superwoman mentality (and cape!) with a feeling that I could conquer the world.

However, not too long after starting, a few months down the road, I was disenchanted, emotionally disconnected, and depersonalized from my job and myself...I could barely recognize who I was anymore, was incredibly unhappy and just wasn't a joy to be around. I had lost my steam and was not living up to the idealistic life I had imagined. I felt like I was losing myself and my purpose as a human being and began considering quitting medicine altogether. I felt like a complete failure and a disappointment. Looking back now, I realize how invalid all my feelings were, but the perfectionist in me at the time tried to fake it until I made it (like many of us are accustomed to doing), but even that was not working as I could sense that I was gradually falling apart. The life and career I had worked so hard to achieve were unraveling, and I didn't know how to fix it. I terribly missed my cheerful, fun-loving self. Was it the pandemic? The incessant workload? High patient census? Constant death? The victim mentality and sense of betrayal from the community toward healthcare workers? The widespread disinformation about COVID? The unrelenting weight of perfectionism? The expectations as a wife and mom, or just a culmination of everything? I was not sure. I just knew something just had to change!

At one point, I realized I was simply going through the motions. Even though I was delivering great patient care, I remember feeling so defeated, worn out, and empty and didn't have anything left to give to my family or myself at the end of the day. Also, the real & heightened fear of bringing the deadly virus home from work to my husband and 3 young kids as I resumed my second shift as wife & mom did not help alleviate my tension. I couldn't juggle all my responsibilities effectively due to how I felt.

As a 2nd year resident, I had promised myself that I would always practice medicine on purpose or not at all. I even created an Instagram page & blog in 2019 called doctoringonpurpose. It was my own reminder to myself not to become like the burned-out, cynical physician attendings that I had heard about or encountered during training. Unfortunately, I had become one of them.

I had arrived at Burnout-ville and just felt stuck. When I think of burnout, I literally think of a burned-out matchstick because that's exactly how I felt. It felt like the world was burning up, and I didn't feel like I was making a difference or an impact anymore. What I had worked so hard to achieve felt forced, dry, and lifeless. My burnout experience had me question everything about my life's mission, vision & purpose as a human being and as a physician. My so-called LIP service felt severely anemic and almost nonexistent at this point. I did not like or recognize who I was becoming and didn't feel fulfilled in my life.

After seeing so many people (young and old) lose their lives prematurely to the deadly virus, I came to a sobering realization that death was an inevitable appointment that everyone would meet sooner or later regardless of the medical advancements or heroic efforts we may attempt and that the time in between one's birth and death day was what we had some control over.

I still remember the look of regret on one of my young patients who reported "not being ready to die" but who still, unfortunately, passed eventually.

That experience left an impression on me. Then, reality hit me. Time was my most expensive commodity. I decided that I needed to live life with more intention and spend my time wisely without regrets. My determination was to live a more impactful life, tapping into my dormant potential and start living up to the most fulfilling version of myself.

I knew I needed to focus on myself and what I could control, which is my reaction to life's unpredictable circumstances, not the actual circumstances themselves. In a unique way, my burnout experience somehow re-ignited my passion for life—it became a necessity for me, not just another cute cliché.

I acknowledged that I needed extraordinary strength, support, guidance, and help outside of myself to overcome. My support from family and friends and faith in Jesus was the anchor that kept me going and literally became the wind beneath my wings. This was the catalyst that spurred me to go on a journey of self re-discovery to further explore what I was experiencing, which turned out to be burnout.

Thankfully, unlike many other unfortunate stories, my story did not end there.

During my road to recovery, I found out about coaching and invested in it. That was a game-changer for me! Coaching helped me address limiting beliefs and flawed mindsets that hindered me while helping me uncover parts of who I am that I had not been aware of.

I connected with some amazing people, including physicians who had experienced burnout as well. I learned A LOT from them. I knew in my heart that I had found my tribe, and the most comforting thing was the knowledge that I wasn't alone, I was supported, and that changed everything. I began to lean into the quiet, resilient strength that I didn't realize I already had.

This realization slowly spilled over into the knowledge & joy that I had the power to define & design my life to be more fulfilling despite the pains of burnout, the pandemic effects & surrounding circumstances.

Working with a physician coach helped me prioritize self-care practices and was also tremendously helpful for me during those times! I got back in control of my life and began to experience deep joy in myself and my relationships even though the COVID situation persisted. It was during these restorative moments that I got the idea and inspiration for my business, VIP LIPPY which became a healing balm for me as I began to tap into my dormant potential to live a more fulfilled life. A new, more joyful me emerged that I like to call my best HER.

Burnout revealed to me that sometimes one's dream could lead to one's greatest nightmare. I hope with my story I can help at least one physician heal and feel less alone should they ever deal with burnout.

Question and Answers

Looking back, was there anything in your childhood or upbringing that you think led to your burnout?

Growing up in Africa's most populated nation did not come without its challenges. The need to strive and succeed was ingrained in us from a very early age by well-meaning adults. There was an intense emphasis on success and education and blossoming in every area of life so deeply rooted in the Nigerian psyche that anything short of the best is almost labeled as a failure. Failure was not an option, and getting B & C grades in examinations was never good enough. The goal was always to get As.

I remember growing up, I was a self-motivated child. I always needed to ace every test or exam to prove I could. I am not exactly sure to whom I needed to "prove" anything, but I found myself constantly striving to work very hard, especially in my academic pursuits.

Fortunately for me, I was raised in a loving family with amazing parents who invested in top-notch, quality education for myself and my siblings, and I had the support to become whatever I wished to be as an adult. Due to the prevalent hardships, unsteady economy, and limited resources available to most Nigerians, I didn't take this privilege trivially. I worked very hard.

When I was about 8 years old, I decided to become a physician after my brother experienced a serious illness that got him hospitalized. With support from my family, I journeyed from Nigeria to the United States about 20 years ago to begin my journey into medicine.
As a recovering perfectionist, this likely was the beginning stages of what led to my burnout at the height of the COVID pandemic – the burden of perfectionism when life happens in unexpected ways.

Did anything occur in your training that led to your burnout?

Nothing in particular omes to mind. I was very fortunate to have trained in a very good program that was very supportive of residents compared to what I have heard about other residency programs. I did fine through the rigors of residency training with 2 young children while having my third child a few days after residency graduation. I even took & passed my ABIM Medical Board certification exam despite postpartum exhaustion and sleep deprivation barely 8 weeks after having a cesarean section during the COVID pandemic.

Did anyone notice and reach out to you?

My personal support system knew the stress I faced with work and life pressures and were incredibly helpful, but no one reached out to me specifically, to my recollection.

How are you thriving today?

I am living my best life and absolutely LOVE it! I have discovered new passions and areas of my life that I didn't even know existed, one of which is my newly found passion and joy as a budding entrepreneur.

My journey into entrepreneurship began as I began to recover from my burnout experience and re-discovered my hidden passions and potential. As a physician, I never once imagined or even considered going into the beauty cosmetics industry…like never! I mean, I love lipsticks and enjoy wearing them, but that's about it.

During the pandemic, even though I was burned out, I always had my lipstick on under the layers of personal protective equipment and masks, I wore as I cared for COVID patients, even though no one could see it. I knew it was there and that's all that mattered. I never left home without lipstick on because it not only boosted my spirits but also somehow made me feel more confident, empowered, and in control to face the challenges & uncertainties each harrowing day presented. It wasn't a huge thing, but it made a lot of difference to me. As they say, it's always the little things that make big things happen.

It was during one of my quiet moments of prayer, reflection, and meditation (an important aspect of self-care emphasized in coaching) that I became inspired by the story of a lady called Hannah in the Bible, a woman who persevered in the face of unspoken prayers, dashed hopes, and unfulfilled dreams until they became a reality. I saw myself in Hannah.

It dawned on me that there were likely other women who, like myself and Hannah, had these same unvoiced hopes & dreams yet kept them hidden, ignored or suppressed to fit into the status quo of societal expectations and life circumstances. I felt the need to disrupt that flawed system and give a voice to every woman's unspoken dream and untapped potential starting within my own circle of influence.

I began to imagine a world where every woman lives intentionally to her fullest potential (think of what a world that would be!). I believe that this dream is possible but begins with addressing our limiting beliefs & shifting fixed mindsets. I am a firm believer that you are what you think & you become what you speak. My LIP service evolved from a focus on myself into a lipstick brand to get that message out to women everywhere, so at that moment, right in the middle of the pandemic, V.I.P. LIPPY was born and officially launched on May 27, 2022!

I still work full-time as a physician and don't have any plans to quit medicine anytime soon. Medicine is a part of my core, and becoming an entrepreneur re-fueled my passion for it.

After my burnout experience, I got passionate about physician wellbeing and got certified as a Physician Peer Coach. Sadly, a lot of physicians are leaving healthcare due to burnout, systemic failures, and of course, considering the difficult COVID burdens on them, yet we need to help physicians remain in medicine now more than ever. I believe all healthcare workers are truly remarkable people and I feel the need to help our physician healers by creating a safe space for their wellbeing. Following my burnout experience, I helped pioneer the Physician Wellbeing initiative for the faculty as well as create the Resident Wellness committee at my institution to forge a culture of wellbeing among the attending physicians and medical residents.

It is my hope that more physicians begin to speak up about the silent pandemic of burnout in medicine and advocate for the wellbeing of all physicians because they matter.

What advice would you give to someone going through burnout?

You are not alone. There are many people like myself who have experienced what you are going through. You are not weird, weak and worthless. There is help even in the MIDDLE of the tunnel! Reach out to someone.

What advice would you give to the facilities and administration that are trying to help decrease the rate of physician burnout?

First, I'd like to say THANK YOU for your efforts and well done! You are doing a great and noble work. Physician wellness is a great business. Investing in the wellbeing of your physicians is just as important as investing in the patients they serve. Keep it up, and your return on investment will speak for itself in due season. Please spread the word, physicians need all the help and support they can get to address this devastating silent pandemic in medicine. A culture of wellbeing should be the norm, not the unicorn.

What advice if any, would you give to the facilities that can do better when it comes to improving burnout rates of physicians (those facilities that appear to have a lack of interest in helping to improve conditions)?

Physician burnout is costly. There are countless studies and reports showing that the quality of care, patient safety and medical errors, patient satisfaction, work productivity, physician retention, suicidal rates & mental illness are only a few of the adverse effects of the increasing rates of burned-out physicians.

If you truly care about your patients, you'd care about the physicians taking care of your patients. Creating a wellness culture and investing in physician wellbeing is no longer an option. It is the wave of the present and future. Please get on board.

About Damilola Babaniji, DO

Dr. Babaniji is a board-certified internal medicine physician by the American Board of Internal Medicine and a former registered nurse with over ten years of combined healthcare experience. She is an Academic Hospitalist and Associate Professor in the Graduate Medical Education department, training residents and medical students at her medical institution.

She is the Founder & CEO of VIP LIPPY, an inspirational lipstick brand that aims to inspire women to live as the best version of themselves. She is also a Certified Life Coach with a special interest in helping burned-out physicians and women through her comprehensive courses and coaching programs.

She is an avid physician wellbeing advocate, and inspirational speaker.

When she is not busy saving lives as a physician, she enjoys spending quality time with her family and friends, participating actively at her local church, reading personal development books, listening to inspiring podcasts, traveling to new places, and learning new things as an entrepreneur while meeting people through the local pop-up events for her lipstick brand.

She lives in the Dallas area with her husband and three children.

www.viplippy.com

Asha Padmanabhan, MD, FASA

"With the 20/20 vision of hindsight, it's easy to see now, looking back, how a gradual change in the way medicine was being practiced was a key contributor to feeling the loss of autonomy, the feeling of being powerless in a system that was gradually being driven more and more towards profit and less and less about patient care.

The first death knell for me was when my anesthesia group, of which I was a managing partner, lost our hospital contract to a large national group that could promise the hospital lower cost to provide care, which we as a small group could not. Going from having some say in how we delivered care, some autonomy, and definitely more respect as a physician to then becoming an employed physician in a for-profit system was definitely challenging.

My next job was when I was hired to be Chief of the Department at another for-profit hospital system. The next 5 years were some of the best of my career as I relished the challenge of becoming the kind of leader I always wanted to have, supportive of my team and standing up for them while simultaneously walking the tightrope of two bosses: the hospital administration, as well as my employer, a large national group that contracted our services to the hospital. I threw myself into the challenges of improving metrics: improving first case on-time starts, reducing surgery cancellation rates, and improving the morale of the department while still keeping patient care front and center. I relished working on these challenges and thrived in that role. I loved the ability to make processes better. The job was not stress-free, considering the fact that most of my coworkers had been in the department for over 10 years and did not take kindly to change.

Added to this was the stress of being a brown female leader of a department in a hospital that did not have many female physicians in leadership positions. The fact that I was an introvert and not overtly assertive and "aggressive" did not help. I was idealistic and full of enthusiasm to make my department a place where people would love to come to work.

Little did I realize that there were people waiting to see me fail and willing to push to see that happen. I found every supposed minor transgression being reported to the CEO instead of being told what I was doing wrong in the first year. I was lucky enough to have a boss who was supportive and helped me through those initial challenges.

Despite all this, I not only survived the first couple of difficult years but by the end of that time, I was repeatedly told by some of my strongest detractors that I had made a huge difference in the department, changing it from a dysfunctional group to a cohesive group that worked together. The next few years were easier, and I believe I did make a difference in the way the department functioned and how the department was perceived.

This was why, out of the blue, when I was asked to step down after 5 years, without any reasons given, without any warning, except a vague "the hospital wants to go in a different direction" I was completely blindsided.

On an intellectual level, I understood that the company I worked for could not gainsay their client, the hospital administration. And they did their best for me and made sure I had a choice of positions available. I made a lateral move to another hospital. Yet I was left with a deep sense of betrayal. That was the first time I truly felt that I was just a number, a pawn to be moved around on the whim of someone who probably did not even know me or the work that I had done. Not having any feedback on what I could have improved or changed was the worst. If I had been told that "these are the mistakes you made" or been given any indication of what needed to be corrected or fixed, I would have taken the feedback, worked on it, and tried to improve. There was none of that. So the rug was pulled out under my feet without ever knowing why.

Knowing that all your hard work and effort, your sacrifices, everything you have done could be taken away so suddenly, without an explanation, leaving a wound that has never been filled.

I moved on to a different hospital and went on to work with truly the best people I have ever worked with, and in that sense, I am grateful for the day I was forced to make that decision: to step down and stay or choose to move. And I am so thankful that I chose the uncomfortable move of starting over.

That move also led to several other changes in my life and new directions that might never have happened otherwise.
But the fallout was that though I loved my new hospital, I was no longer as invested in the practice of medicine as I was before. I love my job, I love my team and coworkers, and yet the spark that I had to go above and beyond was no longer there. I went to work, I smiled, and joked, I was excellent at my clinical responsibilities, yet it was just a job. Something to be gotten through until I could go home. I no longer had the enthusiasm to look at what was not working and figure out ways to make it better. It seemed like I was working on

autopilot. My brain and body knew what to do. My heart just wasn't in it anymore."

Question and Answers

Looking back, was there anything in your childhood or upbringing that you think led to your burnout?

Growing up in a small town in India in a small, close-knit school community, the daughter of middle-class parents, I feel like I had a great childhood. I was expected to study hard and do well at school, but that was the norm as my friends were raised with the same expectations. I feel like that upbringing was crucial for building my self-confidence. My parents were supportive of whatever I wanted to do, and I was a leader in my school community. I was the classic Type A personality.

However, looking back, the seeds of wanting to be the best and do my best were probably sown then, and while it was crucial to motivate me to achieve all the things I subsequently did, I was not prepared for failing. Additionally, growing up in the environment I did, and the way I did, was a utopian bubble because I was not prepared to handle people who were looking to do me harm or have me fail, which I encountered later on in my career. I look back on that younger self as a naive, idealistic young woman who was always looking for the best in people and assumed that others would be the same towards me.

Did anything occur in your training that led to your burnout? Please be specific.

I started my anesthesia residency first in the UK before redoing it again here in the US. And the thing that struck me most with this transition was the difference in attitude towards the specialty of Anesthesiology and Anesthesiologists. In the UK, anesthesiologists were respected and looked up to as the leaders in peri-operative medicine and critical care, and the interactions between the surgical team and the anesthesia team were a lot more collegial. We were a valued and respected part of the surgical team.

When I started training here in the US, what was a completely shocking eye-opener was the attitude of the surgical team towards 'anesthesia' starting with the residents on up, where we were somehow considered inferior. I loved my anesthesia residency program and will always remember my time there, my attendings, and my co-residents with great affection, but I thought at the time that this was a symptom of a malignant surgery program. I was sure that in the real world, when I was an Attending, I would be accorded more respect. Once I started my first job, I realized that a lack of respect towards the anesthesia specialty was not uncommon within the surgical world. And that factor definitely plays into adding more stress at work when you have to frequently defend your decisions to optimize the patient's condition to surgeons and administrators.

Was there anything about the system you worked in that led to your episode (s) of burnout?

Apart from all of the above:
So many factors contributed:
The shift in the way medicine is practiced that I saw in my practice: when I finished my residency and in my first years of practice, I had the time to truly talk to a patient. As an anesthesiologist, I have 5-10 minutes to create a rapport with my patient. And it was easy to do that. If I felt that the patient needed more of a workup, I could delay or postpone without having to explain to multiple people why. But the corporatization of medicine changed the way we practice. Although efficiency is definitely something to be achieved, it can come at the cost of the time I get to spend with my patients. The pressure to keep moving, sometimes feeling like I am cutting corners, makes me feel less of a physician and more of an assembly line worker trying to push patients through.

The lack of respect for my specialty I see from hospital administrators where I feel like they see us as a necessary evil to keep their ORs running and from some of my fellow physicians as well.

The erosion of the care team model and the constant fight to justify the need for physicians to lead the care team rather than have advanced practice nurses deliver care independently.

What helped you overcome your burnout?

I'm not sure I would describe it as having overcome burnout. I think it just hovers beyond the subconscious where most days are fine, and then something happens like you find out about an injustice or an unfair decision, and you find yourself back in the land of not caring.

For me, I found other things to be passionate about that helped me find the fulfillment and joy that I had earlier found in medicine.

During the time I was Chief, as one of the few female physician leaders, I felt lonely and had no one to reach out to who shared the challenges I faced as a woman and a person of color. I started reaching out to other female physician leaders to ask for advice. And as I learned from them, I started sharing what I learned with any female physicians I came into contact with. I started a blog. Then I started creating communities of women physicians who would come together to share experiences. I became passionate about mentoring and helping women physicians because I realized that the only way we could have a voice was to have more women physicians in leadership positions.

When I was going through burnout, these relationships helped me look past what I was going through and realize that I could still make a difference.

I was also getting into leadership positions in my state specialty society, and fighting for physician rights and patients' rights helped me have a sense that I still had something to contribute to better medicine, even if it wasn't in the hospital setting.

Apart from medicine, I was also building a side business in a network marketing company. I learnt skills that I had never learned in medicine, which showed me that I could step outside my comfort zone of medicine. The best part of this endeavor, however, was the supportive community where I saw how people could come together and work together, unlike medicine, where we seemed to work in silos and where I didn't, at the time, find much support.

What I learnt about myself was also that I love the challenge of being an entrepreneur, which led to other business ventures.
Having all these other interests keeps me feeling fulfilled.
And conversely, knowing I have all these other avenues of feeling fulfilled and that I can be enthusiastic about them helps me enjoy medicine more.

Did you have a support system?

I created my own support system. As a female physician in leadership in a small community hospital, I found it was a very lonely experience. I set out to create a community for myself by reaching out to and gathering like-minded women physicians in different aspects of my life, from my state anesthesia society, to national and my local county and ethnic group.

Did anyone notice and reach out to you?

No, I was (and am) very good at projecting a happy and cheerful exterior.

How are you thriving today?

I enjoy my clinical work, my several leadership positions, and my businesses. Through the tough times and through coaching, I have learnt to manage my mindset. I have learnt to look for the gifts in every situation, even if it is not apparent at the time. I have become more mindful. Through my involvement in several physician groups, I have a community of physicians with different interests that keeps me grounded and yet shows me what's possible.

After being coached and seeing the difference it made in my life, I trained and certified as a Coach. Now I am a Career and Leadership coach for women physicians.

I find my coaching work the most fulfilling. Seeing and hearing about the difference I am making in my client's lives, having someone tell me that they now go to work with a 60% positive attitude where they were going in 100% negative, shows me the power and the impact of what I am doing.

What advice would you give to someone going through burnout?

Take care of yourself. Although self-care is a popular buzzword now, actually taking the time to do things for yourself is hard but essential. I have my coaching clients go through an exercise where they rate different areas of their lives and their level of satisfaction with each. And without fail, I see women physicians put themselves last. "I used to love to play tennis but haven't picked up a racquet since I had kids because I feel guilty about spending more time away from them when I already work so many hours." "I don't know when the last time was that I took time to do something I love."
We spend the majority of our day taking care of patients and then our families. When we put ourselves last, it is easy to burnout.

Hire help as much as you can afford. Outsource what you can. You do not have to cook every meal or be at every dance recital or baseball game. You can be better at parenting if you are not coming to it so tired after finishing all the chores.

Saying Yes to everything means saying No to something else.

Learn to say No. It is a complete sentence.

Find something to be passionate about, whether that is a hobby or a project or even working out.

Find a support group or create one if you don't have one.

Hire a coach. There is nothing quite like learning how to manage your mind, your thoughts, and your feelings. I come away from every session with my coach energized and optimistic or with a different outlook on whatever challenge I faced with my coach.

What advice would you give to the facilities and administration who are trying to help decrease the rate of physician burnout?

Put your money where your mouth is. It is no longer enough to tell physicians to build resilience or have them go through programs with meditation/yoga etc if you don't change the root causes: inefficient systems, the drive to do more with less, turning physicians into commodities. I'm not saying metrics are not important, but when they come at the cost of patient care and physician well-being, where is this taking you?

Give physicians the time they need to actually take care of patients. Use ancillary staff as support, not as a substitute.
Create a positive work culture with adequate staffing levels.
Encourage improving work-life balance with vacations, breaks, and flexible scheduling. Provide a place for physicians to rest. Doctors Lounges are fast disappearing and shouldn't be sacrificed.

Provide support like childcare and elder parent support.
Above all, treat physicians as a respected part of the team and not just a commodity.

What advice, if any, would you give to the facilities that could do better?

If you are not seeing the writing on the wall and actively doing something about it, you are going to see the results. Physicians are cutting back and leaving medicine. You might think you can make do with allied staff like NPs and PAs, and it may even be cheaper in the short term, but you will soon find yourself seeing rising costs with more tests and consults ordered, poorer patient care, and higher mortality and morbidity.

About Asha Padmanabhan, MD, FASA
Dr. Padmanabhan is a full-time practicing Board Certified Anesthesiologist, and a Physician Leader in several Leadership positions, including Medical Director of my Department, Vice President of the Florida Society of Anesthesiologists, Chair of the

American Society of Anesthesiologists Committee on Women Anesthesiologists, President and Co-founder of Female Indian Physicians if Florida.

She is a Master Certified Physician Development Coach and a Positive Intelligence Coach. She helps women physicians in achieving professional and personal fulfillment by providing them with the mental skills and resources needed to navigate challenges, stay resilient, and achieve greater job satisfaction.
She is also a podcaster, Speaker, and Author.

www.theleadershiprx.com

Chrissie Ott, MD, FAAP, FACP, CPC

In my first practice out of residency I was in a poor job fit situation. I found camaraderie was difficult to come by, and there was a startlingly transactional tone to the business-physician partnership despite the business being physician-owned. I found myself without a sense of inspiration and an early case of mid-career blahs. I left the practice within 18 months and founded a solo micro practice.

During my 8 years in solo entrepreneurial primary care, I also eventually experienced burnout. Even as I controlled all aspects of my practice, had long visits, shared tea, and provided unimaginable access, including home visits, the challenges of medicine in the US healthcare system became overwhelming... the nature of witnessing the suffering of others with inadequate resources from which to respond is a form of cumulative stress and trauma. I was quite isolated in this role, and while I loved my patients and my practice dearly, I found it unsustainable and not adequately financially rewarding, given the debts and financial delays of medical training. This came into the clearest focus when I finally had our daughter and saw the toll that it took on my ability to remain present in my parenting role.

A particular post-training circumstance that contributed to one of my episodes of burnout (during solo practice years) was infertility. I, like many women in medicine, deferred childbearing until later in life and experienced difficulty conceiving. Without medical coverage for many fertility procedures, my wife and I spent well over $70,000 trying to conceive. We experienced heartbreaking losses and many months of disappointment, and it became extremely painful to care for families who were conceiving and having children with ease.

Following solo practice, I worked as a nocturnist-Hospitalist admitting both adults and children overnight. The intensity of night shifts was, of course, costly to my physical and mental resilience, although it provided some wonderful flexibility for parenting. We had many challenges with administration during this time, as there were multiple contracts we found insulting to our professional agency and accomplishment. As we organized ourselves to respond to these administrative missteps, it became more and more apparent that clinicians needed a way to be heard. This, along with my original intention to begin healing to medicine, motivated me to become the wellness chair for our hospital and a wellness leader in our larger region and organization.

During this time, I was also offered the opportunity to care for medically complex children in residential long term care, sub-acute, and skilled nursing facility for kids. This role evolved into a medical directorship, but not without some significant burnout along the way related to a culture of exclusion and disempowerment to the physician leadership.

Most recently, after realizing a renewed commitment to the healing of the culture of medicine, I took on a much larger, much more visible role in leading well-being work in our organization. Like many others in the healthcare sector, we experienced financial setbacks in the pandemic years, which has caused budgetary limitations to have been difficult to accept as one dedicated to addressing burnout in colleagues at an institutional level. I have had short bursts of burnout in this role, as my work on behalf of others appears undervalued and many of the truths I am working to promote to those in positions of power remain unrealized. The value of working within the system, however, remains a compelling force, and now I am able to draw on a community of wise and insightful physician coaches as well as my own coaching skills. I am clear that this is my Work; it serves my life's mission and delights me, so I remain dedicated to the healing of medicine and the supported emergence of individuals within it.

Question and Answers

Looking back, was there anything in your childhood or upbringing that you think led to your burnout?

One factor I think contributed to burnout from childhood is that my dad tended to be quite critical much of the time. He - like many before and since - was under the impression that motivation and success would come from high expectations and rigor. This was internalized early on and was applied to all future endeavors.

I was a dedicated ballet dancer from an early age and quickly absorbed the culture of discipline and perfectionism, as many do. This resulted in great achievements as well as great suffering in the form of an eating disorder, and with recovery from that condition, early introduction to meditation and mindfulness, consideration of my life's priorities. I realized that I wanted to work in the healing professions and studied massage therapy immediately after high school. With a focus on wellness, I then became a Pilates instructor and chose to major in Human Nutrition and Food Science in college. With these tools for well-being in my toolkit, I set off to medical school, already clear that the medical profession needed a great deal of humanistic reform and healing from the inside. I was determined to bring wellness to medicine even then.

I started two different wellness groups during training- a wellness club for med students and a poetry group in residency. I helped plan and execute a wellness-focused residential elective for fourth year medical students through AMSA's Humanistic Medicine group. Despite having a deep well of wellness resources, I was still vulnerable to the forces that led so many to an experience of existential exhaustion, disillusionment, cynicism, and frustration- the syndrome we abbreviate as burnout.

Did anything occur in your training that led to your burnout?

The training was brutal. I chose a rigorous medical school and field of study, including an extra year of residency and dual board certifications, because I knew that I needed impeccable qualifications if I was to bring change to medicine from the inside. Residency work hour reform occurred during my four year residency, so we went from hundred-hour work weeks to eighty-hour work weeks. Excellence and superhuman resilience was expected even as we faced some of the most intense forms of human suffering around us on a daily basis. We absorbed the implicit part of our training, which taught us we were not to have much in the way of needs. Heavy drinking to blow off steam made sense. I was constantly aware of the inhumane forces around us and used poetry to process much of the suffering I witnessed during those years.

The intensely delayed gratification of medical training leaves most trainees in financially stressful circumstances while working extremely hard jobs for long hours. We are set up to see post-training as the "promised land" where our financial troubles will be resolved, and our many other deferred needs will finally be met. In other words, we are vulnerable to having unrealistic expectations of our post-residency life. Furthermore, we are surrounded by some of the most resilient colleagues imaginable, so we may not notice our own incredible strength as it becomes the baseline for functioning.

A particular set of circumstances in training for me included a painful disc herniation at the end of training, during which I was accused of malingering. Despite having poured myself into my many roles for eight years in the same institution, I departed under a cloud of unfortunate character aspersion. I believe I was targeted in this way for standing my ground in the face of intimidating attendings when patient care was at stake, for successful performance despite some counter-cultural tendencies.

Was there anything about the system you worked in that led to your episode (s) of burnout?

SYSTEM FACTORS
Transactionalism
Lack of control in schedule and other aspects of practice
Length of visits
Prior authorizations and denials of services/ prescriptions
Insurance determined payment and coding requirements
Regulatory Issues
In box demands
Charting demands
Customer service/ entitlement…
Poor life-work balance
Lack of sense of community among physicians

What helped you overcome your burnout?

I have overcome the stuck-ness of burnout in various ways throughout the last 20 years. Sometimes, the change needed was external: I needed to leave the institution I trained in. I needed to leave my first job after residency. Eventually, I needed to leave even my much beloved solo primary care practice. But even those external changes began within…

Each time I needed enough space and time to recognize the sense of unrest, dis-satisfaction… the space to consider and then compare my core values with what I was doing and how it was being done. I believe in integrity, joy, courage, and connection. I believe in existing in creative response to the universe, no matter what. Time spent in reflection or meditation often were the keys that led me to the next right action.

The moments that stick out the most are moments of peaceful warriorship - times when I spoke truth to power without a tone of hostility but with intact boundaries and with clarity. I have found that burnout shrinks in the face of connection. Laughter mitigates burnout.

When I turn to work that is full of meaning for me, I have a sense of renewable energy; this prevents some of the exhaustion and inefficacy that are components of burnout. When I am truly present with patients and colleagues, I am able to resist the forces of cynical depersonalization that can be part of the burnout syndrome. This presence is only available when I have time to do that, which renews my spirit, so balance is key.

Did you have a support system?

The fist layer of my support system includes my incredible wife and a cherished community of friends, chosen family, and loved ones. I am part of a sangha or group of spiritual friends who study dharma and meditate together, and while most of them are not local, their presence and support cannot be overstated. My collaborators and colleagues are another layer of support, and feeling connected to them helps counteract isolation. A third layer are people who provide care to me- my therapist, my coaches, my massage therapist, my house cleaning helper, and more.

Did anyone notice and reach out to you?

I had friends who noticed, I think, but not sure anyone reached out to me formally. I sought therapy early and often.

How are you thriving today?

Today I find myself thriving in my connections with patients and families through enhanced presence, through my work supporting other physicians as a coach and wellness leader, and in connecting with others who are also dedicated to this work. I have job flexibility and variety, and although organizational change is slow and tiresome, it feels like an honorable and worthy goal.

What advice would you give to someone going through burnout?

Don't believe everything you think. You are in a valley without a great view. Ask for help from someone who has been in a similar valley and has a view from somewhere beyond the valley.
Never stop connecting to yourself and to other people.
Make a point to schedule something you regard as play.
Take time off if you can.
Let others know you are having a hard time even though it violates the unspoken rules of medical culture.
Find a way to move your body most days.
Get a coach. Get clear on your non-negotiables AND what is in your sphere of control/ influence.
Recall that you always have choices, even when it appears otherwise.
Work towards a worthy goal, whether at work or in another sphere; find and pursue meaning.

Find your favorite way to experience wordlessness- whether that is a hike, time in nature, meditation, art, or a sauna. Listen deeply to yourself and your body.

What advice would you give to the facilities and administration who are trying to help decrease the rate of physician burnout?

Advice for facilities/ institutions
Ask and measure burnout routinely. Share the data and the response plan.
Demonstrate espoused values with investment in well-being work as part of strategic planning.
Hire a CWO to oversee and report back on your organizational goals related to Clinician distress and engagement. Ensure they are well placed to be well-informed and well-heard relating to organizational strategy formation.
Be sure you have a good safety net of standard supports.
Encourage iterative experimentation and innovation related to well-being.
Fund coaching for your clinicians.
Normalize personal growth work coinciding with professional growth.
Remove stigmatizing language from licensing and credentialing forms.
Provide healthy food and drink options in a designated space for clinicians to take breaks, re-fuel, and rejuvenate. This simple action alone has such tremendous value.

Amplify any and all appreciation for clinical staff - share personal notes of appreciation.

What advice, if any, would you give to the facilities that can do better when it comes to improving burnout rates of physicians (those facilities that appear to have a lack of interest in helping to improve conditions)?

Get familiar with the National Academy of Medicine's National Plan for Healthcare Workforce Recovery.
Read Surgeon General Murthy's Report on the same.
Read Mayo Strategies To Reduce Burnout and other more current publications by thought leaders such as Tait Shanafelt, Lottie Darby's, and more.
Seek guidance from institutions with experience and success.

About Chrissie Ott, MD, FAAP, FACP, CPC
Dr. Chrissie Ott is a physician, well-being thought leader, and certified professional coach in Portland Oregon. She is board certified in Pediatrics, Internal Medicine, and Integrative Medicine. She has worked in group practice and solo

entrepreneurial Primary Care as a Hospitalist and is currently a medical director. She was the first Medical Director of Wellness in her organization and is currently working on bringing coaching to more physicians in her own coaching practice and through organizational avenues. She has completed Chief Wellness Officer training through Stanford and has presented at the International Conference on Physician Health. She speaks to organizations on the topic of burnout and clinician well-being. Chrissie is devoted to supporting the empowerment and emergence of physicians and healing the culture of medicine.

www.joypointsolutions.com

Julia M Huber, MD DipABLM, TIPC

As I write, I'm drinking a peaceful cup of tea, waiting for the sun to rise. Soon my younger daughter will awaken, and we will eat breakfast before she drives to high school. During the day, I will be in my small, light-filled office coaching physicians who are shifting their lives both personally and professionally, healing from the effects of burnout, and making decisions about how long they want to continue to practice medicine and under what circumstances. Many will stay longer in their field than anticipated once they experience relief from burnout, and others will strategize an exit plan either as a job change, full career change, or even retirement.

It has been a long time since I have thought in detail about my own challenges as a physician mom: the deep exhaustion is gone, as is the feeling of depersonalization. Rarely do I look back.

There are many layers to the process of burnout, with many threads that weave the tapestry, beginning with whom we are before signing up for the rigors of medical school. We physicians are hardworking, resilient people and anticipate working long hours and facing the challenges of saving lives head on, and as the daughter of a physician, I knew this intimately from day one. My dad was a solo family practitioner in rural upstate New York when I was little, and on occasion, took us with him on house calls or, when the snow was heavy, he went solo, strapping wooden boards with hand hammered nails at the base as spikes and walking out over the ice, holding his black bag. Ours was a house where our living room was the ER waiting room and where my parents' bedroom turned into a trauma bay one night when a stabbing victim simply opened the door to their house and walked in. This was my normal.

People paid my dad with baskets of vegetables, a crocheted quilt, and odd favors. I learned from the way he treated patients that medicine is a calling. It's an inner need to serve the community and minister one on one by treating illness. Years later, as I sutured up little kids in the emergency department, I would joke and tell them that I grew up thinking that everyone's dad sutured them up in their living room and that, as a mom of two girls, I would be just as careful and kind. And I did get sutured a lot: my big brothers were aggressive, often swinging me around wildly and occasionally accidentally dropping me or one another onto the floor or furniture, so I was used to roughhousing and being "one of the guys". I also had a big sister who looked out for me, and I learned that a sister, or any woman for that matter is the one who has your back, just as you have hers. So I grew up tough but with a team.

In our family we read voraciously, and I loved language, literature, people's intricate stories and characters, the manipulation of words on a page, the magic of opening my mind to other cultures by learning foreign languages, which led to a longing to leave the rural Virginia farm our family had moved to and fly far, far away. Ultimately I did just that: the first plane I ever took was to Switzerland as a high school exchange student. I was sixteen. I often think back to the day I left: it was a quintessentially hot and humid Virginia summer day, so I had on a light cotton sundress with white eyelet trim, my hair in a long ponytail, and my eyes shining with excitement. That year I lived with three different families supplied by the exchange organization. I have very scant memories of the first one. There was substance abuse, and there was domestic violence. So much for chocolate and snow-covered Alps the exchange organization had promised. One morning I packed my suitcase and moved in with another's student's family. I still recall the stinging criticism from the organization and even my peers: everyone decided I was suffering from "culture shock" and not adapting to Swiss standards. This was my introduction to the concept of gaslighting, or the disparity between the actual events and the stories people tell about the events in order to assuage their guilt and feel better about themselves. "Head down, mouth shut" became my motto: I lost my expectation that anyone would understand my experience but was committed to staying out my year, so I soldiered on. To this day, I'm in contact with the second temporary family as well as the third permanent family that hosted me, so I'm glad that my 16 year old self stuck with it. It's this life lesson in resilience that led to success in my medical career, but which in other ways proved to be disheartening in terms of my overall sense of humanity due to the deep trauma I survived.

Not much was known in those days about PTSD. Two years after I returned, I began to have flashbacks and nightmares about the first Swiss family, and left college overweight and miserable, not really understanding that this was a normal response to trauma. I accepted a job offer as a patient advocate and health careers counselor at a hospital in my hometown, where I received on the job training in vocational counseling and professional mediation, and I also joined a support group for those with weight issues and learned to tell the truth about my experiences rather than turn to food to try to forget them.

Patients are our greatest teachers about life and through their complaints about patient care and through my conversations with them, they taught me how physicians could be more successful when they communicate in clear and simple language. The hospital chaplains took me under their wing, and taught me how to sit with a patient and not pity them but show compassion, how to translate the language of medicine into the language of patients and bridge the gap, and how to look each family member in the eye when walking in. It felt good to be part of an administration and hospital system that was committed to everyone providing and receiving the best patient care possible.

A year later, I left my job with the encouragement of a Spanish professor at Bryn Mawr College, who helped me get scholarship money teaching Spanish immersion. I also received a scholarship to lead and translate for a student group in a war zone in Nicaragua, where I met missionary physicians who encouraged me to pursue a medical degree. I graduated with a major in Spanish Literature in 1986, immediately enrolled in an EMT course, was a rescue worker for nearly eight years, and ultimately attended night school to complete premed/post bacc classes and apply to medical school. I arrived with all the tools I needed for success in my field: clear headed, resilient, and with a calling to serve.

Having survived a traumatic event with no support, I have made it my life mission to offer peer support whenever possible. The brief hallway conversations or cups of tea from someone with a listening ear is a way to intervene early, potentially mitigate trauma, and to create openings for people to seek professional help if needed. In college, I frequently volunteered to speak with my peers about navigating stress, weight, and body image; as an EMT, I certified and then volunteered as a critical incident stress debriefer; in med school, I represented my class as one of two elected peer supporters, serving on a peer support committee appointed by the Dean; during residency in the mid 90's, in the absence of any support or wellness programs, I did my best to ask my colleagues how they were doing; as a junior attending I volunteered as a peer litigation stress counselor for a national physician organization in my specialty.

After working one on one with a physician coach for several years due to my own personal burnout in the early 2000s directly related to trying to balance out motherhood and career, I went on to train as a coach in 2009. I now volunteer for several national professional organizations and work privately with other physicians experiencing burnout, especially those near retirement who wish to optimize their health, create an exit plan, and leave a legacy. I the learned firsthand the value of asking for help in the face of thinking you can handle everything, and am confident that coaching helped me stay in clinical practice for many extra years once I was able to make some adjustments to my schedule and also be realistic about what could or could not be changed in various workplace scenarios.

I can't emphasize enough the value of sitting down with someone who completely gets what you are going through. There's vast value in counseling and psychotherapy, and I'm a very strong advocate of folks getting professional help when needed and without any stigma. If you are reading this and feel helpless, suicidal, deeply depressed, or just dead inside, please make the call to the national suicide hotline and reach out NOW at 988. But for those who are at the very beginning of their battle with burnout or workplace toxicity, the very first step is, to tell the truth about it to someone who deeply comprehends the background and the details and who can deeply listen and help you get perspective and brainstorm your own solutions. You don't have to have a trendy name for it.

When I began my career in Emergency Medicine in the mid 90's, we didn't talk much about "wellness". I don't recall anyone using words such as "burnout" or "resilience". I joined a wellness interest section within my professional organization and the very few of us who attended meetings doggedly staffed a "wellness booth" where, thanks to corporate grants, we offered flu shots and stress cards. "Work Life Balance" was a buzzword, and we actually believed in it. Around the country wellness "officers' ' offered yoga on workers' days off and sent in pizza when things looked bad. It would be many, many years before any of us started sharing stories and comparing notes in hushed tones: more colleagues were dying by suicide. One colleague confided in me that they had unsuccessfully tried to resuscitate another physician who died from a self-inflicted gunshot wound on the hospital premises, and this colleague was now suffering from intense PTSD. I learned that around 400 physicians die by suicide each year. Some of my colleagues reported they were not allowed to eat or drink while on 12 hour shifts and not allowed breaks. New physician moms struggled to find a clean place or even the time to pump breast milk as we were expected to work twelve hours plus shifts without any breaks and no clean or private location to pump. One was told to pump in the hallway. Some of my colleagues reported being victims of workplace bullying. To be a regular mom and a doctor was somehow not to be tolerated or encouraged. A few physician mom clients over the years have shared how they were removed from the regular ER schedule or from leadership positions postpartum for no apparent cause, for example. The system disallowed time off to be sick or be home with a family member who was sick. No maternity leave. No vacation time. You don't show up to work, you don't get paid. Emergency physicians functioned as independent contractors hired by outside groups, and I heard reports from out of state colleagues that some of the companies provided delayed or no paychecks to workers for months in a row with no recourse vis-a-vis the hospital. Imagine the stress of working so hard and not being able to support your family or pay your bills. Working for an outside group also meant having no voice on medical staff and no leg to stand on in the face of work scenarios where the employees ruled. "Workplace toxicity". We had a name for it and cold pizza/yoga class on your day off was synonymous with glossing over systemic issues that we, as workers, simply can't fix. Add to that heavy med school debt along with supporting a family for many, and many colleagues throughout the country felt as if there were no real solutions and couldn't really envision a realistic exit. My survival skill to take it without complaint, and try not to bring attention to myself, pay off my debts as quickly as I could while engaging in wellness self care when clocked out so I could best survive the hours and demands of long shifts in the ER with no scheduled breaks, short staffing, and increasing numbers of patients boarding with limited options to transfer even critically ill or suicidal individuals in need of specialty care. Through my coaching, I heard other colleagues share about witnessing the nursing and other ancillary staff burnout with staff shortages creating unsafe patient care scenarios and a blanket acceptance of patient violence as a given. These are system issues and can only be fixed from the top down as long as they are willing to accept honest feedback and creative solutions from those in the trenches, including physicians, nurses, and other healthcare professionals who are experiencing moral injury.

As a segue to retirement, I eventually trained in Lifestyle Medicine and now work for myself, setting my own hours to coach or practice telemedicine from home, where I can be available to clients, patients, and family in a way that honors my personal values and fosters wellness and career longevity. When I started coaching physicians, we mainly looked at how they could engage in self-care when clocked out. Could they improve their anchor sleep in a darkened room? Eat healthier foods, decrease alcohol intake, and get vigorous exercise? What about meditation for stress management? But then I noticed a shift in circumstances and complaints. I realized that the work circumstances that limited us from providing the high levels of care we were committed to were adding unfathomable stress levels. Some of my physician colleagues in other areas of the U.S. advocated vociferously for patient safety and were "taken off the ER schedule" in retaliation, a practice that was highlighted in the press when the Covid pandemic hit and physicians began to speak out about untenable conditions. We began talking among ourselves about the systemic issues that lead to a global sense of depersonalization and exhaustion that typify burnout. There is a deep sense of despair that arrives when, after all this training and commitment, we are simply unable to do the job we not only are trained to do but which we believe in ethically; increasing numbers of physicians are suffering from moral injury, and mitigating these scenarios will require a true sea change not just on a personal but on a systems level if anything is going to improve.

As physicians, we know full well we are resilient. Telling us to be more resilient is blame shifting and is based on the reality of workplace toxicity and moral injury. What I can tell you in my years of recovering first from PTSD and later, recovering from workplace challenges as a physician mom, in addition to my fourteen years of coaching physicians, is that the first step is to tell the truth about what we are seeing and that one single person cannot try to live within parallel realities and stay healthy long term. The next step is to look at what we can change and what we cannot change and must either accept or flat-out leave. Some workplaces are so toxic that even when one person leaves, they are replaced by someone with the same outlook, and this parallel continuity perpetuates workplace abuse. However, there are many instances where patient care is truly placed first, and there are openings for teamwork and innovation: look for these windows of opportunity, and jump through them when possible and keep rolling! There are organizations and staffing companies that are committed to teamwork and problem solving, and if the one you are in is not ready for change, go work for one that is. Protect yourself in writing with clear job contracts with policies around not being fired without cause:

In other words, they can't make you leave just because someone was offended when you blew the whistle about unsafe patient care practices or because the staff is spreading nasty rumors and gossip. Buy short-term disability before you are aware of any illnesses or, if applicable to you, the potential for pregnancy. If you are a new parent, advocate for on-location childcare, maternity (and paternity) leave policies, and turn down positions that do not offer these policies. Have zero tolerance for workplace violence from patients and also zero tolerance for bullying or gaslighting by team members: write it down, report it, and nip it in the bud because it ultimately destroys the mutual trust needed to work together to tend to patients well. Talk to your colleagues and be real with them. Let them know that was a really tough case, a sad loss, an ugly code. Ask them how they are doing and really mean it. Look at your personal values deeply with a peer counselor, professional coach, therapist, minister or other spiritual advisor, or understanding friend or partner. Get real with them so you can get real with yourself; don't be afraid to leave completely, changing careers if you must, retiring if and when you are truly ready, but realize that wherever you go, there you are, as the saying goes, and go toward an exit that feels satisfying to you and not in an effort to run away. Tend to your physical, emotional, and spiritual health: a healthy human is less vulnerable than an unhealthy one, and more apt to make sound long term decisions. There is no reason to play victim once you realize you have options. Chances are, you may enjoy your job more when you are in the place of actively choosing your responses to stress. One day we will all be six feet under, the job over, and it's a lot more interesting to strategize your next steps within your workplace or design an exit than to become too ill or depressed to show up to work or even stay alive. No job is worth your health and happiness: simplify if you must, crunch the numbers, and be willing to do whatever it takes to honor your true self. Our patients need us whole and well. Our families need us whole and well. The world needs you whole and well.

About Julia M Huber, MD DipABLM, TIPC

Dr. Julia Huber coaches physicians in transition, especially those who are nearing retirement. Her approach is trauma aware, and we work at the pace the client chooses with an eye toward feeling grounded and well while strategizing an exit or retirement plan.Credentials: ICF certified life coach; Trauma Informed Professional Coach; Diplomate, American Board of Lifestyle Medicine; Residency Trained/Board Certified Emergency Physician

https://juliamariehubermd.com

Tammie Chang, MD

I was only five years out of my pediatric hematology/oncology fellowship, when I hit rock bottom. When I experienced severe burnout, severe depression, and was actively suicidal, and almost drove my car off a cliff on purpose, driving home after a long end-of-life discussion with a young patient's family on a Saturday afternoon.

It had been over six months of collective struggle for our pediatric hematology/oncology team. Our beloved medical director struggling with his young daughter with metastatic breast cancer, who ultimately passed away. Record numbers of new pediatric oncology diagnoses, relapses, and deaths for our small practice. The struggles of multiple members of our team and their own cancer diagnoses and treatment, and the loss of many of our own family members, including my father-in-law. I hadn't slept well in months. I gained over 20 pounds. I was in a constant state of crisis. And I took all of the responsibility on my own shoulders, as I had been trained to do for years. It's what we do, right? When times get tough, especially for our colleagues and staff, we do everything we can to take care of them. We work even harder. Stopping and resting was not an option. Saying "no" never even occurred to me.

I began to dream of driving my car off bridges and cliffs, initially only to be hurt so that I would end up in the hospital or ICU for a period of time, and then eventually to not have to be alive anymore. All so that I wouldn't have to continue to go to work. Even then in my sleep-deprived, disordered and dysfunctional state I didn't realize how wrong this was. It wasn't until I actively almost drove my car off a cliff that I finally had the moment of realization that I was not ok. I needed help.

I called my boss that day and took an immediate leave of absence. I got help, a lot of help. And that moment has become the catalyst for everything I do today.

Question and Answers

Looking back, was there anything in your childhood or upbringing that you think led to your burnout?

Without question. I'm a first-generation Taiwanese eldest daughter born to immigrant parents, my father an allergy-immunology physician and my mother an opera singer. As their first-born child in the U.S., my upbringing was strict, as it had been for my parents, with very high expectations. I also started playing musical instruments at age 3 and learned the importance of discipline and consistent hard work very early on, by the time I was in kindergarten. By age 9, I was practicing the piano on my own several hours a day, and by the time I was in high school, I practiced for hours late into the night after I completed my demanding homework load at my elite private school. I rarely slept more than four hours a night in high school.

Looking back on all those years, I started my conditioning to push through and put aside my physical and emotional needs very young. Long before I even reached high school. And then, once I was in college and medical school, those habits were already so deeply ingrained.

Did anything occur in your training that led to your burnout?

I don't think my training was any different than that of my peers. In fact, it might have been significantly better than that for many others. I attended a very supportive medical school (Brown Medical School), Med-Peds Residency Program (University of Massachusetts) and Pediatric Hematology/Oncology Fellowship Program, albeit an intense and competitive one (St. Jude Children's Research Hospital). I strongly believe that we are indoctrinated into medicine's burnout culture very young -- as teenagers, as competitive pre-med students, as medical students, and then as impressionable young interns and residents. By the time we are second year residents, our medical burnout culture is deeply ingrained in us.

Was there anything about the system you worked in that led to your episode (s) of burnout?

The specific situation that led to my severe burnout, and ultimately my severe depression and suicidal ideation, is not unique to my health system. It was due to a systemic issue of staffing physicians just enough to cover our inpatient and outpatient services without cushion or back up to cover for medical illness or family emergencies. This is something we see all across healthcare today, not only in the U.S., and across all specialties.

What helped you overcome your burnout?

I took a three month leave of absence. During that time, I focused on the basics of self-care – sleep, good food, exercise, and connection with close friends. I sought counseling help, reconnected with old friends whom I trusted, and discovered the power of coaching. I was lucky enough to reconnect with my Brown undergraduate and medical school classmate, Dr. Luisa Duran, with whom I'd lost touch, and we discovered we both had struggled silently with our own burnout and isolation. A fire was lit within us, and we vowed to find a way to help our friends and colleagues, who we knew must be struggling too. There was no way the two of us could be the only ones. And this was why we created Pink Coat, MD together and have now written two books to help other women physicians to thrive. Creating Pink Coat, MD helped us to overcome our own burnout because our suffering was no longer about us. Instead, we were channeling our own suffering to help others. I deeply believe that creating Pink Coat, MD together saved both of us, personally and our careers.

Did you have a support system?

I absolutely do. I have an incredibly supportive husband. Loving parents. Close and supportive friends and a great community at work. And even then, I still struggled in silence. I somehow seemed ok on the outside to everyone else. I was extremely high functioning, as all of us women physicians are.

Did anyone notice and reach out to you?

Sadly, no. I seemed ok to others.

How are you thriving today?

Today, my life is dedicated to helping us change and transform the culture of medicine – especially for women physicians -- for all of us in medicine today and for our future generations of young women in medicine. We have come so far since Dr. Elizabeth Blackwell became the first woman to graduate from medical school in the U.S. in 1849. And we still have so far to go to achieve equity and justice for women in medicine.

My Why is removing the stigma of mental illness for physicians, and creating a culture of medicine that is sustainable, kinder, more compassionate, and more joyful for all of us today and for generations to come. A culture where asking for and receiving mental health help is viewed as a sign of strength, self-awareness, and leadership – not weakness.

I split my employed work seeing pediatric hematology/oncology patients 50% of the time and as Medical Director of Provider Wellness for our 5000 physicians and advanced practice providers across our health system the other 50% of the time, leading cultural change and evidence-based solutions for organizational well-being. Outside of my employed work, I'm the co-founder of Pink Coat, MD, a digital platform and community dedicated to helping women physicians thrive in their lives and careers, a women's leadership coach, author, TEDx speaker, podcast host, and the co-founder and program director of the American Medical Women's Association's ELEVATE Leadership Development Program for women physician attendings.

If you asked me three years ago what I would be doing now, I never could have guessed my life today. I am forever grateful for this second chance.

What advice would you give to someone going through burnout?

If you are practicing medicine today, you will experience burnout. And know that we know from research that 80% of burnout is due to systemic factors (Collier et al Can Med Assoc J 2018) – not because of a lack of personal resilience. In fact, as physicians, we are among the most resilient of any profession. And yet we have among the highest rates of burnout. We have the highest rate of suicide in any profession (National Institute for Occupational Safety and Health, 2021).

If you are going through burnout, it's because of healthcare and the culture of medicine. Not because you are not tough enough. There is absolutely a way to heal, to thrive, and to find fulfillment practicing medicine as a physician.

What advice would you give to the facilities and administration who are trying to help decrease the rate of physician burnout?

There are exceptional, evidence-based, and proven strategies and solutions to physician burnout. The best resources are:

American Medical Association Steps Forward Program and Joy in Medicine Recognition Program which provides an evidence-based roadmap for organizations seeking to implement programs to directly address physician burnout

Stanford WellMD and the work of Dr. Tait Shanafelt – he has authored over 400 peer-reviewed journal articles and is considered the world leader and expert in physician burnout and organizational well-being

All In Well-Being First for Healthcare

None of this can be accomplished without dedicated FTE and funding for programs. The best first step is to create funding and institutional support for a dedicated Well-Being Medical Director or Chief Wellness Officer, staff, and administrative support.

You will hear from all of us leaders in the organizational well-being space that "Burnout is Local." *Everything comes down to local leadership and culture.* Anything you and your organization can do to foster and create a culture that puts Wellness Centered Leadership at its core will directly improve the well-being and decrease the burnout of your physicians, nurses, and staff.

What advice if any, would you give to the facilities that can do better when it comes to improving burnout rates of physicians (those facilities that appear to have a lack of interest in helping to improve conditions)

Every organization must commit to healthcare worker burnout and well-being as their number one priority. To not do so is short-sighted.

We know that a physician experiencing burnout is two times as likely to make a medical error and at a 17% increased odds of being named in a malpractice suit (C. P. West et al J of Inter Med, 2018).

The cost of replacing one physician due to burnout is, on average $500K - $1million (Shanafelt, et al JAMA 2017).

Physician burnout alone costs the U.S. healthcare system an estimated $4.6 billion a year (Han and Shanafelt et al. Ann Int Med 2019).

One in five physicians plans to quit their job and leave the medical profession altogether within two years due to burnout (Sinsky et al, Mayo Clin Proc 2021).

If organizations do not address physician burnout urgently now, they will experience a critical workforce shortage and significant negative long-term safety, malpractice and financial implications. Investing in physician well-being now is essential to insuring the financial stability of healthcare organizations in the long run.

About Tammie Chang, MD

Dr. Tammie Chang is a board-certified pediatric oncologist, award-winning author, TEDx speaker, leadership coach, podcast host and fierce national advocate for cultural change in healthcare. She is the Co-Founder of Pink Coat, MD, the Co-Founder and Director of ELEVATE, the American Medical Women's Association's Leadership Development Program for Women Physicians, and the Medical Director of Provider Wellness for MultiCare Health System.

She is the award-winning author of Boundaries for Women Physicians, the co-author of How to Thrive as a Woman Physician and the creator and host of the LeadHER Podcast for Women Physicians. She has received numerous awards, including Women We Admire's Top 50 Women Leaders of Washington for 2022, the 2022 American Stevie Business Awards Gold Maverick of the Year and Woman of the Year, the 2022 Stevie American Women in Business Gold Woman of the Year in Healthcare Award, and Health 2.0's 2022 Outstanding Healthcare Leadership Award.

Dr. Chang received her M.D. degree from Brown University and completed her internal medicine/pediatrics residency at the University of Massachusetts and her pediatric hematology/oncology fellowship at St. Jude Children's Research Hospital.

Dr. Chang is an ICF-certified leadership coach and received her coaching certifications from the Co-Active Training Institute and the International Coaching Federation. She has additional training and certifications from John Maxwell Leadership, Gallup CliftonStrengths, Crucial Conversations, and as a Playing Big Facilitator. Dr. Chang lives with her husband, Matthew, and their three fur babies in the beautiful Pacific Northwest: Golden retrievers Gus and Toby, and cat Mimi. Playing Chopin and Rachmaninoff on the piano and being outdoors with her family are the favorite moments in her day.

www.tammiechangmd.com
www.pinkcoatmd.com

Anupriya Grover-Wenk, DO, M.Med.Ed

I grew up in a home that was run in a very authoritarian way. My parents were South Asian immigrants that were constantly in survival mode and often projected their own struggles onto us. There wasn't a lot of empathy to go around, and we grew in the throes of chaos for many years as my parents struggled to establish themselves. Education was a top priority, and there was no room to just pass; if you brought home a 95% on a test, the next thing you heard was, "what happened to the other 5 points?" Perfection was expected in our home and there wasn't much room for error so when you did make a mistake, a lot of shame was induced through chronic lecturing or yelling; there was a lack of curiosity in our home to better understand exactly what all of us were facing because the stakes were so high to succeed. There was so much correction in my home that the connections had been lost. So, when I entered college and the workforce, I was already set up to burnout.

Medical school was the first time I burned out to the point of taking a leave of absence. I had pushed myself to my limits trying to ace every test. As a teen and young adult, I had been chronically ill - colds, flu, chronic fatigue, insomnia, and GI bugs were part of my everyday existence, and they continued in medical school. I was also always on edge and felt like I was sinking into myself if I was not constantly busy or moving.

As a non-traditional student who'd had a career beforehand, getting back into science-based, academic work took time and patience; I felt like I was spending twice as long to understand concepts that others seemed to get quickly. By the Fall of my 2nd year, I was asked to take a medical leave of absence. I wasn't failing any of my classes, but I was not making good decisions for myself and was approached by my medical school administrators, asking me to seek help. I listened, and spent about 9 months in therapy, just trying to understand how I could go back to school with a different frame of mind and a new perspective on my need for validation and perfection. I was grateful for the time to get better and learn more about myself, and I finished medical school and matched into my first choice FM program.

I burned out once again in residency because of the demands I had put on myself to succeed. I had looked at the need for a medical leave of absence in medical school as a moral failing on my part and was determined to make everyone proud. I got very involved in residency and took on a leadership role, and really tried to expand my wings into things that I felt passionate about. I did a lot of mentoring of junior residents and medical students and really found a niche in medical education and medical writing. I was well-loved by the residency and ended up winning several awards before graduation for my leadership work, mentorship, and commitment to medical education. I should have been thrilled, but I was hurting inside. I was dealing with a number of unhealthy relationships, and subsequent decisions, in my personal life. My relationship with my family was falling apart at the seams, and all the hard work I felt like I was doing seemed to be for nothing. The chronic illnesses continued despite being on a number of medications, and I never felt energized or refreshed. In 2015, I started to experience severe fatigue, and my chronic illnesses worsened; I felt like my body was literally failing in front of me, and I could not stop it.

This all came to a head in February of 2016 when I developed an intractable fever, chest pain, and shortness of breath. I finally pushed myself to go to the hospital and was found to have over 250,000 WBCs crushing my heart and a hemoglobin of 4.5: I had end-stage Acute Lymphoblastic Leukemia. Had I not gone to the hospital, I likely would have died that night. I felt like my world came crashing down. For the next year, I would face some really awful experiences, including a lack of emotional support from those I needed it from, my ex-fiancé and I splitting, and what would become a painful chronic pain and infertility journey. Interestingly, however, the lessons I would learn from this period of hardship would prepare me for the next time I burned out, but I would handle it differently this time.

In 2019, I was asked to start a new residency program. I was very excited about this opportunity as I had done a 2-year Faculty Development and Medical Education Fellowship after residency and thought this would be an excellent way to use my newfound skills. Unfortunately, the entire experience did not go as planned. I had an excellent relationship with my Program Director, and we worked incredibly hard to build what we thought would be a chance to create and develop a program that had all those things that we thought would make the residency unique. Unfortunately, the system in which I worked had a very different agenda in mind; things we thought should be requirements for a healthy residency were dismissed by the administrators, promises were left unkept, and the launch of the residency actually angered a number of people including attending physicians that were now forced to teach for very little compensation and without their consent. This created a lot of dissent among many of our colleagues, and we found ourselves putting out fires left and right. We had to massage relationships and calm people down who felt our work was intrusive to their established workday. On top of that, we were responsible for 8 new residents, who needed a lot of support because they had no seniors to look up to. And my PD and I were their only support system. Then the pandemic hit, and we needed even more help and didn't have any. Many of our clinic staff were furloughed, and there were days when we were essentially rooming our own patients, and the practice manager was answering phones. We had new residents that had never done certain things because some of their core rotations had been virtual, and so we had entire skill sets that we had to figure out a way to make up so the residents could actually safely see patients.

Not a day went by where I didn't work a minimum of 10 hours a day, including most weekends. Every time we asked for something simple, it was an ordeal and several hoops had to be jumped through for simple asks like pens, a whiteboard, or even supplying food during an after-hours event. We had very little help, and with time, the shortages got worse. We had difficulty hiring anyone because we weren't sure how someone else was going to fit into the chaos that had been created, and we were trying to shelter our residents from all of it. In the background, our marriages were strained, and we were hardly home to be a part of our families. I had even put expanding our family on hold because I couldn't handle one more loss or one more challenge.

One day in 2021, I found out my dog, who had been gifted to me during my cancer journey and had been part of my rehabilitation, had cancer. It was incurable, and she had at best, 12 months ahead of her. She had brought me out of some of the darkest days of my life and had stopped me from a self-harm attempt, and when I found out about her cancer, I decided that I was going to devote everything to her. My own health had taken a gigantic hit again, and given my medical history, which included a bone marrow transplant for the leukemia, I was at very high risk with COVID before the vaccines came out, and even then, my oncologist wasn't sure what could happen to her patients that had the kind of history I had, if they were to get COVID. I also found myself completely burnt out not only from my work as APD but also with the various heartache that COVID bought to our region: constant deaths, unable to leave the state, long hours, isolation, abusive patient pushback, and divisiveness when it came to education around COVID and the vaccine. I had ended up in the same place again - numb, silent, and exhausted. But this time, given my previous experiences with burnout, I tried something new. I put myself first. And I quit.

I worried about what others would think about it; 'how could a doctor be so selfish when we were already understaffed and needed more help??!! And that too, during a pandemic!' I toyed with my decision for months and felt incredibly conflicted. But if I learned anything from my previous burnouts, it was that not putting myself first and saying yes to everything outside myself had not worked. I didn't understand boundaries and was open to helping anyone, at any time, despite my own need for rest. Every few years, I was going through these severe slumps and setting myself up for failure, given the programming I had developed since childhood. I had catered to others and forgot to take care of myself, and here I was again, unable to function, just living in a shell of myself day to day. I also had gained 25 lbs over the previous 2 years and was experiencing worsening chronic pain, along with self-esteem issues. My husband tried really hard to be supportive and encouraged me to take time off, but nothing felt comforting. Even therapy felt like a chore. But even worse, one of the most important members of our family, and my life, had precious time left.

Leaving my previous role was one of the most empowering and heartbreaking things I've done. I had built that residency from the ground up, and those residents were like my little babies. I had a special place within me for all of them. But I knew if I didn't save myself, I would have nothing left to give anyone. I gave my dog, Jessie, a loving and fully present 6 months. That's all she got, but I was there at every appointment, every time she woke up at night sick, and every time we thought we might lose her. Her death broke me, but I carry no regrets about the time I spent with her at the end of her life. My husband and I rekindled our marriage and moved out of the area to be closer to my family. We now live a life that is joyous and full, and I have started putting myself first. I have learned how to set boundaries and how to say no. I have lost those 25 lbs of physical weight and shed the expectations of pleasing others. I returned to work in an environment that was far healthier for me and reprioritized what was important to me. I now work part-time, practicing medicine in the way I see fit, and on a schedule that, frankly, fulfills my needs first. I have joined a Wayfinder Coaching Program and intend to graduate in August of 2023 and become a certified life coach. I launched my own consulting business and will be working with premedical and medical students to help them get into medical school and residency, respectively. Once I become a certified coach, I hope to be able to expand my business and serve others within the South Asian community that have had similar upbringings to mine and help them find more connections with their families.

When I look back on the multiple burnout journeys I have been on, I realize that all this time, I had the power to heal myself and put myself first. But due to my upbringing and the expectations that come with medical training, I had never learned to look inwards first to my own inner compass and really ask myself what I needed. Since leaving my previous role, I have been able to accomplish a number of really wonderful things, both professionally and personally, and I feel like a new version of myself again. However, this time, I am bringing so much more to the table; my own happiness, a sense of confidence and empowerment, and the ability to thrive and grow with expectations that are set by me and not by anyone else. I feel like for the first time in my life, I have the spaciousness to actually help others as a physician.

Question and Answers

Looking back, was there anything in your childhood or upbringing that you think led to your burnout?

I grew up in a home that was run in a very authoritarian way. My parents were South Asian immigrants that were constantly in survival mode and often projected their own struggles onto us. We grew in the throes of chaos for many years. Education was a top priority, and there was no room to just pass; if you bought home a 95% on a test, the next thing you heard was, "what happened to the other 5 points?" Perfection was expected in our home. There wasn't much room for error so when you did make a mistake, a lot of shame was induced either through chronic correction and yelling, or through a lack of conversation about what could have gone better. I was also chronically ill throughout my teen years and into college and young adulthood. I look back now and realize that so much of that was due to the unhealthy environment at home but also that I was becoming more of a perfectionist and a people pleaser, which was leading to issues with my health, which caused more anxiety and depression, and the cycle persisted.

Was there anything about the system you worked in that led to your episode (s) of burnout?

I think I was set up for burnout, given my upbringing. When you constantly are correcting instead of connecting, and you lack the curiosity to understand the consequences of your actions, your children can end up in a very dark place. Everything I did for 25 years of my life was to please others, whether it be a choice I made to say yes or no to someone/something or a relationship choice. Many of my intimate relationships were a product of aiming to please and get validation in return. For much of my life, I yearned for someone to be proud of me and feel like I had done something right. It wasn't until I started working on myself with real authenticity back in 2017 that I started to undo the damage.

What helped you overcome your burnout?

My cancer journey and nearly dying was the best teacher to show me that life is short and unpredictable. I have lost some friends to cancer in the last few years, and I often ask myself, 'why am I still here?' I don't have an answer to that, but I do realize that, having this second shot at life, I have a responsibility to take care of myself first before I take care of others. I owe it to myself to be able to do what I was meant to do in the way that works for me.

I also have a wonderful husband who loves what he does and inspires me to find my calling within medicine. He is also incredibly empathic and supportive of whatever I want to do to become better or follow a passion. I could not have pivoted without his unconditional love and support. I have a set of friends as well that are so motivating and constantly encourage me to do something unique within medicine. In addition, my dog was like a soulmate - she taught me so much about being in the present and having gratitude for all the possibilities out there. If you see something you want, take a chance because it might not be there later. Life is so fleeting and so precious that we have to be willing to take risks to make ourselves into those that we were meant to be. Jess taught me to be a better version of myself and she left this earth making sure I heard her.

Did you have a support system?

I have some wonderful mentors that have helped me get through some of my hardest days. These include faculty in both residency and fellowship, as well as my program director when I was creating the residency program in my previous role. My husband and I have been together for 4.5 years and as long as I have known him, he has been my biggest cheerleader.

What was frustrating, however, was that when I would speak to the family about this, they thought I was causing my own burnout by "caring too much". And in some ways, yes, I did create my own burnout by not having boundaries and putting others' needs first, but it's not something we are trained in when we are in medical school or residency/fellowship. So many of my residents have learned more about burnout through individual mentoring and having regular discussions about the topic than they ever did in training as a whole. And we are trained to be these altruistic "healthcare heroes," sacrificing so much of our lives to becoming physicians that no wonder we burn out. And women have it harder given the various socialized expectations of them in both their professional and personal lives. So it was frustrating to hear that I was taking things "too personally" when I wasn't sure how to navigate the healthcare system not only for my own wellbeing but for my patients too.

Did anyone notice and reach out to you?

In each of these aforementioned environments, there was someone to talk to, but not everyone, even in my support system, always could see that I was burning out. I masked it well, and in my previous role, outside of my colleague and my husband, no one else reached out. Everyone was drowning together, so the best thing we could do is all cling to our own life vests and scream across the water to make sure everyone else had their life vests too.

How are you thriving today?

I now work part-time, practicing medicine in the way I see fit, and on a schedule that, frankly, fulfills my needs first. I have joined the Wayfinder Coaching Program and intend to graduate in August of 2023 and become a certified life coach. I launched my own consulting business and will be working with premedical and medical students to help them get into medical school and residency, respectively. However, I wanted to gain experience in coaching so that I could help them navigate a very stressful time with a healthy mindset, thereby hoping to have them carry those lessons into medical training. Once I become a certified coach, I hope to be able to expand my business and serve others within the South Asian community that have had similar upbringings to mine and help them find more connections with their families.

What advice would you give to someone going through burnout?

STOP. Look inwards and ask yourself what is causing the chaos within. The answers are within you but you have to stop moving so that you can listen. Learn to get comfortable with being uncomfortable so you can grow and change. Stop keeping your head down as to not stir trouble. Speak up; ask for what you need. Stop trying to please others or meet others' expectations. Stop trying to find your satisfaction by pushing your feelings aside and telling yourself, "it'll get better with time". Stop trying to make administrators happy.

If you give yourself the grace to stop for a second, you'll likely find the things that have led you to burnout. Then you have to take the scary step of putting yourself first even though your training has been anything but prioritizing yourself. You cannot help others if you are hurting and dying inside. Know that you are worthy of having a healthy relationship with your work and that it does not have to come at the expense of your own mental and physical health.

What advice would you give to the facilities and administration who are trying to help decrease the rate of physician burnout?

For women specifically, we need to create flexible working environments. If we are going to continue to ask women to juggle home and family life, we need to honor them by giving them the flexibility to work in a way that is best suited for them. Get them mentorship and coaching because we have a ton of studies that shows that these things work in preventing burnout and allow women to rise in leadership roles.

Start hiring the right people for the right pay. COVID or the economy is not an excuse anymore for understaffing. Stop acting like for-profit systems that are only beholden to the public and the board. Stop hiring APPs as a replacement for us. Give us appropriate pay and admin time. Create flexible working environments. Set boundaries for patients in clinics; if a patient is late to their appt and we have a late policy, the front desk should ask the patient to reschedule, not come back to the doctor and have them beg to be seen to keep your ratings high and patient happiness high. Stop sharing surveys with us, which are often inaccurate, and penalize us for metrics that are unattainable. Let us bill the right way and have educated and experienced coders on the other side that actually know how to bill.

Anupriya Grover-Wenk, DO, M.Med.Ed

Dr. Grover-Wenk is an osteopathically trained, academic family medicine physician who has spent most of her medical career working in medical education. Dr. Grover-Wenk began her career in 2003 after graduating college from Carnegie Mellon University. She went on to work in the investment banking industry and found that the field was devoid of the human connection that she realized would have to be instrumental in her future career. She went back to school and completed her prerequisites for medical school at the University of Pennsylvania, and then started medical school at Philadelphia College of Osteopathic Medicine in 2008. After graduating from medical school, Dr. Grover-Wenk went on to complete her training in Family Medicine at the Jefferson-Abington Health Family Medicine Residency. During residency, Dr. Grover-Wenk was diagnosed with end-stage acute lymphoblastic leukemia and took time off to complete treatment, including a bone marrow transplant. After going into remission and graduating residency, she completed a Faculty Development & Medical Education Fellowship at the Tufts University School of Medicine where she started her Master's in Medical Education and will be graduating with her degree in the Spring. She continues to serve as Assistant Clinical Professor.

After her fellowship, she was selected to build and co-launch the HCA/Tufts Family Medicine Residency at Portsmouth Regional Hospital in Portsmouth,

NH. There, she built the foundation and curriculum for the residency program, served as APD, and recruited the first two classes of family medicine residents.

Dr Grover-Wenk has had multiple articles published in a variety of journals including the American Academy of Family Physicians, Family Practice Journal, and Family Practice News. She has also been invited to speak at various Grand Rounds and Conferences around the Eastern seaboard, where she has mostly spoken about passion topics such as the lack of mentorship and equitable leadership positions for women in medicine, the pressures of medical training on the mental health of budding physicians, and her own experience as a physician and cancer patient. Her work in advocating for more female physicians in leadership led to her being quoted for a story in December 2022 for Forbes Women.

Her master's dissertation is on the importance of mentorship for female physicians and how it can help decrease burnout while also opening up doors for female physicians to go into leadership roles. Much of what happened with over 1.5 million women leaving medicine during the height of the pandemic was due to a lack of resources available to them.

anupriya1013@gmail.com

Susana Santos, DO

I lived my early childhood in Guatemala, Central America during the civil war that violated human rights and made life a daily struggle to survive. Experiencing so much pain, scarcity, and uncertainty made my mother decide to leave everything and migrate to the United States. As a first-generation immigrant, it was ingrained in me that I had to work hard to achieve the American dream. When I entered school, not only did I have to adapt quickly and assimilate to the culture, but I also met the challenge of learning a second language in order to catch up academically. I was a curious child that loved books and dreamt of someday becoming a doctor. I realized the importance of earning an education and knew it was going to take a lot of work and sacrifice, which were familiar concepts to me.

Earning an education and becoming the first one in my family to graduate from college was a big accomplishment. I was determined more than ever to go to medical school and accomplish my dreams. I knew that it was going to be challenging because I was a single parent and was diagnosed with ADHD. I knew that even if I had to work twice as hard, I had the drive and work ethic to do it. Medical school required long days and sleepless nights studying, but I felt privileged to have a seat in class. I was so proud to graduate and matched into an emergency medicine residency program. I moved across the country with my child and only a couple of suitcases. Although I didn't have family in the new state, I had faith that we would be okay. It wasn't the first time I moved far away and started with nothing.

My residency training required an arduous amount of work hours, including multiple 30-hour call shifts throughout the years. I had no balance in my life, but I had the grit and determination to keep going. It was expected of the residents to continue working, to complete medicine floor rounds, notes, presentations, etc. It is common in medicine for residents to be competitive and to outwork or outshine each other. During our last two years of residency, we were allowed to moonlight at urgent care centers and a rural emergency department. I became a workaholic and began working these side jobs during my limited time off. At the time, I thought that working independently was helping me develop my critical thinking skills and eased my transition as an attending physician. In hindsight, it normalized having an unbalanced lifestyle, being chronically sleep deprived, and being exhausted. I continued working a lot throughout my career, accepting extra shifts, and constantly switching night and day shifts for the sake of being a team player. All of this eventually took its toll on my health and personal life.

As a female minority Physician, I always felt like I had to constantly prove that I was qualified, smart enough, and prepared to have been accepted to academic medicine. I had to demonstrate that I have the intelligence and clinical skills to complete my residency program. Taking standardized tests such as the MCAT, Comlex, and specialty boards were especially stressful to me since English is my second language. The months preparing to take these exams were challenging, staying focused despite having untreated ADHD, and maintaining my regular workload. All the hard work and sacrifices I made were rewarded with earning high board scores confirming again that I was qualified to be present in spaces I didn't feel welcome in.

Misogyny and systemic racism is prevalent throughout medicine. Patients often assume I'm a nurse or housekeeping staff even though my name and credentials are displayed on my badge and white coat. Only 2% of doctors in the US are Latinas, the more important issues are why there are such racial disparities among medical professionals and healthcare disparities among minority groups of people. I personally had to overcome multiple barriers to become a doctor then realized that female physicians get unequal pay, less leadership positions, and minimal support for those of us parenting or wanting to have children. In addition, I experienced multiple instances of microaggressions from condescending doctors whose behavior was often overlooked by administrators. The mistreatment by some patients and their family is also disheartening. On several occasions working in the ER, they have threatened and screamed racial slurs directly at me. Administration has done nothing to address the issues of sexism, racism, or safety from verbal and physical abuse.

After completing many years of school and medical training, I was so excited to finally work as an emergency medicine physician in a network of inner-city hospitals. It is an honor to be able to take care of patients of all walks of life, all ages, and for any illness or injury. Then when the covid pandemic began in 2020, I began hearing about a highly contagious virus affecting people in China and the potential of it to spread worldwide. I read every medical update and followed the CDC closely since being a ER doctor puts my staff and me on the frontlines. I watched in horror from afar as New York city became a hotspot for the virus, killing so many patients and medical staff that they used freezer trucks as morgues. I quickly realized that this virus was not like the usual diseases we treat and that there was a high risk of becoming infected and even dying from covid. This was the time to face fear, to go into the unknown, and to serve humanity. I was willing to risk my life to save my patients, but our leadership failed us.

At the beginning of the covid pandemic, there was a decreased number of ER visits. The leadership at the facilities I covered failed to plan for the potential threat of covid spreading and decided to furlough many ER physicians, including myself. They waited until covid affected our communities in high numbers. I came back to work at several ERs in complete chaos. There were so many sick patients, people dying, and no more room in the hospital to admit patients that they were boarded in our ER for several days. All of the local psychiatric facilities were also at full capacity leaving many psychiatric patients in crisis waiting in the ER for several days among the sick and dying. Some of these patients were psychotic with episodes of agitation and anger threatening the safety of staff. The new patients arriving at the ER had to be treated on chairs in the hallways. There was a shortage of nurses, medications, medical equipment, and personal protective equipment such as masks and gowns. We no longer had the support of a unit clerk or scribe, which added more work using an outdated computer system. The ER was staffed by one doctor every 12 hours with the responsibility of treating every patient in the ER and responding to every cardiac arrest code in the hospital. At night, the ER doctor was usually the only physician present in the entire hospital. I was also responsible for supervising midlevel providers and often overtook care of patients. We did everything we could during these difficult times and adapted to every new challenge to save as many lives as possible.

Working in these conditions was not sustainable. At first, I didn't recognize that I was experiencing burnout. I was too busy taking care of everyone else to consider the effects the work was having on me. I often felt frustrated, stressed, and exhausted by the end of my shifts. I became more frustrated by administrators trying to control the practice of medicine, metrics, and rude consultants. The hospital became a hostile and abusive work environment. The hospital leadership and staffing group failed to plan, failed to provide the equipment needed, failed to improve the work environment, failed patients and failed the medical staff working on the frontlines. Corporate medicine and insurance companies are responsible for a broken healthcare system in the US and have become the main cause of burnout for me. The system was broken before the pandemic but became much more apparent in the months that followed. By the end of the pandemic, several physicians and nurses resigned. It became clear to me that sometimes the life we have to save is our own.

Questions and Answers

Anything in your childhood that may have lead to burnout?

Coming from an immigrant family, I learned early to value education and the opportunities I had living in the US. It was ingrained in me that we had to work hard to live and have a better future.

Did anything occur in your training that led to your burnout?

During my training, it was normalized to work many hours and not have any life balance. The expectation that resident physicians take long on-call shifts and to work continuously conditions them. Finishing my medical training with large student debt was a big reason why I continued to work a lot.

Was there anything about the system you worked in that led to your episode (s) of burnout?

Corporate medicine led by business men that prioritize dollars over patient care led to my burnout. Their unrealistic expectations that physicians see more patients, in less time but with minimal resources was frustrating and unsafe.

What helped you overcome your burnout?

My faith has gotten me through dark times and has given me the strength to face fear. I never imagined we would experience a worldwide pandemic. In the midst of the chaos, I prayed and kept hope that we would see better days. I also coped by keeping my mind busy with books and plans for the future.

Did you have a support system?

My family was my major support system that inspired me to keep going. They taught me to be resilient through the most difficult times.

Did anyone notice and reach out to you?

Unfortunately, no since we were all in quarantine and I was living alone.

How are you thriving today?

Leaving a toxic work environment was the biggest change I had to make in my life. I took a sabbatical for a few months to rest and redesign my life. My world changed once I took the time to take care of myself and spent much needed quality time with family and friends. I finally gave myself the opportunity to have balance in my life, and I began loving medicine again. My love for learning allowed me to grow professionally and to create other ways to help patients. This led to formal training and earning certifications in medical aesthetics and obesity medicine.

What advice would you give to someone going through burnout?
If you are experiencing burnout give yourself grace, reflect and pray about it. Realize that there are external factors out of our control that cause burnout. Recovering from burnout starts with taking care of our basic needs, such as eating well and getting restful sleep. Once we have some clarity, we can start to prioritize, plan, and figure things out.

About Susana Santos, DO
Dr. Santos is a board certified emergency medicine physician. She earned her undergraduate degree in biology/psychology from California State University Los Angeles then earned her Doctorate degree from Western University school of medicine in 2009. She was presented with the President Award at Western University. Dr. Santos completed an Emergency Medicine residency at Mclaren Hospital in Michigan and earned board scores at the top of the country. Dr. Santos has done formal training and earned certifications in the fields of medical aesthetics and obesity medicine. She opened the Texas Aesthetics and Wellness clinic in San Antonio, Texas in 2022.

Dr. Santos has dedicated her life to serving communities during their most critical needs and provides care to underserved communities. Dr. Santos has been doing medical mission work in third world countries for more than a decade and will continue this work where aid is needed. She is an Associate Professor with Michigan State University teaching resident physicians international medicine. Dr. Santos lives with her family in Texas and enjoys music, dance, and art.

https://www.texasaestheticsandwellness.com/

Serene Shereef, MD FACS

I remember being fascinated by anatomy and physiology even as a kid visiting my grandparent's farm. I just knew in my heart that being a surgeon was my destiny, the way that I could help others. As a woman of color, I didn't know any female surgeons as a child or young adult to even know if my dream of being a surgeon was "realistic"! I just knew that if I kept persevering, it would all happen just like in my dreams.

I grew up in Southeast Asia and subconsciously internalized many limiting beliefs from my culture and environment. Beliefs that created an internal imperative to please people around me, avoid conflict, and the concept that the "self" should be sacrificed for the community and greater good all contributed to my burnout. Another key belief was the mindset that all problems could be solved by working harder. Whenever there were obstacles popped up along my journey, I pushed any concerns or unwanted feelings deeper into my heart and shuttered the door. I just had to put a "smile" on my face and keep persevering.

I started my general surgery training with a 3 month old infant and as the only person in my class cohort with a baby. Trying to breastfeed, cope with being a first time mom, be present at home, and be the best surgical intern I could be during a time where work hours were just a theory was challenging, to say the least.

My training occurred during a time period where burnout was acknowledged but treated as a problem that affected others, especially those who weren't resilient or efficient. As an immigrant woman of color, my limiting beliefs kept me quiet even during challenging times. I became so good at keeping my struggles hidden that no one realized this was a problem. The stairwells and ends of corridors became my safe space to take a few deep breaths, shed some tears and get my battle gear back on. I regret that I did not speak up or advocate for myself, but I truly believed that I had no choice except to swallow my feelings and to persevere.

As an immigrant, I struggled with understanding all the nuances of the culture and language. Anatomy was infinitely easier than understanding Star Trek & being able to speak the sports lingo or relate to the music in the operating room. Whether I said yes or no, I was wrong more often than not. I learned that in order to survive, I had to hide who I was and what I believed. This habitual pattern of thinking and being only compounded the imbalances in the system for female surgeons despite it being the 21st century.

In the last year of residency [year 7 as I did 2 years of research as was expected], when I chose to go into general surgery practice instead of fellowship and the world of subspecialties, many of my mentors made it very clear their disappointment in my poor choices. Some of them verbally stated this in a public forum that "they are not there to train general surgeons" and followed this up by stopping me from being able to do any significant complex surgeries with them, as previous chief residents had been able to do.

I remember, after a difficult case, being told that I was being disrespectful for having a smile on my face during this difficult moment for the team. I found this especially ironic as I had been up most of the night, and had just finished crying, washed my face, and put on my "pleasant mask" as I thought was expected. This was the moment I realized that nothing I did would ever be good enough, which was a bitter pill to swallow especially coming from mentors that I had admired for many years and had supported me until I decided that I wasn't going to follow their plan for me.

I completed my residency incredibly burnt-out. Unfortunately, I did not recognize this within myself, especially at this point. I was just grateful to survive and complete this chapter. Finally, I was going to be able to take care of my patients and heal from the process of becoming a surgeon. I just had to keep persevering.

I worked in a few different systems thinking that I just had to find the right fit for things to get a little better. Although I was able to grow in my practice by taking care of patients in a meaningful way for me, I quickly realized that the struggles I had during residency still followed my footsteps.

I was volunteered for many committee leadership positions, which I did not feel I could refuse as a junior partner. I wanted to be a team player, so I put on my "smile mask" and did what was requested. I was the only female surgeon in the entire surgery department in one of the systems and realized that there was no one who could remotely understand my struggles. Most had older children and/or spouses who managed the majority of the home needs. What I was struggling with, trying to balance all the expectations on my time, it was not even in the awareness spectrum for most of my partners. I learned that in order to continue surviving, I had to continue to hide who I was and what I believed. This persistent habitual pattern of thinking and being compounded the imbalances in the system for female surgeons despite it being the 21st century. I kept persevering.

I remember one free afternoon when I was taking my kids to run some errands. I was called to cover a trauma, despite not being on call as the on-call partner was in the operating room and no one else was available. So I came to the ER with my young children secured to their car-seats in the back, hoping that my nanny or husband could meet me in the parking lot and take them while I responded to the needs of my department and hospital. No one was happy with me that day, despite my best efforts. I worked harder even than residency, thinking that I just needed to do more and maybe some more for it to be enough. I have days and weeks of my life where I have no conscious memory, exhausted to the depths of my soul, chronically sleep deprived as we also covered our elective patients even when not on-call. I felt guilty for my hidden anguish as I was finally living my childhood dream to be a surgeon. So many people had supported me and believed in me, that I could not voice my struggles.

During this time, I lost one of my best friends from medical school to an unexpected medical event, and a close family member had a devastating medical illness. Both of these incidents shook my foundational belief that if I just did what was expected of me, I had many years ahead of me to live in a more humane manner. I realized that time was finite and promised to no-one. I kept persevering. I tried all measures of efficiency, and willingly accepted less pay to decrease clinic hours. It didn't make any difference because the pager and accompanying full-time responsibilities meant that I had no ownership over my time.

One day I went home after a long weekend of being on-call, and found my 4 year old crying. She had woken up in the middle of the night with a nightmare and knew that once again her mom would not be there for her. After years and years of feeling like I had no voice or choice since I didn't want to abandon my dream of being a surgeon, amongst the fog of post-call exhaustion, I had a moment of clarity. This was my life, and nothing was going to change in all the tomorrow's that I had imagined. Unless I did something. The only question was what was more important to me; to be a surgeon or to be a human. It ended up being a much easier choice than I had imagined. I typed up my resignation letter and handed it to my boss the next day. No one could believe that I would resign without another job lined up or that, after all the work, I was just going to "quit" being a surgeon. I had evidently done a better job than I knew of hiding my struggles. But I could finally take a deep breath, it was over. I didn't have to keep selling my soul to have the privilege of being a surgeon. I could finally take a step back and heal from the journey of being a surgeon.

Once the fog of exhaustion had lifted, I realized that I had exchanged one problem for another deeper problem. You see, I had no idea who I was without my identity as a surgeon. For me, burnout was a crisis of existence. It took time, support from my family, and coaching support for me to learn how to stop hiding myself even from me. I had to let go of my limiting beliefs and my habitual pattern of persevering in an environment that was clearly toxic. I went back home and spent an entire summer with my children for the first time in their lives. We were getting to know each other finally. I started teaching medical students and doing some locum surgical coverage while I explored what I truly wanted to do. At this time, I was completely ready to stop my surgical clinical practice as I never wanted to go back to where I was. My life had been so focused on taking care of my patients, my family, my department, and the hospital that I was rarely even on my own priority list. I thought that losing myself and hitting rock bottom was the worst thing that could happen to me. Ironically, it saved me from never truly loving and taking care of myself.

During my time as a mentor and teacher, I re-discovered my passion and curiosity for learning. I learned to overcome the fear and vulnerability of being seen for who I truly am, instead of the multitude of masks that I had become so adept at wearing. I learned to exercise self-compassion and acceptance of my authentic self. Coaching transformed all areas of my life, and gave me the tools to manage my mind, time, energy & productivity.

In my search for the missing link of wellness in a world focused on pathophysiology and therapeutics, I completed a degree in Health & Wellness. My research and further training including life coach training and certification, positive intelligence, mindfulness, habit-design and productivity systems have all been focused on facilitating life transformation from a space of life design principles, mindfulness and habits. I am so grateful to now use these tools to empower others to find their way out of burnout!

My unique life by design framework combines the energy of mindfulness, self love & self compassion with the scientific principles of habit building, time-design and our unique systems of productivity, helping others live authentically within your signature strengths and create ease and contentment. Through my coaching program, I help others shift from the cognitive thinking model that is thought to be the center of transformation, supporting them to connect deeper into their heart, intuitive awareness and subconscious patterns of thinking, feeling and doing that actually control our ability to change and persevere in a way that is meaningful and authentic for each of us.

I am so grateful not just to survive my burnout, but to thrive beyond burnout. I re-designed my own life with my unique framework, now practicing [and loving] trauma acute care surgery part-time and connecting meaningfully with my patients just like my 11 year old self had dreamt about. I can do this without sacrificing my humanity or feel guilty for wanting more in my life. As my oldest child [aka my intern baby] gets ready for graduating high school, I know that the time and love that I nurtured intentionally has been meaningful for both of us. I witness how he waits for me to return post-call to share his struggles and my middle son saves his favorite memes for us to laugh together or waits to share his favorite Minecraft adventure. I am so grateful for having the option to homeschool my youngest who is now 9 years old and join her in creating a lifetime of memories. I have traveled to so many of my bucket-list destinations choosing not to wait until retirement to do the things that I love. Every moment in our life is precious. I ask myself frequently, "if today was your last day, is this how you would choose to spend it?". I can finally say with deep gratitude, "Yes, I have no regrets. This is the best moment in my life right now. And I am exactly enough as I am"!

For anyone going through burnout, I am holding space for deep awareness and acceptance. I hope you recognize the truth, which is "You are more than enough," exactly as you are now. No extra responsibilities, committee duties, and persevering harder to fill the void within the system is going to change the truth that, as humans, we are worthy and enough in our core foundation without any additional qualifiers. When we accept and nurture ourselves with love and compassion for our humanity, allowing for our truth to be seen whether it is convenient for others or not, this is the space where we can be our imperfect authentic human self, living our truths and creating a life with meaning and purpose. When we accept and allow for our light to shine, the ripple effect allows for others to feel empowered to do the same. Sending love and light to all.

Question and Answers

What advice would you give to the facilities and administration who are trying to help decrease the rate of physician burnout?

Stop suggesting resilience training and physician shaming as a strategy to improve burnout. We are incredibly hard working and optimized on our resilience and productivity with the resources available, we have done everything possible within the system, so the next step is really for the system to change.

Create a group with opportunity for everyone interested to voice their concerns and acknowledge the problems within the system. Explore opportunities for growth and change because the reality is that unless something changes within the system, we are going to see more physicians leaving to pursue other options, including leaving medicine. This is not viable in the long-term for the system. Therefore it is in everyone's best interests to find creative solutions that allow for all or most of the needs to be met for all parties involved.

About Serene Shereef, MD FACS

Dr. Shereef is a trauma acute care surgeon, mom, dreamer, and transformational life coach. She went through severe burnout, struggling to find any semblance of work or life balance. Coaching transformed all areas of her life and gave her tools to manage her mind, time, energy & productivity. Now she is empowering others to find their way out of burnout!

Her unique life by design framework combines the energy of mindfulness, self love & self compassion with the scientific principles of habit building, time-design and your unique systems of productivity. She helps women physicians, who are struggling with burnout & overwhelm to create clarity and design the blueprint for their dream life so they can live intentionally and create their most meaningful authentic life.

https://www.serenitywellnessmd.com

Brittany S. Panico, DO, FACR

I walked out of my office holding back tears. I felt exhausted, alone, relieved, and a whole list of other emotions all at once. This is the second job I have "left" but this time, leaving for good felt harder. This was the last day I would leave feeling angry and let down, the last day I would walk the halls of the hospital as a staff attending, and the last day I would have to share space with a group of people who made my day miserable. With the lyrics from Anna Kendrick's song "Your're gonna miss me when I'm gone" playing in my head, I couldn't help but feel like they were really going to miss me. But I also felt like the very people who would miss me were some of the people who played the largest role in my burnout. And they probably would never know. Or maybe they would know, but would they care? Would anything change, so the next physician who took my place felt more valued and respected?

Burnout is not unique to physicians or healthcare professionals. There are similarities in all high performing careers. But one of the unifying features among those experiencing burnout is the lack of autonomy, the lack of feeling valued, and the expectations to "do more with less". Burnout is becoming the largest contributor to workplace dissatisfaction and the reason for physicians leaving the workforce. Women are burning out at alarming rates. Women in all phases of our careers are experiencing burnout. I have. Twice. I am part of the statistic. We may experience burnout in different ways, though it tends to result in the same thing: the feeling of not being valued in a profession we worked so hard to achieve and gave so much of ourselves for.

The mindset of having one career does not help the burnout saga either. Many of us are products of generations of thinking that you invest in education and training to have one job and that job will carry you through all phases of your life until retirement. There are no specific "promotions" in medicine once you become an attending. It is far too easy to get caught up in the day-to-day repetition of seeing patients and merely showing up to work, working, then going home. Unless you are in an academic setting, or transition into an administrative role, physicians are primarily groomed to take care of people's ailments and we do this every day until we decide we won't any longer. But why do we think this way? Why do we want to spend our 20's sacrificing our energy, ideas, and youth, only to have our 30's, 40's and 50's worn down by the beating of medicine, insurance companies, and corporate managers determining our very worth. If the rest of the world changes and adapts to technology and innovation, why shouldn't we as physicians also change? Why do so many of us feel trapped in careers that lead us to such turmoil?

Hopefully, my story, and all the others like mine, will collectively help physicians see that we have more power than we think. We have the power to overcome obstacles, do hard things, learn new skills, and be whatever kind of physician we want to be.

When I started recognizing the theme of burnout for the second time, I took action to change my path in a different way than I did at first. But for those of us who decide to stay in medicine, how do we prevent burnout from becoming a cycle? Much like addiction or some other unhealthy habit, is burnout the rock-bottom that we reach on our path of high-achieving careers? By telling my story, I hope to share the struggle and success of overcoming burnout so that others can see that there is a way out. The path I found most helpful has been investing in myself: building confidence in my inner voice, confidence in those who support me and believe in me, and joining a community of people who think like me and want more for this world. The grass may look greener somewhere else, but that is a result of the investment in watering said grass. I had to learn what that investment looked like for me. One of the ways we learn what works best is by learning what does not work. My journey through burnout is a compilation of ways that do not work for me.

I trained at the same program for residency and fellowship. I married my husband, whom I met in medical school, after my intern year. We were both at the same program and the comradery we shared helped me immensely. We lived about an hour away from where he grew up and this made establishing our home in Chicago easy. But I was born and raised in Southern California, and the Chicago winters began to wear on me and added to my sense of solitude. I loved the summers but did not take the time to enjoy them because it felt like we were always working. We both excelled in clinically demanding residency and fellowship programs, but the very nature of "survival" established a mindset for me that things would "get better someday." That is the story we often tell ourselves: struggle now so that you will have it better later. The arrival fallacy is one of the largest mindset shifts that I have had to unlearn as I embrace my struggle through burnout.

I started my career as a rheumatologist on the brink of burnout. Or maybe I was vulnerable because of the phase of life I was in. I had my first son during fellowship and struggled every day to juggle the responsibilities of motherhood and preparing for my career. My husband was one year ahead of me in training and would be a cardiology then electrophysiology fellow three additional years. We relied financially on my attending salary, so I started working about 2 weeks after finishing my fellowship. Throughout these next years, we both worked additionally as moonlighters at our local VA hospital. We were literally burning the candle at both ends. I struggled to study and though I was prepared clinically, I was not prepared academically. I did not pass my boards the first time. This was the beginning of my defeat.

My first job started out great. I had wonderful colleagues who became great mentors, our office staff appeared organized and efficient, and I thought I would fall in love with my work. I did love my job for the first few months. Then the honeymoon phase wore off and I started to settle into the grind. As I learned about the business of corporate medical practice, I felt tricked by the façade of the 32-hour clinical workweek. This equated to 4.5 days of clinic. I would arrive to work early and I was able to end my clinical day by 4:30 pm. My perfectionist tendencies kept me at the office later into the evenings, and I would often race to pick up my son from daycare just in time to avoid late charges. I second-guessed myself and my decisions often and was constantly referencing articles and resources to prove to myself that I knew what I was doing. The number of incomplete charts grew, my inbox demands expanded, and my frustration with my office staff mounted as I felt like I was repeating the same silly tasks over and over again without any movement forward. I also got into the habit of overbooking appointments, a habit that feels self-righteous but is only self-destructive to me now.

There was always *more* to do. I felt frustrated that insurance companies could determine how I was going to treat my patients. I learned quickly that peer-to-peer reviews were in fact, never actually my peers. I could not understand how a gastroenterologist could determine if my patient needed an immunosuppressant that was not used in his specialty for a condition that he "had never seen". I succumbed to writing passionate and often angry appeal letters instead, many of which were still denied, and I had to give in and change my plan of care anyway. I was told by my office manager that I was not yet productive enough to have a scribe, so I used dictation in the meantime. This was difficult to do in a shared office space, and I struggled with concentrating on the endless conversations. I constantly had the mindset that I was somehow not doing enough, and this carried over into how I felt about treating patients as well. I also spent an abundance of mental energy dwelling in overwhelm and excuses. I had not developed any other method for coping with my struggles, so they just ate away at me one bite at a time.

I also struggled immensely with criticism and negative feedback. I was used to excelling, and the concept of reviews and scorecards were foreign to me. This was not something that my attendings in fellowship regularly discussed, and as residents and fellows, we were not part of this feedback process. I had to learn how to navigate a review process that was not only public but entirely my responsibility and was not sure how to do this. While my colleagues talked about therapy, I pretended like the reviews did not exist. I refused to read them unless I was contacted by my administration about something that warranted justification from me. This happened several times and ultimately, those patients did not return to see me.

I constantly felt like I was being graded and critiqued by patients on my ability to listen to their complaints, formulate a plan, and provide a treatment, all the while creating a satisfying experience that would be worthy of 5 gold stars. I did not realize how much I let patient satisfaction impact my worth as a physician. I mostly had very positive reviews and was building a clinic of returning and loyal patients, but the ones who were unhappy were not shy about telling the world. I came across Dax Shepard's Armchair Expert podcast and every day on my commute I would soak up the stories of celebrities and how they dealt with fame and online publicity. I started using mental gymnastics routines to look and sound as if I were giving great news to patients I was not going to see back.

I trained at a tertiary care center and was naive about the way clinical practice worked in a community setting. I was no longer seeing patients who had a high suspicion for autoimmune disease but rather was seeing anyone who called wanting an appointment with a rheumatologist. I remember seeing one patient who wanted a complete evaluation for any possible autoimmune disease because she wanted to "make sure" that she would not need the medications she saw advertisements for on prime-time tv. She took the disclaimer to "ask your rheumatologist if this medication is right for you" to mean that she needed a rheumatologist to talk to. I find humor in this now, but at the time, I was breathing fire after she left the exam room.

I also quickly became exhausted seeing patient after patient for chronic pain. I was not seeing the kinds of patients my fellowship trained me for. Every day I walked on eggshells trying to develop a way to explain to angry patients that despite waiting three months to see me, I was not the right specialist they needed. Patients who presented for joint pain most often had osteoarthritis or degenerative disk disease and were outraged that I was not going to treat them with narcotics, after their referring provider told them I would. I developed an early philosophy that I would not prescribe controlled substances, but others in my office did, and this created a tremendous amount of tension. The system I worked for was not in favor of screening referrals and wanted my colleagues and me to see patients regardless of the reason they were being sent. Patients could self-refer, and I would see people for all kinds of requests, normal labs, and vague concerns that were not best suited for a rheumatologist. Meanwhile, patients who actually struggled with autoimmune diseases were often delayed appointments and were, therefore, more challenging to treat.

The lack of support from management fueled my resentment toward the system I worked for. We asked for more support to educate our referring physicians, and the growing number of midlevel providers added to the deficiency of quality referrals. I rapidly learned that our office managers cared more about patient satisfaction ratings and accepting internal referrals for the revenue they created than the reason we were seeing the patients to begin with. Our impact on the community was less important because there was an abundance of rheumatologists in town, and we were there to move volume through the system rather than create a legacy.

After my second full year, I was given a report of my annual collections and I remember leaving that meeting feeling so angry. I brought in seven figures and my salary accounted for about 20% of that. I literally felt like I was drowning, and 80% of my effort was being taken away for a system that did not invest in helping me be more successful. The loss of autonomy was one of the first signs that I had reached my limit.

Meanwhile, I had the looming pressure that I had to pass my boards. If I wasn't studying, I felt guilty about not studying. That entire year I felt like an imposter. I knew I was becoming a great rheumatologist; I had developed a large patient panel and had a good reputation within my community. But I had to pass my boards to keep my job, and that terrified me. I felt like I let my fellowship program down. I was the first fellow to have a child during training, and looking back, I did not have the mentorship or time management skills I needed to thrive academically while dealing with the distractions at home and the exhaustion I felt every day. I was becoming more and more sleep deprived and this fueled anger and frustration with my family and withdrawal from friends. I had never failed an exam, and that feeling was the worst guilt that sat with me for a very long time. I was embarrassed that my peers would think less of me. I carried around an extreme amount of shame that entire year. I did not know how to process those feelings, so I slowly let them devour me. I ultimately passed my boards the second time, and while I was relieved in the short term, my confidence took an eternity to recover.

During this time, I also felt like I was struggling as a young female attending trying to raise a family. Toward the end of my first year, I delivered my second son and was again treading water in the sea of life happening around me. I grieved my independence. I felt like I was giving all my energy to others and was so tired when I would get home that I would often fall asleep holding my kids. I remember waking up so many nights sweating in a panic that I was not doing something that had to be done. I was not enjoying being a mother and certainly was not enjoying my work. I was too tired to have any feelings at all and just lived in a state of numbness.

Between my schedule, balancing open charts and staying at work late, my husband's even more demanding fellowship schedule, and both of us trying to share moonlighting, we were working 6-7 days a week with very little downtime. I often felt like it was "easier" to be at work than be at home because I was so exhausted trying to parent and maintain a household. I would moonlight on the weekends just so I could catch up on charting and other things I needed to do. I would avoid housework and then have panic attacks over the "piles" of things at home. I didn't feel like I had any outlet that would relieve those feelings, so I would work more. It became common that my husband would work an overnight shift and then trade off with me in the morning, or vice versa. We would meet in the parking lot and move our kids into the other car so the other person could work their shift. We justified this because we needed the income for daycare and the ever-looming burden of medical school loans. We lived in a high-cost-of-living suburb of Chicago, and it never felt like we could get ahead. Looking back, this behavior led to my feelings of money scarcity which fueled my burnout even more. I never felt like we had enough to scale back. I knew this phase was temporary, but at the time, I had a hard time seeing any other way.

My husband has been amazing through it all, and I am forever thankful that we both maintained a healthy relationship with ourselves and each other during this time. We even tried to train for the Chicago marathon together as a way to cope with our grueling schedule. But as the miles increased and our days off did not, we could not accommodate the longer runs, and we decided not to race. Nevertheless, I am thankful that exercise did become somewhat of an escape from my less optimistic day-job.

The winter of 2019 was starting to look more positive when my husband accepted a job in Phoenix, Arizona. I was offered a job with the major academic medical center in town, and we would move there after his graduation in July. This was our chance to start over. I had a ticket out of the life I was living. He was going to join a private practice, and I was going to be a full-time clinical faculty. This was my chance to take all the things I wanted to change and start over with a clean slate. I was more comfortable with my clinical knowledge and skills. I had gained experience with a well-respected medical center in Chicago and felt like I knew what I wanted from a job at this point.

Then the world shut down, and everything changed. Literally. From March through July 2020 I was living a new level of survival. I was pregnant with our third son during one of the most uncertain times in medical history. I was back to feeling isolated and overwhelmed. My husband was now moonlighting for the both of us, so I could limit my exposure to COVID while I was pregnant. Both of us remained working full-time during those months of the early pandemic, and my feelings of burnout soared. I was struggling to find childcare for our 2 sons while seeing patients over telemedicine. I envied the mothers who were home with their children, though I felt guilty that I thought work was easier. I struggled with this pregnancy and do not remember much of that time, partially out of fear that something would go wrong and partly because I did not have the mental capacity to enjoy that time. My clinic remained "open" full-time for virtual visits, and although I am proud I provided the care I did for my patients, I was utterly exhausted in a way I had never known before.

We moved from the city we called home for nearly 10 years during the peak of the early pandemic and arrived at a new beginning, only to repeat the same chaos of COVID all over again. Geographically, Phoenix was about 3 months behind what we were experiencing in Chicago, so as the East Coast and Midwest started to improve, the Southwest and West Coast crumbled. I had a healthy and vibrant baby boy but was isolated to keep us safe. I was isolated in a new town where I did not have many friends and was too scared to have family travel to see us. But through this isolation, I was able to really concentrate on what I wanted and how I wanted my career to develop.

I discovered life coaching and participated in a program during my maternity leave that set the stage for my journey to where I am now. Several women I came to know during that time helped save me from spiraling into burnout for the second time. I was prepared for the conversations I knew would come when I returned from my leave. I had new skills to help me cope with stress, a new perspective on finances, and female mentorship like I had never experienced before. I embraced the mantra that that life was happening *FOR* me, not *TO* me. This was a huge revelation because my previous inner voice was very much a victim of my circumstances. Now I knew I had the power to change my perspective just by changing the way I thought about details of my life.

I quickly started working full speed ahead after returning from my maternity leave and was determined to establish systems and protocols to make our clinic run smoother and more efficiently. I now had staff that was screening referrals and I participated in reviewing the patients who were being sent. I felt like my skills were being used more effectively, though our patients were much more complex than the patients I was used to seeing in Chicago. I covered hospital consults two weeks each month in addition to a full outpatient schedule, and this ultimately became my own worst enemy.

I was again not meeting my productivity goals and struggled to piece together patient visits in a system where records were not automatically included in the EMR. I had to learn a new EMR and this was much harder for me mentally than I thought it should have been. It was almost like my brain (and attitude) refused to let charting be easy, and I carried so much drama about this with me. The weight was more dangerous than I realized.

I was not able to decrease clinic time, so I would often come home after a full day, get my kids fed and ready for bed, then go back to round for several more hours. I would do it all again 2 weeks each month. And just like before, my charts were piling up, my inbox messages were not being answered, and my office culture was burning out as well. Every day was a gamble with who would be out sick. Being out sick during COVID meant you stayed home for two weeks, so we never had a full staff, and we were all doing more with less. There were times when my office did not have a dedicated person to schedule new patients or create new charts, so unless the patient was referred from within our system, they could not be seen. This idea that our staff was not cross-trained to fill multiple roles was one of the reasons that propelled me into burnout again. I was not thriving in a culture of "how can we make this better", but rather a bystander on a sinking ship with no way to safety. Despite my efforts to be a leader within my own clinic, my ideas were not welcomed or entertained. Unless direction came from our clinic managers directly, our department was not changing the way things were done.

I resented the fact that my metrics of success were being interfered with by corporate employees, that I could not motivate to change. In the two health systems I have been employed with, my direct physician leader was not tied to my clinic staff. Therefore, I was not a direct supervisor for the staff that worked in my office either. We had two totally separate roles but worked together under different supervisors. My staff did not have loyalty to me, and I could not participate in decisions involving employees in the office. This disconnect is very difficult to overcome when there is conflict.

I started to settle into my role after my first year, but then another curve ball threw me off track. I had restructured my time so that I was not rounding so late every week I was on call, and I was helping implement positive changes within some of the problematic areas of patient care. But our office space was up for renegotiation, and we were relocated without much input about our new office location or clinic flow. When I say that we had little input, I really mean that we had meetings with our management about what we wanted, how much space we needed for our growing clinic, and plans for expansion. But once we moved into the new space, the requests and compromises meant nothing. We moved into a shared multispecialty space that was far too small for our patient volume, difficult for our patients to find, and literally in the middle of another clinic that now resented us for taking up their space. Our patients arrived late for a good portion of the year because our marketing team did not change the address of our office. I was again accommodating patients late throughout the day because they would get lost and finally show up to their appointments demanding to be seen. We had very little support for any troubleshooting from our manager, and the list of grievances became difficult to tolerate. I was utterly and emotionally exhausted *all the time.*

I tried my best to use my coaching skills to work my mindset around these seemingly trivial events, but each time I would feel better for a week, or so then the cycle would start over again, and something else would rattle me. I was now out of my salary guarantee and subjected to our system-wide compensation plan revision. This resulted in a large pay decrease while keeping my clinic time and RVU expectations the same. I was responsible for 4.5 days of clinic and hospital coverage every 3 weeks, thanks to the addition of another physician. My "administrative time" was routinely taken up with urgent patient add-ons because I did not have control over my schedule and regularly booked 2-3 months out. Academic promotion was the motivation to achieve a pay raise, which was still not going to be to the level I was making during my first two years, so the whole model felt futile. How was I supposed to work toward promotion with a full-time clinical obligation, hospital coverage, and the ever-expanding administrative burden that fell on me because my office did not have enough staff to support the needs of our patient volume? The academic faculty advisors suggested administrative buy-out FTEs, teaching roles, or committee participation, as ways to plump up my CV. However, these roles were not at the same pay scale as my clinic time, so the solution was yet another demotion.

Around this time I started thinking of how else I could practice medicine. I was nearing the end of my public service loan forgiveness obligation, and I decided that once my loans were forgiven, I would look for a new job. I invested more time in developing relationships with pharmaceutical representatives and other resources in my community. I joined several online entrepreneurial groups for physicians and learned how others were thriving and practicing medicine on their own terms. I started using social media as a platform to help educate and empower patients with autoimmune conditions and joined several communities of like-minded physicians who are doing amazing things both within and outside traditional medicine practices. I finally felt that there was a purpose to all the struggle I was going through and began formulating my exit from corporate medicine.

I can confidently say that several online (primarily Facebook) communities saved me during this period. I became an avid listener of podcasts and audiobooks, began reading and learning about running a business, and learned negotiation skills that helped me set boundaries at work with my staff and patients. A friend who is a practice owner encouraged me that it was possible to have my own practice. At least if I was going to devote my time and energy into something, it would be my own blood, sweat, and tears. As a corporate employee, my sweat and tears were ignored and seemingly insignificant. I began taking steps to open my own practice and was feeling better about my future. My husband, who has been thriving in his own practice, was proof that physician-owned groups invest in the happiness of their partners and that the collective benefit of the group rewarded everyone. I am learning to modify the way I think about income and wealth. The financial pressure that felt strangling all those years has much lighter grip now.

Currently, as I am writing this story, I am transitioning into a new role within private practice. I do not know what this position will hold for my future, but I do know that the people I am surrounding myself with share a similar vision and drive to provide excellent patient care while maintaining a positive work environment and culture. I am joining a team largely comprised of leaders who left corporate jobs due to experiences similar to mine and have motivation to not repeat bad history.

As I reflect on what burnout means to me, I picture a flame burning only while there is fuel to feed it. The fuel that feeds our burnout is different. It can present in different forms: fire can be large and all consuming, or smolder and taunt. Oxygen is needed for any fire, and when there is either too little oxygen, or too little fuel, the fire burns out. We have the ability to provide the fuel by remaining in the environments that are ripe for burning, or we can leave and start somewhere new where we water the grass that does not burn. We have to put on our own oxygen masks and acknowledge that we have to save ourselves first in order to save others, whether that means our patients, relationships, families, and our own sanity. I feel fortunate that my burnout was more of a slow smoldering fire, but I hope that through my reflections, someone else who is amidst situations like mine can see that there is a way out. We are worth saving. Our stories are worth telling.

Addressing burnout is not a one-size-fits-all approach. I have not been an institutional leader, but I do feel that most leadership is disconnected from the actual work physicians do. Even physician leaders do not have the same responsibilities of the clinic and administrative burdens as full-time clinicians. There are annoyances that can be tolerated by someone who sees patients 1-2 days per week that may seem insurmountable to someone working 4-5 days per week. Recognizing that men and women view work and home responsibilities differently is a start. In my experience, most corporate leaders are men. It is easy to say that we need more women to fill these roles, but there is a reason that these positions are not more routinely occupied by women. I am sure we can all come up with our own reasons we would not want that role.

Therefore, it is up to us to speak up and be honest when we are approaching burnout. More institutions are open to physician coaching, normalizing therapy, and attention to mental health, and part-time roles are now more negotiable than seemingly before. But even these benefits are not replacements for the way physicians are actually being treated on the front lines. Why is it that the people who make decisions about the way a job should be performed are not the ones doing that job? Physicians need to have more input and collaboration when it comes to the conditions we work in and how our offices are structured. We are leaders by nature, and patient care should be the place where our leadership efforts are acknowledged. Transparency and honesty are also key. Women continue to earn less than men in equal roles, and decreasing gender disparity will be a huge step toward decreasing burnout frequency in women. We are amid a healthcare crisis, and if we do not collectively do something to change the culture of how physicians are treated, respected, and valued, we let the suits win. Then everyone will miss us when we are gone.

About Brittany S. Panico, DO

Dr. Panico, DO is a a rheumatologist in Phoenix, Arizona. She is passionate about educating patients with autoimmune conditions and empowering them to live the life they desire despite their diagnosis. When patients are actively engaged and participate in their healthcare decisions, she finds find their outcomes to be much more meaningful and fulfilling.

@AZRheumDoc on IG and YouTube

Christiana Jones, MD MPH

It's hard to tell my story of burnout because it was incredibly painful and lasted a very long time. As early as my third year of medical school, I wanted to quit medicine. The hours were brutal, and the hospital culture was the opposite of nurturing. It was almost like a test of who could survive medical training. Unfortunately, quitting wasn't an option for me because I was on a student visa. If I left school, I'd lose the visa and have to return home to the Ivory Coast, so I stayed. Of course, there were many good moments, but the bad moments were an absolute beat down.

I went on to residency, which was marginally better because residents' work hours were now limited to 80 hours a week. Somehow that didn't make me jump for joy. And then the thing that every physician dreads: I was named in a malpractice claim during my second year of residency. To this day, almost twenty years later, I remember the dread that seized me for months even though I knew I hadn't done anything wrong. The claim was eventually dismissed, but the damage to my confidence was done.

My work hours improved significantly after residency, but my deep-seated dissatisfaction with medical practice persisted. I saw every patient encounter as a potential lawsuit. Like many doctors, I practiced "defensive medicine," ordering more tests than my clinical intuition told me was necessary in order to avoid missing a very unlikely diagnosis. Because doctors are more likely to get sued by unhappy patients, I found myself ordering tests or prescribing unnecessary antibiotics to placate upset patients who I was worried might file a complaint or lawsuit. Despite my dozen years of training, I felt like patients were in charge and dictated the care they wanted to receive, often against my recommendations. That made me angry. But anger has no place in the exam room, so I learned to adopt a mask when I walked in. The distance between me and the people I had taken an oath to take care of grew larger.

At the same time, I was feeling increasing pressure from my employer to work longer hours, work weekends, and see more patients to increase revenue. Employers were getting pressure from insurance companies, and that pressure was passed on to us.

The overwhelming feeling at that time of my life was depression. I felt trapped because I was the sole breadwinner for my family, and I had no clue what else I could do to earn an income. I was only trained for patient care. I knew I was burned out. I was emotionally exhausted to the point I just shut down completely. There was a wall between my patients and me. Even as I went through the motions, I knew I was not being the physician I wanted to be. This wasn't what I suffered through medical training for. I felt like a failure. I cried a lot, alone, where no one could see me. I was never suicidal, but I thought I might die of misery. I was dying on the inside. I had hit rock bottom.

Questions and Answers

Looking back, was there anything in your childhood or upbringing that you think led to your burnout?

As a young person, good grades came easily to me (or so it may have appeared to those who didn't see the hard work I put in). I was viewed as "the smart one" in my family and among my peers. The admiration felt good, and I continued to set and meet my own high expectations. When my parents and maternal grandmother essentially decreed that I was going to be a doctor, I didn't mind. It sounded like the ultimate high expectation as far as careers I could pursue, and I welcomed the challenge. In a home where affection was not physically demonstrated, I saw my parents' pride in my academic achievements as evidence of their love. And so, I worked hard to continue to earn their attention and approval. When I was admitted to Harvard Medical School, my parents' joy knew no bounds. They told everyone they knew what I had accomplished. Even before I had received my medical degree, they called me "Doctor." My mom answered my phone calls with, "Hello, Doctor." My extended family in Nigeria also took great pride in having a doctor (the only doctor) in the family and sought frequent informal consultations. That became my identity in the eyes of my family. Even when I started to have doubts about whether medicine was a path I wanted to remain on, I felt trapped. If I wasn't a doctor anymore, then who would I be to my family? Would they still love me and value me? So, I kept my head down and tried to fight through the challenges, all the while spiraling deeper and deeper into burnout.

Did anything occur in your training that led to your burnout?

My third year of medical school was a serious shock to my system. That was in the era before work hour restrictions for trainees were implemented. One surgical rotation was especially brutal. I arrived at the hospital at 3 AM to begin pre-rounding on my patients and changing wound dressings. Then the team rounded at 5 AM. After that, we carried out our duties for the day, went to surgery, and then had evening rounds between 7:30 and 8:00 PM before heading home. Every fourth night I was on call, so I stayed at the hospital overnight and worked the entire following day till evening rounds before going home, only to return less than seven hours later for the next seventeen-hour day of work. When I was on call, I worked forty-one straight hours, usually with no sleep. I worked ninety to ninety-six hours a week. That was the beginning of the road that led to burnout for me. After the year was over, I took a year off of medical school to recover. I got my Master of Public Health degree and spent three months out of the country at the Albert Schweitzer hospital in Gabon. I did return to finish medical school and went on to residency.

Was there anything about the system you worked in that led to your episode (s) of burnout?

Medicine is full of high achievers, people who are intrinsically motivated to do the right thing for our patients, often at our expense. Most doctors can identify with putting patient care first, ahead of self and even family. This general selflessness is exploited by employers, patients, and insurance companies. I came to resent the excessive workload and intrusion into my family life and its detrimental effect on my physical and mental wellbeing. I'd be in church or at the dinner table with my family and my pager would go off for the third time in an hour. I remember feeling such anger and depression at the thought that this would be the rest of my life.

What helped you overcome your burnout?

Ultimately, what helped me overcome the burnout was to leave medical practice entirely. It took years. I tried a change of scenery by taking a locums assignment in New Zealand. I tried switching from office-based family medicine to an urgent care clinic, then telehealth. I tried reducing my hours. But it wasn't until I left patient care entirely a year ago that I've started to breathe freely again. In retrospect, family medicine was not a good fit for me as I am a massive introvert, and 25 to 40 patient encounters a day were incredibly draining without adequate opportunity to recharge. Who knows, I might have done better in a different field of medicine.

Did you have a support system?

I knew I wasn't alone in the way I felt. Talking to other doctors helped but didn't address the problem. Wine dulled the pain but the relief was short-lived. Eventually, I saw a doctor and got on anti-depressants which helped. My family and friends supported me as best they could. I also journaled a lot. Writing about my struggles in my journal was my therapy and how I eventually found the courage to leave medical practice.

Did anyone notice and reach out to you?

I became very good at masking my perceived inadequacy. There I was, making good money in a career that is generally held in high regard by society. How could anyone sympathize, I thought? Even when I tried to talk to someone outside of medicine, they couldn't really understand. So I made sure no one noticed how unhappy my life had become.

How are you thriving today?

Finding my way to thriving was a process. First, I got a certificate as a life coach. I thought I might help physicians dealing with burnout. Then I tried my hand at writing. I self-published three novels before shelving that endeavor. I enrolled in pastry school and spent several delicious months rediscovering an earlier passion. And now I've landed on real estate. I'm a realtor and investor and really enjoying it. Who knows if this is the last thing I'll try? All I know is that I am now living life on my own terms, and there is nothing more fulfilling than that.

What advice would you give to someone going through burnout?

Talk to a physician coach. Not only do they understand what it's like to be in medicine, their job is to help you analyze your situation, figure out what change you need to make, and help you throughout the process. Don't try to go it alone. Certainly, talk to family and friends but recognize that their understanding and, therefore, ability to advise you on professional moves, may be limited.

If you're feeling depressed or have noticed increased alcohol and/or other substance use, talk to a doctor or therapist.

Rest. This is non-negotiable. Take whatever time off you need, whether it's a week or three months or whatever time frame, to breathe, recover, and begin to think more clearly of a way forward.

What advice would you give to the facilities and administration who are trying to help decrease the rate of physician burnout?

The patient is not always right. Support your physicians. Let them know you've got their back.

Allow whatever flexibility in scheduling is needed for work-life balance, including less than a full time schedule with benefits.

About Christiana Jones, MD MPH

Christiana Jones retired from family medicine in 2022 after fourteen years of practice. She is a realtor and real estate investor in Dallas, Texas, the author of three medical fiction novels, and can be found living her best life with an epic romance novel in one hand and a delicious homemade French pastry in the other.

www.weknowtx.com/ChristianaJones

Tamara Beckford MD MS

How does a tiger hunt its prey?

The tiger creeps slowly, lying low and in camouflage. When the tiger is close enough, it springs, attacking its prey and taking it down. The same can be said of burnout. It sneaks upon you. It is like a tiger lying in the thick bushes, waiting for its prey.

I remember when I became serious about pursuing medicine. I was in high school and spoke with my classmate's dad. He was an Ob/Gyn. He asked one powerful question: "are you sure you want to be a doctor?" I was a bright-eyed 16-year-old, excited about joining the ranks of the coveted healer, so I said yes. Dr. Jenkins cautioned, "medicine has changed a lot since I became a doctor. However, I will give you one piece of advice. Never let your work enter your home. He said to keep "your work at work." It was almost as if he could read the future.

As I went through different phases of medical school and training. I kept his advice in the back of my mind. Once I graduated from medical school and completed an emergency medicine residency, I remembered his advice. I kept repeating the phrase, "keep work at work." I promised myself I would not bring any challenges from work home. My home would be a sanctuary. It will be a space filled with peace, joy, and love. Free from the stress and the uncertainty of medicine.

The first few years were good. I enjoyed getting to know my colleagues at work. I contributed to the team, joined committees, and shared thoughts on how we could get better. I came up with ideas to help improve the flow because I was excited and thought we could improve healthcare for all of us. Fresh out of residency, I had all the grand ideas and would share them with anyone who would listen.

I worked a lot during that time. Like most physicians, I had six figures in student loans that haunted me. If shifts were open, I would take them. Any time of day or any time of night. I would work weekends and holidays. As a result, I never took vacations longer than five days. Looking back, all that work was rooted in fear. The fear of not having enough. I feared going back to the days when I had to choose between paying for parking or turning up the heat in my apartment. I had to make those decisions because I was broke as a resident. There was also the fear of defaulting on student loans. I learned that I would still need to pay back my student loans if I became disabled and could not work as a physician. As a result, I was motivated to get the financial albatross from around my neck.

I continued working nonstop because I wanted to get rid of my debt. The focus consumed me. Then one day, I noticed that I was becoming grumpier and angrier after completing shifts. I wasn't upset at the patients but became annoyed. I am unsure when I started to experience these feelings. I no longer wanted to share my ideas with the team at work because I thought my opinions did not matter. I moved from being fired up about working additional shifts to not wanting to go to work. I didn't have the words for it back then, but today, I know those were the classic signs of burnout.

I tried to identify the exact factors that led to this feeling but couldn't pinpoint them. It might have been when the administrative team re-arranged the department and eliminated privacy for doctors. Of course, this happened without consulting any of the physicians on the team. I went to work one day and was told about the change. This was just another act that frustrated me. As an emergency medicine physician, I am used to interruptions and working quickly, but implementing an obstacle to my efficiency was problematic. I needed to have an area where I could focus on developing a treatment plan for life-or-death situations. Maybe it was the loss of autonomy and the fact that folks with no medical training offered opinions on the best way to treat patients.

It might have been the constant policy shifts and the fear of losing my job over one mistake. Policies like the "three strikes" rule for physicians. If I made any three errors, I could be terminated. Lucky for me, I was informed in writing that I was on strike one, so I better be careful. I explained what happened, but the senior leaders did not seem to care. I was merely a cog in a wheel. A number in a system, and I was treated that way.

It might have been when the toxic culture started spreading, and bad behavior was allowed. In one instance, a senior leader in the system tossed an item at my superiors. If they did that to them, what would happen to me when they got mad? How would they react if I said or did something they didn't like? I had a feeling it wouldn't be good. I knew it was time for a change.

Looking back, it happened during the first 5 years after residency. As I mentioned, burnout is tricky, like a tiger nestled deep in the tall bushes, creeping towards its unsuspecting prey. That is how burnout pranced upon me.

How can I help others avoid the same experience? I have several pieces of advice. As you approach the post-residency life, I urge you to take a few moments to reflect on the "wants" you delayed for your medical education. Create a bucket list of all the experiences you want to pursue. Rank the list in order of priority and start working down the list. I would also remind folks to practice self-care. You can't pour from an empty cup so fill your cup before pouring into others.

Why? Because during those first few years, you will find yourself "wanting" to accomplish tasks such as paying off your loans and adding to your formerly empty bank account. You might even need a cushion to help others in your family. Because of the immense financial pressure, you will likely say "yes" to more shifts and not place any boundaries around work because you always need to be available. You are earning more, but life might become dimmer. You may even be upset and unable to enjoy the fruits of your labor.

As time passes, you find yourself financially stable but unhappy. You find yourself cranky and exhausted. You have been there for everyone, neglecting to ask for help. You do this at work and the same at home. You feel like you must be the superhero. You can do it all by yourself. You place expectations on yourself based on your "gender role." You tell yourself, "my mother was able to work full-time, keep the house clean, cook a fresh meal daily, and was attentive to her family." I should be able to do the same. So you try to live up to those expectations.

The anger builds, and you complain even more. The advice you were given, "keep work at work," becomes meaningless. Like that low-lying predator, the tiger slowly snuck into your house and attacked you. You didn't even see it coming. You look around, and all you see is what is wrong at work and home. You have now entered into the deep realms of burnout.

How are you thriving today?

I am thriving. I am the CEO of UR Caring Docs where I help companies reduce employee burnout and create amazing cultures. I also host a weekly show where I get to interview my physician colleagues across the world.

About Tamara Beckford MD MS
Dr. Tamara Beckford is a physician, speaker, and CEO of UR Caring Docs, where she helps companies build amazing cultures and reduce employee burnout through self-care workshops. She hosts the Dr. Tamara Beckford Show, interviewing physicians

about self-care, wellness, and their lives inside and outside clinical medicine. To date, she has interviewed 170 physicians across the world. Globally, the podcast named after the show ranks in the top 5% of podcasts. Dr. Beckford has presented about the importance of wellness on many platforms, including Power to Fly, Scale Your Business Summit, The Grants Professionals Association, CenterPoint Energy, Physician Coach Support, and Blaze Virtual Summit. She has been featured on 60+ podcasts. In 2022 her content was viewed over 1 million times on social media. Dr Beckford is a success coach and co-author of the book Made For More which will be released in January 2023. The New Jersey Academy of Sciences recognized Dr. Beckford as a COVID-19 Hero for her work during the pandemic.

www.urcaringdocs.com

Cecilia Minano, MD, MPH

I have known since the 3rd grade that I wanted to be a doctor. I did not have any role models in my family, but I knew I enjoyed helping people and I had always excelled in school. I was raised by a single mother who was surviving to provide for my two brothers and me. She worked hard, but was easily frustrated and angry and never seemed to pay too much attention to us. I was fortunate to have a love of education from a very young age and escaped into the fantasies and stories of books. I think I compensated for my internal anxiety from a young age by working hard and studying around the clock. I always recall being very judgmental of myself, always seeing my flaws and having negative self-talk. I always believed I would fail, but I kept trying.

When I embarked into medicine, I was thrilled, but felt like an imposter throughout my education and training. I was highly anxious but compensated by studying the material hard so that I had a strong medical knowledge foundation for questioning on rounds or taking exams. When I matched into internal medicine, I was also dealing with a divorce privately, so I was emotionally a wreck when I was home. I had never really "failed" at anything, so this felt like I had hit rock bottom. I finally shared my experience with one friend because I thought if I didn't, I would surely drop out. He thankfully didn't judge me as I expected, and we grew to be each other's support until he dropped out of the program. I was devastated as he was one of my closest friends, and I barely had many growing up. The remainder of my training was a daze as I was chronically sleep deprived. I applied for chief resident, and when I did not get that position, I felt like a total failure, and my self-critical self took center stage. I began to isolate myself for the remainder of my training and just pushed myself to get through. I do recall an attending who reached out to discuss my annual progress and admitted to her that I was depressed, and she had me see a therapist who helped me begin to process my emotions.

I had always been interested in gastroenterology and had completed research throughout my residency, but I did not honestly think anyone would write me a letter of recommendation. However, this same attending who directed me to therapy months earlier now approached me about applying, so I decided to try once. I matched into a competitive Fellowship and was elated, but that was short lived. The hours were long, and I became, even more sleep deprived. I recall some attendings were nice, but there were a few hostile ones that seemed to judge me more harshly and enjoyed putting me down especially in public areas. I constantly felt judged and criticized and wondered why the environment could not be more collegial. I was thankful not to have to go to my graduation as I had just had a baby because there were so few there that I felt supported me.

I continued to face burnout well into being an attending. It was when Covid hit that my anxiety hit an all time high and could not be contained. I was not sleeping, often crying, having more self-judgment, and showing up negatively at home to my husband and kids. I remembered meeting a surgeon at a wellness conference a few years prior who told me about coaching, so I decided to become a client of coaching. I knew how much it had impacted her, and I needed a change. It has been truly transformative and has allowed me to pause before reacting and helped me learn how to process my emotions. I have learned how to create boundaries for myself at home and at work, implemented more self-care, and begun to dream again. I have since now become a coach to help others transform their lives.

Questions and Answers

Looking back, was there anything in your childhood or upbringing that you think led to your burnout?

I come from humble beginnings and a single Mom household. My Mom worked very hard to provide for us, but did not raise us to be open to discussing difficult emotions or experiences, including being immigrants, growing up in high crime and gang-related areas, and having an absent Dad. I internalized my own anxiety and fears and became an overachiever, perfectionist and people pleaser. For most of my life, I have been my worst critic and over judged myself for perceived internal flaws.

It was not until I came to coaching that I realized the language I was using toward myself was filled with shame, guilt, anxiety, and fear and never anything positive.

Did anything occur in your training that led to your burnout?

For me the culture of medicine definitely heightened my already existing burnout. It seems to idolize overworking, limited self-care, not taking time off when sick or caring for a baby, etc. I felt like I was running at warped speed throughout my training, and if I did not keep up, I was failing. Since I was not perfect at everything, I believed myself to be internally flawed, but I overcompensated by trying to keep up, studying hard, and being a people pleaser. There was little conversation or processing to be had about difficult experiences with patients or attendings, patient deaths, and negative criticism during presentations or journal club. I harbored many negative feelings toward myself and they stuck to me to the point where I even became clinically depressed, even more, anxious and isolated myself.

Was there anything about the system you worked in that led to your episode (s) of burnout?

I think the overall culture that pushes you to always try and achieve the highest standard, teaches you to never make mistakes because it's so costly, and never regards taking time off, all while being sleep deprived inadvertently breeds burnout. The irony is that we are supposed to be kind and compassionate for our patients, yet we, the doctors, are not provided that same level of care and compassion. I recall several times being ill but being advised to "deal with it." I think burnout is multifactorial. It includes the individual's characteristics, i.e., perfectionism, hard working, people pleasing. It also includes the work culture which believes in self-sacrifice, putting everyone else first, working even if you are emotionally or physically exhausted.

What helped you overcome your burnout?

I have an amazing husband who has been my rock through residency and Fellowship. I did not divulge all my negative experiences but just having someone there to support me while I cried or stayed up late to finish a presentation made all the difference for me. I realized that I was showing up in a negative space to my husband and children and that I had to change.

Did you have a support system?

Even though I am a coach, I still have my own coach to process all of life's ups and downs. It is my life line to get me through daily challenges. I also rely on the support of my husband, kids, and friends. As someone who, for most of her life, was very reserved with friendships, I now bask in having relationships that are truly meaningful.

Did anyone notice and reach out to you?

In my residency, I was thankful that during my annual review my attending "checked in with me," and I felt her caring heart. I was able to confess that I was depressed and needed help, and she provided me with resources and checked in on me periodically. For the first time, I felt I was able to exhale deeply and process my emotions.

How are you thriving today?

I am purposeful with my life now. I carve time for my coaching, family, vacations, work, journaling, movement, and sleep. I consider these pillars of my wellness. I enjoy coaching, collaborating with colleagues on coaching, and journaling. I am currently coaching 1:1 clients with burnout and with mind-gut issues. I find the coaching work transformational for my clients and fulfilling for me.

What advice would you give to someone going through burnout?

Please get help because there is hope you can change. You may not realize you are in burnout until you hit rock bottom and are feeling unhappy, frustrated, anxious, angry, and overwhelmed while trying to balance it all. It is definitely NOT your fault, and you can change. Give yourself permission to embark on this truly transformational journey.

What advice would you give to the facilities and administration who are trying to help decrease the rate of physician burnout?

It is not enough to just check-in with your residents. They need coaching from an external resource to help them gain life skill resources that will help them succeed.

What advice if any, would you give to the facilities that can do better when it comes to improving burnout rates of physicians (those facilities that appear to have a lack of interest in helping to improve conditions)

We still have a crisis of medical doctors committing suicide, so this is of utmost importance for the medical community.

About Cecilia Minano, MD, MPH
Dr. Minano helps high achieving professionals overcome burnout by using a mind-body approach. She helps them enhance their own internal cues by building up their own resilience toolkit that helps them overcome negative beliefs and teaches them about nervous system regulation using the soma or body.

www.ceciliaminanomd.com

Payal Ghayal MD

When I was running around in clinic on a busy fall day, my medical assistant came to share some special news with me. Her daughter was pregnant, and she was going to be a grandma for the first time.

I was so happy for her, and it made me think, "When was the last time I got my period?" It's been a while, and we did want to start trying for our first. I thought it wouldn't hurt to check. Yup- exactly what you thought. I was pregnant, and I had no idea how long it's been.

I was excited and a little anxious because work was super busy, and on average, I worked 6 days a week, around 60 hours on average.

Of course, I was going to keep this secret to myself until I was in my second trimester, but I didn't know how much energy it was going to take out of me.

I go to work a few days later, and I'm the only doctor in a small pediatric office. Everyone was sick, and tons of kids needed the flu shot. Back then, I gave every vaccine that our practice administered myself because we didn't have a nurse. At the end of the day, I saw the total number on our census- 72. Yes, you read that right!

I was exhausted, hungry, and nauseous all day. But of course, I was back in the office 12 hours later to do it all again. Within the first hour I knew something wasn't right. After completing a 12-month WCC I walked out of the room and started seeing spots. My legs gave way and I had to sit down in my office chair with my legs up on the desk. The staff came and checked on me. They didn't understand what was going on but were super stressed because every exam room was full, and the front was full of young families with kids.

I went home despite resistance from my boss, who was out of the country on a family vacation. It was then I realized that maybe I wasn't going to be able to perform my best anymore, and it wasn't going to be accepted. I somehow managed the next 9 months and decided to take a 3-month maternity leave which I would have to use FMLA and unpaid. I was married to a fellow, so that would be a major hit to our monthly budget.

Now let's fast forward 3 months post-partum. I had a healthy baby boy whom I loved and adored. But he also was the reason I never slept longer than 2 hours at a time and looked like a zombie. I chose to breastfeed and despite the initial struggle, we were able to make it happen. As I mentioned earlier, my husband was in a malignant cardiology fellowship which meant I was on my own for all the feedings and 95% of the childcare. We had no money and no support other than my parents, who came to help while working a fulltime job cross country.

I knew my boss was going to ask me if I was all set to come back, and the answer was "NO". I didn't know how I was going to see 50 patients, work 12 hours, pump every 3 hours so my chest didn't explode, and then come home and be up all-night nursing and caring for my baby.

When my boss called and asked about my plan, I told him about my dilemma. I was so anxious and felt like I was going to meet resistance, which is exactly what happened. They wanted an answer right away, and there would be no changes to my schedule because it would affect productivity. Even if I was given the option to ease my way back with fewer days, the expectation was to produce the same, if not more.

I didn't want to give up nursing my baby. I felt like a hypocrite helping other moms care for and feed their babies the way they desired but I couldn't do the same. It didn't sit well with me. It didn't seem fair.

On the one hand, I wanted to do what was best for my son, and on the other hand, all I could think about was letting my practice down. It made me physically sick to think about the conversation I would have to have with my boss.

Despite all the anxiety it created, I knew something had to change. I had to choose between nursing my baby and being a doctor.
I choose to be a mama then, but I still remember the disappointment on the other side of the phone. My boss was angry, and I felt like I couldn't even ask him to be a reference in the future. If I was a man, this would've never been a problem.

As women, moms, and doctors, we are asked to choose between purpose and passion.

Questions and Answers

Looking back, was there anything in your childhood or upbringing that you think led to your burnout?

The Asian first generation immigrant upbringing led me to put my head down and work hard to earn acceptance by superiors, colleagues and patients.

Did anything occur in your training that led to your burnout?

I had co-residents who had babies during our 3 years in Peds residency. I recall so many negative comments directly and indirectly towards them. I also saw them overcompensate for their "time off" with a newborn at home and minimal to no sleep. So when I started my first attending job and found out that I was expecting, I felt panic immediately. All I could think about was how this would affect everyone else and what they would think of me. I didn't enjoy the pregnancy or the post part period because I had to figure out how to do two full-time jobs simultaneously- mom and doctor.

Was there anything about the system you worked in that led to your episode (s) of burnout?

I worked in a very busy private practice where I saw almost 50 pediatric patients in a day. I was as a solo doctor working for a larger family medical business. There was a lot of emphasis on productivity and very little time to recuperate between patient encounters. I remember when I first found out I was pregnant, but the office staff didn't know I saw 72 patients in 12 hours during flu season. There was no other coverage, and my boss was out of town. I had so much pressure to come back the next day. I felt like I had no choice.

What helped you overcome your burnout?

Hiring a life coach and going through the process of certification to become a coach was the most transformative for me personally. It helped me differentiate between the stories I told myself and the reality of what was really true.

Did you have a support system?

I didn't have a support system when I was burnt out but later built a village of women who came from different seasons of my life.

Did anyone notice and reach out to you?

Nope

How are you thriving today?

I am more than thriving now. I live in the present and have hope for my future regardless of what happens and how others show up. I feel empowered and on a journey to loving and accepting myself more and more each day. Having a personal coach, exercising, journaling, meditating, and connecting with friends helps me find fulfillment.

What advice would you give to someone going through burnout?

Don't suffer alone. Being open and vulnerable is not easy but extremely transformative.

What advice would you give to the facilities and administration who are trying to help decrease the rate of physician burnout?

Stop shaming women for procreating. Don't ask women who have just had a baby to pretend it never happened.

Payal Ghayal MD
Dr. Payal Ghayal, is a certified life coach for women physicians and an Integrative Pediatrician. She helps women physicians start advocating for themselves and experience greater fulfillment and happiness. Payal received her coach training at The Life Coach School and is currently working with women of all backgrounds looking to meld two cultures to create their own identity. She truly enjoys coaching women of color who identify as first or second-generation Americans.

www.payalghayal.com

Santisree Tanikella, MD, FAAP, ABIMH, ABOIM

I'm the youngest of three children. My parents were immigrants from India. Their path, like many immigrants, was not easy. They both worked very hard to create a safe, happy, prosperous home environment for us. My father did research and worked for a pharmaceutical company. He often worked long hours, and there were days that he'd leave in the morning, not to be seen again until midnight. My mother, who initially studied education in India, changed course and studied all over again to become a nurse. She worked night shift so that a parent was always available 24 hours a day/7 days a week for us. My parents tried not to trouble others or depend on others for help and always aimed to be totally self-sufficient. As an example, I never had a nanny or babysitter. They tried to save as much money as possible. We rarely ever went on vacation or spent money on things that were frivolous.

Both of my parents were perfectionists in their own ways and had high expectations for themselves. I think the combination of perfectionism, the constant pace of their lives, and sheer exhaustion led them into burnout. One day, my father was helping me with my homework (I must have been about 9 years old) and he strongly advised me never to trust anyone, because they might one day steal my work and be given credit for my achievements. I guess he had recently been in an incident with a coworker or a superior who had done this to him. It was clear that that, too, had contributed to his burnout.

Cue me. That was the norm that I grew up in.

From an early age, I knew that I had wanted to become a doctor. I was 5 years old, eating dinner and watching a TV sitcom with my family. In that particular episode, the main character, a doctor, delivered a baby and I thought that was just magical. I knew at that moment that I wanted to help children and their families thrive by teaching them how to live healthy, joyful lives.

I am told that I was a very conscientious child, thoughtful, and well-organized. I worked hard to get good grades. I received compliments on these qualities all the time. Of course, as a child, who doesn't want compliments? My sister tended to be a little more free-spirited, and this sometimes got her in trouble. I hated getting in trouble and I did my best to avoid it. Indian culture prizes a prototypical girl/woman who holds certain qualities: Being intelligent and accomplished. Being artistic. Being good. Being quiet. Being nurturing. Not ruffling others' feathers. Diplomacy. Always looking happy and put-together no matter how you felt on the inside. When I exhibited these qualities, I'd receive praise. I tried hard to embody these qualities.

I recognized in high school that in order to get into medical school, there were more people I needed to please. I now had to hit all the possible check boxes that my college and medical school interviewers would be looking for. I pushed myself when it came to academics. Check. Clubs – I joined several and tried to function as well as I could in all of them. Check. I worked in a doctor's office after school – first as a volunteer, and then later as a paid member of the team. Check. When I was in 12th grade, I became a certified EMT and volunteered on an EMS squad. I carried a pager and would answer calls in the middle of the night. Check. Then, of course, standardized tests. That was a grueling check. Earning college credits. Check. It was a struggle to balance all of these things and still be a normal teenager.

I learned about joint 7-8 year Bachelor and MD programs as I was entering 12th grade. I was motivated and applied to 10 such programs. I interviewed at colleges and medical schools simultaneously. The fellow 12th graders I met on the interview trail were remarkable. My heart sank. I immediately felt 'less than,' and could no longer think of myself and my accomplishments as amazing. I was fearful that I wouldn't meet the cut. Somehow, I did make the cut and felt incredibly blessed for it. My hard work had paid off.

I went on to an all-women's college. Being at a small school allowed me to develop myself in a way that I don't think would have happened at a larger institution. Academically, I worked hard. My college professors cared about my progress and encouraged me. The perfectionist and high achiever in me got stronger. Luckily, I had incredible friends to keep me balanced. During our senior year of college, a few of us went to Omega Institute's Women & Power conference. It was life changing for us to hear stories and lessons from other women, many of whom were authors and leaders with a global presence. Their stories were humbling and inspiring and called each of us to action. They were examples of what was possible. We carried their wisdom with us as we each moved into a new phase of our lives.

I went on to medical school. I was proud and excited. But medical training was a different beast. It demanded precision and perfection. Most of the subjects have very concrete answers that are either correct or incorrect. What muscle is this? What's the physiology of that? What medications can treat high blood pressure? What's the pathway for the Krebs cycle? Lots of memorization. Lots of tests. Lots of self-imposed mental flagellation when I messed up. I had felt like I had a good handle on things when I was in college, but now the amount of material was starting to feel impossible to put my arms around. I put a great deal of my time and mental energy towards training. My self-esteem was starting to tank again. I was physically and emotionally exhausted. I started to prune time away from my family, friendships, and hobbies so that I could focus more on school. In doing so, I felt like I had started to lose pieces of my identity.

By March of my 1st year of medical school, I began to feel disenchanted. The material we were learning felt mechanistic. Was this what medical school was going to be like?? It was all about the human body and how it worked (of course), but very little about the human being itself and all the things that came with it. What about personal belief systems? Spirituality? Motivation to make changes to become healthier? Would we learn more about this later on in the curriculum?

I felt trapped and there was this overwhelming need to go as far as I could from that place. In between college and medical school, I had started to read books about Ayurvedic Medicine, and I was intrigued. Ayurveda is a traditional form of medicine practiced in India, which dates back 5000 years, and it quite literally translates to "the science of life." There was nothing like Ayurvedic medicine in conventional western medicine. I decided to follow my urge. I arranged to do a medical rotation in India in the summer between first and second year of medical school through Child Family Health International. The rotation took us through clinics that practiced Ayurveda and other healing modalities, including Naturopathy, Yoga, Reiki, and Homeopathy. I applied for and received grant funding from the Arnold P. Gold Foundation to help pay for the expenses. In exchange, I was to create a lecture series teaching my fellow medical students about each of these modalities. The commonality between all of these healing systems/modalities was that there was a strong emphasis on emotional and physical wellness, and the treatments were individualized to the patient. The patient was treated like a human being and not just a machine where the focus was on one specific part that was perceived to be broken. I remember hearing the term "supratentorial" being used pejoratively towards patients on clinical rounds here in the States when their ailment had no physiological basis. With these other healing modalities, however, the patient's suffering was not only taken into account but treated seamlessly alongside their physical illnesses. Human suffering was a part of their illness, not a pesky obstacle that was in the doctor's way. This more expansive worldview on patient care fueled my ability to complete my medical training. It started to mold the type of physician that I wanted to become.

I went on to do a residency in Pediatrics, and being around children gave me new life. The long, grueling hours and the compassion fatigue, however, wore at me. Twenty-four-hour call was never just 24 hours... sometimes it'd be upwards of 30+ hours without sleep, trying to function at my highest throughout. Still trying to serve the sick. Trying not to harm the children despite being foggy of mind at 4 am. Being a shoulder for parents to cry on when their child was suffering. I was blessed and cursed all at once. Sometimes, my senior residents or my attendings would say things that would shake my confidence. The physical and emotional exhaustion limited my ability to maintain good self-care. I was lucky, though, to have some good friends and some supportive attendings who saw me for who I was and what I was capable of.

I think one of the most formative moments I had was while rounding in the Pediatric ICU. One of my patients had passed away during morning rounds and was being cared for by the attending, who was on overnight. Here I was, standing on the other side of the ICU in front of the day team, including the attending and my fellow residents who were fresh and ready to receive information about the patients from overnight. Though we couldn't see the family, I could hear the parents of the child crying and wailing, their grief echoing through the halls. I knew that the overnight attending had just pronounced this sweet 8-year old boy dead. Everyone looked at me, expectantly, to learn about the next patient on rounds... as if everything were totally normal. As if they couldn't hear what was happening. I knew at that moment there was nothing for me to physically do for that child. I wanted to say my goodbyes to the little boy who was my teacher. I had held the hands of the mother intermittently during the night, and so badly wanted to be there for her in those final moments. Yet, here I was, rounding with the day team. I felt torn. Crushed. The field of medicine requests that you keep your composure during times like these so that you can continue to serve your patients. This was a moment in which I felt our system was truly broken. We did not stop to share a moment of silence. We did not even acknowledge what was happening on the other side of the PICU. The lack of compassion weighed on me. After the death of a patient, we were given the option to do debriefing. These generally happened a week or so after the patient's death. They were always scheduled during clinical care hours. It was never protected time. Looking back, I struggled with these barriers. I could have/should have gone for my own personal healing... but I didn't, partially because I was always so overwhelmed with the demands of that day that I didn't feel like I could pull away without falling behind. I was also afraid of what others might think of me, and I didn't want anyone to perceive me as 'weak.'

After graduating from residency, I went into General Pediatrics. I loved watching kids and their families evolve. I loved being able to empower moms and dads, especially as they took their first steps into parenthood. I loved being able to teach kids about their health through play. I loved working with teens and helping them navigate their new-found emotions. Building relationships with these patients and their families was a joy, and I felt a renewed sense of purpose.

After I had my first child, though, I began to feel burned out again. My son rarely slept through the night. Night after night of, severe sleep deprivation took its toll. Soon after, my husband had left the state to pursue fellowship. I moved in with my parents, and was grateful for the care they gave my son while I worked full time. About 18 months into this arrangement, my father became very sick. Juggling motherhood, being a dutiful daughter to my parents, and being my father's medical advocate was exhausting. Managing my emotions and my mother's needs after my father's death proved difficult. I was very good at keeping my composure during periods of high stress, but this came at a cost. Months later, I began to experience health problems of my own and I realized I had to shift my energy toward making positive changes in my life. I had no idea how big the ripple effect would be.

I decided to pursue fellowship in Integrative Medicine. What's Integrative Medicine, you ask? The Academic Consortium for Integrative Medicine and Health defines it in the following way: "Integrative medicine and health reaffirms the importance of the relationship between practitioner and patient, focuses on the whole person, is informed by evidence, and makes use of all appropriate therapeutic and lifestyle approaches, healthcare professionals and disciplines to achieve optimal health and healing." I received training in lifestyle modification, dietary supplements, botanicals, mind-body medicine, and learned how to interweave these with current conventional medicine practices to help optimize patient outcomes. There were additional bonuses with going to this fellowship. I learned about self-care and self-compassion. In fact, it was built into the curriculum. I also met a group of like-minded, beautiful souls whose mere presence gave me hope during one of the darkest periods of my life.

I went on to create a clinic in Pediatric Integrative Medicine. I had a lot of fear around what people would think of me when I started this process. Would they think that I had changed? That I had 'gone soft'? That I wasn't practicing real evidence-based medicine anymore?

In this process of stepping into my true self, both as a human being and as a physician, I realized that I could no longer make everyone happy. There were some people (medical professionals, parents, and patients) who were very happy with what I could offer them, and others who appeared to be in blatant disgust. Those who weren't in agreement questioned my professionalism and criticized me – sometimes to my face, sometimes behind my back, and sometimes in front of colleagues within the medical community. This hurt me to my core but eventually became a life lesson for me. My supporters – for whom I am forever thankful – encouraged me to fight for what I believed in. I believed in myself. I believed in my ability to help others by expanding my skillset in medicine. I believed in my ability to provide compassionate care to people who were suffering. I believe that the medical system could evolve into a better healing environment for its patients. And, so, I marched on.

Around this time, I started to learn about life coaching. Coaching ultimately transformed the way that I functioned within my world. It changed the way I related to myself, my family, and my friends, for the better. It provided me with a community of caring individuals who embraced a growth mindset. It helped me to further step into the person I hoped to become.

Question and Answers

What helped you overcome your burnout?

Looking back over the past 25 years, there are a few themes that repeatedly popped up. These factors helped me overcome burnout at various stages in my life and thrive again:

Community
A sense of purpose
Listening to myself without judgment
Acknowledging and meeting my personal needs

Did you have a support system?

I wasn't very vocal about how burned out I had become. Because of the high demands of training, I didn't always make time to reach out to my close friends. I also worried that, even if I did, they wouldn't totally understand. My boyfriend at the time (now my husband) went to medical school and residency at the same time as me but was in a different program. We often talked about our experiences. I was glad that we could understand what the other was going through. The downside was because we were both going through it, the stress of training, and later, our careers, became normalized. In other words, we were living in it for so long, we had forgotten what normal was.

I mentioned before the importance of community in my life. During medical school, I had learned about the American Medical Student Association (AMSA). AMSA had a section on Humanism in Medicine. They held weekend-long retreats 1-2 times a year. The planners for these retreats had a gift for creating a space for a healing. Knowing that there was a community of healers out there who could hold and encourage each other was one of the most pivotal parts of healing my burnout. I later became a planner for these retreats. Being able to collaboratively create healing environments for others (and myself) was rewarding.

How are you thriving today?

The self-confidence that I have gained over the past few years has helped me to open my life to new opportunities. Even when things seemingly go wrong, I am able to bounce back and see the lesson that it presents, instead of perseverating over the negative.

I continue to serve patients at my Pediatric Integrative Medicine clinic. The patients that come through the Integrative Medicine clinic are generally medically and/or socially complex, and they often have associated anxiety or depression. This can severely limit their ability to lead normal lives. Their caregivers come to me at a point where they are seeking out holistic care. I take great pride in being able to offer such care.

I also became a life coach. I created a business called Integrative Approaches to Mastering Wellness, which is dedicated to helping individuals (including physicians) heal from burnout and perfectionism. I utilize my knowledge of life coaching and mind-body medicine to help others reduce stress and increase self-compassion.

What advice would you give to someone going through burnout?

My greatest piece of advice is to know that you're not alone. Even though it may feel at times like the workload and expectations are so heavy that you can't even pick your head up – take that one last grain of energy to pick your head up and take a look around you. You may be surprised to know that there are more people rooting for you than you could ever imagine. We are here, ready to help and support you.

What advice would you give to the facilities and administration who are trying to help decrease the rate of physician burnout?

I think the first piece of advice I'd give is to recognize that we all want to have lives outside of our careers. The culture of medicine has taught us that self-sacrifice is something that is worthy of praise. The reality is that self-sacrifice is not sustainable and can damage our personal lives and professional lives.

As a primary care provider, 15 – 20 minute visits aren't always enough time, especially when you have medically/socially complex patients, patients that don't speak English, new patients, or patients who are being discharged from the hospital. The doctor-patient relationship, to me, is one that is sacred. A factory-model healthcare system does not allow room for meaningful relationships between healer and patient. As a result, many physicians experience burnout because their purpose for coming into medicine has been displaced by a financial model that's often designed by non-physician administrators and insurance companies.

Also, phone and email messages can take hours to complete, especially for primary care providers. This is something that most practices ask their physicians to do in addition to direct patient care. Physicians generally don't get paid for the time that is spent on these messages. That means there are several hours per day, several days per week that physicians are not getting reimbursed for their work - of course this would contribute to moral distress. Time should be carved out of the workday so that these messages and lab results can be addressed. This will allow physicians to go home to their families on time and allow for self-care.

If you want to enhance our productivity, having a scribe would be amazing.

Lastly, having access to professional coaches can help decrease emotional exhaustion, decrease burnout, improve quality of life, and increase resilience for physicians. (Dyrbye LN, Shanafelt TD, Gill PR, Satele DV, West CP. Effect of a Professional Coaching Intervention on the Well-being and Distress of Physicians: A Pilot Randomized Clinical Trial. JAMA Intern Med. 2019 Oct 1;179(10):1406-1414. doi: 10.1001/jamainternmed.2019.2425. PMID: 31380892; PMCID: PMC6686971.)

What advice if any would you give to the facilities that can do better when it comes to improving burnout rates of physicians (those facilities that appear to have a lack of interest in helping to improve conditions)?

Physicians are the cog in the wheel that earns money for the whole system. If the institution can help them, they will be more likely to provide their best work.

Losing a physician to burnout and having to sign a new one can cost an organization a significant amount of money. It is easier and more cost-effective to work with the physicians that are already present.

This article published in the Journal of the American Medical Association (JAMA) states these ideas beautifully:

"Understanding the business case to reduce burnout and promote engagement as well as overcoming the misperception that nothing meaningful can be done are key steps for organizations to begin to take action. Evidence suggests that improvement is possible, investment is justified, and return on investment is measurable. Addressing this issue is not only the organization's ethical responsibility, it is also the fiscally responsible one." (Shanafelt T, Goh J, Sinsky C. The Business Case for Investing in Physician Well-being. JAMA Intern Med. 2017 Dec 1;177(12):1826-1832. doi: 10.1001/jamainternmed.2017.4340. PMID: 28973070.)

About Santisree Tanikella, MD, FAAP, ABIMH, ABOIM
Dr. Tanikella practices General Pediatrics and Pediatric Integrative Medicine. She is a Clinical Assistant Professor in Pediatrics. She graduated from Drexel University College of Medicine, completed my pediatrics training at the Children's Hospital of Montefiore, and pursued a fellowship in Integrative Medicine at the Academy of Integrative Health and Medicine.

Dr Tanikella has a special interest in Mind-Body Medicine, and have additional trainings in meditation, Mindfulness, Biofeedback, Hypnosis, Reiki, and Ayurvedic Lifestyle. She also obtained training as a life coach through The Life Coach School. She has always had an interest in the area of emotional wellness. She has presented at lectures, workshops, and retreats geared toward physician and healthcare provider wellness since 2007 and have found this to be a truly rewarding experience.

There is an intimate relationship between emotional wellness and one's personal beliefs. I am fascinated by the roles that upbringing, culture, psychology, and spirituality play in how a person defines themself and the world they live in.

Coaching has taught me how much my beliefs allowed me to achieve success. It also taught me how much I had been limiting myself. Some of these limiting beliefs were unknowingly created by me. Some of them were taught to me, whether it was through my family, culture (both Indian and American culture), friends, TV, movies, and books.

I didn't even realize that my beliefs about myself and my place in the world were restricting me. I had inadvertently put myself into a glass cage. Everything inside my cage looked amazing to the outsider who was looking in. And yet... something didn't feel right to me. When I started to become aware of the self-limiting beliefs that were present, all of a sudden, the glass cage began to crack. Soon after, every wall shattered, and so did the proverbial glass ceiling.

I'm grateful for what I have learned. I am excited to share what I have learned with you.

Whether you are seeking to restore wellness and balance to your life, or you are ready for massive transformation, I would be honored to help you on your journey.

Thank you for reading my story. I hope my words have provided you with a sense of comfort and inspiration.

iamwellmd.com

Chinyelu E. Oraedu M.D. (Dr. Yel'Ora)

In the stillness of the night, all I hear are crickets! I have been propped up in bed for hours.

Wait a minute, I can hear a second sound. Whistling, wheezing, with bouts of a hacking cough. Oh No! The sound is coming from my airway. It sounds like a musical instrument was buried deep in my lungs. Slowly, I realize, I cannot breathe.

I muster some energy, and I walk across to my parent's room. "we need to go to the emergency room again". Asthma!!

This was my 10-year-old self who experienced nocturnal asthma symptoms at least 2-3x/week. We did not have a home nebulizer. My standard medications were Ventolin and Aminophylline. For flare-ups, I was placed on injectable hydrocortisone. This was in the mid-1980s in a quaint university town Nsukka in South Eastern Nigeria. My parents settled here after they returned from Birmingham, United Kingdom. In the Casualty Room (same as ER), I was always treated by this knowledgeable female physician who used the limited resources at her disposal to render excellent care. This kind doctor made such a lasting impression on me. I decided at 10 years old that I wanted to be a medical doctor.

I started my life staying awake at night due to asthma symptoms. Thankfully, today, I no longer have nocturnal symptoms and rarely do I need my inhaler. I know my triggers- smoke, dust, cold air & grass.

Zipping through elementary school and secondary school, I was an A student. Very competitive. In elementary school, I loved creative writing. I wrote a lot of poems and short plays, which earned me awards and recognition in school. For Secondary school, I went to an elite All Girls' Boarding School. Initially, I hated boarding school till I became a senior. The perks associated with being a senior in a Nigerian boarding school were limitless. You enjoyed extended personal time after lights out, and frequent outings into the big city. The junior students revered and adored you (this helped massage a few weak egos). I completed Boarding school with straight As in my final Certification Examination. I applied to Medical School and was accepted.

The commonality in my childhood till my early adult life was my tenacity. I was never a quitter. I remember the voice in my head that says "No rest till success is achieved". I was so madly driven even as a young kid.

By Medical school, I began to notice the waning in my tempo. My medical school was highly competitive. Full of the brightest and smartest minds. Being a natural storyteller, I enjoyed my Internal Medicine clinical rotation. I loved taking a detailed history and formulating differential diagnoses. My witty side helped me connect with patients and families at first contact. I realized I was a People's person. I loved to talk and listen to people. The long 7 years I spent in Medical school allowed me to make a lot of friends. Nowadays, we communicate on social media from different parts of the world via a class WhatsApp chat group.

Next, I graduated from medical school. Chi Chi (as I am fondly called), you're now a medical doctor. What is your next move? Relocate to the U.K. or America or remain in Nigeria?

I traveled to America. The cycle repeats again. "You need to pass the USMLE before you can practice in America". This means more studying, more testing, and countless sleepless nights. Finally, I made it!!! I applied to Internal Medicine Residency and got accepted in a prematch. Did I tell you, I traveled for my interviews while pregnant with my twin boys?

Now my deeper story about burnout.

The dictionary description of the term "Burnout "means, literary "to be forced to stop working because you have become ill or very tired from working too hard".

For many years, I played multiple roles-wife, mother, daughter, doctor, community member, and volunteer parent seemingly perfectly. I never faltered. But inside, I knew I had to hit the snooze button.
I started my IM residency when our twin boys were 4 months old. I had a nanny and a teenager who was the nanny's helper. We had no money at that time. We had limited choices for childcare. Also, I was commuting from Long Island to Brooklyn on a daily basis. My parents were living and working in Muscat, Oman. They could not care for our kids for an extended time.

I remember being the only black girl in my first-year internal medicine class. I felt I had a shitty schedule, working on most holidays. It was almost impossible to switch schedules for personal events. The fact we had to do scutwork in Residency added another layer to an already stressful situation. I started to feel exhausted but did not seek help in Residency. I do not remember at any time my program offered mental health and wellness services to the residents.

Post Residency, I started my first job as a Hospitalist- Nocturnist. One of the decisions I made early in my life as a teenager, I did not want to be totally dependent on anyone if there was a viable alternative. My husband works in New York City while we live in Connecticut. I opted to work nights because I did not want the stress and anxiety associated with erratic childcare coverage. Secondly, I wanted to participate in our young kid's early school life. Whether I was the mystery reader, parent chaperone during school trips, or holiday parent class volunteer, I showed up maybe tired, but I cherished those moments. Seeing the joy and happiness on my children's faces made this sacrifice totally worthwhile. Thirdly, working nights meant I could use my daytime hours to learn and grow. I could learn a side hustle and continue my night shift till "my side hustle becomes my main hustle". I could save more money and make investments in stocks and real estate.

While working the Night shift, I became comfortable being the sole nocturnist in my hospital. Though initially anxiety provoking, over time, I mastered my routines and developed a great camaraderie with the night ancillary staff, including the nurses. The job became easier and more doable. As my workload increased (overnight admissions and cross coverage), my personal dissatisfaction started creeping up.

As the years rolled by, I began to feel irritable at home and unfulfilled at work. I looked into other options including pursuing a fellowship in Hematology & Oncology or an MBA in Health Policy. I started working as a per diem dayshift hospitalist as I wanted to participate in multidisciplinary rounds and engage more with my peers. I was tired of being invisible, "everyone sees and reads your patient notes, but no one has ever seen you in person".

Moving on, I also covered some daytime shifts at the Outpatient Pre-surgical Optimization clinic affiliated with my hospital. Was working outpatient the remedy for my distressed soul? While juggling all my various roles and thinking deeply about the true meaning of happiness and job satisfaction, COVID happened in March 2020.

The whole world stopped!!! My kids and husband were home 24x7. The alarm went off.

Dr. Yel'Ora what do you want to do for yourself? Focus on YOU

I started working with a Fitness & Nutrition coach. I lost a lot of weight and built muscle. My director graciously accepted my request, so I switched over to being a Part-time Hospitalist-Nocturnist. I felt alive again. The same feeling after I visited the ER during my nighttime asthmatic flare-ups and I was able to breathe freely again.
Gush of air out, No bronchospasm. No whistling.

I had been waiting for many years to finally EXHALE.

Nowadays, I am working on creating my platform which will focus on the challenges faced by Night shift workers. Dr. Yel'Ora- Lifestyle & Obesity Coach for Night shift workers. I am embracing the rigors involved in entrepreneurship- the good, the bad, and the ugly. I intend to tackle the issue of obesity among night shift workers. Do you know that night shift workers have almost 3 times higher association with abdominal obesity, independent of age and gender, compared to day shift workers?

My perceived mess is now my authentic message.

My final message to everyone is, "Do not focus on your job description, day shift or night shift, rather look further or deeper into the values and principles you've acquired at your current job". How do you prepare for your next step? I think Entrepreneurship may be the antidote for my burnout at this stage of my life.

The energizer bunny has finally been deactivated. Welcome, Dr. Yel'Ora, a physician and more....all about People, Medicine, and everything Glam.

Question and Answers

Looking back, was there anything in your childhood or upbringing that you think led to your burnout?

I had a bi-continental childhood. I describe myself as a Trifecta because I was born in the United Kingdom, nurtured in Nigeria, and now I am reaching my full potential in the USA.

My childhood was loving, and I was cocooned and closely protected by my parents as most African parents do. I was born in the United Kingdom during the time my parents were foreign students under the sponsorship of the British Council.

My father also narrated the story of his life to my 5 siblings and me. Yes, I come from a large family (4 sisters and 1 brother). My paternal grandfather was a subsistence farmer. He spent his meager lifesaving on my father's secondary school education. This was money he had set aside to use for a Chieftaincy title. Despite his lack of formal education, he knew the value of education. His manifestations of abundance and success came to fruition through my parents.

I grew up in a family where a lot was expected from you. Being the second child, I was always up for any challenge. I was more daring, extroverted, and highly intuitive, and my demeanor got me into trouble a few times. In many ways, including physical appearance, I am a daddy's girl. A few of our former neighbors tease me about my well-known jingle, "I want my daddy, my daddy come back". The entire neighborhood always knew whenever my dad stepped out of our home.

As a child, I wanted to be successful because that meant I could help more people. I wanted to repay my paternal grandfather who sacrificed the highest societal recognition (Chieftaincy title) in order to ensure my father got a great education at a renowned Secondary school.

As a child, I had a lot of drive, resilience, and motivation. Though there were times when I had self-doubt, my drive to be successful superseded my personal introspection. I was an energizer bunny without batteries.....but for how long I can continue like this?

Did anything occur in your training that led to your burnout?

Heading into Residency in New York, I was stressed out. Training in a new environment as a foreign graduate, starting Internal Medicine Residency with 4-month-old twin boys coupled with my daily commute from Nassau county to Brooklyn heights, NY were my daily challenges.

These factors all mashed up together, and exponentially contributed to my mental and physical exhaustion. Unbeknownst to me, I did not recognize the early signs of burnout while I was in Residency. I think Residency Programs need to identify overt and covert biases and micro aggressions which occur within their programs. Having a handle on any unfair treatment at their institutions may help curb the feeling of burnout among new and older resident physicians.

Was there anything about the system you worked in that led to your episode (s) of burnout?

I do not blame the system for my feeling of burnout. There were organic and manmade processes that were contributory. By organic, I mean I started residency with 4-month-old twins. This situation is anxiety provoking for anyone even with maximal support from your employer or family. Manmade processes refer to imbalances and implicit biases which exist in the workplace environment.

Thinking back into the archives of my mind, I remember being the only black girl in my class. I felt I had a shitty schedule, working on most holidays. It was almost impossible to switch schedules for personal events. The fact we had to do scutwork in Residency added another layer to an already stressful situation.

By the following year, I made a positive impression on my attending. During the next interview cycle, a few more black females and one male were offered spots in my Residency program. Their familiar faces were a welcome addition to my tribe.

I completed Residency with my peers despite the additional birth of my daughter two months prior to my graduation from Internal Medicine. She was born via a cesarean section the day after my USMLE step 3.

Alas!!! I checked one major accomplishment off my list. No more kids!!

Remember, I told you I was an energizer bunny. I have so much energy and enthusiasm for life. My mantra is " Stop only when the mission is accomplished".

What helped you overcome your burnout?

I realized I could not change the situation. COVID was real and the illness was ravaging the whole world in 2020.

I saw a friend of mine from college on social media. I noticed she was very physically active. Lots of biking, swimming, and running. I reached out to her, and she introduced me to my Coach. I worked with Ms. Liz, my Weight loss and Nutrition coach. I channeled my mental fatigue and negative emotions towards transforming my body and mindset. I embraced exercise and healthy eating.

Did you have a support system?

Yes, I have a strong support system around me. This includes my husband, immediate family, and my siblings. Also, I have close friends who live nearby and internationally. With the help of social media, friends are just a few time zones away.

Did anyone notice and reach out to you?

Not really. My colleagues always wondered how I was coping with 3 kids, a husband, and my night shift work schedule. The stress of the Pandemic in early Spring 2020 affected me, including my fellow nocturnists. We supported one another through this difficult ordeal.

How are you thriving today?

Thank God. I am happier and healthier today compared to 13 years ago when I completed my Internal Medicine Residency.

At the beginning of the first fiscal quarter, in October 2020, I decided I could no longer continue working as a full-time hospitalist-nocturnist. I needed to change my work schedule. I had hit rock bottom. My program director was gracious and supportive. He approved my request to decrease my hours to 0.57 FTE. Overall, I needed to have more control over my schedule so I could spend more time with my family.

I wanted to practice medicine on my own terms, doing what I loved and making money. Nowadays, I show up at work rejuvenated with a lot of ideas for new quality improvement projects I would like to review in the hospital in 2023. Working at a teaching hospital with medical residents is also very gratifying. Teaching the residents and midlevel providers on the few nights I worked at the hospital no longer seemed like a chore unlike before. I felt a renewed sense of purpose and a deeper commitment to my job.

In addition to my Part time hours, I also work per diem at the Outpatient Pre-surgical Optimization Clinic. The hours are flexible, and I would not trade my peace of mind for any regular full-time job at this current time.
Having worked nights for 13 years, I focused on my own story. My "WHY". I was ready to face the prospect of entrepreneurship head-on. Did I think long

and hard? What am I good at? What mess do I manifest that I could transform into my message? I want to be an entrepreneur. These questions triggered some deep thinking and self-reflection.

My experience made me an authority in this "uncharted territory". No one was specifically catering to people who cover the Night Shift. My mission is to create a Health and Wellness platform for Night Shift workers. "Dr. Yel'Ora; Lifestyle & Obesity Coaching for Night Shift workers". My vision is to provide supportive educational resources about the health challenges associated with night shift work. Targeting metabolic diseases such as DM, HTN, Obesity, and Heart disease. Other conditions include Cancer, Sleep Deprivation, Dementia, Anxiety & Depression, and Endometriosis to mention a few. Studies have shown that with dedicated monitoring, night-shift workers can thrive and survive. They can minimize (but not eliminate) the detrimental health effects of night shift work. A recent survey showed that over 40% of people who work the night shift are enrolled in school.

As per the U.S. Bureau of Labor, over 9 million adults work the night shift. This includes Healthcare workers, Public Safety officials, Service Providers including IT engineers to mention a few.

Nowadays, I spend more time with my kids being a regular mom. Currently, I am taking sewing classes with my 13-year-old daughter. We both share a love for fashion and textiles. Having more time to volunteer at my kids' activities also gladdens my heart and gives me a real sense of purpose. Also, I started creative writing, mostly short plays. I belong to a community of professionals who are passionate about teaching their American children about their Igbo cultural heritage.

Being a Trifecta, I take pride in my multi-national identity. I want my children to know about the Igbo tradition and customs. Igbo people are one of the three major tribes in South East Nigeria. They are known for their entrepreneurial acumen. Few months ago, I wrote a short play that was acted by the kids in our Igbokwenu community. The kids reenacted the steps involved in a traditional Igbo marriage through drama and storytelling.

I am happy and thriving in 2022. I look beyond the horizon. I see opportunities for innovation in Medicine and other specialties. Beyond helping night shift workers, I want to improve my writing ability and someday write a fictional story that will have a movie adaptation. I am a champion for female empowerment because when you "educate a woman, you indeed educate a nation".

What advice would you give to someone going through burnout?

Please stop! Remove the stressor! Then, look inwards at yourself. Next, re-set, re-adjust, re-start and re-focus. Do not continue in your old ways. Seek help, whether therapy or personal coaching.

What advice would you give to the facilities and administration who are trying to help decrease the rate of physician burnout?

My personal opinion is geared towards changing the workplace culture by genuinely promoting employee Health and Wellness. As we all know, a lot of female physicians left the job market. I propose employers or team managers meet quarterly with their staff members to rejuvenate and recharge their passion and optimism towards their duties or jobs.

In my opinion, team meetings have morphed into gatherings where physicians are reminded about metrics, deadlines, and new responsibilities. As we commonly say, "the reward for work is more work".

Being a Hospitalist-Nocturnist, I deeply care about all night shift workers, including Healthcare workers. The rate of burnout among nightshift workers in the emergency or hospitalist department is astronomically high. These jobs are very stressful at baseline and post-pandemic, and a lot of Healthcare systems are unable to hire or maintain nightshift staff.

Culture eats Strategy as Peter Drucker aptly proposed.

What advice if any, would you give to the facilities that can do better when it comes to improving burnout rates of physicians (those facilities that appear to have a lack of interest in helping to improve conditions)?

I feel some institutions may minimize the impact burnout may have on their staff physician productivity. Conversely, some employers recognize the need to help their physicians remain healthy. Happy people tell other people (including new prospective hires)about their supportive work environment.

I think the greatest indicator of potential burnout is when there are unclear job expectations between the employer and the employee. When people feel like they are unduly taken advantage of at work, their morale fades and enthusiasm falters. Over time, they lose that zest or momentum for work and life.

I feel that physician recruiters can play a pivotal role in addressing burnout also. They sometimes act as the "conduits" between the physician and a potential employer. They are the ones who "present" the job to you initially in some cases. They play a huge role in ensuring physician retention by making sure they match a qualified candidate with the right job opportunity. Facilities should only work with knowledgeable recruiters who are transparent and uphold the tenets of their institution.

Ensuring you have adequate and competent staffing at your facility will help minimize burnout. Rapid employee turnover is always a red flag and signals an issue with staff development and retention. Understaffing is one of the commonest causes of job dissatisfaction.

Inefficient workflow due to obsolete Electronic Health Records (EHR) or unnecessary clicks leads to physician dissatisfaction due to the length of time spent on documentation.

Facilities should assist physicians, if possible, with bureaucratic bottlenecks involving patient insurance authorization and prescription coverage.

Lastly, institutions should identify physicians who have worked at the same job for several years. They may be at risk for having a complacent attitude to work which is seen "when employees tune out, cease to think and merely follow a routine". Also called "Autopilot mode". Another new terminology mostly used by the Gen Z generation "quiet quitting" is the art of not taking work too seriously.

Ask your older employees, "how are you coping, are you ok?" Their answers may surprise you.

About Chinyelu E. Oraedu M.D.(Dr. Yel'Ora)

Dr. Chinyelu E. Oraedu, also known as Dr. Yel'Ora, is Board Certified in Internal Medicine.

She graduated from the University of Nigeria. The first indigenous university was founded in 1960 after the country's Independence.

She completed her Internal Medicine training in 2009 at SUNY Downstate in Brooklyn, NY.

She practices medicine in Connecticut in the outpatient setting as well as inpatient as an academic hospitalist/ nocturnist. Being a versatile physician, she also enjoys working as a Physician Advisor/ Utilization review, where she reviews Patient records and ensures the Insurance companies compensate the hospital promptly for the quality care they provide.

She is an Adjunct Professor where she mentors a group of Medical students.

Dr. Yel'Ora has over 20 years of working experience as a physician in Nigeria, Oman, and the United States.

Member of professional societies, American Medical Association (AMA), American College of Physicians (ACP).

Being a physician who works the night shift predominantly, Dr. Yel'Ora recently embarked on a total lifestyle makeover. Deciding to hold myself accountable for my weight gain and not blame my work schedule has been a game changer. "I am intentional about the way I live my life."

She is working on creating a platform that brings more visibility to the Health, Social and Personal challenges associated with the Night Shift.

Dr. Yel'Ora is also the best-selling author of The Warrior Women Project- an Anthology she coauthored about Immigrant women. The book's purpose was to limelight the incredible stories of 22 exceptional, tenacious Immigrant women who sacrificed a lot in their pursuit of a better life far away from home. The book serves as the Holy Grail for anyone who plans to emigrate from any part of the world.

In her spare time, she loves to write short plays and poems, travel, spend quality time with her family and friends, and read books related to personal finance and investing.

She loves her family and friends and believes that one can only experience true happiness through selfless service towards others.

She is married, and they are blessed with three beautiful children-16-year-old twin boys (Kobi and Dumeto) & Kaira, my 13-year-old daughter.

Her fearless, intuitive, and highly enterprising alter ego comes to her rescue whenever she feels despair or terrified about an idea. She's always cheering her up, reminding her, "you cannot quit."
 Do you know she's afraid of heights? While working on overcoming her fears, she tried Bungee jumping in Cabo San Lucas, Mexico.

Next on her bucket list, Skydiving someday!! So watch this space!

Dr. Yel'Ora lives by the mantra, "Doing the hard things in life prepares you to be successful.

Her life is a Trifecta: born in the United Kingdom, raised in Nigeria, and now living in the US...Global citizen spanning three continents!!!

www.dryelora.com

Winnie Mar, MD

Looking back, was there anything in your childhood or upbringing that you think led to your burnout?

As a child, I was expected to achieve and taught not to rock the boat. I did not know how to set boundaries and wanted to please everyone.

Did anything occur in your training that led to your burnout? Please be specific.

I developed limiting neck problems which later on I would find out is due to Ehlers-Danlos syndrome. I was not able to wear the lead apron to do certain procedures, which was problematic for training and also call coverage. Driving was too painful, so I lived across the street from the hospital. I was also told to think about quitting radiology by my program director to do something less physically demanding, like pathology. These limitations motivated me to work extra hard to prove that I could do the work. Even over 10 years after training, I felt I still had to prove myself and I think this was one reason why I kept working through years of increasing pain, fatigue and suffering.

Was there anything about the system you worked in that led to your episode (s) of burnout?

I think in all of radiology, there is a push for more and more RVUs to make up for decreasing reimbursement in order not to have to take a pay cut. I would think that the push for more RVUs is also present in most other specialties as well. In particular, my section seemed to have to take the brunt of the work (for example, we took all the evening shifts, and other sections reserved weekday scan times so that more of our scans were performed on weekends).

Describe your period of burnout. What did burnout look like?

For me, burnout showed up as worsening health due to underlying Ehlers-Danlos Syndrome. I had gotten to the point of barely being able to walk around my home, and then, only in a walking boot. I hadn't been able to use a computer without significant pain for three years and had hired assistants, paying thousands of dollars out of pocket to allow me to continue to work. Due to pain, it took me longer than others to get the work done, especially when required to work on-site with a less optimal computer setup. On those days, I would save a lot of work to bring home so I could work in less pain but that resulted in more fatigue.

What helped you overcome your burnout?

I enrolled in a coaching program with empowering women physicians (EWP) and realized I had a choice. I decided to take some time off, thinking I would go back; however, I felt so much better than I have in years, I have not gone back yet, and it has been a year and a half. I'm not sure if leaving work is a good answer to help overcome burnout in general, but in my case, it was very beneficial to my health, and now I am able to walk and live again without constant high-level pain.

Did you have a support system?

My husband. Physical therapists, therapists, coaches, and friends.

Did anyone notice and reach out to you?

Not really. Actually, I was pretty good at hiding how much suffering I was in. However, I went to work in bilateral wrist braces, sometimes in a wheelchair, and by the last few months, also a cam boot. I never really talked about it except to my chair when I had reached the point where I needed to work entirely remotely and then when I couldn't do it anymore. Many people were surprised when I finally decided to take some time off.

How are you thriving today?

I am able to walk 10,000 steps some days now, and I just physically feel so much better and feel like I have my life back. I am still working on my health, doing my PT exercises, and going to multiple appointments a week. I am still looking for some work that I can do, without going back to pain, to fulfill that aspect of my life.

What advice would you give to someone going through burnout?

It's ok to take the time that you need for yourself. The patients and other staff will be able to carry on even if you take time off. You need to look out for yourself as no one else usually does. It's ok to say no, to ask for help, and set boundaries when you need it.

What advice would you give to the facilities and administration who are trying to help decrease the rate of physician burnout?

More staff needs to be hired. One reason for my burnout apart from my health was increasing workloads due to a lack of funds to hire more attendings, as well as imbalances in work distribution between sections. Facilities can also invest in ergonomics and offer more help to those who ask for help. There was one IT person who tried his best to help me. Other than that, I was told by others that I should just go get injections for my hands or that I wasn't able to have a different computer setup because everyone gets the same thing.

What advice, if any, would you give to the facilities that can do better when it comes to improving burnout rates of physicians (those facilities that appear to have a lack of interest in helping to improve conditions)
Hire more staff, and don't ask or expect a person to do the jobs of two or three people.

About Winnie Mar, MD

Dr. Mar is a former academic radiologist who is thinking of becoming a coach, specializing in disability/chronic medical issues or money. She has a blog on perfectpitchfi.blogspot.com which will be updated.

winnieaz@hotmail.com

Ololade "Lola Day" Akintoye, MD

Looking back, was there anything in your childhood or upbringing that you think led to your burnout?

As the oldest child in an immigrant family, you are automatically expected to be responsible for your younger ones. Not in a bad way, but it is a role that you were destined/ born into, and I take pride in it. However, because of that responsibility, the past me tend to felt responsible for all and everything instead of delegating.

Did anything occur in your training that led to your burnout?

As a neurodivergent, I needed structure, but instead of structure, I got more work, and I did more work to over compensate for the deficiencies of not being able to finish in a disorganized environment. Training #1 was amazing because I had structure and Camaraderie was the culture, graduated and almost forgot I had ADHD, so I went into my next training program expecting the same support and camaraderie. This was not the case. You asked.... Did anything??? I would say it was EVERYTHING. Medical culture in this particular training program was not female-friendly at all. While I was blessed to have been at 3 different training programs, this one in particular was where I experienced burnout.

Was there anything about the system you worked in that led to your episode (s) of burnout?

There was a lack of support for a woman with young children. I also did not have any family around. I TRULY FELT ALONE! The expectations were unrealistic, and there was no room for complaint. Because our attending never complained, when we completed our training, we became an attending that does not complain. We are not fair to our colleagues and fellow doctors. We do not give the grace we give to our patients to ourselves.

Describe your period of burnout. What did it feel like?

My burnout was an accumulation of many events and not one sentinel event.

I remember once, I wrote my actual work hours, and I got called into the fellowship director's office for not being efficient with my time. I asked my senior fellow how they never went over work hours on their report. He said I have been working 8 am to 5 pm for the past three years. So guess what? ... I also started working ... "8 am to 5 pm"... on my work hours report. So I over worked and had less time for rest and a break. It came to a point my body gave up. I had chronic migraine for one month straight and still came to work, and as I was driving home one day, I swerved into a ditch. I was pregnant with my second child at the time. I felt horrible! Medicine was almost destroyed my life! I knew something had to change!

In retrospect this was a blessing in disguise.

I was about to graduate, but I made a commitment to myself.

It was either I quit with three months left to graduate from fellowship or make a decision about what I wanted out of my life.

I asked my self...
WHO do you want to be?
WHY do you want to be that person?
HOW do you want to be that person?
I looked back at my 1st training program, why was a successful there?

I wanted to be an amazing physician that was great with her patients and excellent in her knowledge; without sacrificing my health or my family.
I decided at that time academic medicine was not where I wanted to be.
I decided my life, family, and future were more important than accolades.
This may be great for others, but it truly was not my vision or my purpose in life.

I graduated and went on to an amazing advance program who had the same culture I knew I needed. I also went in with a sense of clarity.
I had time boundaries, rest boundaries and support.

This led me to look for attending jobs that supported the life I wanted...

All I wanted was to be an amazing physician without sacrificing my children and/ life.
This should be standard not the exception!
Thankfully I now work as an attending where it is the standard, and I have continued to practice time boundaries, rest boundaries and get support.

What helped you overcome your burnout?
I created my vision and goals for my life

I said NO more often
I sought therapy & coaching
I became a productivity and burnout coach helping overwhelmed women.. and most recently added ADHD coach because the majority of my clients have ADHD

Did you have a support system?

In the third training program I was in, I had a mentor who was an amazing clinician and researcher. Showed me it could be done, but she also showed me "it took a village". She taught me to have a support system paid, borrowed, or physical.

Did anyone notice and reach out to you?

In medicine, No.. but my mother knew something was wrong and would always tell me to remember why I went into medicine.
My "Why" saved me!

How are you thriving today?

I am a Life coach that specializes in productivity, Goals to fruition/success coach, burnout, and ADHD in women.

What advice would you give to someone going through burnout?

-Awareness of the situation
-Get support
-The Power to create the life you want is your hand.

What advice would you give to the facilities and administration who are trying to help decrease the rate of physician burnout?

Hire coaches that can be on retainer for your physicians. Burnout is not solved by just one lecture. You may need to have weeks of coaching to unlearn past beliefs and create new strategies.

What advice, if any, would you give to the facilities that can do better when it comes to improving burnout rates of physicians (those facilities that appear to have a lack of interest in helping to improve conditions)?

Burnout actually decreases productivity, so if you don't care about the life of your physicians, I know you care about the bottom line.

About Ololade "Lola Day" Akintoye, MD

Dr. Ololade "Lola Day" Akintoye is a life strategist/ coach who specializes in productivity/ goals success, burnout, work-life harmony, time management, and ADHD/ executive function coaching. She coaches ambitious women who have a busy life or busy brain (ADHD) how to focus on what they need to do (responsibilities), so they can thrive and have time for what gives them joy (life). She believes if you learn efficient ways to focus on the necessary things, then you can have time to enjoy the important things.

www.lollietasking.com

Puja Aggarwal, MD MBA

"Ribbit, Ribbit," my dissecting partner Maddy said in an effort to scare me as I nervously cut open the heart of the lifeless frog in front of me. I didn't have the heart to dissect the frog, mainly due to a phobia of reptiles. Once I got the hang of dissection, I liked dissecting it. "Dissecting the frog doesn't scare me," I said while she looked back in disgust at me that her prank didn't work. I continued my love of science in AP Biology classes in high school when I decided to become a physician.

One month after finishing high school, I started my 6 year combined B.S./ M.D. program at the young age of 18. Quickly, I formed bonds with 35 other students in the same combined program as we knew we thought we would be together for 6 years throughout the program. My penchant for dissection continued through to my first year of medical school, dissecting the human brain. Learning all the pathways of the brain and spinal cord and how each one controlled a different part of the brain. From then on out, I had decided to become a Neurologist. I graduated from medical school at the age of 24. I had expected that residency was going to be demanding, with sleepless nights on call, exhaustion, and poor self-care, but I also knew this was a short period of time.

My first real Attending job started at the age of 28 at a small academic institution. I was enthusiastic about starting but also nervous about being the one making the decisions. In the beginning, I felt confident rounding on consults and teaching trainees. Shortly after, imposter syndrome plagued me, like most female physicians at some point in their careers. I felt like I was doing a good job at providing care for patients, but I felt nervous about answering medical students' questions. I thought to myself, "What if I don't get it right?" or "Should I be taking care of patients?" I wasn't sure that I should have been a physician. In addition, I had felt a void as I had not completed a fellowship which I always wanted to. By chance, I found an open position for a fellowship in Clinical Neurophysiology and decided to take it. I feared the response my current department was going to have when I decided to submit my resignation. After receiving my resignation, I received the updated call schedule to reflect my being on call for 6 weeks during the last 3 months of my time there. However, this reinforced my decision to leave this practice in.

I found an open fellowship position in Clinical Neurophysiology at an Ivy League Institution in NYC. The change was definitely difficult at first, going from being the one teaching medical students and residents to being the learner. But I gained a great background in EEG reading and Epilepsy through the fellowship. I thoroughly enjoyed my time living the big city life going to Central Park, Broadway shows, Museums, and eating at the best restaurants. During my fellowship year, I tied the knot and became pregnant within our first year of marriage. Looking to move away from the big city due to the pregnancy, we moved to a smaller city in Pennsylvania. I decided not to work for the first year of my child's life. I gave birth to my daughter just a few months later and tried to be a stay-at-home mom. However, this only lasted a few months due to my restlessness and desire to get back to work.

I started the interview process for my second job as an Attending physician and was in the contract negotiation stage. Before signing the contract, I offered to take on 4 weeks of extra continuous EEG call without extra compensation so the new job would like me. My people-pleasing tendencies were present in full force. I wanted people at my new job to like me as a physician by volunteering to give up four full weeks of my time for free! Who would do that? People Pleasers, that's who. People-pleasers do things to avoid conflict, even if they change who they are to the core. I didn't even know what EEG called entailed, but I signed up!

In my first year in the position, I was taking 14 weeks of calls, often taking two weeks of call straight. The Neuro ICU resident paged me at 3 am, my first week of EEG call to check up on a patient with new involuntary movements due to a concern for seizure. I reviewed the last 7 hours of the patient's brain waves, trying to ascertain if there were, in fact, seizures. It took me 90 minutes to review the EEG, at which point I was ready to pass out. Exactly fifteen minutes later, I was paged again to ready another EEG. Doing this day in and day out led to insomnia. I couldn't sleep if there were pages and also couldn't sleep in anticipation of a possible page. At work, I would ruminate about making mistakes, and at home, I thought about my work. I was unable to show up for my family as I was not fully present. Work consumed me on my call for weeks, and the fatigue lasted for one week after call. This pattern continued for months during my first year as an attending.

December was around the corner, and we all know that brings the obligation of attending a department holiday party. Begrudgingly, I attended the work holiday party with my spouse at a posh country club. We walked in the door and were greeted by the leaders of the department. One head physician said, "Hello, thanks for coming–Uh! Happy Holidays!" I couldn't believe it! The physician had forgotten my name and had just hired me 6 months prior to the party. Maybe I was being overly sensitive but for a leader of your department to not know who you were was disappointing. I had been trying to please co-workers at this new job to no avail. My people-pleasing effort had failed miserably, and I felt horrible about myself.

My second year working was no different–in fact, it was worse. I was pregnant with my second child but was not taking care of myself. I again was not as active or eating well. The work environment was worsening by the day. Toxicity was rampant from the receptionist to the office manager. We had a high turnover, with receptionists leaving after a few months and MAs leaving the office to return to their previous jobs. Work was affecting my ability to practice self-care in my second pregnancy. Upper management wanted me to take most of my call for the year prior to maternity leave, but I said I was unable to do this. I gave birth halfway through my 2nd year of practice there. Thankfully I had a non-traumatic delivery and delivered a healthy baby boy. I clearly stated that I would try my best when I came back from maternity leave and finished my contracted call.

"We can't pay you any more money for the renewal of your contract," management said when I asked for more compensation at the end of my 2-year contract. My response was, "Well, can you decrease the call amount?" to which the answer right away was, "No. We need someone to take the call." There was no room for negotiation in an already chaotic department with multiple Neurologists leaving. After a short deliberation period, I decided to leave a job that was not willing to accommodate me.

I had all the classic signs of burnout–irritability, job dissatisfaction, insomnia, and anxiety. However, "burnout" was not a commonly used word in 2016. In hindsight, it is easy to see I was experiencing burnout, but hindsight is always 20/20. We are taught as physicians to put the patient first above all else, but to what end? Should we sacrifice ourselves and provide substandard care? Or should we prioritize our own health to better serve patients? This ingrained mentality cost me my own physical, mental and emotional health.

Physicians should make decisions and take action to serve themselves first. If something is not working out, don't be afraid to ask for change or leave if a change is not happening. I have found a balance in my personal and work life, now practicing clinical medicine and coaching female professionals with burnout. I went from being scared of the frog to "eating the frog" or facing adversity and prioritizing myself and my family first in my life.

Question and Answers

Looking back, was there anything in your childhood or upbringing that you think led to your burnout?

I was the daughter of immigrant parents from India who came to the United States with very little money. Both were very loving and caring. Education was stressed from a young age to get the highest grades. I felt an innate need to please both parents by obtaining high grades from elementary school to high school. Daughters of immigrants from India often have the need to do things to please their parents. I was no different. Through college and medical school, I continued those behaviors.

Did anything occur in your training that led to your burnout?

The system was suffering from the loss of several Neurologists and high turnover. From the time I had started, several neurologists had left over the two years I was there. The leading cause, from what I understood, was that physicians felt the department was unwilling to make changes to decrease workload, including calls, changing the way the clinic worked to make it more efficient, and other issues. These same issues contributed to my burnout in addition to my own tendencies.

I had people-pleasing tendencies in addition to wanting to be a perfectionist. These qualities contributed to me second-guessing myself, not feeling confident, and ultimately experiencing burnout. The perfectionist in me wanted to do well on the EEG call. I used to try to read every second of every continuous EEG, which can prolong my time awake at night. This led to poor sleep on call and contributed to my burnout. My people-pleasing tendencies, as mentioned in my story, is another example.

What helped you overcome your burnout?

Coaching helped me to overcome burnout. I had heard of coaching before but didn't actually know what they did. My coach at that time helped me to realize how the negativity in my mind had become pervasive in my life. With introspection, I was able to learn to develop thoughts that served me in my life and do what I wanted. I started to prioritize myself and finally had time to myself after experiencing burnout.

Did you have a support system?

My support system included my sister, who was also a physician, and my mother. I was able to easily speak with both of them about my trials and tribulations. My sister was always available to lend her ear to me. She understood the difficulties of being a physician.

Did anyone notice and reach out to you?

No

How are you thriving today?

What work are you doing that you find fulfilling?

I am thriving today by prioritizing my self-care--exercise, eating healthy, and spending time with my family. I am able to have a girl's night out with my daughter or spend time with my son. I have the time to do the hobbies that I want to. I have found a current balance of clinical medicine that makes me feel fulfilled in addition to coaching female professionals with burnout.

What advice would you give to someone going through burnout?

You are not alone in experiencing burnout. The occurrence is very high among female physicians. It is not your fault. Seek help from your physician, counselor, or coach. Prioritize your health--mental, physical, and emotional--over your job. Employment can come and go. You only have one life to live and won't get that precious time back.

What advice would you give to the facilities and administration who are trying to help decrease the rate of physician burnout?

A positive work environment promotes psychological safety, higher job satisfaction, higher rates of staff retention, and more productivity.

Here's how to promote a positive work environment:

Have open lines of communication: Check in with your employees weekly by asking how they are doing, how is their workload/productivity and what can be done to make the organization a better place to work. Psychological safety is important for an employee to be able to bring up issues.

Build a community at work: People need a sense of belonging and a shared common goal that happens in a community.

Develop strong leaders: Start from the top by developing leaders who listen to others.

Be transparent: Don't try to hide things from employees. A sense of secrecy promotes a toxic work environment.

Prioritize your employees over customers: Allow employees to take time off without fear of retaliation, and have outside speakers come in and educate them about physical, emotional, and mental health. Institute coaching programs or other outlets to allow your employees a safe outlet to speak about their experiences.

What advice, if any, would you give to the facilities that can do better when it comes to improving burnout rates of physicians (those facilities that appear to have a lack of interest in helping to improve conditions)?

A toxic workplace leaves people feeling psychologically unsafe, where they cannot speak up about their concerns for fear of retaliation. A negative workplace environment has higher rates of burnout, anxiety, depression and poor productivity, job satisfaction, and results. A toxic work environment involves poor lines of communication, high workload, values mismatch between employees and employer, a lack of community/appreciation/fairness. According to an MIT Sloan Study in Forbes from January of 2022, a toxic work culture is the leading cause of people resigning from their jobs. Please start making the change to keep physicians in clinical practice.

About Puja Aggarwal MD MBA
Dr. Aggarwal is a Board Certified Neurologist/Epileptologist, Neuroscientist with 14 years of experience as a Neurologist currently practicing in Orlando, FL. She is a Leading Authority in Organizational Wellness. She educates organizations and individuals on how to improve engagement and gain the clarity needed to boost productivity in the workplace while still cultivating the importance of each individual in an organization.

Dr. Aggarwal is also a Certified Executive Coach who helps burnt-out female professionals to stop people pleasing, let go of perfectionism and self-doubt to become more empowered to learn to say "no", set boundaries, and be self-confident. She started her business, Zenful Brain Coaching, in 2021 during the height of the pandemic. Dr. Aggarwal has been featured in Authority magazine, Medium magazine, iHeart Radio, and Radio America, ABC 15, WebMD, and several other media outlets. She has spoken at several local, state, national and international events about mental health.

www.zenfulbrain.com

Radhika Sharma, MD, FACOG

Looking back, was there anything in your childhood or upbringing that you think led to your burnout?

I was born the third of 3 children. I was the 'baby' in the family. Yet, from a young age, I often felt like I faced an intense amount of pressure. I cannot remember exactly where it started, but I will say this: for as long as I can remember, I felt as though I required approval from the elders around me. Did this have a cultural basis? I am sure to some extent. But I believe that even from infancy, we have a tendency as individuals. My tendency was towards garnering approval based on my actions. I believe that my locus of control was very much affected by my external world from a young age. I remember that disapproval from those in a position of power or influence directly impacted the way I viewed myself. Whether this was related to respect, education, mannerisms, or the way I spoke. The majority of my life decisions from a young age that were made by me or for me were related to how others would view me.

I feel as though the competitive spirit which helped me become successful in many areas of my life also hindered me. I often felt as though whatever I did was not enough. This led to working harder at school and putting in more hours at practice. However, I never felt like it was enough. I believe that the constant pressure I placed upon myself, and the feeling of never being good enough, directly contributed to my burnout.

Was there anything about the system you worked in that led to your episode (s) of burnout? Please give specific examples.

What do you think caused the burnout?

I had the opportunity to be trained in a very well-rounded residency program.

I had great teachers.
Based on my foundation of striving for excellence, this served me well in residency. I worked long hours. I tried to 'be better' than the rest. I sacrificed sleep and physical and psychological wellness because that's what I was 'supposed' to do to be the best Obstetrician/Gynecologist I could.

I remember specifically being told by one of my senior residents that I was holding a needle driver "in a weird way." I became obsessed with this and would stay after my scheduled hours had finished and spend hours practicing how to hold and drive my instrument until I had calluses on the insides of my hands.

I would go home, often feeling defeated, only to put in more time reading until I fell asleep on the couch, often forgetting to eat.

I don't share this part of my story as a point of 'feeling sorry' for myself, but rather a point that the drive for perfectionism from an early age impacted the way I looked at myself as a resident physician. This directly impacted my journey to burnout. If I was not the best, it wasn't good enough. If I wasn't liked by patients, attendings, fellow residents, or nurses, it wasn't good enough. If I wasn't receiving external validation about my performance from others, this wasn't good enough.

These were all factors that played into the way I practiced when I got out of residency training.

See, where I believe we falter as physicians in training is that we don't focus on the "humanity" of being a physician. In residency, the focus is on becoming robotic, suppressing our feelings of inadequacy, and working despite them rather than through them.

Seldom are we reminded to take time for ourselves or focus on things outside of residency.

I know in my specific residency program, I had wonderful mentors but very few individuals who helped us focus on life outside of residency. Reminding us that this was a snapshot in time and that life outside of training was extremely different.
Fast forward to 4 years of training.

I came out of residency, and much like many other physicians, I was excited and extremely nervous. Yet I continued to work at the pace of residency. My husband, who is also an Obstetrician/gynecologist, and I decided to take a position at a rural hospital secondary to my return of service required by my Visa. We were excited. We would be working together, we were building a practice from the ground up, we were getting paid well and we would be working towards our goal of paying off our student loans. These were the Pros, and I thought: "Everything is going to be just fine, we just have to keep working hard. We can make this work"

What we didn't take in to account: the hospital that had promised 'in good faith' a 1 in 4 call, starting and building a practice with minimal business knowledge, that there was life outside of medicine. What we did not realize was that we were a cog in a wheel. That although we had the best intentions for our patients, the health system had an agenda on what they needed from us regardless of what we wanted.

(One thing we did have at the institution we started at was autonomy. I realized later that this was imperative to continue to be successful in all facets of medicine. More on this later.)

Regardless, we kept our heads down.
Both my husband and I being International Medical Graduates, had an additional load on our shoulders. We had known previously that this load existed, but we did not realize how this would affect us in clinical practice after residency. Despite being Physicians that had both completed residency and were competent, we continued to have to justify to the world around us why we went the route of leaving Canada and the USA to practice medicine. Having to justify who you are, despite your skill in practice, despite your kindness and empathy. We had these same feelings when we were matching into residency. However, we thought once we were on 'the outside,' surely we wouldn't be judged as harshly. Unfortunately, we were wrong. These additional stressors contributed to feelings of inadequacy. I, even more than my husband, found myself questioning my ability. Questioning why patients even cared and what I needed to do to reassure them. It took me back to the loop of questioning: Am I good enough? Am I worthy? Maybe they are right.

I spent a lot of time trying to push away the feelings of inadequacy, and the feelings of loneliness by continuing to work, by continuing to grow the practice, and by serving the community. I continued to not pay attention to what I needed, whether it be physically or emotionally.

I will say although I did go into practicing medicine as a service to the community, I fast started to feel as though I was a "servant" to the community and that my needs and feelings did not really matter. I started to realize that although the institution I worked for cared about me being in the office, the way I practiced, and how many hours I worked, they seldom cared about how I was feeling.

Even when my husband and I decided to start a family, one of the main concerns was how quickly I was going to be back to work. Being a Visa Holder, there were statutes in place that did not even make me 'eligible' for maternity leave. In order to take time off with my new baby, I would have to take all my sick time or paid time off. In addition, this would increase my return of service and leave me with no time for myself, for my family, or in case of emergency. This was not an additional stress we had anticipated.

My husband and I made the decision that we would have additional help at home and that I would return back to work shortly after having our first child.

In addition, I was studying for my Oral boards, which I took 2.5 weeks after having our daughter.
And then I went back to work.
And I went back to call.
And now I was a mom.
I felt myself continuing the pace of work I had before, however, spreading myself more thin. On top of the pressures of being a physician, I was also a new mom, a wife in a small town with minimal support.

I put pressure on myself, thinking that I had to continue to prove myself even more now. Because I did not want to be judged by my peers, by administration, or by my patients. As much as I related to patients regarding their own stories as New Moms, I found that this was often a façade. I didn't know what they were going through. I couldn't relate.

I was up with my baby through the night, but I did not have the downtime to learn how to be a mom. To find a way to "balance" my work life and home life.

I yearned for a connection and did not know where to find it.
Work continued to be daunting, but it was manageable. My husband and I now had our family and continued to have good days and not-so-good days (just like anyone else). We brought up safety concerns to the administration, ideas to help grow the practice, and ways to improve work-life balance for our staff and for us. However, most of these ideas were met with consideration but no change. See, what I learned from this part of our journey was as a physician, I was no different from any other member of society in one way. I wanted to be heard. I wanted someone to respect my ideas and recommendations. I wanted to grow, but it was difficult to do so under the sturdy hand of an Institutionalized medical practice. At the end of the day, I did not feel I could fault anyone directly, and I did not want to. I realized that at every level, someone was answering to someone else. (Even the CEO had to answer to the Board and the Board to the shareholders.) Even my ask to add blood products to our lab was met with a challenge because it would be too expensive and a waste to bring the blood products to an area where they weren't likely going to

be used in time. (The helicopter at our hospital was flown daily to the neighboring city to transport patients, but we could not have blood available in the case of an obstetric emergency to help prevent catastrophe.) And even this, I could manage in my head until the catastrophe hit.

That's when I started to see the first signs of burnout. We had had one too many "near misses" and "Swiss cheese" events. "We will do better, get better training, better equipment." "This was a fluke situation, this almost never happens, and you are a hero." These are the things I heard from administration at all levels, and started to realize that change wasn't coming, help wasn't coming. I did not care what I was being told. I did not believe that change was coming. I did not believe that help was coming. I did not believe it was important to anyone for me to get home to my family in a timely fashion. I was driving revenue for the hospital. And I was told there was good legal backing should the "unlikely event" occur.

I told my husband that I could no longer go forward with working for this institution. I was concerned for our wellness of ourselves but more importantly of our careers. Even at that time, I hadn't realized what this compilation of events was doing to my overall physical and mental health. Under a large pile of debt, I was still worried about work, and of course, there was the concern of monetary loss.

My husband being as supportive as he always had been, asked some hard questions but ultimately agreed that our time at the Critical Access hospital was coming to an end. We completed my Visa requirement and started to look for a new position.

Like other physician couples, we realized we were an asset, but we also yearned to find the 'right fit' for our family.

We were approached by a previous colleague about an offer. It was in an area we hadn't been. We had just become pregnant with our second child. We were vulnerable, we were tired. I was especially vulnerable and yearning for connection and companionship. I wanted to work around other women physicians who could relate to me. The colleague who approached us was "just like me." She, too, was growing her family. She mentioned finding a place to call home. Where we could all work together with a similar mindset and grow our families. After all, "it takes a small village to raise a child," she quoted to me.

We visited a quaint small town in the Midwest of the country. Like a swooning teenager, everything about the town and the practice drew me in. I loved the children's activities, I loved the comraderies, and the office was pretty and new. There appeared to support not only from ancillary staff but from the administration and the neighboring towns.

I managed to overlook specific burnout risk factors like "the number of patient contact hours," who was making the call schedule, and how we would split holidays. I "forgot" to look at if my husband and I could operate together from a safety perspective. I glazed over the fact that 'autonomy' was barely existent in this practice. And lastly, I completely glossed over when our soon-to-be partner mentioned we were the "last to be called because I had no one else." I was vulnerable and leaped at the chance for a change.

And so, in the beginning of the pandemic, in my first trimester of pregnancy with my second child, we drove across the country and moved.

Big dreams in our heart, we had found our home. This was going to be our place. The community was welcoming, and the town was charming. There were events for the kids. It seemed like I was starting to make a connection with the community.

And then it started, like a record on repeat.
First it was little: policing the number of hours worked, asking why I wouldn't be present at lunchtime meetings when that was the "expectation." I was noticed to be rushing at the end of the day, ten minutes before my day ended. (Keep in mind our set schedule templates required me to have openings until 10 minutes before the end of the day). This was not touting the line that the organization was hoping to. My partner, who was in a similar circumstance, had no problem working grueling long hours, staying after clinic, coming in on days off, and spending hours at night to complete charts. After all, she was a mom, too, if she could do it, why couldn't I? Why wasn't I doing the same thing? These were often the questions I was asked in the first 6 months of being at the organization.

When I asked to change certain aspects of my schedule when seeing patients in order to be more efficient and also see more patients, it was met with resistance.

When I asked to alter the call schedule so my husband and I could take a long weekend off together or take a holiday, there was always something that had to be paid upfront or paid back on the back end.

As time went by, I realized the negative reviews were rolling in. I was CONSTANTLY being told about the accolades of my counterpart and how I continuously had patients who had concerns that they wanted to be addressed about Dr Sharma.

I felt like a "delinquent" being called down to the Principal's office on multiple occasions, Oh, and did I mention I was pregnant in the middle of the pandemic with my second child: New Job, New town, one child under 2, and our new partner out on maternity leave.

But even then, I did what I Knew. I put my head down and continued to work. I tried to see more patients. I tried to bend more and be available more. I wanted to be accepted and liked. I wanted a full schedule so I could prove that I was a "great" doctor like my counterpart. I wanted the administration to see that I was good and worthy. (Again, I was looking for external validation that I would not find). I came in when I wasn't on call. I started being ALWAYS accessible to the patients, despite being exhausted and emotionally fragile.

And then it happened. I had my second child, and I took time off. I started to reflect on what was important to me as an individual.

I started to feel a sense of not having accomplished much: So what I was in my early 30's and a successful OB/GYN. So are other people? They seem to be doing fine. Why am I struggling?

My constant self-doubt started to show at work. It led to arguments at home with my husband that I created because I was mirroring my own feelings of inadequacy.

I would dread going to work. I would purposefully drag my feet getting in to see my first patient. I felt weighted moving from room to room and had minimal conversations with ancillary staff. I would go and have lunch in my car or even just leave in the middle of the day because I could feel the stress piling up around me like blocks. I started to withdraw. (Another cardinal sign of burnout.) I withdrew from my family, my friends, my spouse, and from my patients. I found it difficult to find empathy and understanding, even at times when it was most necessary. I found myself rushing through my day in order to feel like I was breaking free at the end of the day, even if I had a mountain of charts left.
My husband started to worry for my mental health. He started seeing a side of me he had seen during residency. And he was brave enough to approach me about it.

I was defensive. I felt as though I was doing just FINE. I remember saying: "this is normal. This is what all new moms go through." And one day, he asked me: do you still love what you do?

And I remember feeling highly vulnerable, "No, I said."
I remember feeling defeated in that moment. How could it be that the one thing that had defined me for so long, the thing I worked towards for as long as I could remember, was not fulfilling? I remember the feeling of defeat was followed by fear, panic, and anxiety. I felt as though the weight of the world was even heavier on my shoulders as my mind scrambled to think of what I was going to do next.

I'll tell you this; it took me several years of going back and forth to realize the answer that was sitting in front of me all along.
I needed a Break.
I needed some time to figure out what I wanted.
I realized that I had spent so much of my time and effort focusing on getting to the goal and feeling successful when I got there that I forgot to live life along the way.
I have spent the last year since leaving Full-time practice allowing myself to heal.

I gave myself permission to grieve the loss. Now I did not believe that I was walking away from medicine forever, but what I did recognize is that I was walking away from practicing medicine and living life based on others' expectations.

It became readily apparent the longer I spent time away from full-time practice that for the years of my life that I had been working towards becoming a "successful obstetrician/gynecologist," I Had completely lost sight of what life was outside of medicine.

And this is not just in the medical field. Many of us are raised in societies and cultures that believe that accomplishments and accolades are what drive success, prosperity, and happiness.

What I am learning, and want to share, is that the goalpost needs to keep moving. We owe it to ourselves to be happy in our everyday and not be working toward an end goal. As it is mentioned in the popular book "Atomic Habits," outcomes are actually a lagging indicator of our successes.

What I want to share is that taking your time, stepping away, and reevaluating what your life is, is okay and is oftentimes necessary.
If I had not stepped away from full-time practice when I did and spent the last year finding what drives me, I do not think I would have been able to go back to medicine.

So fast forward to our present day. In the last year, I have gone back to practicing Obstetrics & gynecology. And I realize how much I love it. I absolutely love taking care of women and their health and wellness.
Even with the decision to leave practice, this has not decreased the challenges that have come up in my life. However, I feel different about them now. I face my challenges differently, with my priorities being myself and my family. My family has been challenged secondary to my husband and me alternating between remote work areas. Yet, we are finding more joy this past year than we have previously. I have learned that saying "No" is a strength and that setting boundaries are necessary for not only my success but the success of my family.

I created a vision board because, for the first time, I feel that I am looking forward to the future and realize I can create it the way I want it to be.

Why did this change? It is not that I did not "like" my job anymore. It is not that I did not want to be an Obstetrician/Gynecologist any longer. It was neither of these things. It was that I was burnt out. I was exhausted from a toxic work environment. I had lost sight of what I wanted my purpose to be.

In this last year, I have not only found more time for myself, but I have also found more time with my family. I play with my children, enjoy date nights with my husband, and am mindful of where I am using my time.
I often find myself laughing with colleagues at work. I find waking up to go in for an early shift or working overnight is enjoyable. I don't mind working late because it is on my terms. I have rediscovered empathy and connection with my patients and my colleagues.

I have instituted the practice of self-care as necessary and have Penned it into my schedule daily whether this is journaling, movement or talking to a friend. Whether it be taking up a new hobby, painting or working in my garden. It has become a time that people in my life know is non-negotiable.

Burnout happens. It is hard, and it often feels like you are carrying the weight of the world on your shoulders. You may feel that you will not be the person you once were, and you may feel like you won't find joy again.

I am here to tell you: I have been there. I have felt alone. I hope if this tells you anything, it is that you are not alone. That you can move forward through burnout. You are meant to live the life you dreamt of, even if that dream changes.

About Radhika Sharma, MD, FACOG

Dr. Sharma is a obstetrician/gynecologist and a life and wellness coach. She is the founder of BusyOBees. She helps you challenge your thoughts, feelings, and doubts, in order to uncover the life you want to live.

https://busyobees.com

Mously Le Blanc, MD, FABPMR

I remember being at the office. I was trying to hold it together and get through the day. It was difficult to focus on my work. My mind kept shifting from thoughts about my home life and to the tasks before me. My thoughts were racing. My emotions went from sadness to anxiousness to numbness. I sat waiting for the next patient to be roomed by the medical assistant. My thoughts and feelings getting heavier and heavier. I remember feeling my emotions boil over in an interaction with the medical assistant. In the next moment, I found myself yelling at her. This was completely unlike me. I never had so much as raised my voice ever and had always been nice, calm, professional, personable, and perfectly poised at work. I surprised everyone and myself as well. It felt like I had an out-of-body experience where I found myself looking at myself, thinking, 'What is wrong with me?!'

Weeks before this moment, my life as I knew and loved it came crumbling down. The illusion of happiness and contentment faded when I realized my spouse was not whom I thought he was, and I realized I had been living in an illusion. I didn't know what the fate of my marriage and family would be. Suddenly my perfect life that included the house, the car, the titles, the Ivy League pedigree, the career, the marriage– all meant nothing. It all felt empty and meaningless. I was walking around as a hollow shell of my former self. I felt like the rug had been suddenly pulled from underneath me, and I wasn't sure what to do or how to make sense of my new reality.

I never hated my job. I actually loved my patients and the specialized work I was doing. While there were stressors and frustrations with the hospital system and management, I felt pretty blessed. But once things fell apart at home, my tolerance for work environment toxicity became an all-time low. Everything and everyone pushed my buttons when before, I could always smile through my frustrations. Suddenly, I became aware of how toxic this work situation had become. Prior to that, I seemed to walk around work and life with rose-colored glasses. I was too easily satisfied, content with the bare minimum, accustomed to pleasing others, and never stated my needs to others. In medicine, we're taught to never let others see us sweat, to cry alone, to face life and death situations, and simply walk into the next patient room with a smile. It certainly didn't help that I grew up in a household where I wasn't allowed to show emotions, was highly criticized and I never felt good enough. As an overachieving perfectionist people pleaser, I was fully accustomed to suppressing my needs and always being the good girl. I didn't realize how much I was tolerating and how toxic the work environment was until I couldn't take any more on my plate.

When I was ready to say 'no more' to drama and toxicity in my personal life, I finally woke up to the reality of the degree of toxicity I was experiencing at work. My personal life crumbling was my wake-up call. It was the violent removal of my rose-colored glasses, and I could no longer look away and smile. It was my inner child screaming, "look at me!".

At that moment in clinic, after yelling at the medical assistant, I knew I could no longer continue on this path. Something had to change, and it needed to change - not now but right now. This was the moment I realized I was burnout and I needed help.

That's how I found my way to coaching, something that I had never heard much about previously. But I didn't walk in through the front door, so to speak. Rather than admit defeat and ask for help, I did the doctorly (or martyrly) thing of signing up to become a life coach to help others when I knew the person who actually needed help was ME. But in true people-pleasing form, I convinced myself that I was only able to receive help if it was in service to others. Despite walking into coaching through the back door, the next 8 months of training to become a coach radically transformed my life.

I learned the importance of filling my own cup on a daily basis rather than expecting other people or a job to fill it for me. My cup was empty, and I needed a fill of self-compassion, self-acceptance, and self-care- all of which were completely foreign to me.

I learned to connect with my inner emotions and experience emotions rather than living a life numb to emotions. In medicine, we are trained to ignore our emotions, to be professional, and to endure the tragedies we face at work. The problem with numbing out to endure the hardships of medicine is that you equally numb yourself to experiencing the beauty of life. Passion, love, excitement, and joy become muted, and life feels unfulfilling.

I learned that the key to a joyous life is gaining clarity about what I truly wanted- not what I was told to want or what I was expected to want by society, family, and friends. I learned to connect to my heart and my emotions by asking myself, 'what are you feeling, and what do you want?' I would ask myself that over and over until I had absolute clarity on what my heart desired. In medical training, we are routinely asked to ignore our needs- physical such as bathroom, food, and water breaks, and emotional needs. Therefore, I needed to reprogram my mind by learning how to thaw out my numb heart and connect to my body. This allowed me to feel into my body so that I could make decisions from a gut level knowing. Essentially, I learned how to trust and tune into my body for wisdom after spending decades ignoring my body and intuition.

After discovering the tools of coaching and filling my inner cup of joy daily, I journaled about what I truly wanted and what would make me radically happy. I imagined what my best life would look like and how I wanted my work life to look in detail. I was simply dreaming big and audacious dreams, not even thinking it could ever really happen. Within a year of writing that journal entry, I found myself living that dream life. I no longer worked at my stressful academic job, I doubled my salary while decreasing my clinical time in half, and I had full autonomy working for myself. I no longer felt overwhelmed or helpless. I was no longer burnt out. I was thriving.

With my newfound freedom, I was free to explore my passions for travel, explore hobbies such as golf and horseback riding and build a coaching business helping female physicians to say yes to living a happy and fulfilled life without sacrificing their health, wealth, or relationships. As a former people-pleasing perfectionist, I help female physicians remove their 'good girl' masks to live authentic lives connecting inwardly to their intuitive compass to lead them to true happiness.

About Mously Le Blanc, MD, FABPMR

Dr. Mously Le Blanc, is a highly awarded and sought-after medical doctor, holistic intuitive healer, and coach. Dr. Mo received her medical degree from the University of Pennsylvania and completed her residency training in Physical Medicine & Rehabilitation at Columbia and Cornell University Hospitals. She has been recognized as a Top Doctor multiple years in a row and has earned many teaching and patient care awards. She is an author, podcaster and motivational speaker that has been featured in the media including CBS, FOX and SHIFT Network. She is the founder of Holistic Health and Healing, dedicated to holistic and intuitive healing and coaching. As a master teacher of reiki, neurolinguistic (NLP) and akashic record readings, Dr. Le Blanc takes a holistic heart-centered approach to healing that addresses the mind, body, heart and soul by incorporating energy healing techniques with coaching to quickly and effectively empower women to transform their lives.

In her experience as a doctor treating cancer and chronic pain patients, she has witnessed directly how emotional trauma and burnout result in physical manifestation of pain and illness. She empowers successful women experiencing burnout and betrayal to get off the hamster wheel of overwhelm to find self-acceptance, balance and courage to create a life they love on their own terms so that burnout is a thing of the past. She discusses her healing methods in her book entitled, "Unleash the Healing Within: How to stop relying on things outside yourself to heal yourself". She enjoys curating retreat experiences and VIP days to take clients on deeply transformative journeys to connect within and heal their past trauma.

www.unleashthehealingwithin.com/coach

Robyn Tiger, MD, DipABLM

About 15 -20 years ago, I began developing a series of symptoms that seemed unrelated:
Migraine headaches with intense vomiting
Tinnitus so loud I could barely sleep
Vertigo from a simple head turn
Bleeding gums
GE reflux
Body pain – felt like "the tin man" every day
Intermittent paresthesias –hands, feet, left side of the back
Poor digestion—abdominal pain and bloating and poor bowel habits (diarrhea & constipation)
Insomnia
Exhaustion
Full of anxiety, overwhelm and doom
Suicidal ideation

At the time I was practicing diagnostic radiology, married to a wonderful man with two beautiful children. We had "all the things" and looked perfect on the outside, but I felt like I was dying on the inside. I went to many specialists: GI, neurologist, periodontist, psychologist….was put on many meds…." a pill for an ill"…had many blood tests (all neg) and many imaging studies (all neg). I had to talk myself into getting out of bed each day and hide how I was really feeling from my family and friends, and co-workers. Nothing made me feel better. The meds made me feel worse.

I lost three physician friends to suicide and saw a fork in the road… didn't want to end up like them. Started looking outside of western medicine for help since western medicine wasn't working. I was already exercising a lot (probably too much) and eating a healthy vegan diet, so those weren't my issues. I heard more and more about yoga & meditation and thought those were for "those other people" as I was a "gym rat," but I finally decided to cave and give them a try as I had nothing else. So I signed up at a local studio for a 101 course, and even though I was quite skeptical, an unbelievable shift happened after the very 1st class. I felt calm, balanced, focused, and in control, and I was no longer exhausted! Over time the symptoms that I described began to dissipate. I reviewed the medical literature to find that there were many studies documenting the benefits of yoga & meditation and I was shocked to never have heard of this. So my symptoms were related to a whopping case of chronic stress, nothing I needed any pills for at all. I was the only physician to correctly make my diagnosis.

Over time ALL of my symptoms resolved completely by utilizing self-care tools we were never taught in training.

I went on to study to be a yoga teacher (200 hours) and then further to become a certified yoga therapist (1000 hours) as well as a certified meditation teacher to continue my own healing and to help others learn what I had learned. I added to this body-based education life coaching to work with a mindset which was also very helpful for me. I had a firsthand understanding that a whole-person approach to well-being was what I and others needed, and I wanted to provide the missing education in physician training to prevent and relieve what I went through.

Question and Answers

Looking back, was there anything in your childhood or upbringing that you think led to your burnout?

Lack of coping mechanisms with trauma.

My Father suffered from manic depression and died from suicide when I was seven years old (I remember the day clearly....), that side of my family disowned us (my 2 sibs and me), and I never had any therapy or help processing.

Did anything occur in your training that led to your burnout?

During training, the call and hours were difficult at times, doing 2-3 36-hour shifts/week and working 6-7 days/week. There were also issues with sexual harassment and no consequences when reported. It was exhausting trying to avoid the culprits and losing sleep over inappropriate behavior and fear of further incidents. So many of us now learned that others were also experiencing it decades ago. We didn't really talk about it much back then, as we had no support and feared consequences.

Was there anything about the system you worked in that led to your episode (s) of burnout?

As a radiologist, we initially were in a reading room with films -- it was very intellectually stimulating and fun sharing cases with each other and collaboratively reviewing cases with teams of physicians that would do "radiology rounds," enabling the best diagnoses and treatment plans.

Then when everything switched to PACS it all changed. This isn't what I signed up for. We were just hamsters on a wheel dictating into a machine with voice-activated transcription at a computer in a dark room alone. It was very isolating and lonely, and harder to make the best diagnoses.

Additionally, the quantity was being prioritized over quality. Taking time to review prior cases, speak with patients, speak with referring clinicians, and ask another for help, were all frowned upon. More was better, even if inaccurate. This caused even more work for me because I had to check other people's work who cut corners, and clinicians would trust me to read and over-read their patients and family's cases as they didn't trust others since I was "old school".

Did you feel that you had a support system?

Support only in friendships and spouse for listening (although I didn't ever tell the whole story).
No real support system at work or medically.

Do you remember any specific incidents where your burnout was apparent?

Intermittent paresthesias:
I couldn't feel the biopsy gun in my hands during breast biopsies
I couldn't feel the knife while cutting up vegetables
I couldn't feel the steering wheel while driving

Making mistakes:
Delayed Disney trip because of extreme migraine with vomiting
Showed up in the wrong airport terminal for a family trip on Christmas day
Showed up for a show on the wrong day (thought someone was in our seats).

Did anyone notice and reach out to you?
no

What helped you overcome your burnout?

Fearing I would end up like three physician friends who died from suicide
Looking into the eyes of my then two small children and husband
I decided to seek help outside the box of traditional western medicine, which wasn't working, and learned tools in yoga therapy, meditation, trauma, somatics, and life coaching

How are you thriving today?

My daily self-care routine is non-negotiable!
Each morning I start my day with meditation, yoga therapy & exercise.

I get regular coaching for my mindset, keep a plant-based diet, abstain from alcohol and caffeine, and feel amazingly grateful each and every day!

I am a physician well-being coach, founder of StressFreeMD, and lead faculty + and subject matter expert in stress management for a large lifestyle organization..

I love teaching physicians a whole-person approach to stress relief and well-being, including bottom-up (body-based) and top-down (mindset) tools so they can live their best lives through my programs, presentations, and a podcast. I am happy to be able to provide CME for all of my teachings as physicians deserve to have this education compensated.

What advice would you give to someone going through burnout?

You are not alone
It is not your fault. You just were never taught how to really take care of yourself.
You can feel better all by yourself--you just need to learn how
If you are suicidal, please get help.
Free Physician Hotline**1-888-409-0141**.

What advice would you give to the facilities and administration who are trying to help decrease the rate of physician burnout?

Provide required self-care education sessions AND pay for them + CME
Give more time off, fewer hours
Create community

What advice, if any, would you give to the facilities that can do better when it comes to improving burnout rates of physicians (those facilities that appear to have a lack of interest in helping to improve conditions)?

Show them the research.

About Robyn Tiger, MD, DipABLM

Dr. Tiger is lead faculty and subject matter expert in stress management for a large lifestyle medicine organization, host of the StressFreeMD Podcast, a medical society Healthy Healer Partner, an app self-care key opinion leader for surgeons, a specialist for first responders, and is on faculty to teach yoga therapy & meditation for trauma certification.

She received her BS degree in Natural Science and Psychology from Muhlenberg College. She earned her MD, completed an Internal Medicine internship and Diagnostic Radiology residency at the Medical College of Pennsylvania and also completed a fellowship in Body Imaging at Thomas Jefferson University Hospital.

Her strong desire to help physicians grew out of her many years in medical practice experiencing and witnessing firsthand the need for physician self-care education. She is deeply passionate about successfully guiding physicians to become the best versions of themselves and live their healthiest, most fulfilling lives!

https://www.stressfreemd.net/

Anonymous, MD 1

Looking back, was there anything in your childhood or upbringing that you think led to your burnout?

I think that "never being enough" was something that I heard in my head a lot. Even when it was 99%, it was not perfect.

I did not really consider myself a perfectionist, but the more I write / journal and experience day-to-day life, I realize that although I may not be a "perfectionist", I definitely hold myself to some out-of-this-world (Superhuman) standards sometimes. I do believe that it is, in part, due to having a stay-at-home mom that seemed to " DO IT ALL."

Comparing myself to my own mother is something that I still struggle with. By no means do I think she is perfect in every way. But – I do compare my mothering and wife-ing to the way she did it.

Did anything occur in your training that led to your burnout?

I love medicine, and I had full buy-in to the way we were trained. Now – I have some other thoughts about it. At the time of my training, I felt that the hierarchy and exhausting hours in training were not unreasonable. I knew it was temporary, but I also believed it was necessary. I now know that it is far from helping doctors to thrive and be successful once residency is completed, and it is not geared to help us lead a life that is sustainable - to being good at more than one thing and, more importantly, being content. I do feel that the "not good enough" thoughts did serve me in school, college, medical school, and even residency. But –those same thoughts have now become detrimental to my happiness.

Was there anything about the system you worked in that led to your episode (s) of burnout?

I feel that my own thoughts were definitely part of the feelings of burnout. I already worked part-time, so I didn't know why I was having feelings of burnout, and I told myself I could NOT have feelings of burnout because there was no reason – I worked part-time and part-time doctors can't be burnt out.

The culture of medicine did not have space for doctors who were interested in doing anything other than seeing patients, day in and day out. And then find "extra time" to do the documenting and messages etc. As a primary care doctor, there is almost MORE non-patient care that happens on a day-to-day basis than actual face-to-face patient care, and that does not fulfill the soul.

What do you think caused the burnout?

My own thoughts of self-worth were negative and low.
We were 1 year into the pandemic, and mistrust of doctors and angry patients regarding the vaccine probably didn't help. When we were heroes for the first few months, it felt pretty amazing, and it felt like maybe the system would FINALLY change. But when it didn't, the disappointment in our government, the system, and humanity seemed to take over, and I felt completely helpless – like many others I know.

Describe your period of burnout in depth. What did it feel like? What did burnout look like?

I was irritable and angry and frustrated at patients AND about the system.

I loved patient care and still do. But the negatives (non-face to face patient care) started outweighing the positives.
The "highs" I got from taking care of patients didn't last as long as they used to and no longer felt worth it.

Do you remember any specific incidents where your burnout was apparent?

I had a "meltdown" at work about my schedule, and I started thinking things like, "they don't value me because of x y z reasons."
Then I had to climb myself out of that. I realized that it wasn't THEM that didn't value me. It was ME that didn't value me.

Did anyone notice and reach out to you?
No

How are you thriving today?

What work are you doing that you find fulfilling?
I LOVE coaching
I am coaching and practicing medicine and taking a sabbatical next year to explore other opportunities and a creative side that I didn't even know existed in my brain.

What advice would you give to someone going through burnout?

You are not alone. We can help, and we want to help!
We need doctors, and we need to prevent burnout! We want to help doctors stay in medicine and do so ON THEIR OWN TERMS!

What advice would you give to the facilities and administration who are trying to help decrease the rate of physician burnout?

Just start talking about it. It is not just about money. Increasing salaries and bonuses help, but it does not solve the problem, and it is not long-term.

Acknowledge that it is happening and that the system is the way it is, and we are not just pawns in the system.
It will take time – that is what I am starting to realize. We are all part of the history of improving the conditions for future doctors.

Anonymous, MD 2

My story of physician burnout occurred when I was working at a county hospital with a Level 1 trauma center. The county hospital had grown into a full hospital system with multiple hospitals and many satellite offices. Like I would suspect exists at any government job as well as large hospital systems, there was bureaucracy and multiple layers of regulation. I was coming from private practice and was bracing myself for the lack of flexibility but took the job in order to return to my hometown.

I was hired to cover a specific subspecialty call for which the hospital did not currently have coverage. There was one physician trained in my subspecialty who was near retirement that worked at the hospital very part time, around 4 days a month, and didn't take call. From my understanding, there were previously physicians who had their own practices but were hired and worked part time for the hospital system. The hospital system at some point in the past shifted to hiring full time staff physicians so when I arrived, most physicians were hospital staff employees without their own practices outside the hospital system. I agreed to take a 24/7 subspecialty call and would not take my general specialty call, which was written in my contract.

The call contributed to my burnout, but probably not in the way you would think. It wasn't about working too many hours or lack of sleep due to call. There were residents who provided call support. Most of the time, surgical cases were scheduled for the coming week and not performed overnight. Cases may be added on at the end of the day or on the weekend but I never started a case past midnight. This is standard for my subspecialty and even during fellowship, there was only one case where we operated overnight and that was an unusual circumstance.

My burnout was insidious, as I think is the case with many people. It's hard to pinpoint when I first started feeling burnout. It really felt more like frustration with the system, both the hospital system and the healthcare system as a whole.

There was frustration with errors in scheduling patients. For example, a patient would be scheduled with me instead of the regular physician when they were returning for follow-up of chronic disease. I regularly checked my next day's schedule to try to find and reschedule all the patients that shouldn't have been scheduled with me.

There was frustration with staff support. A lot of the staff I worked closely with were great. The lack of staff support was more of a systems issue. There was a culture of, "well that's the doctor's job, I can't do that." One example was when I was paged by a nurse regarding a patient's antibiotic while I was on vacation. I asked her to switch the antibiotic and the reply was she couldn't do that; the doctor has to handle all medical prescriptions. In contrast, when I was in private practice, any calls to the pharmacy would be handled by staff under my direction.

There was frustration with not being able to get surgical instruments or supplies. I had to carry my own bag of sutures to ensure I had the correct suture for call cases or if I operated at a different surgery site than my home site. There were times I did not have an instrument I needed for surgery and had to improvise. This was most common when doing cases from being "on call" but even happened for scheduled cases at my regular surgery center. I had to attend multiple committee meetings to request and get approval for surgical implants I used for my surgeries. I was informed when I was hired that there was a specific surgical equipment available only to find that it was a different system than I was told and that system didn't do what I needed. That system was also so old it was no longer serviceable by the manufacturer. In order to get the equipment I needed, I had to conduct a trial of all similar equipment from multiple vendors and have the equipment evaluated by any surgeon who may use that equipment. After organizing the trials with the vendors and all the surgeons, a process which took a significant time investment, I was told the budget had been set aside to purchase the equipment. Months passed and it never came. I had to tell patients I couldn't do their surgery due to lack of equipment and refer them elsewhere. This was sometimes problematic due to the patient's insurance or financial situation.

There was frustration at the ability to deliver healthcare. As the county hospital, we were the safety net for patients. However, helping patients get the medications they needed was often a hurdle. We weren't allowed to speak to drug reps, much less take free samples to give to patients. It felt useless to see a patient, who could have their appointment with me for free, but to be unable to treat their condition because they couldn't afford or get access to the medication.

There was frustration with billing those patients who choose to have implants or procedures not covered by insurance and pay out of pocket. I would have patients tell me they keep calling to try to pay and couldn't find anyone who would take their payment. They were worried about having their surgery canceled or that they wouldn't get their desired implant without paying. This added more work for me to try to solve the problem. It also disincentivized me from discussing specialized implants or promoting cash pay procedures, which if done effectively, would have been financially beneficial both to my employer and myself.

There was frustration with my direct supervisor, who had specific ideas of how she wanted me to practice. She wanted me to personally evaluate patients in the emergency room who had been transferred by another hospital for specific specialty care. She denied my request for a two-week vacation that was made 7 months in advance unless I found another sub-specialist who was willing to accept any patients while I was away. She expected me to continue to coordinate care for patients while I was on scheduled vacation contrary to our discussion regarding call coverage prior to when I accepted the position. There were other conflicts that arose as well.

Before long, I found myself that person sitting in my car in the parking lot before work, dreading actually walking into the building to start my day. Each day felt like an endless merry-go-round of seeing patients and doing bureaucratic tasks. Like so many physicians, I stayed late finishing charting and responding to my in-basket. I was no longer connecting with my patients or my work as a physician. I no longer had a sense of accomplishment at work. Though I was working less hours than during medical training, I felt worn out and drained in a way that I did not feel during residency, fellowship, or my prior physician position.

I started to plan my exit strategy. I thought of starting my own private practice. That's when the COVID-19 pandemic hit.

The pandemic was a blessing for me in many ways. It allowed me to slow down. I went to working one or two days a week, seeing urgent patients only. Since I was on call 24/7, I wasn't forced to use up all my sick days and vacation days while other physicians were furloughed. I also didn't get assigned to work outside of my specialty. I got to exercise more, enjoying long bike rides in the park.

The pandemic was also when I first learned about physician coaching through the Leverage and Growth Summit and heard Dr. Sunny Smith. I started listening to The Life Coach School podcast and joined Self Coaching Scholars. I connected with more physicians online through physician Facebook groups including the Leverage and Growth Accelerators and Female Physician

Entrepreneurs. My mind was opened to amazing endeavors other physicians where pursuing outside of practicing medicine. It changed my perspective on what was possible in my own life.

Question and Answers

Looking back, was there anything in your childhood or upbringing that you think led to your burnout?

My parents instilled the desire to be a high achiever, which I consider to be overall positive. My mother really wanted her children to be physicians, and I was the only one who actually went to medical school. I didn't choose medical school to make my mom happy, though the prestige of being a doctor likely did influence my career choice. I grew up as a very independent child with a fierce desire for freedom and autonomy. My burnout really resulted from lack of autonomy in my work situation.

Did anything occur in your training that led to your burnout?

I personally enjoyed my time in residency and fellowship and didn't feel burned out at all during my training. That being said, I think the medical culture of training with the constant messaging that, "the patient comes first" contributes to physician burnout. By constantly hearing, "the patient comes first," there is the additional message that you don't come first to yourself. Your family doesn't come first. How many times during training do we skip meals, or grab a quick but unhealthy snack instead of having a healthy meal? How many times have we been expected to work beyond the brink of exhaustion? My first time being on call as an intern, I worked 30 hours and didn't even have enough downtime in the evening to take out my contact lenses. Putting work first is celebrated in medical training. Putting oneself first is considered selfish. It's not surprising that so few doctors take the time for self-care.

What do you think caused the burnout?

The lack of autonomy and lack of a voice within the system is the largest contributor to my burnout.
While I was able to give input on how many patient slots and when the slots should occur on my schedule, I had no control to make different types of patient slots. I could not have a slot for a new patient, an annual return patient,

an acute follow-up patient, a post-op visit, or a surgical consultation. Every patient got placed in a generic time slot. A post op visit generally takes a fraction of the time a new patient or surgical consultation takes. This made it very difficult to get any reasonable flow on clinic days. Some days I would get very behind and other days I would be twiddling my thumbs depending on the type of appointments that were scheduled.

When we started operating again after elective surgeries were shut down due to the COVID-19 pandemic, the system only tested some patients for COVID-19 prior to their surgery. This was determined by a committee without input from surgeons. There wasn't an appeal process or any way I could find to request my surgical patients be tested prior to surgery. Instead, I operated with their entire face exposed. There was one patient who came in for their post-op visit complaining of symptoms consistent with COVID-19. He was tested that day and was positive for COVID-19 and likely was positive on his day of surgery. This meant I spent close to two hours being within 2 feet of an unmasked person with COVID-19. At least I had a N95 mask to wear during surgery.

What helped you overcome your burnout?

Coaching ultimately was the key to overcoming burnout for me. Shifting my mindset to focus on what I could control, instead of constantly thinking about all the things out of my control, made a big difference. I shifted how my clinic ran and worked on devising a schedule that was better given the limitations of the system. Ultimately, I decided to leave that particular work situation.

Did you have a support system?

My husband was and is my biggest support. He always said I could quit and didn't have to work. Financially, that wasn't really in our best interest. I was the primary breadwinner making more than double his income.

Did anyone notice and reach out to you?

I don't think anyone I know would have thought I was burned out or said I was burned out. My physician friends were spread out over the country. I didn't have any physician friends that I saw in person when I was experiencing burnout.

How are you thriving today?

I've made really large changes in my life. I'm now working part-time as a physician in a private practice setting. I started my own coaching business where I help other physicians, some with burnout and some with other goals. I'm more mindful of my time and how I want to spend my time. I review my goals and values regularly and strive to live based on those goals and values. I still find treating patients fulfilling, especially when I can "fix" their problem surgically. I really find coaching physicians fulfilling. One coaching session can turn around years of programming with a shift of mindset. I love those moments when I see a lightbulb go off.

What advice would you give to someone going through burnout?

You are not alone. It's not you, it's the system of medical training and healthcare. But if you are a physician, you have done hard things. You can overcome burnout and redesign your life into one that you love. Life is a blessing and every day is a gift. Get the help and support you need. There are people out there who can and want to help you. Don't be afraid to invest in yourself, either with time, money or both.

What advice would you give to the facilities and administration who are trying to help decrease the rate of physician burnout?

Create avenues where physicians can relate their concerns where they feel safe to do so and where they feel they will actually be heard. Consider bringing in a coaching program. There are peer reviewed publications that show that coaching reduces burnout in physicians. Cleveland Clinic Foundation has been vocal that they believe their coaching program has potentially saved them $133 million by decreasing physician turnover. Coaching for Institutions designs physician coaching programs for hospital systems.

Medical Malpractice-Laura Fortner, MD

The Truth About Physician Burnout and Medical Malpractice-
I remember like it was yesterday; the pain was so gut wrenching. I just returned home from a 36-hour on-call shift. My five-year old son excitedly ran up to me and hugged me. Then he pulled back and looked at me with bewildered eyes and said: "Mommy, why are you here? You are never home." My dream of being a physician was turning into a nightmare.

I was emotionally and physically exhausted from working 80-100 hours per week. I had three children ages 5, 3, and 1, but I felt so disconnected from their lives. Just prior to my son's message, I broke down in my Sunday school class as I shared that I had to miss something in my son's kindergarten class. I was definitely on the path to physician burnout.

The heart-breaking encounter with my son provided fuel for the proverbial snowball: my life was spinning out of control. In 2004 I discovered that parents of a child whom I delivered in 2001 intended to sue me for malpractice because their son had autism. They came to my practice to retrieve the records, and soon after, I received a certified letter stating their intent to sue. Fear gripped me, and thoughts bombarded my mind that my practice was in jeopardy.

Could I lose my job, income, and license to practice? The burnout I was already feeling, coupled with this letter of intent, convinced me that I should search for some other career outside of the medical field. I was feeling that I was not cut out for medicine and that I was an incompetent doctor. Therefore, in 2005 I launched a successful entrepreneurial business, which generated an income stream that allowed me to quit my private practice by 2007. However, for several years after that, I did work part time as an OB/GYN. These life choices were all a reflection of the negative thoughts that I had about myself and my capabilities as a doctor.

As the years passed by, I lived with constant low-level anxiety and uncertainty of the unknown. I was riding an emotional rollercoaster, fearing my future, my job, my finances, and my reputation. I had so much self-doubt that I even would second-guess my clinical decisions. Doctors have a deeply ingrained belief that they can do no wrong, which is directly linked to the Hippocratic oath. In that oath a physician pledges to "prescribe only beneficial treatments, according to his abilities and judgment; to refrain from causing harm or hurt; and to live an exemplary personal and professional life." Even though 99 percent of doctors in high-risk specialties can expect a malpractice lawsuit, they have the belief that it will not happen to them. If it does happen, doctors are expected and warned not to talk about it with anyone. This perpetuated feelings of isolation, fear, shame, and self-doubt. Not normalizing this experience in our culture creates dysfunction, and this inhibits the healing process.

My fears became a reality when I was finally served papers in 2013. I went through two years of depositions and legal haggling before the case was dismissed in 2015. The parents had a year to re-file their complaint. Right before the year expired, a sheriff rang my doorbell and delivered the papers. My kids were with me at the door as he handed me the envelope. With a pounding heart and shaking hands, I put the kids in front of the TV and ran to my bedroom and sobbed.

At this point in the litigation, my lawyer and the insurance company representatives recommended a jury trial because the legal team was convinced without a doubt that I followed standard of care. Furthermore, scientific evidence does not support that autism is caused by birth injury. It was here, however, that I hit another roadblock. I experienced the inequity of the justice system when the judge decided not to allow a Daubert motion, which is used before the trial to examine the validity of the scientific evidence to be presented by expert witnesses. Therefore, an expert witness was allowed to testify using a theory (Cranial Compression Ischemic Encephalopathy) that contractions during the course of a delivery can cause birth defects and autism. At this time, this theory was being perpetuated throughout the country with no scientific evidence to support it. Someone just arbitrarily made it legal medicine vs. medicine as a standard of care.

As a result, I lost the case and was devastated that the plaintiffs were awarded $11 million. This is why cases are settled instead of risking the outcome of a jury trial. The entire system needs to be changed because normal jurors do not understand medicine.

Through the years I did not realize that I was experiencing Litigation Stress. Ninety-five percent of physicians suffer from this, which creates negative physical and psychological reactions from being involved in a lawsuit. This may lead to Medical Malpractice Stress Syndrome (MMSS), characterized by extreme symptoms of anxiety, depression, feelings of worthlessness, and suicidal ideation; MMSS is an actual disorder cataloged in the DSM codebook.

Upon first being served with the papers, I experienced feelings of heightened anxiety, fear, worry, nausea, and heart palpitations. I struggled with negative thoughts about my ability and reputation, believing that I really did do something wrong. I had a hard time eating and sleeping: everything would bother me. For example, when I would treat patients, I doubted my medical judgment. I also worried what would happen to my family if I could no longer support them. This rollercoaster of emotions continued for years. As time went on, it would dissipate until suddenly an email would appear, and the triggers of the syndrome would be set in motion again.

Since litigation for medical malpractice lawsuits can continue for years (the average case being 4.9 years), physicians exhibit behavioral changes because of burnout, litigation stress, and MMSS. Some of these behaviors include constantly ruminating on the details of the case, overworking to prove self-worth, turning to drugs, alcohol, overeating, and having affairs and relationship problems. Often doctors will procrastinate charting and will second-guess everything, such as doubting their diagnoses, ordering more tests than needed, and consulting the opinions of colleagues, etc. All of these are buffering mechanisms causing the physician to engage in defensive medicine. Furthermore, the depression caused by MMSS can lead to suicide. Approximately 400 physicians die by suicide per year, making it one of the top occupations leading to taking one's life. After years of physician burnout, medical malpractice is like the last straw that breaks doctors. It is like layering a cake having malpractice as the top layer with such a weight that it destroys it all.

In polling other physicians concerning their thoughts on burnout and malpractice, I found that their experiences were similar to mine. One doctor stated, "It becomes part of the paralysis, part of the loud, very loud, loud, self-doubt that becomes a tidal wave when we are empty and without support and when so much is demanded of us. Another responder defined it as a constant struggle: "We wonder what zebra monster is lurking in a patient, even when the current diagnosis fits…beating ourselves up over this constantly, questioning ourselves." Other descriptions included soul crushing, life altering, a major headache, and something ever present and looming.

For a long time, I recognized that I needed someone to help me. However, doctors are trained that they do not need therapy and should have the strength to deal with any situation. It is ingrained that doctors are weak and incompetent if they need counseling or psychological help. Furthermore, most applications ask if a doctor has participated in therapy or were treated for depression, which could jeopardize future employment.

Nevertheless, I was introduced to a psychotherapist who worked with first responders regarding traumatic events. We did EMDR, a form of memory reconsolidation designed to transform how I was thinking in order to get me out of the downward spiral of toxic thoughts and feelings. This helped me for a while. Nevertheless, during the ongoing trial, I also tried a traditional therapist. This was unsuccessful because she did not understand the physician's world or my life.

As a last resort shortly after the trial, I started listening to a podcast about how our thoughts create feelings, affect our behaviors, and influence our lives. I hired a coach who used this methodology. I was given the tools to rewire the tracks of my brain. This coaching enabled me to heal myself and to be at peace. At last I was unleashed and had certainty about myself and competence as a physician. In fact, when I started to heal and regained my confidence, I transitioned to becoming an OB hospitalist.

It is always darkest before the dawn. The result of all this pain and suffering made me determined to offer peace and hope to rescue others from the downward spiral of medical malpractice. It was clear to me that God wanted me to use my struggles to comfort doctors in the same situation. Consequently, I became a certified malpractice coach and started my own business. My clients have offered positive feedback stating that their sessions with me helped them to regain confidence and provided hope and peace of mind regardless of the outcome of the lawsuit. Specific coaching skills and memory reconsolidation helped me and others in the same situation to be overcomers.

Dr. Laura Fortner is a board certified OBGYN, speaker, certified life coach and founder and CEO of The Med Mal Coach. She currently practices as an OB hospitalist in Northeast Ohio. She graduated from University of Pennsylvania and completed her medical degree from the University of Toledo College of Medicine. During her career she got hit with a medical malpractice lawsuit and realized there were no resources for physicians to turn toward to help them navigate the legal system and the emotions of isolation, shame, fear, anxiety, anger, and self doubt. Through her journey of healing, she created a process to help physicians overcome medical malpractice and adverse outcomes. Her unique process helps physicians step back into their greatness. Helping them feel confident, self assured, and peace no matter the outcome.
www.themedmalcoach.com

Surviving Burnout as a Family By Dr. Carrie Atcheson, MD, MPH and Rev. Dr. Eric Atcheson, MDiv, DMin

My husband Eric almost sprinted through the door, shut it behind him, and leaned back on the closed door panting, as if he had just escaped mortal danger and was now preventing his foe's entry into our home. Grizzly bears are uncommon in Alabama so I was really confused by his body language.

It was Saturday where we had nothing particular going on, dogs and our kiddo were playing in the background, and the only sound outside was the airbrakes of the garbage truck rounding the bend. And yet, my wide-eyed husband, radiating nervous energy while holding biscuits in one hand and a blueberry iced latte in the other.

"Hi?," I said, looking at him quizzically. Still leaning on the door, he held my gaze and then just hung his head, shaking it from side to side. He slowly managed to peel himself off the door, take off his shoes at the front entry, and slump down at the dining room table. He finally spoke: "I think I just had a panic attack - there was someone there who looked just like someone from work."

We were almost a year into a move from the Pacific Northwest back to the East Coast so that Eric could accept a call - he's a minister, so that's what they call "taking a job" - to serve an established congregation with good resources and great intentions. As a minister's family, we had been in discernment about this move for about nine months before he interviewed and took the job.

The move brought us closer to both of our families, and, despite the COVID-19 pandemic, we had found neighbors, shops, and outings that made us feel more settled more quickly than other times we relocated. We had just moved out of a rental, having bought a house we loved in an area we loved in the toughest real estate market in a couple of decades. My clinical anesthesia job was pretty fantastic, and I was about to accept a leadership position at a local non-profit to complement my clinical work and my desire to do more racial justice work.

On paper, life was good, but clearly something was not right if seeing someone from work could trigger such an extreme psychological event for my dear husband. Panic attacks aren't that common in our household, in fact, I don't think he'd had one in the 7 years we'd been married. He has been living with major depression since he was a teenager, and for the majority of his adult life, has been stable on medication and therapy. The pandemic had brought out his more anxious and obsessive-compulsive traits, but nothing I had noticed as debilitating. And any anxiety I feel in my pretty chill life manifests as excessive productivity - I'm a former EMT turned trauma anesthesiologist, so I love chaos, and high-stress situations are my happy place.

So how did the two of us get to family grizzly bear high alert on a Saturday morning? And more importantly, how could we find our way out of these woods? This is likely not any kind of spoiler, but Panic Attack Day signaled the start of acknowledging that my husband Eric was deeply burned out at work - not just stressed out, not just "dealing with the pandemic," but really and truly burned out.

It turned out the combination of normal new job challenges, pandemic related challenges, and interpersonal and online harassment in the absence of structural support at work lead to a situation where he felt isolated and unsafe in what should have been his safest space, the congregation he served. After asking for help, trying to facilitate change, and providing all the normal spiritual and theological services of a minister, he realized his only option was to take a step back from active ministry, and he exited his call about six months after Panic Attack Day. As his partner, I only realized after-the-fact how much he was white-knuckling it through every day. He was fully in survival mode, experiencing all the textbook symptoms of burnout: exhaustion, decreased engagement in the work that is his life's calling, feelings of negativity and cynicism towards his work, and the resulting decreased professional efficacy.

It turned out that getting out of the woods was only the beginning of the journey. The real question for our future was: how could Eric be better equipped to recognize the difference between real and perceived grizzly bears, and how could I be better equipped to support a survivor of a bear attack? More than a year later, we're still fleshing out the full answers to those questions, but we have learned a lot along the way.

In this chapter we are going to reflect on what went well and what we could have done better during these past few years of burnout build-up, burnout fallout, and burnout recovery. This will be an uncommon conversation between the supporting partner and the partner experiencing burnout. Burnout recovery in our family is ongoing, but we wanted to share our experiences in the hope that our story might help other families surviving this epidemic of professional burnout together.

What Went Well: The Supporting Partner's Perspective

For me, the things that really helped us through this tough time are divided into things I did for myself and things I did for my partner. The reason I like this division is that it forces me/us to acknowledge that it's not only the partner who is experiencing burnout who needs care during recovery. The supporting partner has to take care of themselves in a really intentional way. Sometimes taking care of myself seemed incongruous or unnecessary because I actually felt fine, but I realized that being over-filled sometimes is what enabled me to live through the days when Eric was at an unexpected low.

The days when I was feeling depleted by normal life things (work, family, parenting, tragedy, grief, mood), and I didn't listen to and ask for what I needed, intentionally filling or overfilling, those were the days when his mood or needs would catch me off-guard. That's when I would bottom out and succumb to poor communication (inevitably saying something I'd regret) or to physical exhaustion, making me vulnerable to getting sick or to poor self care. So here are the things that helped me personally as the supporting partner:

1. Having a great counselor. The help of a good counselor or therapist has always been key for me as a person with no mental health problems. It's helped me deal with normal human stressors in a healthier way, and I've always felt supported through big life events (moving, having a baby, job transition, deaths in the family). I have met regularly with a counselor or therapist for the last decade.

Specifically during the time of Eric's burnout, my counselor helped me work on boundary setting, assessing what I needed and how I could get it, and supported me in dealing with my own normal life stressors. I have experienced excellent care with counselors and therapists with social work, nursing, and psychology backgrounds. On average, it's taken me 1-2 months to connect with a good counselor or therapist, so my advice is always: have one before you need one.

- Partner's reflection: Being raised by lawyers, I would sometimes hear, "It is easy to make fun of lawyers until you need one." I think the same can be said of therapy. It is sooooo easy sometimes to mock therapy as navel-gazing or psychobabble…until you need it yourself. As opposed to merely venting to friends–which I also highly recommend–therapy can give you a trained, more removed perspective that can be invaluable in sorting yourself out as you are experiencing, and trying to heal from, burnout.

2. Getting endorphins, Vitamin D, and dopamine boosts on the regular. Working out regularly, getting outside, and seeking the company of my family, friends and pets has been key to my ability to support Eric during his burnout. I have also had to be okay doing these things by myself.

Eric is more of an introvert, so sometimes a morning at home or a solo walk on the treadmill listening to a podcast really fills his cup. Not me! I need action, fun, sun, sweat, and raucous laughter. I have had to go out of my way to seek these things out safely during the pandemic. Sometimes it has meant random trips to local attractions, and sometimes it's meant rearranging days off so I could make the 6 hour drive to see my extended family in North Carolina. Almost every Monday or Tuesday, it's meant getting up between 4:30 and 6:30 so I can get my work done, get some water, get some coffee and work out with my trainer.

- Eric's response: In the ministry world, a lot of these measures are referred to as "self-care." And while self-care is great, it is mostly a preventative measure, and it has its limits. You cannot expect it to work miracles. Self-care is for staving off burnout, not addressing burnout that is already present. When you are so beset that your vocation is causing you panic attacks, disassociation, or other deleterious impacts, there is only so much you can expect bubble baths and nature walks to do. And saying that is not meant to negate their value, but to clarify the ceiling of their value.

3. Saying "Yes!" to help. Whether that has meant accepting random invitations to dinner or offers of extra childcare from my parents or putting effort into hiring and keeping great folks to help out with housework, the help of our team has been key. We would not have survived the dark days of early recovery without some help with the laundry. Don't get me wrong: the mental load of being the mom-parent, a full-time working professional, and the person in the family with the natural strength of logistics/planning is still overwhelming at times. But knowing that there are some things that are taken care of and some things I can ask for help with is ahhhhh-mazing.
    ◦ Eric's response: I think this is something that ministers and other helping professions can have trouble with accepting, because we are called to lead but only from a position of servanthood. I think another way to look at this–especially around childcare–is a matter of community. We have been profoundly fortunate to have family who are not only able but

eager to help care for our daughter, and that is not something everyone has. Quite simply, we could access a level of assistance that many people cannot, and I think saying that aloud is important.

4. Putting the bar all the way on the floor so it could be easy to step over. I let go early of the concept of perfect birthday parties, having a well-dressed family all the time, having the house straightened for company, or going on elaborate vacations. I see my colleagues jet-setting away to Egypt and Japan, having lovely family photos taken, and enjoying their well-designed homes. These things are outside of our logistical and financial abilities during this season, so t-shirts, driving vacations to visit family and friends, and home-made birthday scavenger hunts are the right fit for us. This was the first year I tried to take family photos, and it was almost an unmitigated disaster. Duly noted - I will stay in my lane with the simpler plans next year!

Eric's response: Goodness, it was not like we were feral! I think it is really important to remember that this all took place during the covid-19 pandemic, and so jet-setting around the world with a child too young to be vaccinated was not advisable to begin with. I suppose in that regard, if I was going to flame out, the pandemic was the time to do it–it was not the only reason we were not living out a picture-perfect life. At the same time, I know my burnout definitely added to the strain in so many ways, which is something I had to come to terms with, make amends for, and forgive myself for.

There were specific ways in which I helped Eric that I think really made a difference. These included:

1. Encouraging him to take a sabbatical job. Even though it ended up being a heavy lift for the family scheduling-wise, I was supportive of him taking a job working at a local wine & spirits shop right after he stepped away from ministry. This is something that is very much outside of his area of specialty, not particularly feeding into any career goals, but I recognized it as a passion & hobby of his, a place to kind of get back out there, so I was supportive. I remembered that, a few years ago, we went to Scotland, and on our way home, he said with a dreamy look in his eyes, "Maybe when I retire, I'll give distillery tours." So, even though I felt cautious about someone with depression and a family history of alcohol abuse working in the wine & liquor industry, I trusted my gut and my belief that getting to fulfill your dreams earlier in life is an incredible opportunity.
    - Eric's response: I think I saw the benefits of this most on display as I searched for my next position post-sabbatical job. It

was like night and day compared to my job search as I was burning out on church ministry. During the latter, I applied to over one hundred positions over a span of several months, with precious few interviews and no offers. At that point, taking a sabbatical job felt like it made a great deal of sense, because I was clearly not bringing the right energy, presence, and focus to my job search. My several months at the shop were not always easy, but afterward, I applied for and got my hospital chaplaincy position in what felt like record time compared to the drawn-out slog my previous job search had become.

2. Scheduling a solo retreat for him right after he exited his job. I took what felt like a huge risk at the time and made reservations for Eric at a beautiful Benedictine monastery in Cullman, Alabama right after his last Sunday at his church. I knew it would have the perfect thing for him because it would be:
    - Economical - he believes that saving money makes things more enjoyable, so I knew a vacation or resort would only stress him out as he was exiting his job.
    - Spiritual but not religious - because he had experienced some recent trauma in his church job, I knew he would need some space from our own religious observances. He had some professors in seminary who were Benedictine, so there was a nostalgia and comfort there for him, without it being directly related to our Protestant traditions and practices.
    - Isolated, but not rigid - some people really benefit from lots of external structure when they are vulnerable. A silent retreat, meditation center, or bootcamp might be the right thing for them, but I knew it wasn't right for him. He likes structure but independence.
    - A good space for reading and writing - he gets a lot of comfort and benefit from reading books and from doing his own writing, so I knew having a space for this would be therapeutic for him.

As you can see, I put a lot of thought into this retreat, so that was really something I felt set him on a better course after he exited his job. It kind of feels good to talk about it here because I kept it very quiet as it was happening.
- Eric's Response: Most of my theological education took place at Jesuit and Dominican seminaries, and I cherish my memories as a student at those divinity schools. So even though I am a Protestant minister, monastic Catholicism is very much a comfort zone for me, and I needed just a bit of that to begin my recovery from burnout. More broadly, I think when you are entering or exiting a time of recovery–such as a

sabbatical, or rehabilitation from an injury–it matters to build in some sort of travel experience if possible to remove you from your day-to-day environs and give you no other excuses or pretexts to avoid healing.

3. Putting aside my "fixer" tendencies to try and listen sympathetically more. This is something I don't come naturally to. Like many physicians, many women, and especially many female physicians, I am a fixer. I see a problem, I make a quick risk-benefit calculation, and I formulate a plan of attack. As you can imagine, for Eric, being the object of a constant barrage of plans of attack, eventually just feels like being under attack.

So I had to do and am still doing *a lot* of work on stepping back and just letting him be, trying to listen and laugh with him. Of course my success at this was and is variable. One of the tools I used is a mindset practice that I call "Marie Kondo face," where I can look at a person or situation that from, my perspective, is rife with opportunities for improvement, and just gaze lovingly at it appreciating the good intentions that went into its creation. I have practiced "Marie Kondo face" many times during Eric's burnout and recovery.

- Eric's response: For me, and perhaps for many of us, seasons of survival and seasons of self-improvement are often mutually exclusive. It can be just too much to do deep work on yourself when you are just white-knuckling it and trying to make it through each day. It is not that I am not interested in bettering myself as a regular practice, but that my emotional, mental, and spiritual resources with which to do so were a) profoundly diminished, and b) all being surged toward the aforementioned goal of just putting my head down and taking life one day at a time. In addition to your partner or significant other giving you the grace for your burnout to be a season of survival rather than self-improvement, give yourself that grace. Self-improvement can and will come when you are able to apply the lessons you learned from your burnout experience moving forward.

4. Focusing on gratitude. During our darkest days of parenting during the pandemic, we had a family practice of giving our kiddo her bath and sharing three things we were grateful for. It was something that just kind of evolved as a family behavior because of opportunity. In the bath was one of the only times our rambunctious, very verbal baby was contained. It was very challenging and painfully intentional at times. Eric had to dig deep for one or two, let alone three, things some days. I had to cultivate silence to give him the space (not my natural state). The practice fell out of favor as our life and needs evolved, but I think it

saved our marriage to a certain extent, and I kind of hope we come back to it in a different season.
- ○ Eric's response: I remember those three gratitudes practices well, as I sat on the toilet seat in Sadie's bathroom and scrounged my burned-out brain for stuff I was grateful for that day. I had actually thought the other day about bringing a version of it back for when we say grace around the table, to each of us offer a gratitude before saying the blessing, as a way of giving thanks to God for those gratitudes on top of our usual pre-dinner prayer. When everything around you seems terrible or closing in, forcing yourself to focus on what is not either of those things can be a really edifying daily practice.

What Could Be Done Better: the Supporting Partner's Perspective

Hindsight truly is 20/20, and when it comes to relational well-being, to thriving within and through community, there is no one prescription that will work for every family, every time. But, again, our intention is that in our reflections, you might hear some truth about your own pathway. So here it is - these are the things I know I could have done better in supporting my partner during burnout and recovery:

1. Acknowledge my own needs. As a physician, I trained to be really good at putting my own mental, emotional, and physical needs aside to deal with the current emergency. The call of my stomach or bladder, my own response to attending a stillbirth, my worries about a family member or financial situation…these can wait until the urgent need has passed. The problem with leaning on this training while supporting a partner experiencing burnout is that the need is ongoing. The need escalates and dies down in an unpredictable pattern. So, for the first year or so, I bottled up my needs or pushed them to the margins of our family life. I realized I was doing this two ways: first, if a need was big enough and had been deferred long enough, it made itself known. An ignored knee injury required surgery, a cold on top of poor sleep became pneumonia, or a need for respite or recognition long deferred came tumbling out of my mouth in frustration at exactly the wrong moment and became a fight. I also deeply recognized the deferred needs once they were met. I so dearly enjoyed a Zoom drawing class I took at noon on Saturdays as it met a need for creativity and a break from weekend caregiving. A flood of well-being overcame me after a belated birthday trip with friends met my need for celebration, fun, and fellowship with my nearest and dearest. In her book The Way of Integrity (The Open

Field, 2021), Martha Beck says "Above all, please learn to trust your inner teacher, the burst of relaxation and freedom that rings through your whole body." I'm trying to do better at trusting the wisdom in my positive emotional responses, or as Martha Beck calls it my "inner teacher."

- Eric's response: This was a particularly difficult dimension for me to come to terms with–that my spouse had needs that I was not in a place to help her meet because of my burnout. If you are used to being a high-functioning, names-taking, business-taking-care-of type of individual, it can be an unspoken but still highly important component of how you perceive yourself, and the loss of that can be profound. Simply writing those words of acknowledgement was hard for me to do, but a person's family not getting the best from that person is an extremely common denominator in burnout experiences, and so I think it needs to be discussed more openly.

2. Stating the positive stuff out loud. During the time my husband was experiencing burnout, I was mostly enjoying life. This differential in our daily experiences and the nature of running a busy family meant that, often, what we were sharing or talking about was problem-focused. Sometimes it just didn't occur to me to say out of the blue, "man, I had a really great day - this one patient really amazed me" or "The $50,000 grant I wrote got funded!"

And, though I recognize the error in this thinking now, sometimes it felt like I would be rubbing salt in a wound, sharing my good day with someone who was having a bad day. We were pretty good at sharing parenting gems or good moments, but even this goes awry sometimes because of a differential of enjoyment of parenting during different stages. For me, parenting a toddler is mostly enjoyable, while for my partner and co-parent, I know his favorite age is going to be when she is a voracious reader, fully potty trained, and more likely to sleep through the night. I know at times, my reticence to share my positive experiences contributed to an impression that my assessment of our life together was a negative one. Also as Martin Seligman notes "When we take time to notice the things that go right - it means we're getting a lot of little rewards throughout the day" (Learned Optimism, Pocket Books Paperback, 1992). This is one thing, I'm trying hard to course correct because I was missing a lot of opportunities to reward both of us.

- Eric's response: Burnout does not just make it tougher to celebrate the good stuff, it makes it tougher to even realize that the good stuff is still taking place. In that regard, a partner or significant other recognizing the victories is not only *not* "rubbing salt in a wound," it is reminding the person experiencing burnout of the good that exists beyond the wound. But when the wound is deep, severe, and ongoing, it can be all we are capable of perceiving.

3. Better communication about finances. In the depths of Eric's burnout, I made a unilateral decision to refinance my student loans. Alone in the living room on a Friday night, I filled out the online application and just got it done. Financially, it was the right decision, taking advantage of the lowest interest rates, but from a relationship perspective, not trusting Eric's emotional abilities to handle the discussion fostered some distrust that we are still working out. We definitely can and could have been much better about making this a part of our family life.

I personally let my personal experience with shame after losing income during the shutdown of elective surgeries during the pandemic, color my perception of Eric's shame at losing income. Of course, Brene Brown calls me out on this: "We judge people in areas where we're vulnerable to shame, especially picking folks who are doing worse than we're doing. If I feel good about my parenting, I have no interest in judging other people's choices. If I feel good about my body, I don't go around making fun of other people's weight or appearance. We're hard on each other because we're using each other as a launching pad out of our own perceived deficiency." (Daring Greatly, Penguin Random House, 2012)

- Eric's response: Finances can be especially fraught around the topic of burnout, both because burnout operates fundamentally from a place of scarcity and because in order to recover from burnout, you may need to leave your job as I did. And there can be a great deal of shame indeed around that, again if you perceive yourself as a successful go-getter, or even if, like me, you struggle with the traditional image of the man as the provider for his family, whatever the cost. But in order for me to continue to provide not just financially but emotionally for my family, a change had to be made. Financial unsustainability and emotional unsustainability go hand-in-hand more frequently than I think we want to acknowledge, again in part due to that power shame has over us.

What Went Well: the Perspective of the Partner Experiencing Burnout

Because I am married to such an action-oriented doer and executor, I had the space to sort of fall apart a bit and not function as highly as I once did in our family system. My roles of grocery shopper, dishwasher, weekday cook, and dogwalker (among others) became a bit more time-consuming for me, I made mistakes and forgot things more frequently, and I simply was not bringing my

A-game home to my family. In those moments, and when she had the bandwidth to spare, Carrie volunteered to take some of those tasks of my to-do list.

As an expression of care and as a way to give me a bit of slack with my own expectations, that meant a lot. Continually feeling like I was not living up to my own expectations wore me down as my burnout progressed, and I would project those feelings onto my spouse, as though she must be displeased with me because I was displeased with myself. Her acts of service as gestures of care would communicate to me that this was not the case.

More deeply, the acknowledgement that I would need to leave my job and vocation behind for a while, and the encouragement to do so with the knowledge that our family would be okay, was perhaps my first real step towards liberation from burnout. Never underestimate the importance or power of such reassurance, if it is something you can offer from a place of truth and care.

What Could Be Done Better: the Perspective of the Partner Experiencing Burnout

If there is one thing I could communicate in all of this, it is that burnout is, at its core, not a matter of overwork but a loss of right relationship with your work. In other words: burnout is relational. Overwork can definitely contribute to burnout, but it really is much more than that.

Mourning that loss of relationship is work, especially when you are in the midst of experiencing that loss. It is a little like watching a loved one slowly die–you are mourning their loss even as they may still be alive. And it is those acute moments in which you are in survival mode, just trying to make it through for your own sake.

In those moments, having loved ones press you to improve yourself can be really difficult to experience, and ironically can add to the relational nature of burnout, because your relationship with your work or vocation has already been deeply altered, and in a perverse game of dominoes, your relationship with your partner or spouse stands to be altered as well.
So ultimately, what could have been done better I think comes down to tending to the relationship and not just tending to your partner's function in the family unit. I greatly appreciated those acts of service which took stressors off my plate, but that addressed the symptom of me not functioning as highly as I once did. To really tend the relationship piece, deeper work is required, and that

deeper work in turn requires a purposefulness and determination that I simply did not have at the ready. I think we are still surveying some deferred maintenance on our relationship that I hope for us up-prioritize going forward.

Conclusion

There is not much to say here but that both of us wish you well: wherever you are on your journey through burnout and whether you are the supporting partner or the partner experiencing burnout. Because of our negativity bias as humans, when we hear about relationships being strained to breaking by the experience of one partner surviving burnout, we tend to think having everything shattered by burnout is the norm. It definitely happens, and, if it's time for partners to part ways because irreparable damage has been done to the relationship, that's okay and healthy. We wanted to tell you our story, a story of two very imperfect humans holding things together through a lot of bad days, surviving burnout as a family.

Carrie Atcheson, MD, MPH

Dr. Carrie Atcheson is a private practice anesthesiologist, nonprofit executive, digital educator, and multigenerational family member, which makes her simultaneously very busy and obsessed with rest. She is a professional sleep-maker and anti-anxiety warrior for her patients, and - by virtue of her medical training, innumerable busy nights on call, and journey with a colicky baby - she is also an expert curator of her own personal rest. On a good day, she can be found reading a novel in the bath, and on a challenging day, she can be found wearing one hat on top of another. She deeply believes perfect is a verb and not a noun.

https://thesabbaticalschool.org/

About Dr. Eric Atcheson

Rev. Dr. Eric Atcheson is an ordained pastor in the Christian Church (Disciples of Christ) and the author of two books: Oregon Trail Theology: The Frontier Millennial Christians Face —And How We're Ready (Church Publishing, 2018) and On Earth as it is in Heaven: A Faith-Based Toolkit for Economic Justice (Church Publishing, 2020). Eric is a church minister by training who has dedicated himself through his preaching, speaking, and writing to his calling as a prophetic and pastoral voice rooted in the Scriptures. A wordsmith and storyteller, Eric believes in the grace and truth found in the logos, the Word. His preaching and teaching on God's Word aims to reflect that grace and truth. And as a descendant of Armenian Genocide survivors, Eric's ethnic identity is woven into his passion for social justice and human rights. Eric lives with his wife, daughter, and their two dogs, and he loves exploring the Birmingham area's many parks, trails, and other outdoor spaces with them.

https://www.ericatcheson.com/about

How it All Started By Sharon T McLaughlin MD FACS

I had wanted to be a doctor since I was a teenager. Never do I recall saying that I wanted to be anything else. Never could I have imagined I would get to the point where one day, I wanted to walk away from it all.

At the age of 13, I was diagnosed with Non-Hodgkins lymphoma. This was a difficult time in my life. I struggled with the change in my appearance and living a life different than my teen friends. It was at that time that I had a conversation with God. It went something like, "let me live and I will become a doctor."

School was not easy for me or at least getting all those A's. It seemed to me that I had to put in more time than others. In high school, a teacher mentioned that it appeared I had dyslexia. Feelings of Imposter syndrome would creep in throughout my career. I was highly motivated though and those A's came. There was a drive deeply rooted in me that at times I questioned myself where it came from. I finished with a degrees in biochemistry in 3.5 years. My persistence did pay off. I was overjoyed when the first letter of acceptance to medical school came and more followed.

My intention was to become a pediatric oncologist, but when I rotated through surgery, the fast pace and ability to heal with my hands changed that path. I applied for orthopedic surgery with a plan to specialize in bone tumors. Many people told me "don't not go into surgery", it is not a place for women. I did not listen, I wanted to follow my own dreams

I didn't match into orthopedics, and I was heartbroken. I took a transitional year in a general surgery program and reapplied for orthopedics the following year, and still didn't match. I did a second year in general surgery. Although I don't know if this is an official term, the residents referred to our program as a "pyramid program" which means they took in more residents in than they finished.

From the beginning, there were 3 residents who were told they would finish if they continued to meet the requirements. One resident decided that general surgery was not for him. Another resident did not meet the requirements and was asked to leave, and another spot opened up in that residency program. I was one of the residents offered a spot to complete the 5 year general surgery program and was thankful to secure a position. The resident that was asked to leave the program went on to commit suicide. There has always been some guilt carried inside me because of this...what if I didn't get the spot and he stayed?

There were not many women in my general surgery program. The hours were long and grueling. I don't remember having a difficult time with the attendings and many of them went out of their way to support me. However, I do remember that a couple of the residents were not kind. There were minor differences in how we were treated. I wasn't a guys guy who could carry on a conversation about sports.

Looking back as a whole, I would say the residents who had the happiest marriages were the most supportive. I finished the program in good standing, with the support of the chairman of surgery (thank you Dr. Tortolani and Dr. Abumrad).

I went on plastic surgery fellowship. There wasn't the same support as I found in general surgery. I thought that no matter what I did it was not good enough. There were plastic surgeons who I preferred to work with where I felt I could just be me, and there were a handful I preferred to avoid. One surgeon confronted me about this, suggesting that I didn't like working with him, I was thankful he recognized this. The feeling was not mutual. To my surprise he proceeded to blow up in the middle of the operating room hallway. I have a motto, don't ask unless you want an honest answer. It appeared women would get yelled at more often than men in this program. It seemed to me that there were more jokes made about us than a willingness to help.

I was outspoken at times which had repercussions. One day my junior resident and I were performing a breast reduction with a voluntary staff plastic surgeon attending who was supervising but not scrubbed in. We typically ordered lunch on these days, and he covered the bill. I thought we had removed enough breast tissue. The attending surgeon did not think so and asked me to remove some more, and I did. This went on and on. He then told me to remove more, at which point I declined. He was angry and asked me to step away as he went to go scrub in the hallway. My junior fellow leaned in and said I don't think we are getting lunch today. Humor helps all! Any thoughts on what the patient said to me afterward?

I mentioned earlier that I had Non-hodgkins lymphoma when I was 13 with radiation to the chest wall. Reports were coming out showing an increased risk of breast cancer. For me, it was 34% given the age I was when I received radiation. I started with screening mammograms. There were some changes from the year prior. Probably not cancer, but they would need to do more testing. I elected for a bilateral mastectomy with reconstruction. My program director did not want me to have the surgery as I was in training. I had a week's vacation and thought this was the best time to do it. I had good insurance from the state as I was in training, and who knew what the future held? I said I would be back in a week. I was

I did a case when I came back. Usually, at the end of the case, the plastic surgeon would leave, and I would bring the patient to the recovery room. This time this particular surgeon stayed. For a second, I thought it was to help me move the patient onto the stretcher, as I knew I shouldn't being doing any heavy lifting. He didn't help. He stood there and watched. I made sure not to wince in pain, but I would be lying if I said it didn't hurt like hell to roll the patient off the OR table. I looked at anesthesia to make sure they were ready and said let's go without ever looking his way.

Those 2 years in plastic surgery were rough for me. The thoughts of being judged all the time left me with a feeling of inadequacy and I was concerned about my performance as a surgeon.

Thereafter, I took a position as an attending in a busy plastic surgery practice and I was thankful for this opportunity. The staff were wonderful to work with, and I had a good working relationship with the senior plastic surgeon. I did all the call for the practice 24/7, which was fine at first because I was able to pay off my school loans, but after I met my husband, I knew I wanted a more stable life.

I opened a solo practice. I enjoyed skin cancer reconstruction on the face and built my practice around that. After I had my daughter, things started to change. The work-life balance became extremely difficult. I wasn't working set hours because I had to wait for the Mohs surgeon to finish their part before I could close the wound. Some of these wounds could not be closed in the office which required taking the patient to the operating room, these were now add on cases to the schedule going all times of the day. As time went on, the cases that I was getting called in on were more complex, and the schedule was chaotic.

Managing the staff, the practice, the patients, my marriage and mommying were becoming more difficult. I was too much in control in the office, I didn't know how to let go and when I had to let go, there were mistakes. I was tired of managing the staff and being pulled in many different directions, it was just too much.

My father became sick around ten years into my practice, and at that time I reassessed. I asked myself, Is this really what I wanted? I kept this to myself. I didn't understand why I was having these thoughts. I had worked so hard to get where I was. I felt guilty about having these thoughts, I thought back to the surgeons who had trained me. I felt I would be doing a disservice by leaving the field. For most of us, it takes a jarring event to step back and ask, "Is this what I really want."

For the next couple of years I was in limbo. I was there but not present nor was I enjoying life to its fullest. I had made a promise to myself when I was sick many years earlier that I would have gratitude and appreciate each and every day. I wasn't practicing this promise I had made to myself. My marriage was struggling. I felt like I was not a good mother, and my practice was too much too handle. I questioned my skills, my performance, and I thought I had lost my edge.

Around that time, I was asked by the CMO of one of the hospitals I had privileges to do quality assurance reviews. I said yes but walked away from that conversation in tears because I had no idea how I was going to add one more thing to my plate. The little things that had to be done now seemed like immense tasks and it was all just too much.

I was experiencing burnout, but I didn't know that this was what it was, so I didn't know what to do about it. I didn't have a hard time sleeping. I just felt pure exhaustion. I started having diarrhea, a lot of diarrhea. There was blood, and I needed a bathroom open at all times during office hours. Then the diagnosis of ulcerative proctitis came (an autoimmune disease). I felt stressed and felt like I was barely hanging on. I did not have suicidal thoughts but I wanted it to all go away. Everything starts with awareness.

The opportunity to do case reviews. You know, the one that had me in tears was my ticket out, or at least I thought it was my ticket out. I knew I wanted to be a better mother. I knew I had to work on my marriage, and I knew the practice could be better but I couldn't do it all, not then, anyway. Walking away from the practice seemed like the easiest thing to do. Yes, even after all of those years of training. I knew that I didn't want to do this for another 10 plus years, let alone another 20 years. I was done.

I clearly remember my last day of operating, I had 5 cases and will cherish those for the rest of my life. People ask, "Do I miss it?" I do, but I don't miss all the chaos that went along with it. Have I thought about going back? Yes, I have, but not in the same capacity. I am looking into this now.

I took a position in utilization management after I left my practice and was doing consulting on the side. The job wasn't the best as far as pay and hours, but it helped me recover and heal. I gained more experience and then applied for another job that had higher pay. I have been with that company for 9 years.

Walking away was hard on so many levels. I thought I was a failure. I felt totally alone without a support system. There were many questions from my husband, my sisters, and some of my friends. Not the friends in medicine because they understood it. I wasn't sure why I was doing what I was doing but I knew my time in clinical medicine had come to an end. So when those questions came as to why I was leaving medicine after all the years I had spent training and building up the practice, I wasn't ready to answer them. I needed to figure this out myself first. I found the questions irritating and just made me feel worse because no one seemed to understand what I was saying or how I was feeling. The questions were repetitive to the point where I needed to say, "This is my life, and I get to choose. No one gets to make these choices other than me."

For those of you who are doubting yourself, know that you are not alone, and you don't have to walk through this difficult time alone. Ask for help and get support (resource section). Coaching has exploded in this area because of the high rates of physician burnout.

There are a number of supportive groups out there. I started the Female Physician Entrepreneurs group so that women physicians could come and learn about business and know that they have options. When you surround yourself with others who are taking steps and moving forward, you are more likely to do the same. Additionally, a like minded community helps normalize what you are going through because you feel heard and understood. Isn't that the point of life to belong?

Question and Answers

Looking back, was there anything in your childhood or upbringing that you think led to your burnout?

My parents were loving, and our home was open to everyone. The only thing that came to mind was that I was an anxious child. My parents had lost their first child and looking back, I would say that my mother had anxiety as well as depression. This anxiety has followed me throughout my life. Anxiety was one of the reasons I doubted myself towards the end of my time in my practice. I always thought the worse would happen when operating. There were a lot of "what ifs."

Was there anything about the system you worked in that led to your episode (s) of burnout?

I was in private practice so I can't blame the system per say.

Working with the insurance companies was not always easy, but for the most part it was not the system. It was me.
Looking back, I could have done things differently.

For one, I am a people pleaser. I give to the point that I am exhausted. Having boundaries and the ability to say no is imperative for our survival. People will take as much as you let them take. It might not be intentional, but you set the precedence.

I would have spent more time hiring and had a trial of testing to ensure they would be a good fit. I could have had a better onboarding process for my staff. I expected them to just know. I would have had PDFs and videos to help train them. I would have fired earlier than I did. If something feels off, go with your gut.

What helped you overcome your burnout?

My time away from practice and the feeling of having less on my plate. My process was a long one. My goal was to find a job that was not as stressful. In retrospect, I would have sought guidance from a coach had I known they existed at the time.

How are your thriving today?

I am thriving today by stretching and trying new things. I have built up a community and have found support. This book is an example of what is possible if you are open to trying new things and knowing that there is another side of burnout, one where you thrive.

Do I still doubt myself-Yes, but I know that this is a part of everyday life and the only way to grow is to push through those uncomfortable moments. I ask for help often and I help others by offering a podcast, a blog, and a Youtube channel. We have also done summits and fundraisers. I truly feel the sky is the limit. When you take the time to network, you never know what doors will open. Open those doors for you never know where they will lead.

About Sharon T McLaughlin, MD FACS

Dr McLaughlin is a board certified plastic surgeon with training certification in medical coding (inpatient and outpatient). She is a speaker, podcaster and blogger. Dr. McLaughlin is the founder of Female Physician Entrepreneurs Group. Our mission is to help women physicians learn more about business so that they can build profitable businesses and have the freedom to live their best life. We do summits, fundraising and workshops. We come together for projects like this book and hope to cover more topics such as perfectionism, boundaries, and Imposter syndrome.

Our community is strong, with over 9,000 women physicians. I am blessed that my message as well as the members who contributed to "Thriving After Burnout" can be shared with many.

https://fpestrong.com

Resources

Physician Support Line is a national, free, and confidential support line made up of hundreds of volunteer psychiatrists joined together in the determined hope to provide peer support for our American physician and medical student colleagues as we all navigate our professional and personal lives.
1-888-409-0141.

AMA STEPS Forward® Program. AMA STEPS Forward® is a collection of strategies designed to help you improve your practice. The AMA can help you improve your practice in the areas of efficient EHR use, physician burnout, and more.
https://www.ama-assn.org/topics/ama-steps-forward-program#:~:text=AMA%20STEPS%20Forward%C2%AE%20is,%2C%20physician%20burnout%2C%20and%20more

AMA-Joy in Medicine™ Health System Recognition Program. The Joy in Medicine™ Health System Recognition Program is designed to spark and guide organizations interested, committed or already engaged in improving physician satisfaction and reducing burnout.
https://www.ama-assn.org/practice-management/sustainability/joy-medicine-health-system-recognition-program

Mayo Clinic-Program on Physician Well being was established to conduct and promote innovative research focused on physician well-being. Research led by the team has established that physician burnout threatens the quality of patient care, patient satisfaction, access to care, and physicians' lives.
https://www.mayo.edu/research/centers-programs/program-physician-well-being

Stanford Medicine WellMD works to orient the entire organization around creating the cultures and practices that reduce burnout and drive professional fulfillment rather than placing onus on the individual physician.
https://wellmd.stanford.edu/

Final Note

Thank you for reading our book. When we decided to do this project, the word burnout came up. Some members were tired of the term and thought it placed the blame on the individual physician. I agree. From a marketing perspective, I thought burnout needed to be used in the title.

For those going through a tough time, you are not alone. Reach out to the co-authors.

For hospital administrators, the numbers speak for themselves. Please look at the resources I have included to help decrease burnout. I kindly as that if you take this initiative on that, you give protected time.

For the payors, we know that patient care is better if the physician is not burned out. I hope to see a scoring system put in place that would have higher reimbursement for facilitates that had lower burnout scores.

Female Physician Entrepreneurs Group

Over 9,000 women physicians learning how to build profitable businesses

"If you want to go fast, go alone, if you want to go far, go together"

FPE.Strong.com

and on Facebook https://www.facebook.com/groups/FemalePhysicianEntrepreneurs

FEMALE PHYSICIAN Entrepreneurs

Acknowledgments

To my husband, Robert, who understands the need for me to take on a project like this book which provides purpose and meaning in my life, thank you for all of your support.

To the members of the Female Physicians Entrepreneurs Group, you have been by my side and lifted me in many ways, whether it is a summit, workshops, fundraising, a holiday guide, or writing a book, you jump in without asking. Thank you.

To the women physicians who graciously shared their stories, this project could not have been done without you. Thank you from the bottom of my heart.

To Dr. Gigi Abdel-Samed, thank you for graciously offering to provide workshops on burnout.

To Dr. Shilpi Pradhan, you are a lifesaver. Thank you for expertise, guidance and willingness to help with this project.

To Mackenzie Weber, thank you for editing and helping with formatting. Thank you for saving me time and showing me that persistence will get the job done.

To Dr. Radhika Sharma Curtis, thank you for the title suggestion and for helping with this book as it evolved.

To Dr. Avian Tisdale, who so graciously offered the opening line of her talk "Do No Harm, Means Us Too". Avian, that is your line, and I do not doubt that it will be used as you continue to help other physicians.

To Dr. Natalie Schwartz, thank you for your support and friendship. You lent reassuring words when I needed them most.

To YOU, who are taking the time to read this. Change starts with awareness. I hope these stories shed light on the levels of burnout that we are seeing and why women physicians are leaving medicine.

Made in United States
North Haven, CT
23 May 2023